D1445792

OTTER~
COURTRIGHT MEM~

Courtright Memorial Library
Otterbein College
Westerville, Ohio   43081

DICTIONARY OF
SOCIOLOGY

DICTIONARY OF
SOCIOLOGY

TONY LAWSON & JOAN GARROD

Series editor Ian Marcousé

FITZROY DEARBORN PUBLISHERS
LONDON · CHICAGO

Copyright © 1996, 2000, 2001 Tony Lawson and Joan Garrod

This edition based on *The Complete A-Z Sociology Handbook*, second edition, first published in the United Kingdom by Hodder and Stoughton Educational, 2000

Published in the United States of America by
Fitzroy Dearborn Publishers
919 North Michigan Avenue
Chicago, Illinois 60611
USA

All rights reserved including the right of reproduction in whole or in part in any form

A Cataloging-in-Publication Record is available from the Library of Congress

ISBN 1-57958-291-5

First published in the USA 2001

Typeset by GreenGate Publishing Services, Tonbridge, England and Alacrity, Banwell Castle, Weston-super-Mare, England

Printed and bound in Great Britain by The Bath Press

PREFACE

The *Dictionary of Sociology* is an alphabetical text designed for ease of use. The major concepts that you will come across in your study of sociology have been included. The dictionary therefore constitutes an important reference work for sociology students, helping them to grasp the basic concepts of the sociological approach.

Each entry begins with a brief definition. This should help you gain a good understanding of the concept in a precise way. The length of an entry usually depends on the relative importance of the concept and often on the degree of controversy it arouses. Entries therefore try to provide illustrative examples of the concept or introduce you to the major points in support or criticism of it. Illustrations and tables have been provided where they help you to understand the concept.

Your understanding of sociology can be increased by making use of the cross-referenced entries. These are to be found in italics either in the main body of an entry or in parentheses at the end of the entry. These cross-references direct you to related concepts. The authors have restricted the use of cross-references so that important linkways are highlighted. By looking up cross-referenced concepts you will gain a more complete understanding of the issues you are exploring.

While the dictionary is therefore a text that will aid your study of sociology, it is important to recognize that it is not a textbook. This means that you will require further reading to complete your grasp of the subject. However, the more substantial entries will give you a sound introduction to the debates and issues in which sociologists engage and will provide a handy reference when you come across concepts about which you are unsure. It also makes sense to check the entries of concepts that you think you know, to make sure you have a good understanding of the basic tools of the sociological approach.

Most importantly, we hope that you enjoy using the dictionary on a daily basis and find that it is an invaluable resource in your studies. We have certainly enjoyed compiling it.

Tony Lawson and Joan Garrod

ACKNOWLEDGMENTS

Though we have worked closely as a team, we could not have carried out the work for the dictionary without many invisible supporters, too numerous to mention. However, we would like to record our gratitude to Ray Garrod and to Tim Gregson-Williams for their encouragement. The most important thanks should go to the hundreds of students we have taught over the years who, through their questions, have honed our sociological understanding. Nevertheless, we recognize that sociology is not an exact science and that not everyone will agree with the way we have defined every concept. We have taken every care to be as factual as the subject allows and any mistakes are our responsibility.

abortion: the termination of a pregnancy by artificial methods. It has been the subject of often violent disagreement about the morality of allowing legal termination. This has been an important debate for sociologists to study. The debate arouses such passion that *new social movements* have been founded on the back of the debate.

absenteeism: when workers take time off work without any real reason. The degree of absenteeism in a company is difficult to determine, because it is problematic to decide, for example, whether a worker absent from work with "a bad back" is genuinely sick or taking time off without good cause. The degree of absenteeism is sometimes used as a measure of *work satisfaction.* For example, a great increase in absentee rates on the shop floor following a change in work practices may indicate unhappiness with the new arrangements. (See *industrial conflict.*)

absolute poverty: the lack of the basic necessities (food, shelter, and access to clean water and medical care) with which to sustain a healthy existence. Absolute poverty tends to be associated with certain developing countries, but it can be argued that this type of poverty also exists in many developed *industrial societies* among the destitute and the *homeless.* (See *poverty of lifestyle, relative poverty.*)

absolute rate of mobility: the total number of movements up and down the *class structure* within a given period. It is distinct from the *relative rate of mobility.* The absolute rate since World War II has been large, with a great deal of upward social mobility occurring. (See *forced mobility.*)

abstracted empiricism: a term used by C. W. Mills to describe the collecting of empirical evidence for its own sake without the context of a *theory* to make sense of it. (See *theory.*)

academic machismo: the domination of education by men, and agendas set by men. (See *androcentricity.*)

accommodation: the process whereby different social groups come to live together peacefully without resolving their differences or losing their distinct identity. It is often used in describing the mutual tolerance of different ethnic groups living in the same society. (See *assimilation.*)

accounting process: the way in which individuals have *common-sense* understandings that "account for" or make sense of the activities they undertake. In the sociology of organizations, the accounting process has been used by Garfinkel, among others, to show how individuals in a *bureaucracy* have a common-sense understanding of how bureaucracies work, which they employ to make sense of what they actually do in their everyday lives. That is, individuals call upon the concept of bureaucracy when they try to explain what they are doing in their work lives.

acculturation: the process by which a group takes on the behavior and values of a dominant culture; also the way in which different cultural groups influence one another's cultural patterns.

achieved status: a position in society that individuals gain through their own efforts, rather than being born into. In modern industrial societies, education is the main way in which individuals can achieve a particular *status* through acquiring qualifications. The greater the importance of achieved status in a society, the more open that society is likely to be. (See *ascribed status.*)

achievement: an ideological formation of industrialized societies, which states that individuals ought to be rewarded for their efforts and attainment, rather than for being born into a particular background. The idea is important ideologically because it provides the *legitimation* for industrial societies. The education systems of industrial societies are based on the idea of achievement; that is, by being provided with the opportunities to fulfill their abilities, children will rise in the social structure to their appropriate position, according to their *talent.* (See *ascription.*)

achievement principle: a principle developed by Offe, argued to be a central ideological construct of contemporary society, which states that rewards given to individuals in capitalist societies are a result of effort or qualifications, rather than *particularism.* However, Offe argued that the achievement principle cannot work in practice because of the multiskilled nature of contemporary societies, in which there are so many different skills that the notion of a *hierarchy* of skill becomes meaningless.

act: the basic unit of social life, and a unit of behavior that usually involves some purpose or meaning attached to it by the person carrying it out (the actor). (See *behavior.*)

action: one of the basic concepts of sociology, a term to describe the capacity of the individual actor to do something. The concept implies a contrast with instinct, where *behavior* is unthought. Action therefore implies intention or meaning, with the actor being purposeful in what he or she does. *Giddens* argues that action should also be seen as implying two other things:

- that everyone is a highly skilled, knowledgeable agent
- that everyone is a capable human agent. That is, action implies the capacity to do otherwise, to choose not to do the action but something else instead.

action research: where sociologists introduce planned changes into people's behavior, so that the effects can be studied. It is often to be found in classroom research, where changes are introduced in the attempt to improve educational attainment.

action theory: a perspective that begins from individuals and the way that they interact with each other to create society through their everyday actions. It is in contrast to structural theories, which begin at the level of society. There are many forms of action theory, and although they have a long history, they rose to prominence in the 1970s, in reaction to the dominance of *functionalism.* Action theories are *voluntaristic,* in that they emphasize the free will of the individual and the view that the activities of individuals make a difference in society. (See *dramaturgy; ethnomethodology; phenomenology.*)

active audience: a term that describes the receivers of media information and suggests they should not be seen in a passive way, but as actors who interact with media material and are influenced by the social context in which they view content. Past experience, current *beliefs*, family, and friends are examples of factors that intersect with media viewing.

active citizen: a term used to describe the duties and responsibilities of a member of society toward others. The concept is associated with *New Right* sociologists, who argue that rather than being concerned with their rights, citizens should focus on how they can contribute to the well-being of society in an activist way. It is therefore a contrast to the idea of a *dependency culture* and constitutes a moral commitment by citizens to their compatriots.

active society: see *postindustrial society*

activism: see *political participation*

actor: see *act*

adaptation: one of *Parsons' functional prerequisites*, a term to describe how societies adapt to the external environment and shape that environment to their own ends. In practical terms, Parsons was referring to economic institutions such as factories. (See *goal-attainment; integration; latency*.)

adequate at the level of meaning: the idea that, in order to be a proper scientific study of society, sociology must take account of the intentions and motivations of the individual. This view was strongly put forward by *Weber*, who followed Dilthey in arguing that, unlike the *natural sciences*, the social sciences need to examine both the subjective and the objective worlds.

adhocracy: a type of organization in which individuals come together in teams to solve organizational problems, creating their own rules as they go along. (See also *organismic organizations*.)

administrative criminology: an approach to crime that rejects theoretical understandings and focuses on the manageable prevention of crime. It advocates measures such as closed circuit television to facilitate crime prevention and detection.

adolescence: an imprecisely defined period between *childhood* and adulthood. Many important physical changes occur in this period, but most attention has been focused on the emotional and behavioral problems allegedly associated with the teenage years in modern Western societies. In many simple societies the period is marked by *rituals*, with ceremonial *rites de passage* marking the transition between childhood and adulthood.

adult baptism: a practice particularly associated with those religious *sects* in which converts are regarded as having been "born again," and undergo a ceremony of baptism, often by total immersion, to symbolize the washing away of sins and the process of rebirth.

advanced capitalism: see *late capitalism*

advertising industry: the sector of the business world devoted to promotion of sales through favorable publicity and marketing. In sociology, the term is used to denote the powerful position of advertisers and marketing personnel in the *postmodern* world. Postmodernists argue that, in contemporary society, surface images are just as powerful and important as any underlying forces that structural sociologists might identify. In a postmodern world advertising is therefore more than just the promotion of products; it is an important part of reality in its own right. By promoting certain images and *discourses*, advertisers help to shape the reality in which individuals live and mold their *identities*. Advertising companies are also, however, concerned with making profits and therefore they form their own industry, with their own *culture* and *structure*, providing employment and income for a large number of people in *capitalist* societies.

affective action: an element of *Weber's* typology of action, a term for behavior carried out at the whim of the individual, without thought. It is also known as emotional action, and was seen by Weber as characteristic of premodern societies, where *rationality* was less common as a source of behavior.

affective neutrality: where emotional life is controlled and under constraint. It was said by *Parsons* to be one of the important features of modern societies that emotions became privatized, with fewer public displays of emotions such as grief. (See *affectivity*.)

affectivity: where emotional life is carried out publicly, with little restraint. It was identified by *Parsons* as one of the *pattern variables* associated with traditional societies. (See *affective neutrality*.)

affirmative action: a series of programs designed to increase the prospects of minority groups by preferential treatment. Measures range from granting government contracts to minority or female-owned companies to providing target quotas for companies or universities to attract minorities. Affirmative action is under attack from members of the *New Right* as part of the *"whitelash."* They argue that affirmative action programs discriminate against white males in the labor market. (See *positive discrimination*.)

affluence: literally meaning prosperity, and used in sociology to describe the relative prosperity of groups who previously may have been poor, in particular the working class and the young. Affluence has often been associated by conservative commentators with "having it too easy" and has been cited as one of the reasons for increases in *juvenile delinquency* and the loss of respect for established authority.

affluent worker: a type of worker that developed in the postwar era characterized by relatively high wages compared to those of the traditional manual worker. Affluent workers were the subject of keen sociological interest in the 1960s and 1970s, to see whether they would develop middle-class characteristics. Sociologists such as Zweig argued that such workers were becoming middle-class and that the future of industrial societies would be to have a large middle class and a small working class. Goldthorpe and Lockwood argued that affluent workers were becoming a new type of working class rather than middle class. Other sociologists suggested that the attitudes exhibited by the affluent workers had always been held by the group of skilled workers known as the *aristocracy of labor* and therefore were not new at all.

age: the biological basis for *age groups*, which describes the journey between birth and death in years. While there is an objective factor to age, in that any person has been alive for a fixed number of years (though this may be lied about), there are important subjective factors involved also. For example, how old a person feels may not correspond to his or her biological age. There are also important *social construction* aspects to the concept of age. (See *generation*.)

age at marriage: the median (average) age of women and men at the time of first marriage. This is influenced by a number of social and economic factors. In many Western societies, men are on average some two years older than women when they marry for the first time. In general, the median age at marriage has risen significantly since World War II. This rise is partly attributable to the growing trend among young people to cohabit before marriage and also reflects the greater likelihood that many women will wish to establish a career before embarking on marriage. (See *cohabitation*.)

age group: a socially constructed collection of people who are seen by society as occupying a similar position according to their age. Such groups are differentiated from others primarily on account of their age. For example, adolescents would constitute an age group in the US, but would not necessarily do so in other societies. Different societies therefore construct age groups in different ways and treat members of age groups differently, according to custom, tradition, religion, opportunities, etc.

age profile of the population: a breakdown of the population into different age groups. The age profile of a population has a significant effect on many other aspects of a society, including economic development and the way in which resources need to be allocated. Problems can occur if there is too great an imbalance among the different age groups, such as a disproportionate number of young people, as is the case in many developing countries, or elderly people, as in many Western industrialized societies. (See *aging population*.)

age sets: groups of people of a similar age who have shared status and roles. Age sets are usually found in simple or nonindustrial societies, where the transition from one age set to another is often accompanied by *rites de passage*.

ageism: negative feelings toward, and/or discriminatory behavior against, a person or group because of their age. The term is almost always used to refer to such feelings or behavior toward older people. In many developed countries, finding employment can be difficult even for people still in their forties, and the older age groups are increasingly stereotyped as having physical and mental disabilities despite the fact that many of them are healthy and lead active and fulfilling lives. In some societies, such as ancient China, the elderly have been viewed as a valued and respected group whose accumulated wisdom could be used to benefit society. It is notable that, despite ageism, some groups of people, such as politicians and judges, continue to wield power and command respect at a much greater age than the majority of citizens. (See *aging population*.)

agency: a term used by *Giddens* to indicate human action that has the possibility of transforming social arrangements, through the intended or unintended consequences of that action. Agency also has the effect of reproducing structures as well as containing the possibility of changing them.

agenda-setting: manipulation by the news media who bring certain issues to the forefront of public debate by choosing to give them prominence in their reporting. The power of agenda-setting is important, because it allows the media to determine what we should think about, even if we reject the particular line taken by the media with which we have contact. The process occurs because the news is socially constructed through a whole series of choices in the news-gathering process. Decisions are taken all along the line from the actual event to its eventual appearance in the media, any one of which may lead to the item being "spiked." Editorial control is the final and crucial stage in deciding how prominent a story should be, if it is to appear. (See *gatekeepers.*)

aggregate: a term used in sociology to depict a collection of individuals that does not have some formal or informal structure. It is used to distinguish collectivities such as groups, which always have an internal structure, from chance collections of individuals, which are thrown together in fortuitous circumstances.

aggression: see *frustration-aggression theory*

AGIL: the four systems needs of society identified by *Parsons* and referred to in this way by their initial letters: *Adaptation, Goal-attainment, Integration,* and *Latency.* (See *functional prerequisites.*)

aging population: a population in which the proportion of people aged 65 and over is increasing. This is a common feature of most industrial societies, and is a result of relatively low birth rates and increased life expectancy. There are considerable implications for society arising from this pattern. There will be a significant shift in the *dependency ratio,* and consideration will need to be given to the cost of retirement pensions and the health and housing needs of the aging. However, it is a mistake to see this pattern only in negative terms. Many retired people have a reasonably large disposable income, and form an important consumer group, particularly of leisure goods and services.

agrarian societies: societies in which the major form of *employment* is agriculture. Agrarian societies are characterized by subsistence farming and traditional, settled social relationships, with low rates of geographical and *social mobility.*

agribusiness: a term to describe the development of farming away from small family-owned businesses with a notion of stewardship of the land, toward a system where large farms are owned by absentee companies and are farmed only for profit. Agribusiness is associated with the extension of capitalist relations of production from the factories of the towns to the farms of the countryside. Agribusiness has been opposed by many traditional farmers because it leads to nontraditional practices that are claimed to ruin the land. However, the efficiency of agribusiness in producing cheap food has led to its inexorable rise.

Agricultural Revolution: a period of great change in farming, that began in Britain in the early 18th century and spread to other parts of Europe, when traditional land patterns and production methods were subject to fundamental and far-reaching changes. In terms of the pattern of land ownership, the enclosure movement destroyed the strip-farming methods of the feudal system, in exchange for the development of larger, privately owned agricultural units. Production method changes included the introduction of increasingly efficient and sophisticated machinery and rotation methods, which allowed the production of larger amounts of food to feed the growing population of the towns.

ahistoricity: having no sense of history. In sociology, this has been a critique of functionalist thinking, which tends to take an existing society as the best one possible, with little feeling for the past and how societies have developed into their present state.

aid: a blanket term for various kinds of assistance given to *third-world* countries by the *first world*. Aid covers the direct transfer of financial resources, such as charitable donations, the transfer of material goods such as industrial plant, and the provision of loans and credit. Aid can be given by individual countries or by international organizations such as the World Bank. Sociologists are interested in the way that aid affects the *development* of the third world. There is disagreement among sociologists as to the most effective use of aid.

- Some *modernization theorists* see aid as the main vehicle of development in the third world, with the emphasis on large infrastructure projects.
- Some "green" sociologists argue for intermediate development aid, with resources going to smaller, locally sustainable projects.
- Some *dependency theorists* suggest that aid is used mainly as an instrument of policy by the first world, with projects that assist the first world being financed to exploit the resources of the third world.

AIDS (Acquired Immune Deficiency Syndrome): an illness that has raised a number of important issues for sociologists. Initially identified as exclusively associated with homosexual men, AIDS increased the *stigmatization* of this group. Some even saw what they referred to as "the gay plague" as a form of divine retribution. The "at risk" category was then widened to include intravenous drug users, another group held in generally low social *esteem*. Recent statistics of the actual and projected incidence of AIDS, however, show a fall among homosexual men, a continued rise among intravenous drug users, and a growing increase among the heterosexual population. Sociologists have focused on AIDS as an example of a *moral panic*, on the further stigmatization of certain groups in society, on how people who have AIDS or who are HIV-positive cope with this, and how it has altered the doctor–patient relationship. The inability (as yet) of the medical profession to find a cure, and the fact that many AIDS patients are articulate, well-educated, and successful people, has meant that the usual power relationship between doctor and patient, in which the doctor is the more powerful partner, has undergone changes. (See *epidemiology*.)

alienation: according to *Marx*, the result of capitalist organization of industry that increases the separation of workers from the fruits of their labor. Central elements in the condition of alienation are the separation of workers from their tools and from the final product. Alienating conditions stem from the ownership of the *means of production* by the capitalist class, who therefore control the conditions of work, as well as expropriating the *surplus value* of the worker. The conditions of work that are alienating are increasing mechanization and specialization. These transform the active satisfaction of the worker in work into passive resentment at the monotony of work. Alienation is therefore the totality of the objective conditions of capitalist production, which translate into subjective features of deprivation, loss of dignity, sense of a lack of wholeness, and most of all, a feeling that one's life is controlled by impersonal forces. (See *anomie.*)

alienative involvement: the way in which individuals are committed to a society in which *coercion* is the mechanism of control. Because individuals share a common threat, they are likely to be committed in a way that does not engage their feelings. Such an involvement is likely to be limited and to lead to weak feelings of loyalty to society from individual members.

allocation process: the way in which individuals are sifted and sorted by the education system to produce different types of workers for the economy. The crucial part of the allocation process is the certification of individual students, which codifies the skills they can bring to work. However, there are also nontangible factors in the allocation process such as cooperative ability, work discipline and attitudes, and other personality traits. Schools are concerned with the development of these nontangibles as much as they are about the actual knowledge that they give students.

allocation role: the capacity of the education system to select individuals and place them into appropriate occupational positions.

allocative control: the power to determine the resources given to particular activities in an organization. Sociologists have identified allocative control as the more powerful form of control in companies. By being able to decide the distribution of priorities, those who hold allocative control can influence the direction of the organization in a strategic sense. Owners of companies do not therefore need to control the day-to-day activities of the company in order to retain control over what goes on. Allocative control insures that the interests of those who hold such control are met. (See *managerial revolution; operational control.*)

allopathic medicine: the type of medicine primarily associated with Western industrial societies. It is based on the principle of finding a treatment (usually a drug) with an opposite effect to the symptoms of the disease or illness to counteract these symptoms. Recently, more Western doctors have shown an interest in, and sometimes a willingness to prescribe, *homeopathic medicines.* (See *etiology; germ theory of disease.*)

alternative medicine: a general term to describe those forms of treatment that are not recognized by the official medical profession. These include acupuncture and aromatherapy, among others. The boundary between mainstream and alternative medicine is constantly shifting. (See *allopathic medicine.*)

altruism: a feeling that places the welfare of others above a person's own interests. Comte saw the development of altruistic feelings as a measure of the civilized nature of a society, influenced by positivistic values.

altruistic suicide: self-inflicted death where the integrating forces of society are so powerful that they overcome the individual's instinct for self-preservation. This form of *suicide* is usually bound up with the concept of *honor* and involves an over-identification with the group. So, soldiers performing hopeless rearguard actions are committing altruistic suicide. (See *hara-kiri*; *suttee*.)

American Dream: a central ideological construct of the US, that offers all Americans the chance to pursue their own happiness. Its main promise is that any individual can rise to the top of American society if he or she works hard enough and has the talent. It is the openness of opportunity that the American Dream promises that insures the allegiance of the many diverse groups in the US.

amplification of deviance: the idea that the media, through their reporting activities, contribute to the escalation of activities of which the majority population disapproves. The process begins with an actual event or phenomenon, which the media report and headline. The reporting arouses concern in the majority of the population, who demand that something be done about it. The police respond by placing more resources in the area of concern, consequently catching more individuals committing the illegal activity. In reporting this development, the media give the impression that the number of occurrences of the initial activity is on the increase. Individuals who are predisposed to the initial illegal activity may then also gravitate to the places where reporting is taking place, thus actually increasing the incidence of the phenomenon. The amplification of deviance can be represented as a spiral. (See *folk devils*; *moral panic*.)

Reporting increased incidence

Increased police activity

Moral panic

Creation of "*folk devil*"

Media reporting

Initial event

Amplification of deviance spiral

amtshere: identified by *Weber* as the code of honor developed by officials of the *state* for the proper conduct of their roles. It includes a highly developed sense of duty, allied with a belief in the technical superiority of official qualifications, which allows such officials to be the true interpreters of the national interest, rather than politicians, who have party interests at heart.

analogy: the use of a comparison to illustrate a social phenomenon. The classic analogies in sociology are the comparison of society to a biological organism or a machine.

anarchism: a political philosophy that advocates social life without the *state*. It argues that rules of social life should be negotiated between the participants of interactions rather than being imposed by an alienating state. While it is usually accused of being disruptive of social arrangements and leading to disorder, anarchism claims to be about setting up an alternative social order, based on individual freedom, with each person taking responsibility for his or her own actions.

anarchy: the condition of being without *social order, state* justice, or the force of law. Anarchy is similar to the *state of nature*, though it is the result of a breakdown in or overthrow of the apparatus of the state, rather than a hypothetical position.

ancient society: a term used by *Marx* to delineate the period of history associated with slave-based production and usually identified with the Greek and Roman civilizations.

androcentricity: viewing things from a male perspective or being biased toward male points of view. In the sociology of education, traditional textbooks are said to be androcentric in that they encode a particular masculinity and femininity, in which females are seen as subservient and passive. (See *malestream sociology*.)

animism: a belief that plants and animals are endowed with a spirit, or life force, usually accompanied by the idea that people must learn to live in harmony with the animal world. In some societies, certain plants or animals are regarded as particularly sacred, and are the object of *rituals*. (See *totemism*.)

anomic suicide: self-destruction resulting from the lack of social regulation in society. It is related to the appearance of *normlessness* in society, for example in times of crisis or in times of rising prosperity. In both cases, there is a loss of social identity and control, which results in increased *suicide rates*, as individuals are frustrated by the nonrealization of their expectations.

anomie: a concept used by *Durkheim* to describe a society in which individuals do not have any firm guidelines about the way to behave with each other. This *normlessness* is characteristic of those societies in which *individualism* predominates, with no counter-values of social *solidarity* to tone down the emphasis on individual satisfaction, at the expense of others.

antagonism: in sociological research, where a *respondent* shows hostility to the interviewer or to the topic under question. Antagonism can taint the results of sociological inquiry as it creates resistance by the respondent.

antagonistic cooperation: a feature of *pluralist theory of industrial relations*, in which the opposing sides of management and workers in a company work together only in so far as it is necessary to achieve whatever their aims are. They therefore engage in conflict in a restricted way.

anthropocentric: looking at phenomena from the viewpoint of the human race, in contrast to other species. The term is used to denote a selfish perspective that does not take into account the interests of the other species that share the planet. It is thus mainly associated with the *new social movements* that surround the issue of *environmentalism*.

anthropologically strange: a label given when treating a familiar situation as if it had never been encountered before and therefore needs explaining as a completely alien phenomenon.

anthropomorphism: the attribution of human characteristics to animals or other nonhuman forms, especially supernatural beings.

anticipatory socialization: the process whereby individuals alter the patterns of their behavior to conform to those of a superior social group in the hope of joining it at a later time.

anticipatory widowhood: a term developed by Jacobsohn to explain why many middle-class women are reluctant to retire from work early, when their husbands do. Their reluctance is based on the apprehension of isolation should their husbands die before themselves, which statistically is likely to happen. Women in work therefore remain more attached to their work relationships to keep contact with the non-domestic world, should they be left as widows.

anticlericalism: a political attitude that is opposed to the church's interference in politics. It is particularly strong in France and Spain, where a strong Roman Catholic church has attempted to influence *social policy* over such issues as education, abortion, and morality.

antiracism: a particular approach to *race* relations, which argues that the important issue is the prejudiced attitudes in every one of us, and therefore that racist groups and opinions should be confronted and challenged at every opportunity. Though it has led to a particular form of education, antiracism has many manifestations, from challenging racist groups for control of the streets, to agitating against discriminatory legislation. (See *antiracist education.*)

antiracist education: education that actively tries to combat racism and prejudice and promote positive images of people from different ethnic groups.

antisexism: policies and behavior consciously geared toward the prevention of sexist images, language, and practices. It is likely to be a combination of legislation and initiatives such as *antisexist education* programs.

antisexist education: education that actively tries to combat *sexism* and sexist practices in schools, e.g. by insuring that all students have equal access to the curriculum, by using textbooks and other teaching materials that do not contain sexist language or images, and by raising the awareness of students to sexism as an issue.

apartheid: the system of racial segregation that operated in South Africa until the 1990s. Apartheid was maintained through the use of force and legal sanctions, which included imprisoning its opponents such as Nelson Mandela. It was the release of Mandela that heralded the end of apartheid and the emergence of universal democracy there.

apolitical: the condition of being uninterested in politics. The term is usually applied to women and the young, but many sociologists have been critical of this view, arguing that it is better applied to the vast majority of the population, who exhibit little interest in politics beyond voting.

apprenticeship: the provision of on-the-job training for young people, leading to a craft or skill. Apprenticeship programs are often conducted by the relevant unions, in arrangement with vocational high schools and local businesses. (See *training.*)

appropriate technology: see *intermediate technology*

appropriation: the taking of the *surplus value* of the labor of the nonowners of the *means of production* by the owners, to be disposed of as they see fit. The exploitation of the subordinate class is a central feature of capitalist society according to the Marxists. It is achieved by capitalists forcing the laborer to work beyond what is necessary for survival and then taking away the value of the excess for their own. (See *labor theory of value.*)

arbitration: the appointment of an independent person or group to try to bring two parties in a dispute to an agreed compromise. It is a feature of *industrial relation*s and is often carried out by independent agencies.

archeology of knowledge: the methodology associated with Foucault, which consists of peeling back the additions that time places on social and cultural ideas to reveal the origins of those ideas in their socioeconomic context. Foucault was particularly interested in using the archeological method to examine the development of conceptions of punishment and of sexuality in society.

areligiosity: the state of being without religious belief and thus without religious practices. It is claimed by some sociologists that the extent of areligiosity is growing as *secularization* becomes more widespread. However, this claim is disputed.

aristocracy: a traditional ruling class, whose power over society stemmed from its control of agricultural production. The power of the aristocracy reached its climax in the feudal system, but it was slowly supplanted by new social groups emerging from the Industrial Revolution. However, many aristocratic families were also in the forefront of industrial developments and remained individually powerful. The aristocracy in some countries, such as Great Britain, still retains enormous *wealth* in the form of land and is held in high regard by many subordinate groups in society.

aristocracy of labor: that section of the skilled working class who see themselves as separate from the rest of the working class on account of their high level of skill. They tend to be status-conscious and instrumental in their attitudes. Their labor union organizations tend to defend the pay differentials of the aristocracy of labor over other less-skilled workers. (See *deferential workers.*)

arranged marriage: a marriage in which the partners have been chosen by the respective parents and in which the bride and groom will often not have met until shortly before the wedding ceremony. Although now mainly associated with Eastern cultures, arranged marriages used to be quite common among the aristocratic and royal families of Europe, where marriages were seen as alliances between families and groups, and as a way of creating or perpetuating dynasties rather than securing a romantic attachment between two people. Defenders of arranged marriages today argue that they are much more likely to last than relationships based on physical attraction and notions of romantic love, while critics say that many such marriages are unhappy, and can be particularly hard for the women involved, who may be completely subject to their husbands and mothers-in-law.

artifact: an object produced by a *culture*, which can have an existence beyond the life of that culture. Although artifacts are usually associated with physical objects, sociologists also recognize nontangible artifacts such as ideas, which can also survive the culture that produced them.

asceticism: the practice of self-denial of worldly comforts and pleasures arising from a belief that this is a means to religious salvation. Traditionally, in Christianity, the monks and nuns were those who practiced asceticism, often by a complete withdrawal from the world. However, after the Reformation a form of Protestant asceticism developed in which self-denial was practiced without withdrawal from the world. Indeed, with the notion of the "calling," this self-denial was applied to work, with the result that a group of people emerged who worked hard, but reinvested the profits of their labor rather than spending them. (See *Protestant ethic.*)

ascribed status: a position in society that is the result of a fixed characteristic given at birth, such as gender or class of origin. (See *achieved status.*)

ascription: where an individual's status is fixed by the social characteristics with which they are born. These characteristics may be a person's gender or ethnicity. They may also be the social standing of the parents. (See *achievement.*)

ascriptive sociopolitical deference: the acceptance of a high-born social elite as being particularly fitted for high political office. The central idea is that this elite is "born to rule." (See *political deference; sociocultural deference.*)

Asiatic stage: one of *Marx*'s eras of history, distinguished by the hold of the *state* over schemes of irrigation and the ownership of the land by self-sufficient village communities. Though there is little empirical evidence to support the existence of the Asiatic mode of production in any widespread way, the term was used by Marx to indicate the relative stability of societies in Asia, in contrast to the dynamic societies of western Europe. It has been criticized as a Eurocentric view of development.

aspiring professions: see *personal service professions; semiprofessions*

assembly-line systems: a form of production in which the product is sent down a continuously moving line, with workers arranged down the line performing a limited number of routine tasks. The classic assembly line is associated with automobile production during the 1960s. Sociologists are interested in the effects of assembly-line production on workers' attitudes, and it is often seen as the most alienating form of *technology*. High levels of *strikes* in the automotive industry have tended to confirm this view. (See *continuous process production; craft industry.*)

assimilated workers: those members of the *working class* who aspire to be members of the *middle class,* economically and socially, and are accepted by the middle class as their social equals. The accepted worker is said to be assimilated into the middle class. (See *socially aspiring worker.*)

assimilation: a view of *race* relations that sees the host community as culturally homogeneous and the task of the immigrant community to be absorbed into the host community as quickly as possible, by adopting host features. Sensitivity to cultural differences is minimal so that ethnic minority *culture* is disparaged. It can lead to the minority community being dissipated through tactics such as *busing.* (See *cultural pluralism.*)

association: see *Gesellschaft*

atheism: a belief that God does not exist.

attempted suicide: an unsuccessful act of self-destruction. Sociologists are interested in attempted suicides because they give access to the motivations of would-be suicides. However, in exploring the intentions of attempted suicides, sociologists have found that it is very difficult to determine what is a serious attempt at self-destruction and what is a cry for help. (See *gambles with death.*)

attenuated extended family: groups of kin who have relatively little contact with each other. They include students and young people in the process of moving away from their family of origin, and also those whose jobs or geographical distance from their families make it difficult to keep in regular contact. (See also *dispersed extended family*; *local extended family.*)

attitude: a frame of mind that persists over time and predisposes the holder to view things from a particular angle and with a particular slant. Attitudes are learned through experience and *socialization*, but are not unchangeable.

audience: used in the sociology of the media to denote the recipients of any media content, not just of movies or theater. Thus, sociologists would describe the readership of a newspaper as its audience, because it receives the messages that the producers of the media content wish to get across. Some sociologists are critical of the term as it implies, with its image of sitting in an auditorium listening to a concert, a passive reception of messages.

audience dependency: a term to describe the relationship that modern audiences have with the media. It is based on the view that, with the advent of the *mass media*, people increasingly rely on the mass media not only for their knowledge of the world, but also for the interpretation of particular events. The mass media are therefore seen as increasingly powerful, with the ability to significantly shape people's ideas, and therefore behavior. Others see this as a flawed view of *audiences*, arguing that people are not passive and uncritical receptors of media messages but "filter" and even transform them in the light of their existing opinions and beliefs.

audiovisual evidence: the wealth of material, now available to the sociologist, that relies on the relatively new technologies of tapes and videos. It includes photographs, videotapes, and audiotapes. For example, the cameras now located in city centers provide a rich source of ethnographic material for the sociologist.

authoritarian personality: a term developed by Adorno to indicate that attitude of mind based on the belief that society is a system of domination and submission and that some individuals are born to rule and others to obey. Authoritarian personalities can be of the dominant or the submissive kind – that is, they can expect to be obeyed or expect to obey.

authority: the possession of *power* that is seen as legitimate by those over whom it is wielded. Accepted authority can be subdivided into two major types:

- Sacred authority: this can be invested in the personnel of the church, temple or mosque, or in the holy documents that a religion holds. The authority held by religious tradition is often unchallengeable and can lead to *fundamentalism.*

- Secular authority: this is often associated with political leaders and the legitimate organs of government. Political authority can also be attached to great political leaders who, through their *charisma,* can attract legitimated support.

autobiographies: written accounts of people's lives as recounted by themselves. Autobiographies can form a useful source of information, but it should be remembered that they are usually written only by those who are sufficiently well-known for their life stories to be of interest to others, and that the events recounted will be selective. (See *documents; life histories.*)

autocracy: strong rule by a single person. It usually indicates a society governed arbitrarily, with little democratic accountability, where the ruler can make decisions without recourse to anyone else. Autocratic rule is often used in contrast to democratic rule.

automation: a system of production in which human beings take a supervisory role and the main process of production is carried out by machines alone. There are several types of automation:

- transfer automation, which links different machines in a continuous process
- techniques of automatic control over production, with no feedback mechanisms
- computerization, where complex work tasks are controlled by computers through feedback loops.

Automation is a key area of study for sociologists of industry, as the effects of increased automation on society are likely to be long-range and fundamental. Much interest has focused on the effects on jobs, with some sociologists predicting that automation will lead to massive job losses and the creation of a society in which there are large numbers of unemployed people. Other sociologists argue that automation both destroys and creates jobs, with the newly created jobs more highly skilled than the jobs destroyed. Another area of interest has been the effects of automation on the *consciousness* of those who work with it. Some sociologists suggest that automation decreases *alienation,* as it frees workers from the more routine aspects of work, leaving them to concentrate on more creative aspects of work. Others suggest that automation leads to even more alienation, as workers are reduced to "appendages of the machine" with little control over their own work.

autonomy: the freedom of individuals to act in certain circumstances. Sociologists use the concept of autonomy in different contexts. Autonomy in the workplace is associated with the ability of workers to set their own pace of work and organize its activity to their own liking. In terms of *professions,* autonomy is one of the defining characteristics, in that professionals theoretically have the freedom to offer the best advice to the client, irrespective of any other pressures. Professional autonomy is defended vigorously by the professions, but is under constant threat from the bureaucratic forces with which they may work.

avoidance relationship: where an individual seeks to keep out of the way of another for usually deferential or ritualistic reasons. The classic avoidance relationship is between *caste* members and the Harijan (the so-called "untouchables") in India, where contact with the latter by the former is believed to lead to a ritual pollution.

B

babble of experts: a phrase that describes the state of knowledge in the post-modern world, in which a large number of apparently knowledgeable people offer contradictory opinions about the major issues facing society. For example, there are so many conflicting views about whether the "greenhouse effect" is or is not happening that we cannot reasonably know which view is correct. (See *information overload*.)

backlash vote: the support for the racist parties of the right by mainly, but not exclusively, working-class whites, who are reacting against the presence of ethnic minorities in their localities. The strength of the racist vote varies but is most significant in local elections when the *turnout* is low. It tends to be concentrated in white areas on the edges of high concentrations of ethnic minorities.

balkanization: the process whereby any organization or structure is split up into smaller separate parts, with limited connections between them. It refers to the historical development of the Balkans in Europe, which changed from being dominated by a few empires to forming many smaller states, as those empires broke up. In sociology, balkanization can refer to labor markets, where jobs are divided into different sectors with little interchange among the parts or it can refer to an organization where the levels are split from each other and kept separate by the need for qualifications to advance to different parts.

bandwagon effect: where *opinion polls* suggest that a party has a lead in voting intentions or that there is a surge in support for one party at the expense of the others, and other voters are thus tempted to support the winners by "jumping on the bandwagon."

base: see *substructure*

batch production: a manufacturing process in which goods are manufactured in small numbers. It is usually associated with craft skills or small manufacturing companies, employing skilled workers and fairly simple machinery.

batches: the way in which individuals in *total institutions* are dealt with, that is, in large groups. Given that in a total institution there is usually a small number of staff looking after a large number of inmates, social life has to be organized so that a great number of inmates can be processed quickly in any activity, for example eating.

bearers of the mode of production: a term developed by Althusser to indicate that individuals' actions are determined by their position in the production system. It has been criticized for denying individuals choice in their actions, because it implies that an individual's position in the relations of production controls the actions he or she can take.

bedroom communities: rural residential areas where urban workers buy up property and commute to work, leaving towns and suburbs quiet and empty during the day. The search for some idyllic countryside retreat is part of a myth that has had a hold over the consciousness of many urban dwellers.

behavior: as distinct from *action*, behavior is the events that individuals engage in, which may or may not be intended and planned. Behavior thus has several sources, from emotions, through instinct, to rationality. It does not have to involve purpose in the consciously planned sense.

beliefs: things that we hold to be true. The term is often used in the context of religious beliefs, which are usually concerned with beliefs in a *supernatural* power or powers, and are linked to ideas concerning the origin of life, the meaning and purpose of life on earth, and what happens after death.

berdache: a practice among native Americans, in which individuals choose their gender role irrespective of biological status.

Beruf: the calling or vocation of the professional. The Beruf defines part of the *ideology* of professionals, who claim that they carry out their job not for the good rewards they receive, but because they have a calling to practice. It is this ideology of service that informs professionals' own view of themselves. Critics of the Beruf argue that it is a smoke screen to justify the professionals' high salaries.

bias: a deviation from some assumed "truth" or objective measurement. Bias in sociological research can arise at any or all of a number of stages, e.g. in the research design, the method of *sampling* and/or the choice of group to be studied, when designing *questionnaires*, in *interviews*, and in the analysis and interpretation of results. Some sociologists argue that the use of quantitative methods is less likely to lead to bias than qualitative methods, but others strongly disagree. It is probably the case that truly unbiased research, whether in the natural or social sciences, is impossible to achieve, and that the methods chosen will themselves influence the nature of the results. (See *objectivity.*)

bilineal descent: where inheritance and descent are determined through both the male and female lines. (See *matrilineal; patrilineal.*)

biological analogy: used mainly, but not exclusively, by functionalists to compare society to a living organism. The idea is based on the similarities between biological organisms and social formations. In it, society is seen as a functioning entity with an existence of its own, but composed of many parts that contribute to the well-being of the whole. The analogy has been criticized because it leads to the assumption that all parts of society have a positive function to perform for society as a whole, and critics point out that some parts of the social "body" are dysfunctional rather than functional. The analogy is drawn from biology, but other critics point out that if Darwinian selection is taken as the biological analogy, then conflict would be the main feature of the analogy rather than the interdependence of interrelated parts. (See *cybernetic analogy.*)

biological deviant: an individual who displays *deviance* as a function of biology. According to *Durkheim* deviance would occur as a natural event, even in a perfect society, because individual consciences vary enormously according to genetic inheritance and the variation in social contexts. The purpose of the biological deviant is therefore to fix the boundaries of what is acceptable in any society. The biological deviant operates on the margins of society's approval.

biological naturalness: in answering the question, "why do people choose to interact with their kin?" some people refer to the idea that "blood is thicker than water." This implies that, in some basic sense, *family* is a natural phenomenon and more than just the accident of genetic inheritance.

biomechanical model of health: a dehumanizing model of health and illness in which the doctor is viewed as a mechanic treating a defective machine. This model, associated with Western industrial societies, tends to ignore links between mind and body, physical and mental well-being. Its characteristics are:

- a focus on treating the symptoms of a disease rather than finding its root cause
- belief that a particular disease is caused by a particular germ (also known as the doctrine of specific *etiology*)
- a focus on the individual as the site of disease and the object of treatment, rather than considering the wider social, psychological, and environmental milieu of the patient
- a belief in the objectivity of medical knowledge and treatment, and that the most appropriate place for treatment is in a medical environment.

Critics argue that, by its focus on the effects of disease on the body, and on treating symptoms, the biomechanical model of health has diverted attention away from the social and environmental causes of disease and poor health.

biopower: used by Foucault to refer to the activities of the modern state that are geared toward the control of the bodies of its citizens. Biopower can take many forms; for example, the collection of statistics by the state on the incidence of disease is a manifestation of biopower, as the state attempts to control the health of its members. Another is the classification of activities as "normal" or "abnormal," which channels the behavior of citizens into acceptable practices. (See *disciplinary technology*.)

birth rate (crude): the number of live births per thousand of the population per year. As the number of births is expressed per 1,000 people, this enables a comparison to be made between countries of widely differing population sizes. Although the availability of reliable contraception is of obvious importance to the birth rate, social factors such as religious beliefs, the level of literacy, employment opportunities for women, norms governing "ideal" family size, and views on the relative importance of males and females also have a crucial effect. Different countries show markedly different birth rates, with developed regions of the world generally having much lower birth rates than developing regions (see below). Some demographers argue that, as the total population obviously includes those who are not in the childbearing category, (males, very young, and elderly females) and as the proportion of people in these categories might differ considerably between populations, a more accurate way of measuring birth rate is the *fertility rate*.

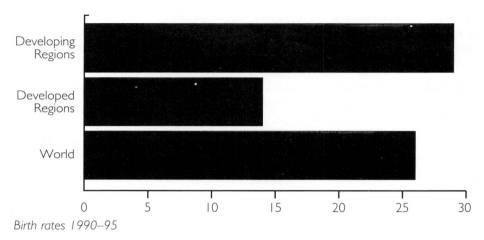

Birth rates 1990–95

births outside marriage: the number of births to women who are not in a legal state of *marriage* at the time of the birth. This number has increased significantly since 1960, and by 1990 had risen to more than one in four births. However, a large proportion of unmarried parents live at the same address, indicating that many of the parents are in a stable relationship. Much of the increase can be attributed to the growth of *cohabitation*. In addition, the younger the mother, the more likely it is that she will be unmarried.

black: a general term used to describe those of African descent. It was developed largely as part of the black consciousness movement of the 1960s, in which pride in being black was developed in contrast to the feelings of inferiority associated with slavery. The "black power" movement was the most radical aspect of 1960s' black consciousness, aiming for increased political and economic power for African-Americans in an otherwise racist and unequal society.

black box view: an approach in the sociology of education that takes for granted what happens in schools and looks to the family or wider society to explain under-achievement. The black box view has been criticized for ignoring social processes within schooling and in particular what happens in the classroom.

black-coated worker: a term applied by Lockwood to clerical workers in Britain. It reflects the traditional clerical "uniform" of a long, black coat.

black economy: see *informal economy*

black feminism: a branch of *feminism* that focuses on the particular concerns of black women. It is argued that, as well as experiencing the disadvantages that apply to all women in a *patriarchal* society, black women face a further form of discrimination, *racism*. They are thus doubly disadvantaged. (See *liberal feminism*; *Marxist feminism*; *radical feminism*.)

black legend: a term used by Pollack to describe the view that children before 1900 were treated as young adults. She argued that this was not a true account of the way children were treated. Rather, her research showed that children were recognized as having need for play and affection and that they were treated as children, not just as little adults.

blasé attitude: a term developed by Simmel to describe the urban sophistication he found in large cities. It was manifested in a "seen it all before" attitude, in which the individual affected never to be surprised by the many novel events witnessed in the city.

blue-coated workers: a term used to describe the police. It is used to indicate that the police are concerned with pay issues, *status* considerations, and working conditions just like other workers.

blue-collar workers: a term for manual workers and therefore the working class. It is used in contrast with *white-collar workers*.

blurring boundaries: associated with *postmodernism*, this refers to the weakening of the traditional distinctions among different phenomena, as the *rationality* of modernity gives way to a loss of certainty. For example, traditional academic thought was carried out within disciplines where the boundaries between subjects were fairly clearly drawn. In postmodern thought, academics draw on materials across many disciplines, often in creative ways, to develop new modes of thinking.

body: in sociology, a term not just for the physical aspect of the human being, but also for a social construct, influenced by social processes and negotiated in inter-action. The sociology of medicine has been particularly interested in concepts of the body, especially with the rise of postmodernist theories in the 1980s. For example, Foucault argues that the way people conceive of their bodies is influenced by *discourses*, which define appropriate body shape and the ways in which bodies may be kept healthy and free from disease.

body language: the communication of sentiments, ideas, or emotions by gestures, facial expressions, and posture. Some of this communication is deliberate (e.g. waving goodbye) but much of it is unconscious. Individuals become very skilled at interpreting the body language used in their own culture, but mistakes are often made when interacting with or observing people from other cultures, where the same gesture or expression may have quite a different meaning.

Booth, Charles: a Victorian businessman and social reformer whose detailed survey of people in London at the end of the 19th century provided detailed statistical evidence of the extent of urban *poverty*. Booth used the concept of the *poverty line* to define and measure poverty, and his pioneering *social survey* showed that almost a third of the people in a large part of London could be defined as "poor." (See *Rowntree, Benjamin Seebohm.*)

border pedagogy: a term developed by Giroux, based on the notion that teachers should be recruited to transform the prospects of working-class children by focusing on resistance to dominant ideologies and the crossing of traditional subject divisions to show, for example, that works of literature are situated in specific social and historical settings, rather than only being interpreted in a particular way.

boundary maintenance: in functionalist sociology, the tendency of a *social system* to preserve its position in relationship to its external environment. It is therefore a defense mechanism for systems to maintain their own position and insure survival. (See *reification.*)

bounded rationality: a term used by March and Simon to suggest that action is never totally logical, but is limited by the partial knowledge the individual may have about a situation. Because no one individual can know everything about a set of circumstances, there must be areas of uncertainty and chance involved in the decision-making process.

bourgeoisie: one of *Marx*'s two main classes in society, described as the owners of the *means of production*. According to Marx the bourgeoisie are not just an owning class but by virtue of their ownership also a *ruling class* in capitalist societies. That is, economic power gives access to political power.

bricolage: in the sociology of youth culture, the borrowing of aspects of different styles of dress, music, and behavior to form new styles. Youth subcultural styles therefore give nods in the direction of particular cultures and modes of dress, but are creative in the pastiche of *style* that results.

bride-price: in certain societies, a gift from the bridegroom and his family to the father and family of the bride. The higher the *social status* of the bride, the higher the bride-price will be. The handing over of the gift is often the sign that the marriage is legally established. The notion of the bride-price is most often found in societies in which there is *patrilineal* descent, where it forms the means to attach children to lineages.

brute being: a term used by Merleau-Ponty to describe the shadow side of the human character. In existential sociology attention should be paid to this darker side of humanity, with its passions and thoughts, about which the individual rarely tells others.

Buddhism: an Eastern religion which predates Christianity, that is based on the teachings of the Buddha, "the enlightened one." With its emphasis on self-denial and the finding of inner peace through meditation, Buddhism has attracted a growing number of adherents in Western societies, many of them people tired of the "rat race" and what they see as the growing materialism of Western, consumer-oriented societies.

buffer zone thesis: the argument that the amount of mobility at the manual/nonmanual line is marginal and that this line forms a barrier to mobility. While this is a traditional view of the class structure as a relatively closed one, the increase in middle-class occupations has had the effect of temporarily increasing mobility rates across the manual/nonmanual line. However, the long-term effect of the occupational changes has been to produce a relatively homogeneous working class, whose *self-recruitment* is high.

built environment: a term that covers sociological interest in urban planning and architecture and their interrelationships with individuals and society. The interaction between people and the space that surrounds them is a particular interest of postmodern sociologists, but the built environment has a more general appeal to sociologists as a reflection of and background to the cultural values and activities in which people engage.

bureaucracy: a particular form of organization that is characteristic of *modernity*. The concept is associated most of all with the *ideal type* of bureaucracy developed by

Max Weber. In this ideal type, Weber defines a large number of features of bureaucracies that can then be used as a measure of how bureaucratic real *organizations* are. These features include:

- a series of official roles that are organized hierarchically
- roles that are bound by rules defining what may or may not be legitimately done by an official
- laid-down procedures that theoretically cover all situations that may face the bureaucracy
- officials being subject to strict discipline
- meticulously kept records
- a clear separation between what is official and what is personal.

Weber claimed that bureaucracies are the most efficient form of organization. Critics of bureaucracy have argued that they are more suited to a situation where there is predictability, for example in producing standardized goods for a mass market in which demand for the goods will be steady. Bureaucracies are said to be less efficient in the postmodern world where there are *niche markets* demanding specialized, tailor-made goods. When bureaucratic organizations survive in inappropriate situations they become *dysfunctional.*

bureaucratic personality: a term developed by Blau to indicate how individuals working in a *bureaucracy* tended to develop similar habits, skills, and reflexes in dealing with their clients. This personality was one of the factors contributing to the *dysfunctioning* of bureaucracies, as the bureaucrats became inflexible and unable to respond to new or changed conditions. (See *impersonality.*)

bureaucratization: the process whereby society becomes increasingly subject to the control of bureaucratic organizations, with a consequent loss of freedom and *individualism.* The concept is particularly associated with *Max Weber,* who believed that modern societies were distinguished by *rationality* and that one consequence of this was the dominance of *bureaucracy.* The result was that modern societies were subject to an "*iron cage*" of bureaucracy that stifled freedom and controlled the lives of individuals.

burgesses: identified by Watson as those individuals who are upwardly mobile in a particular locality. They rely on local opportunities to "better themselves" and utilize local networks in achieving movement. (See *spiralists.*)

busing: the transportation of schoolchildren to nonlocal schools to insure an ethnic mix in schooling. Busing was developed in the late 1960s to avoid the so-called ghettoization of inner-city schools and the consequent problem of low achievement. After much opposition from both black and white groups, the practice was abandoned in the 1980s.

cabal: a term used by Burns to describe a network of aspiring individuals in an organization, who use their influence with each other to further their own careers. (See *clique.*)

calculability: the ability for social actions to be predicted by an individual as a result of their regularity. Calculability is a basic prerequisite of collective action. Working together would be difficult without some calculation by an individual as to the likely responses of those with whom he or she is working. Individuals make such calculations on the basis of a whole range of factors, from previous experience to the rules of the *organization* in which they are working. Calculability, however, is not foolproof because actions can have *unintended consequences* as well as desired outcomes. (See *exchange theory.*)

calculative involvement: the way in which individuals are committed to a society where there is a self-interest operating. Since individuals make a rational calculation to come together in society, they are likely to be committed in a way that engages only their self-interest. Such an involvement is likely to be conditional and lead to negotiable feelings of loyalty from individual members to society. (See *alienative involvement*; *moral involvement.*)

Calvinism: a form of Protestant *Christianity* with a strong commitment to self-control, self-denial, and the conscientious assumption of the duties and obligations arising from work. Work was seen as another way of honoring God, with the emphasis on hard work, a sober and modest lifestyle, and saving rather than spending money. These ideas, collectively referred to as the "Protestant work ethic," led *Weber* to argue that Calvinist values had a major influence on the development of industrial capitalism. (See *Protestant ethic.*)

capital: in economic terms, the money, machinery, and plant needed to produce goods. In sociology it is often reified to represent a social force in its own right, with its own *class interest.* Capital is therefore supposed to operate in predictable ways that often produce *exploitation* as well as great wealth. Capital is thus the contradictory concept to "the workers."

capital accumulation: to *Marx*, the central dynamic in capitalist society and the process whereby capital is expanded, so that further investment and therefore profit can be made. Capital is created by exploiting workers and expropriating the *surplus value* of their labor. This capital is collected in fewer and fewer hands, which then employ it to create further capital through increased exploitation.

capitalism: a type of society in which the private ownership of the *means of production* is the dominant form of providing the means to live. Capitalism is a "system" – that is, it has a series of interlocking structures that together function to produce a particular way of living and producing. What distinguishes capitalism from other types of society is the emphasis on the rights of property and the individual owner's right to employ capital as she or he thinks fit. The development of capitalism has been a focus of sociological interest, with some arguing that there is a common path of capitalist development, produced by the logic of the maximization of profits. Critics of capitalism have attacked its reduction of all relationships to monetary value and its apparently alienating tendency. Supporters of capitalism claim that it is through the harnessing of the profit motive that the "good life" has been provided for so many people. (See *late capitalism.*)

carceral organization: an institution in which individuals are held for treatment or punishment and in which they spend 24 hours a day for a set period. The usual examples given are prisons and asylums. Sociologists are interested in these because they are an extreme situation, in which the collectivity is more important than the individual inmate. They thus represent a *case study* for situations where free will is limited but never extinguished. (See *total institutions.*)

career: the progression that individuals go through during the course of their lives. It is usually associated with an occupation, but in sociology the term is used more widely. Sociologists are interested in the way that the concept of a career has changed under the impact of post-Fordist developments in industry.

carers: a term usually applied to informal carers, i.e. those who care for people with some kind of disability, usually relatives or neighbors, outside the system of medical or care institutions. In areas where a policy of *community care* has been applied, the number of these informal carers, the majority of whom are women, has increased. The largest category of dependant is that of parent.

cargo cult: one of a number of *millenarian movements* that existed in New Guinea in the 1930s. Cargo cults shared a belief that by engaging in particular rituals their followers would insure that the millennium would be accompanied by the appearance of a miraculous cargo of trade goods. Cargo cults arose at a time of social and political dislocation linked to successive waves of *colonialism.*

case study: a detailed in-depth study of one group or event. The group or event is not necessarily representative of others of its kind, and case studies are sometimes used as preliminary pieces of research to generate *hypotheses* for subsequent research.

cash-nexus: a term suggesting that the only bond between employer and worker is the wage paid by the former to the latter. Where the cash-nexus is dominant employers and workers have no other obligations to each other and workers develop an instrumental attitude toward their work, in which a certain amount of effort is expended for the reward that is given.

caste: a social class within the *stratification* system of India. The system is based on four traditional groups organized in a *hierarchy* and originally based on an occupational classification. The system is now hereditary, with caste being determined at birth by parents' caste membership, and cannot be changed during a lifetime. The system is a complicated one with the four main castes being subdivided into thousands of "jati," or subcastes. The four main castes from top to bottom are:

1. Brahmin; 2. Kshatriyas; 3. Vaishyas; 4. Sudras.

Standing below the castes are the Harijan, who are literally "out-caste" and who occupy a position in society that makes them the object of much discrimination.

casualization of the workforce: used to describe the increasing numbers of workers who are employed on a part-time and/or temporary basis. The growth of casual labor is associated with the development of *post-Fordism* and the *dual labor market* of *core workers* and *periphery workers*.

category: a logical class in which to group phenomena. In the case of sociology, categorization is one of the main ways in which sociologists seek to understand the social world.

catharsis effect: the idea that watching violence on television or in the movies relieves feelings of frustration and therefore contributes to the reduction of violence in the real world. (See *stimulation effect*.)

caucus: a meeting of members of a political party for the purpose of deciding policy or nominating members for office. The term can also be used to describe the members themselves, often in the sense of "a group within a group."

causal explanation: a statement that accounts for the existence of a phenomenon by identifying the events and factors that led to its occurrence. They are very difficult to establish in sociology because of the complexity of social phenomena and because human beings have enough free will to change the cause and results.

censorship: the banning or restricting of public expression regarded by those in authority as potentially dangerous to that authority or the system of which it forms a part. Most censorship is carried out by political or religious authorities.

census: a method of counting and characterizing the members of a population at a particular time. In the US a full-scale national census has been taken every ten years since 1790. As well as counting the number of residents, census returns may also ask for other detailed information. When published, data from the census are widely used by a number of organizations, including the government, and prove an invaluable source of information, particularly for predictions of health and other social trends. However, a census will always have a certain nonresponse rate, despite follow-up work and the fact that people are required by law to provide information. It is estimated, for example, that the US population in 1990 was undercounted by 1.6%.

center: in the political spectrum, a term to describe the ideas and organizations that stand in between *right-wing* and *left-wing* ideas and emphasize the individual and freedom. They range from social democracy to the old-style Liberal parties in Europe; in the US, the term "center" is commonly used to refer to the less ideological and more pragmatic wing of each party.

center–periphery models: a view of social phenomena that characterizes divisions between a strong, stable core and a weak, vulnerable surround to that core. It developed as a conception of world economies, where the core was seen as the industrial, mainly capitalist societies of the West and at the periphery were those countries of the *third world* dependent upon and dominated by the countries of the core. The analysis has since been applied to many other social phenomena, such as the labor force. (See *core workers; periphery workers*.)

central business district: one of Burgess' urban zones, which represents the economic heart of the city where business and commerce are conducted. While the CBD is still important in the life of cities, developments such as out-of-town shopping and business parks have undermined the centrality of the CBD to the economic success of the city. (See *urban zones theory*.)

central life interest: a term used by sociologists of work, in particular Dubin, to describe the main focus of concern in workers' lives. It was initially used in the debate over how important work was to factory workers. Some sociologists claimed that the informal groups that grew up on the factory floor were the most important part of workers' lives – their central life interest. Others argued that the home was the central life interest of workers, who were mainly instrumental in their approach to work.

central value system: the collection of beliefs and attitudes that make up the important core of a society's consciousness. The central value system is seen by functionalists as a key element of social solidarity and one of the main ways that individuals are integrated, through agreeing on the most important values in society.

centralization: the process whereby *power* becomes more and more concentrated in the hands of the few, as local sources of power and influence are neutralized and stripped of their capacity to make a difference. The process of modernization can be seen as the increasing centralization of power in the hands of national government officials and the emasculation of independent sources of oppositional power.

ceremony: a set of symbolic and ritualistic actions performed on appropriate occasions that are intended to express shared feelings and attitudes. Many important ceremonies are connected with birth, marriage, and death and also with the transfer of power, such as a coronation or the swearing-in of a president or chief.

certification: the granting of qualifications by appropriate examining bodies. In sociology there is also a wider meaning of certification, referring to the process whereby societies recognize the abilities of individuals through the qualifications they obtain. Certification is a crucial power of professional bodies who through the granting or withholding of certificates determine who can and who cannot become a practitioner.

chalk-and-talk: a method of teaching in which the students are relatively passive, the teacher controls the pace and content of the lesson, and few, if any, resources are used other than the teacher and the blackboard. This method is often contrasted with so-called progressive teaching methods. (See *discovery learning; experiential teaching.*)

change: see *social change*

channels of influence: the focus of lobbying work by *pressure groups*, this describes the power centers of society that, if persuaded to a course of action, can translate influence into action. By charting the channels of influence that pressure groups act upon, sociologists claim that it is possible to map out the power centers in a society.

chaos theory: an explanation in science that argues for the difficulty in establishing invariate laws because of the operation of chance and long causal connections in the natural and social worlds. The classical conception of chaos theory is where the fluttering of a butterfly's wings in one part of the world may, through the operation of chaos, lead to a hurricane in another part. While this may seem far-fetched, the central idea is that actions can have unintended consequences long after they occur and in seemingly unconnected phenomena through long chains of events.

charisma: the attraction exerted by a powerful personality. In sociology, charisma was identified by *Weber* as one of the sources of *power* in society. It led to a particular form of social organization, which was based on the whims of the charismatic leader, from whom all *authority* flowed.

chauvinism: the possession of strong ideas associated with extreme forms of nationalism and national pride. The word comes from Nicolas Chauvin, a French soldier in the Revolutionary and Napoleonic armies, and is often used to imply intolerance of those from other nationalities. It is also used in the context of male chauvinism to describe beliefs in the innate superiority of males and the corresponding belittling of females.

check-book voting: a model of voting that argues that one of the most important factors in deciding how people vote is their concern over which party will bring the greatest financial benefits to the individual and his/her family. (See *instrumental voting.*)

Chicago School: an important school of sociology between the two world wars, which was prominent in the development of urban sociology. It was largely based upon a study of the fast-changing nature of Chicago, and also on the theoretical development of *symbolic interactionism,* associated with Cooley and Mead.

child care: in simple terms, the provision of care for the young, but in sociology, it has other aspects, such as whether child care is carried out by the biological parents or others. There has been an increase in professional child care since World War II, as more and more mothers have gone out to work, whether in a *single-parent* or dual-parent situation. Sociologists are interested in the effects that this has on children as they grow up. They have also focused on the reasons why women are seen in society as having primary responsibility for child care and the ways that this has been challenged and changed in recent years.

child-centeredness: in a family, the way in which much activity and emotional energy is focused on the children, rather than on adult desires. It developed with the emergence of the *nuclear family* form and stands in contrast to previous forms, where children were allegedly less important in the structure of the family.

childhood: a state that in sociological terms is both socially and chronologically determined. The concept is used to refer both to a period of time during which a person has not yet reached adult status and a set of beliefs regarding what it is to be a "child." The French sociologist Philippe Ariès argued that in medieval Europe children were both perceived and treated as young adults, and that the notion of "childhood" as a separate status as we know it developed with the creation of a formal education system. Throughout the world there is a wide variation in notions of childhood and in some countries children remain an important part of the labor force, not always legally. The Victorians idealized childhood as a time of innocence, in which moral development should be a prime concern, and the development of psychology in the 20th century emphasized the importance of the childhood period to the development of the adult personality. There are many current concerns regarding the physical and sexual abuse of children, and the *state* has powers to protect children, even to the extent of removing them from their family. (See *black legend.*)

childrearing patterns: a reference to social class differences in ways of bringing up children. Research by John and Elizabeth Newson in the 1960s and 1970s showed that such differences existed, with middle-class mothers more likely to follow advice from health officials and reference books, and working-class mothers more likely to rely on advice from their mothers, sisters, and friends. Middle-class parents were found to apply a more consistent approach to discipline, whereas working-class mothers showed a more arbitrary approach, veering between indulgence and strictness. Bernstein also identified social class differences in childrearing, with middle-class mothers more likely than working-class mothers to use language to control their children's behavior and to give reasons for their decisions. Bernstein believed that this particular use of language was one way in which middle-class children learned to use the *elaborated code*.

chiliastic movements: organized groups, usually religious in origin, that look toward the passing of the present order and the end of the world as we know it. They tend to be enthusiastic in their services and welcome the transformation as the culmination of history.

choice: the ability to make decisions between alternatives in a free and unconstrained manner. Choice is traditionally an important concept in the sociology of *poverty*, in the sense that the poor have very little choice. However it has more recently become a central concept in *postmodernism*, where the extension of choice has been fundamental to the development of postmodern societies. The idea of choice has therefore been extended from decisions about basic foodstuffs to the choice of lifestyles in which the postmodern individual engages.

choice of method: in sociological research, the choice of a particular research method or methods, which may be influenced by a number of factors. These are sometimes defined in terms of constraints, either practical or ethical, but the following may also exert an influence on choice of method:

- time – some methods, such as *covert participant observation*, can be particularly time-consuming
- money – both the amount of money available to the sociologist and its source (e.g. a specific research grant, government, or private funding)
- access to the group being studied – is this easy, difficult, or even dangerous?
- the nature of the group being studied – factors such as their degree of literacy, their willingness to take part in research, the amount of time they have available will all need to be taken into account
- the nature of the subject matter – personal, sensitive issues may not lend themselves to a written *questionnaire* with standardized questions
- the kind of data required – do the end-users of the research need quantitative, statistical data, or more qualitative information?
- theoretical perspective – does the researcher or the person/group for whom the research is being conducted have strong positivist or interactionist leanings?
- gender – it is increasingly acknowledged that this can exert an influence on the method(s) used; these influences include physical space (there are

some places where either men or women cannot easily conduct research), and female sociologists in particular sometimes face resistance from male bosses or colleagues to their attempts to conduct the more unstructured types of research often favored by women.

Christianity: a monotheistic religion that emerged in the Near East and came to dominate the religious and civil life of Europe. Through *colonialism*, it spread to many other parts of the world in various different forms of Protestantism and Catholicism.

church: a well-established, bureaucratically structured religious organization with values that tend to be conservative and to support the established order in the society of which it is a part. Membership is usually by ascription, i.e. people are formally admitted into the church at birth. The term is usually used to refer to Christian churches. (See *denomination; sect.*)

church attendance statistics: figures covering attendance at church on the major Christian religious festivals, particularly Easter, and/or measures of the frequency with which members of society attend church services. Other statistical measures include the number of infant baptisms, the number of marriages solemnized in church, and Sunday school attendance figures. These statistics show, particularly for the Protestant church and the major *denominations*, a steady decline, particularly since the end of World War II. This is often used as evidence that *secularization* is taking place, but there is considerable disagreement regarding both the reliability of the figures and their interpretation.

circulation of elites: a term used to describe how *social change* may occur where there is a single unitary elite monopolizing *power*, suggesting that the only possibility for change is the replacement of one *elite* by another. The concept therefore denies the possibility of democratic control in society. Where there are elections, the circulation of elites suggest that the only avenue open to electors is to choose which elite they will be governed by. Circulation may occur by the replacement of individual members of the elite by others, such as when younger members replace the older, or it may occur through a peaceful transition from one elite to a new rising one. Alternatively change may be violent, with the overthrow of one elite by another through *revolution.*

citizenship: both the legal right to count oneself a member of a particular state or commonwealth, and ideas concerning the relationship between an individual and the *state.* Generally, notions of citizenship involve defining the rights and the responsibilities of both the state and its citizens.

city: a large urban area, which is usually a focus for the surrounding countryside. Cities have always been of enormous interest to sociologists, because they are often exciting and vibrant places, with a great deal going on. They are also associated with social innovation, so that new ways of living are constantly being developed. Cities are also places of conflict and struggle between different social groups, so they are places of *contestation.*

city planning: a development scheme to create environments in urban areas that meet the needs of different urban groups, and develop urban spaces in a systematic way. Sociologists are interested in the way that the results of city planning affect individuals and groups within these spaces. The results of city planning decisions by *urban managers* can be the disruption of communities, the creation of pedestrian space, the death or revitalization of city center shopping areas, etc. Castells argues that city planning is about, firstly, *social control*, as it siphons working-class populations into specific areas of cities, and secondly, about creating an urban environment that is conducive to the creation of *wealth*, by building roads, communications, etc.

civil liberties: personal and social freedoms that are guaranteed by law unless, in a particular set of circumstances, the exercise of these freedoms is deemed to be against the common good or public interest. When these freedoms are claimed and/or enforced through the legal or administrative system, they are usually classed as civil rights.

civil religion: where secular symbols such as flags and national anthems function to promote social solidarity in the way that religion has traditionally done. *Durkheim* used the term to indicate that there were *functional equivalents* to religion in every society, even those that did not have a single or unifying religion.

civilization: a term that describes a complex cultural and social entity, usually covering more than one society or nation-state. Thus sociologists define Western civilization as the cultural *artifacts* associated with capitalist industrial societies of the 19th and 20th centuries and encompassing such values as democracy, tolerance, liberalism, and so on.

civilizing process: the ways identified by Elias in which history can be seen as the progressive ability of humans to control their emotions. Elias showed how different standards of behavior (decorum or etiquette) come into existence and create a more civilized human being.

clan: a *descent group* that claims membership from one side of the family only.

clash of cultures: a notion in the sociology of education that identifies the cause of *underachievement* of working-class and ethnic minority children as the difference between the expectations and practices of the school and the values and attitudes of students from particular backgrounds. In the case of the working class it is argued that the middle-class *ethos* of the school, with its emphasis on *deferred gratification,* does not go well with the more hedonistic culture of the working class. A criticism raised against this approach is that it tends to lump all schools and all working-class children together, when there are important differences within each category. (See *cultural deprivation; cultural difference theory; cultural reproduction.*)

class: see *social class*

class boundaries debate: one of the continuous disagreements in sociology, concerning how many social classes there are in modern societies and where the distinctions between them should be drawn. It was developed as a reaction to the Marxist division of capitalist societies into two major classes and some unimportant intermediate classes. Critics have argued that this is a simplistic view of a complex social phenomenon and therefore theoretically more social classes should be identified. *Common-sense* views tend to divide the *class structure* into three – the upper, middle, and working classes – but sociologists are interested in how these can be justified in terms of the social situation in which members find themselves. Different sociologists have therefore developed various schema of social class, which seek to divide society into a specific and often different number of social classes according to some objective criteria. (See *contradictory class locations.*)

class-centric: having a view that is biased because it is taken from a particular position in the economic structure. Middle-class sociologists are often accused of being class-centric in that they view the problems of the *working class* from their own particular class position.

class cleavage: see *partisan alignment*

class conflict: see *class struggle*

class consciousness: where workers have an awareness that they have an interest in common with all other workers and bind together in collective organizations to pursue those interests. This leads to struggles on the political level, as class-conscious workers seek to change their common material conditions. (See *labor union consciousness; status consciousness.*)

class culture: the shared meanings and patterns of behavior associated with a particular *social class.* The Marxist view of this is that socioeconomic factors lead to different classes having different patterns of meaning; therefore it is questioned whether an overall shared *culture* exists in society. Class culture arises out of shared interests. Others disagree, and argue that there is a dominant culture that all members of society broadly share, irrespective of differences that may arise from other characteristics such as *age,* class, or *ethnic group.*

class dealignment: represents the situation, especially in Great Britain, where the connection between occupation and political support for a particular party declines. The traditional British alignment has been between manual occupations and Labour voting, and nonmanual work and Conservative support, but this has changed in recent years.

class-for-itself: where members of the *working class,* as a *class-in-itself,* recognize that they share interests with all other workers and take political and industrial action to further their interests. *Marx* saw the state of being a class-for-itself as a crucial step on the road to a revolution in which the working class would seize power and change society in their own interests. (See *class consciousness.*)

class formation: the Marxist view that the private ownership of the *means of production* determines the allocation of *political power* in society, and leads to the two groups, the owners and the nonowners of production, having different *class interests,* resulting in a struggle with one another. These three elements, namely the ownership of the means of production, the distribution of political power, and the conflict between groups, together lead to the formation of two opposing classes.

class fragmentation: see *fragmentation theories*

class imagery: the way that individuals and groups see society as divided according to levels of subordination and superordination. The main types of class imagery are proletarian, deferential, and pecuniary.

class-in-itself: a term developed by *Marx* and Engels to describe the situation where groups of workers have enough in common materially to share a similar objective class position. The basis for a class-in-itself was urban living, where large numbers of individuals were brought together to work in large and small factories. Thus, the material aspect of these workers' lives showed great similarity, and at the time that Marx and Engels were writing, also much poverty and misery. The concept is used in conjunction with *class-for-itself.*

class interest: a term used to denote, for each of the collectivities that exist in superordinate and subordinate positions in the economic hierarchy, the social policies and political developments that benefit them, as opposed to others in different positions. For example, it is supposed that having a left-wing government is in the working class's interest, because it would introduce reforms that would benefit them. These interests are real in that they reflect the material and economic circumstances of each class.

class structure: the distribution of groups in society according to criteria such as ownership/nonownership of the *means of production*, control or noncontrol over work situations, and whether the group sells or buys labor power. Traditional class structure is conceived of as a *hierarchy*, in which the largest social class is also the lowest. However, postmodern societies are alleged to have developed a different class structure, in which the largest social class is in the middle of the class structure. This can be represented as in the diagram below. (See *new middle class.*)

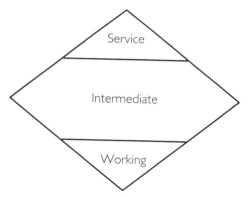

Class structure

class struggle: the conflict between economic groups which, according to the Marxists, is central to historical progress. *Marx* saw class struggle as the important dynamic in society, causing *social change* through the resolution of the contradictions between the interests of the *proletariat* on one hand and the *bourgeoisie* on the other. The struggle between the classes occurs on a number of levels, from the day-to-day economic conflict through the political to the sometimes violent revolutionary conflict.

classical criminology: the traditional approach to crime, associated with the 18th and 19th centuries and founded on the belief that all people were criminal by inclination and that therefore there must be strict controls and punishment for wrongdoing. The classical criminologists assume that there is a basic antisocial instinct which society must control in order for there to be *social order*. There are thus no mitigating circumstances that might excuse the individual from crime.

classical sociologists: a term used to describe the great early sociologists, who developed and set out a distinctive way of looking at society. The canon of classical sociologists usually includes *Comte, Durkheim, Marx,* and *Weber,* but may also include others such as Saint-Simon, Henderson, Vico, and Tönnies.

classification: see *taxonomies*

classroom interaction: the relationships and subsequent behavior that occur within the classroom and can have a powerful effect on both teaching and learning. Interactionists in particular have focused on the importance of this process, and have looked at the interaction between teacher and students, and among groups of students. It is a view of education that sees it as a dynamic and constantly negotiated process, rather than the simple imparting of knowledge to students by a teacher. (See *labeling theory.*)

clearup rates: the proportion of crimes reported to the police, that are subsequently processed in the criminal justice system and deemed to be "solved." (See *crime statistics.*)

client mode of production: a term used by Marxists to indicate a productive capacity that lies outside of the main capitalist *mode of production. Domestic labor* is one such client mode, which reproduces the labor power of the workforce.

clients: an increasingly common term used to refer to individuals and groups using particular services. These services include professional services such as health, education, and social care, and a range of other services such as leisure and entertainment.

clinical iceberg: a term to describe the idea that only a small proportion of symptoms, usually under 10%, is actually reported to doctors. This underreporting throws doubt on the use of *morbidity data* in the investigation of illness.

clinical sociology: a term used mainly in the US to describe an approach to the subject that is aimed at intervention to solve social problems. This interventionist approach is associated with federal funding of programs to alleviate *poverty.*

clique: a term used by Burns to describe a network of marginal individuals in organizations, who form *solidarity* friendships for mutual support. Those under threat of losing their jobs may therefore form cliques to give each other reassurance. (See *cabal.*)

closed questions: questions that allow the respondent only a specific range of answers, e.g. Yes/No/Don't Know.

closed shop: the situation in which being a member of a designated *labor union* is a condition of employment. The closed shop was made illegal in the US by the Taft-Hartley Act in 1947. In Great Britain, it came under increasing restriction during the 1980s, with only a few now remaining. Sociologists are interested in how the closed shop served the interests of both labor union leaders and employers. Closed shops simplified negotiation and also gave the union a role to play in work discipline.

However, the idea of the closed shop became increasingly unpopular as the ideology of *individualism* became more dominant.

closed societies: societies in which there is little *social mobility* in the *class structure.* Closed societies tend to be very rigid, with individuals spending their lives in the same social position into which they were born. *Status* is therefore fixed by hereditary characteristics and is given by the status of the parents. (See *ascription; open societies.*)

cluster sampling: a form of *sampling* in which the *survey population* is first divided into smaller groups, or clusters, from which *random samples* are then drawn. Cluster sampling is usually used when both the population and the desired sample size are particularly large.

coalition formation: a formal relationship between two *organizations,* which may range from written agreements to merger. The term is used by Thompson and McEwen to indicate one of a range of ways in which organizations might influence each other. (See *competition; cooptation.*)

coca-colonization: the process whereby American industry comes to dominate the economies of other countries through the penetration of their markets by American big business. The franchising of American products in other countries, while retaining overall control of the product, is a central part of the neoimperialist process. (See *McDonaldization.*)

code: see *language codes*

code of ethics: one of the defining characteristics of a *profession* that regulates activity *vis-a-vis* the public. The code of ethics therefore sets out the moral dimension of a profession, setting standards of proper behavior and providing guidelines for issues such as fixing charges.

coding: the way in which sociologists give numerical values to respondents' answers in order to ease the analysis of data and establish correlations of statistical significance. The development of the computer has made coding an important part of the research process and permitted the development of sophisticated mathematical models of society.

coefficient of aggravation: a term used by *Durkheim* to suggest how prone to *suicide* a particular individual might be. It was calculated by the level of involvement of individuals in integrating social contexts. Thus children leaving home increased the coefficient of aggravation of married women, who in this way lost an integrating context. (See *egoistic suicide.*)

coercion: literally, force. Sociologists are interested in the way that coercion manifests itself in society. It can either be overt, as in the direct use of the police or army to control populations, or indirect, through the threat to use force. Coercion can also take a legitimated form in the law and justice system. Marxists argue that capitalist societies are coercive by nature and beneath the velvet glove of the institutions of the law lies the iron fist of the military.

cognition: the process of thinking. It is an important aspect of mental life and constitutes the conscious thought processes as against the unconscious. (See *affectivity.*)

cognitive dissonance: where there is a lack of fit between the views of an individual and the ideas in the media content to which they are exposed. Festinger argues that this is psychologically uncomfortable and that the individual will seek to reduce the dissonance, largely by selectively choosing more consonant material. (See *selective exposure.*)

cohabitation: a situation in which a couple lives together as man and wife although not legally married. This is increasingly common in Western countries, both among young, never-married couples and among men and women separated or divorced from previous spouses. Statistics show that people are more likely to cohabit before second marriages than before first marriages. Many cohabiting couples later marry and while it might be expected that their "trial marriage" might help to insure a lasting relationship, figures show that couples who have cohabited have higher divorce rates than those who have not.

cohesion: literally, sticking together, it is used in sociology to describe the *integration* of a society into a unified whole. (See *solidarity.*)

cohesive mass segregation: an explanation for the high *strike-proneness* of certain groups (e.g. miners). Kerr and Siegel argued that it was the relative isolation of large numbers of workers in a single-industry town or village that led to high levels of striking. The *solidarity* that working and living together with few alternatives engendered, led to a strong propensity to act together to pursue aims.

cohort analysis: the investigation of a group that shares a similar demographic characteristic, usually age. Cohort analysis is particularly used in the sociology of gender, where children born in the same year may be followed through the education system in order to chart the changes and constancies they experience. Cohort analysis is important for the *comparative method*, where two different cohorts may be contrasted and compared for differences and similarities.

Cold War: the situation that prevailed after World War II, when the major communist and capitalist countries (especially the Soviet Union and the US) were in strong confrontation with each other, though not directly involved in warlike activities against each other. The Cold War was thus in a sense fought by proxies in the *third world*, especially through civil wars between those sympathetic to communist ideology and those hostile to it. The Cold War ended with the collapse of *communism* in eastern Europe and the Soviet Union in the late 1980s, so that even though communist regimes survive, most notably in China, communism is widely seen as having "lost the war." (See *end of history.*)

collapse of communism: the momentous events of the late 1980s that saw the overthrow either peacefully or violently of the communist regimes of the Soviet Union and eastern Europe. The symbolic end of the *Cold War* came with the dismantling of the Berlin Wall. Communism continues to survive in its eastern form in China, North Korea, and Vietnam, and in the Western Hemisphere in Cuba.

collective bargaining: the negotiation between workers and employers through organized representatives on each side. It is in contrast to individual bargaining, where single workers might seek to negotiate conditions and wages. By banding together, workers hope to receive better conditions and pay through a system of collective bargaining. For the employers, collective bargaining simplifies the process of setting conditions and pay, though it also holds the possibility of industrial action. (See *institutionalization of conflict*.)

collective behavior: the actions of people when they operate together, for example in a crowd or a mob. Collective behavior usually implies the loss of individual will in the psychology of the group, which takes on characteristics independent of the sum of the individual actions within it.

collective conscience: a term used by *Durkheim* to denote the existence of a social and moral order, exterior to the individual and acting upon him or her as an independent force. It is the shared sentiments, beliefs, and values of individuals that make up the collective conscience and in *traditional societies* forms the basis of *social order*. As societies modernize, the collective conscience weakens and *mechanical solidarity* is replaced by *organic solidarity*.

collective consumption: a term developed by Castells to denote the services that need to be provided to keep a workforce healthy and rested. Collective consumption therefore guarantees the reproduction of *labor power* by insuring that the workforce is housed, rested, materially content with the system, and ready for a day's work. It is composed then of the agencies of the *welfare state*, which provides health care, education (both vocational and ideological), housing, transportation, and leisure for everyone in society. Critics of this concept, such as Pahl, argue that it is a very vague one, as it is unclear whether Castells is writing about the welfare state or all goods consumed.

collective orientation: one of *Parsons' pattern variables*, which suggests that in *traditional societies*, shared interests are more important than individual ones. (See *self-orientation*.)

collectivism: a political philosophy that covers a range of ideas united by their advocacy of the communal control of the *means of production* and distribution. The most common form of collectivism is associated with direct *state* control of industry, as opposed to *industrial democracy*.

collectivities: a general term to cover any grouping wider than the individual. They may range from friendship groupings to the membership of the Rotary Club. The advantage of the term is that it implies that groups are built up from individuals collected together and do not have an existence independent of the individuals.

colonialism: a system in which dominant countries control and exploit foreign colonies. The term is usually used to describe the way that European countries once controlled much of Asia, Africa, and Latin America. The heyday of the colonial system was in the late 19th and early 20th centuries, when the British, French, Dutch and, until World War I, Germans held large empires in the Southern Hemisphere. Sociological interest in colonialism has centered on the way that laws were used to establish dominant trading positions for companies in the colonial powers and the way that state power was used in a systematic way to exploit indigenous populations. The main tactic used by the colonial powers was "divide-and-rule," by setting different elements within the colonized areas against each other. The eventual drawing-up of "national" boundaries by the colonial powers, without heed to history, *culture*, or language, aided this policy. The legacy of this policy is said to be the tribal and ethnic troubles that still affect much of Africa and Asia.

coming out: the process whereby lesbians and gay men reveal their sexuality to a public *audience*. It is a fairly recent phenomenon, dating largely from the growth of more radical political and social movements from the 1960s on. It is interesting to the sociologist because it involves social as well as psychological aspects. For example, the audience for the process may be confined to a few friends and not to family, or to the public at large. It may signify a personal commitment or a political statement. (See *outing*.)

command economy: a concept describing the control of the *state* over the *means of production*, so that all investment and marketing decisions are made by central state agencies in contrast to the market. (See *mixed economy*.)

commodification: the tendency for goods, services, people, and relationships to become subject to the principles of the market and thus reduced to a monetary value. It is seen by Marxists as a fundamental feature of capitalist development and a sign of the increasing *alienation* associated with *late capitalism*.

commodity fetishism: where goods are valued for their monetary exchange value rather than the practical use to which they can be put. Marxists see commodity fetishism as a feature of the consumerist ethic of developed capitalism.

commodity form of incorporation: a term used to describe the way in which an oppositional subculture is neutralized by capitalist society, through the conversion of *subcultural signs* into popular, mass-produced objects. The classical example is the transformation of the fashion of street punk into high fashion. (See *ideological form of incorporation*.)

common sense: what everybody knows or assumes. In sociology, common sense is used as a contrast to sociological knowledge, which sometimes challenges common sense and provides evidence that things are not always as people assume them to be. Common-sense explanations are therefore contrasted with sociological explanations, with the latter providing a more solid basis for knowledge.

common-sense knowledge: see *everyday knowledge*

common-sense world: the world that everybody knows and takes for granted. It is the world where *action* is taken without deep thought but as part of the everyday activities of individuals. The knowledge of the common-sense world differs from scientific knowledge in three ways:

- Science is more formal and systematic, being precise in the way that observations are carried out. Observation in the common-sense world is haphazard and arbitrary.
- Science is more rigorous, allowing itself to be subject to critical scrutiny.
- Common-sense knowledge is practical for short-term solutions to everyday problems. Science goes beyond the pragmatic to form theoretical knowledge, which may be drawn upon for practical purposes.

(See *everyday knowledge*.)

common values: where people share the same set of opinions concerning the proper way to live. In any society there needs to be at least a minimum of common values if that society is to persist. Where common values are lacking or where the *consensus* over appropriate behavior breaks down, there is likely to be conflict. Whereas in a society a degree of *conflict* is necessary to prevent it ossifying, the existence of common values insures some continuation of society.

communal economy: the exchange of services in a locality that does not rely on the exchange of cash. This can exist in either a semiformal or an informal form. In the case of the former, a good example would be a baby-sitting circle in which tokens are exchanged for hours sat. For the latter, services are exchanged through friendship groupings on a basis of expertise held.

commune: a form of "family" living in which a group of individuals, either related or not, live together and hold property in common. There are various forms of commune which vary in the amount of communal property they hold. Some for example bring up their children with all adults of the commune as the social fathers and mothers. The classic commune is the Israeli kibbutz, which emerged as an attempt to forge a new way of living in the aftermath of the Holocaust.

communication: the transfer of information between individuals or groups, and a fundamental feature of the human condition. Human beings communicate much more extensively than other animals, both verbally and symbolically, and are distinguished by their ability to use technology to reach mass audiences. (See *mass media.*)

communism: a political and social arrangement in societies characterized by state control of the *means of production* and a monopoly of *political power* by the Communist Party. Derived from the work of *Marx*, the implementation of communism involved totalitarian control of society. The empirical manifestation of communism was in the Soviet Union and the socialist societies of eastern Europe until their collapse in 1989–90. Communism continues to dominate in the People's Republic of China, North Korea, Cuba, and Vietnam.

communitarianism: an idea developed by Etzioni in response to the individualism of the 1980s. It stresses the importance of the community to ordered living, and the responsibilities as well as the rights of individuals toward the social.

community: a central concept in sociology, used by both the *classical sociologists* and modern sociologists, to describe a certain type of social organization in which there is a strong sense of *identity* among individual members of the community. As with many sociological concepts, it has been defined in different ways by different sociologists:

- as locality – a given geographical area is the basis for identity
- as a local social system – a set of relationships usually, but not always, found in a given locality
- as a type of relationship – a sense of strong shared identity, which may be geographically dispersed.

Communities can therefore be based on day-to-day contact, religious belief, ethnic identity, national feeling, etc.

community action: where locally based groups organize themselves to achieve objectives in a locality. It is usually associated with disadvantaged groups who seek redress for their grievances through self-help organizations. They also tend to look for funding to national or local government to help achieve their objectives.

community care: a policy of deinstitutionalization that removes certain groups of people from institutional care into the care of the family and the wider community. The policy has been applied to certain groups of people with mental disorders or disabilities, and the elderly. Supporters of the policy argue that it is not good for people to live in institutions unless they really need to do so, as it robs them of their dignity and independence. While most people would agree with this, critics of the policy are concerned by what they see as the inadequate resources often provided for good quality care by families and communities. Many families find themselves unable to cope with members suffering from mental disorders, particularly schizophrenia, and it is argued that government provision for mentally disabled and elderly people is insufficient. (See *carers*.)

community integration: a concept put forward by Kerr and Siegel to explain the low *strike-proneness* of some industries, which argued that where industrial communities were connected to the rest of society in several ways, they had less of a propensity to strike.

community politics: political activity within the community that is focused on local campaigns and issues.

community power: a term used to describe the patterns of control of local areas or neighborhoods. The concept was developed to cover those sociological studies that investigated whether there were local *elites* in control of local communities, or whether power was pluralistically dispersed among different groups.

community studies: a collective term given to a series of examinations of different localities, mainly of working-class occupational groups such as miners and fishermen. The studies, mainly carried out in the 1950s and 1960s, provide a documentary account of the experience of traditional working-class communities and in particular the male working population within them. The focus of much of the community studies was the ideologies and consciousness of members of the community. The studies have been criticized because:

- in focusing on work, they ignored the experiences of women
- they made contradictory class images into simplistic class-conscious stereotypes
- they were ahistorical, ignoring the shaping of these communities by the relationships between capital and labor.

commuter zone: the outer edges of a city and its satellite towns which, according to *urban zones theory*, are the main residential areas for middle-class workers. These areas are characterized as "bedroom communities," being largely empty during the day as workers travel into the city to work, and having limited recreational opportunities in them for the workers who return at night.

comparative method: sometimes used as an alternative to an *experiment,* a method that analyzes two or more different groups or institutions in terms of their similarities and differences, often with reference to statistical data. It is usually used with large groups, sometimes whole societies (e.g. *Durkheim*'s work on *suicide*) although research in psychology has used the comparative method on a study of a relatively small number of monozygotic (identical) twins reared apart. While comparative studies can yield interesting results, there is a problem of *validity*. There are usually so many different *variables* involved that it is impossible to draw definitive conclusions.

compensation thesis: a thesis developed by sociologists of *leisure* that argues that the main function of leisure is to make up for the frustrations that individuals experience in work. Conversely, those whose jobs are interesting do not seek compensation and therefore downgrade the importance of leisure in their lives.

compensatory education: education that has as its main aim the overcoming of perceived deficiencies in a child's education. This education is often delivered in the form of special programs, such as "*Head Start*" and "Project Upward Bound." The concept of compensatory education for the culturally deprived child originated in the US in the mid-1950s, and quickly became a popular way of explaining the relatively poor educational performance of certain groups of children, notably blacks and Puerto Ricans. The programs, which received considerable financial support from the federal government, developed an increasing emphasis on the preschool years. Critics of the view that lack of educational success was a result of the "wrong" *culture* and *values* in the homes of some children argued that it diverted attention away from the real problem, which was that of *poverty* and lack of opportunity, and it also assumed that the culture of black and Hispanic Americans was inferior to that of white Americans. Some of the original "Head Start" children were surveyed in later life, and did not show significant advantages over similar children who had not taken part in the program, but there is disagreement regarding the interpretation of the findings. (See *positive discrimination*.)

competences: a term increasingly used in the context of vocational education and training to refer to those skills of which the effective demonstration renders a person able to be certified as "competent."

competition: in economic terms, a situation where industries with the same product vie with each other to attract customers to their particular brand of product. Competition is also a central ideological concept for capitalist societies, as it is through competition that industry remains efficient.

competitive interest theory: an answer to the *problem of order*, which states that *society* is the unintended consequence of interaction. It proposes that in order to compete effectively and fairly for the satisfaction of desire, we must have a minimum of justice and rules, because we need order to trade.

complementary leisure: a situation where work generates neither enthusiasm nor hostility and therefore the leisure pursuits undertaken are unaffected by work. It is usually associated with routine office work, where much leisure activity is carried out at home, such as watching television. (See *extension leisure, oppositional leisure*.)

compliance: see *normative power, utilitarian power*

compound family: a complex web of relationships, based on marriage and kinship, that is a feature of high-divorce societies. As the *divorce rate* increases, family relationships become more intricate, to include stepfamilies as well as those related directly by blood or marriage. (See *reconstituted family.*)

comprador state: a term to describe a *state* in the *third world* that is a client of a *first-world* country. The implication of the term is that the governing *elite* of the third-world country is so tied in to the interests of the first-world country that the former is not truly independent. Underdevelopment theorists argue that the advantage of a comprador relationship over direct *colonialism* is that the illusion of independence satisfies nationalist opinion in the third-world society, which might otherwise be hostile to the interests of the first-world state.

computer technology: a system of technology consisting of a range of machines and applications, based on digital code and microprocessors, through which many millions of operations per second can be processed to achieve programmed ends. The development of computer technology has revolutionized the way that we produce goods and services in society and also affected the lives of millions of individuals, for example in the appearance of personal computers in our homes. The continuing development of computer technology should be one of the most important factors shaping the 21st century.

Comte, Auguste: a French sociologist writing in the first half of the 19th century. Comte developed the idea of *positivism,* and believed that societies were subject to the laws of social and intellectual development, which he believed were as much "laws" as those in *natural science.* He argued that societies passed through three stages, the last of which was the *positive stage,* characterized by rational thinking and rational government. Many of Comte's ideas influenced the development of *functionalism* in sociological thought. (See *metaphysical stage, theological stage.*)

concentration: a term used by sociologists of the media to describe the way in which the media industry is increasingly dominated by a small number of large companies. Initial interest in concentration was focused on Britain, where the collapse of independent local newspapers and the shrinking of ownership in the national press meant that fewer companies were dominating media output. More recently, concentration has taken on a global dimension with increasing domination of the global media market by a few huge businesses.

concentric zone theory: see *urban zones theory*

concept: a term that carries a specific meaning and stands as a halfway house between empirical facts and fullblown theories. Concepts are often used as a shorthand for more complex descriptions of social reality. Each discipline develops its own set of concepts which can sometimes be seen as the jargon of the subject. Nevertheless they are indispensable for describing and explaining the subject matter of a discipline without having to go into long descriptions each time they are employed.

conflict: a form of disagreement; used in sociology to indicate the struggle among the different interests and social groups in society. The concept implies that social life is based on coercion, and generates hostility and even violence. Society is therefore fundamentally divided into sectional interests, which compete with each other by various means to protect and extend their own positions. *Social systems* are therefore full of contradictions and are subject to constant change. (See *consensus.*)

conflict theory: a general term covering a number of sociological approaches, opposed to *functionalism* and sharing the idea that the basic feature of all societies is the struggle among different groups for access to scarce resources. They range from the Marxist emphasis on class conflict over economic resources, to the Weberian emphasis on the struggle among different groups over *status* and *power*, as well as *wealth.*

conformity: according to Merton, specifically where individuals are able to achieve their goals through legitimate means. As their socially defined wants are met in appropriate ways, conformist individuals do not need to turn to deviant activities to satisfy their wants.

conglomeration: the bringing together of companies in different sectors to form one overarching company with "fingers in many pies." Conglomerates are of particular interest to sociologists of the media, who see a small number of companies with interests in many different sectors of the industry. (See *diversification.*)

conjecture: a logical suggestion as to why something is happening in the way that it is, which can then be subject to experimental testing. The notion of conjecture forms an important part of Popper's view regarding science and scientific method. (See *falsification; natural science; refutation.*)

conjugal: a concept referring to husband and wife. (See *conjugal roles.*)

conjugal roles: the roles played by a husband and wife within a marriage, with particular reference to the *domestic division of labor.* Elizabeth Bott suggested that there were two main types of conjugal role, *segregated* and *joint*, which her research showed to be associated with the working class and middle class respectively. Bott predicted that as the *norms* of the middle class "filtered down" to the working class, conjugal roles would tend to become increasingly joint, though this does not seem to be borne out by the evidence. As "conjugal roles" is a term that technically applies to married partners, and taking into account the increase in *cohabitation*, it is increasingly common to refer to the *domestic division of labor* rather than conjugal roles. (See *new man.*)

connotation: used in *semiotics* to indicate the associations produced in an individual by a particular signifier. For example, the connotation of the signifier "torch" might be light, conservatism, heat, caves, etc. (See *denotation.*)

consanguinity: relationship based on descent from a common ancestor. The line of descent may be lineal (i.e. a direct line of descent) or with no direct line.

consciousness: that part of the human mind that is self-aware. In sociology, the term consciousness is used particularly, but not exclusively, by Marxists to indicate the individual's awareness of his or her position in the social structure of *society.* Consciousness also extends to awareness of place within the environment and with the internal workings of the individual's own mind. It is thus our knowledge about the world.

consensual view of need: a shared view of what is required to reach and maintain a minimum standard of living based not on subsistence but according to the prevailing norms of society. In the research for their 1985 book *Poor Britain*, Mack and Lansley took a *representative sample* of 1,174 *respondents* and asked them to categorize a range of goods and services as either "essential" or "luxuries." They found a high degree of consensus regarding items considered necessities. The list of necessities established in this way formed the basis of defining *poverty* for Mack and Lansley; people with an enforced lack of three or more items on the list (excluding public transportation, a yard, and a television) were deemed to be in poverty, as they were unable to reach the minimum standard of living as agreed by a majority of the sample. (See *index of deprivation*.)

consensus: literally meaning agreement, a term used in a wide sense in sociology to describe those perspectives that stress the essential cohesion and *solidarity* of society. Consensus is based on the assumption that *norms* and *values* in society are generally agreed and that social life is based on cooperation rather than *conflict*. There is usually a legitimate *authority* involved in policing the consensus, which also guarantees that societies tend to persist.

conservatism: a political or social philosophy that is oriented toward traditionalism and preserving the structures and ideals of a society's past, while adapting them to the present. Modern conservative theory has become associated with the free market and the defense of capitalism.

conspicuous consumption: the use of goods and services to demonstrate actual or symbolic membership of a particular social class, especially one of high *status*. The goods and services therefore usually fall into the luxury class. Conspicuous consumption may occur in any society, but is particularly associated with consumer-oriented societies in which status is closely associated with the ownership of particular material goods. An example of conspicuous consumption is the wearing of designer clothes that carry the easily visible designer label. However, this is only effective if people can recognize which are the high-status, luxury goods, so advertising and marketing play an important role.

conspiracy theory: a theory based on the idea that individuals in power act together secretly in order to preserve their own interests against the interests of the rest of society. Classic conspiracy theories include the belief in a global plot to dominate international and domestic politics by the *military-industrial complex*, the Zionist movement, or the capitalist class.

constituency: a geographical unit or district that makes up an electoral area. A constituency contains electors bound together in a unit that, as far as possible, has some sense of *identity* or logic.

constitutional typologies: an explanation of criminality that relies on the body-type of the individual as a predictor of the tendency to criminality. Of the body-types identified by Sheldon, it was the high-energy mesomorphs (hard and round types) who were most led into criminal activity. This did not suggest that all mesomorphs were criminal, but that they were more likely to engage in delinquency. The theory has been criticized because it does not identify the mechanism whereby the body-type is translated into particular actions. It may also lead to *stereotyping* of certain individuals on the basis of their appearance.

constitutive criminology: a postmodern approach to the sociological study of crime. It recognizes both the constraints on people's actions and the freedom of choice they have. It therefore takes into account factors such as a person's past, their present condition, and their biological and social backgrounds, which may limit their ideas and actions, while insisting that there is still freedom for the individual to make decisions whether to carry out legal or criminal actions in any circumstance.

construct: in sociology, any *concept* or explanation that helps individuals to understand the world around them. The term is used to indicate the artificial nature of the linguistic device being used. For example, the concept of social class is a construct, which helps sociologists classify and explain stratified societies.

consumer model of voting: see *rational choice model*

consumer power: the ability we all have as buyers of goods and services to fashion the patterns of distribution in a society. While the individual purchaser may have little consumer power, the millions of consumer decisions made every day shape the economic fortunes of different businesses and the country as a whole.

consumption: a term used to describe the ways in which individuals use goods and services. Whereas sociologists have traditionally been interested in production, focus on consumption has increased since the 1980s. Arising out of the increased *leisure* in society and a renewed focus on lifestyle as a determinant of *social class,* consumption has become a major item of sociological research in many different areas. These range from a focus on consumption patterns by different social groups, to an interest in the sociology of food and cuisine.

content analysis: a method associated with the study of the media, in which researchers define a set of categories and then classify the material under study in terms of the frequency it appears in the different categories. It has been used to study newspaper coverage of different types of crime, relating the extent of coverage (in column inches) to the actual incidence of the various types of crime. One of the problems of content analysis is the difficulty both of defining the categories and of allocating the material to the appropriate category.

contest mobility: a form of *social mobility* based on the assumption that some education systems operate in a meritocratic fashion. The concept was used by R. Turner in the 1950s to describe the social mobility that he believed to operate in the US, as a result of the fair and open competition found in American schools. Turner has been criticized for an overly idealistic view of American education, and for ignoring the impact of *social class* on social mobility. (See *meritocracy.*)

contestation: a process described by Mandel, where workers come to challenge the rights of *capital* to determine the conditions of production. Mandel argued that, with the increase in *automation,* it would be impossible to continue to increase the real wages of workers. Therefore, the standard of living of the working class would decline and workers would begin to challenge the prerogatives of *capitalism.* (See *late capitalism.*)

contingency theory: an approach to *organizations* that examines the influence of the *environment* and *technology* (contingent factors) on organizational behavior and structure. The importance of this perspective is that it rejects the search for the "most efficient" form of organization, in favor of exploring the variations that responses to the environment invoke in organizations.

continuous process production: where goods are manufactured without being touched by human hands. It is usually found in the chemical and drugs industries where the transfer of the materials from one part of the process to another could be dangerous if humans were exposed to them.

continuum: in sociology, a representation of social phenomena that suggests that there are numerous variations between two opposite characteristics. It is usually drawn as a straight line, with the opposites at either end of the line. Along the line may be placed variations of the opposites, and where they are placed will suggest their relation to other variations. This can be seen in the following:

Illustration of continuum

contradiction: a term used by Marxists to describe situations in which there are disjunctions between social structures when there should be a fit. For example, Marxists argue that there is a correspondence between schools and the economy, so that schools prepare students for the world of work. However, schools are constantly changing because there are always contradictions between the type of workers an economy needs and the type of workers that schools produce. This is because capitalist economies are constantly changing under the dynamics of capitalist laws of economic development.

contradictory class locations: a term used by Marxist Olin Wright to describe those positions in contemporary capitalist society that are not part of the *bourgeoisie*, *proletariat*, or *petty bourgeoisie*, but are semipermanent locations of the *class structure*, along the dimensions of economics, politics, and ideology. The contradictory class locations are determined by a whole range of processes, such as whether a group has credentials or skills that are valuable in the labor market or some supervisory powers in the workplace, as well as whether its members are owners or nonowners of the *means of production*. These positions are only semipermanent because they are subject to change as powerful economic, ideological, and political forces act upon them. The idea has been criticized because, despite its apparent objective classification of occupations, it actually relies on the coding decisions of sociologists as to where particular occupational groups appear. (See *semiautonomous employees*.)

control group: a group within an experiment matched as closely as possible to another group, the *experimental group*. With human groups the matching features may include age, gender, social class, ethnic group, region, etc. The difference between the control group and the experimental group is that the control group is not exposed to the *independent variable*, that which is thought to be the cause of what is being investigated. Therefore if any differences emerge between the two groups it can be assumed to be because of the independent variable. The use of control and experimental groups is widely used in medicine to test the effectiveness of new drugs or a different kind of treatment. It is often much easier to control the different variables and to measure the outcome in cases like these than it is in sociological research. (See *experimental method*.)

control theory: used in the study of crime to suggest that illegal activity takes place when society does not control sufficiently the naturally base appetites of human beings. Though it can take very crude forms, leading to calls for harsher punishment, control theory has developed in many more sophisticated ways, which recognize the complexity of the relationship between control and freedom and the importance of internalized control, as well as punishment, as limiting factors on criminal urges.

conurbation: a geographical area that covers several local boundaries but forms a continuous urban region.

convergence theory: an explanation of societal development that identifies a process whereby heterogeneous cultures develop and change in the direction of a greater likeness to each other as they industrialize. Convergence theorists argue that in important respects, industrial societies must be similar, because they adopt similar arrangements for performing important social functions in the most effective way. Convergence theory has been criticized on three main counts:

- It ignores the starting points of industrial countries, which means that they have different cultural preferences and will therefore end up in different industrial states.
- It sees the US as the most advanced industrial society and therefore assumes that industrializing societies are converging on the American model.
- It is a crude determinist theory, ignoring the importance of political decision-making in determining social arrangements for important social functions.

Convergence theory has had a resurgence since 1989 with the collapse of the Communist regimes in the Soviet Union and eastern Europe. (See *one-way convergence, two-way convergence*.)

conversational analysis: a method associated with *ethnomethodology*, in which the *common-sense* rules of everyday talk are uncovered by examining the speech acts of individuals talking with each other. For example, conversational analysis might uncover the rules associated with the timing and legitimization of taking turns in conversation. Conversational analysis has also revealed gender differences; in mixed groups, males frequently interrupt females, who tend to stop speaking and allow the male to continue. Males are more likely to make statements of fact, while females are more likely to be tentative, e.g. "I think that ..." or "Isn't it true that ...?" (See *sociolinguistics*.)

cooperation: where action is shared to achieve common goals. Even in high-conflict situations, some minimum of cooperation is apparent, for example in the shared principles of the Geneva Convention. (See *conflict*.)

cooptation: the situation in which two or more *organizations* are related through the same individuals having directorships in each of them. Though there may be no formal relationship between the organizations, some sociologists suggest that multi-directorships mean that there are informal contacts which can lead to coordination of some spheres of activity.

coproduction: the process in late capitalist societies whereby the *state* and its citizens act together to administer society. The postmodern condition of late capitalism so fragments society that the state can no longer administer society effectively on its own. It therefore recruits the citizens into coproduction, to enable the cooperation needed to insure the smooth running of society. For example, the self-assessment of tax payments, rather than assessment by state employees, is one form of coproduction.

copycatting: the process whereby accounts of events in the media encourage people in other areas to copy the behavior reported, leading to an increased incidence of the original behavior. It has been used, for example, in explaining the outbreaks of urban violence that periodically sweep some cities. However, critics argue that the copycat theory is insufficient on its own as an explanation, as violence does not break out in all cities following the reporting of an initial riot.

core characteristics of the professions: those features that delimit a profession from other occupational groups. (See *professions.*)

core functions of the family: those functions believed to be the basic, essential functions performed by all family units. Murdock, an early functionalist writer, argued that the four basic family functions were:

- the sexual
- the reproductive
- the socializing (Murdock referred to this as "education")
- the economic.

According to Murdock, the sexual function performed by the *family* was the social control and expression of the sex drive. All societies have rules governing sexual activity, particularly with regard to who may marry (and have legitimate sexual relations) with whom. These rules are believed to be functional in that control of sexual relations helps to avert the conflict that might arise from totally free access to sexual partners, particularly if these relations are devoid of social responsibilities. Societies also have rules about the socially acceptable expression of sexual feelings and activities, which again, according to Murdock, helps to avoid conflict.

The reproduction function refers not only to the obvious fact that children are born into families, but that the rules governing *marriage* and *family structure* insure that children are seen as the responsibility of a particular group of adults, either the parents or, as in some societies, a wider group of kin. This helps to insure the survival of children, and thus of the society.

The *socialization* function is seen as particularly important, as it is this process that enables children to function as members of their own society and insures that the *culture* is passed down from one generation to the next.

The economic function refers to the work performed in family units. In simple and nonindustrial societies work is largely devoted to the provision of food. This is sometimes referred to as the "production function." It has been argued that, in industrial societies, where few families produce their own food and household goods, the economic function is one of consumption rather than production; that is, families buy and use goods rather than produce them directly.

As in many modern industrial societies, many aspects of family functions such as welfare, education, and leisure are increasingly performed by more specialized agencies such as hospitals, schools, and leisure organizations, it has been suggested that the family has lost many of its functions and has become correspondingly less important as an institution. However, others including *Parsons* maintain that this has made the family more specialized, and that its remaining functions are more important to society than ever. A criticism of the functionalist view of families generally relates to the assumption that families are, by definition, "good" both for society and for individual members. Sociologists such as Vogel and Bell, Leach, and Laing point to the many ways in which families can be highly dysfunctional units for some people, filled with tension, misery, and even violence. (See *universality of the family*.)

core workers: in post-Fordist production methods, the highly skilled workers who form the permanent members of the workforce. The cost of training and maintaining such workers is high, so they are rewarded well in order to insure their loyalty to the company. (See *periphery workers*; *post-Fordism*.)

corporate crime: lawbreaking by the executives of large work organizations, which occurs as a matter of routine in the daily discharge of their duties. Corporate crime is committed in the pursuit of *organizational goals* and the effects of it are to cause injury, sometimes fatal, and financial loss to members of the public. To theorists of corporate crime such as Box, the well-publicized effects of such crime, like the poisonings at Bhopal, are merely the tip of an iceberg, because the pursuit of profit denies the rights of others who might stand in its path. His point is that corporate crime is not abnormal but a consequence of the everyday activities of organizations as they go about their normal business.

corporatism: a situation where organized economic interests are intimately connected to the *state*, so that political decisions are shaped by the major industrial, financial, and commercial groupings in society.

correlation: a mutual relationship between *variables* so that one is affected by the other. For example, age and visits to the doctor are both social variables. If a study were made of a group of people and information obtained about their age and the number of visits they had made to the doctor in the past year, these variables could be examined to see whether or not there was any connection. If the *sample* were sufficiently large, it would probably be found that, the older the person, the greater the number of visits to the doctor. This would be a positive correlation, i.e. as one variable (age) increased, so did the other (visits to the doctor). Population studies have shown that, as the level of literacy in a population rises (particularly among women) the average number of children born to a family falls. In this case, as one variable (the level of literacy) rises, the other (average number of children born) falls, so we say that there is a negative correlation between the two variables. We must be cautious, however, in attributing a causal relationship to correlating variables. It would not be possible to claim that the ability to read and write in itself causes the birth rate to fall; rather, it is the effect of a more literate population on the whole economic and social structure of a society that exerts an influence on the desired number of children. (See *spurious correlation.*)

correspondence principle: developed by Bowles and Gintis to suggest that what happens in schools mirrors what happens in the workplace, so that education can be seen as a direct preparation for the child's future role in an unequal *division of labor*. For example, they argue that the system of rewards and punishments in schools echoes that of the workplace. More importantly, children of the middle class receive a different education from that of the working class. In the case of the former they have a more independent type of schooling, which prepares them for more managerial jobs in the future. For the latter, schools emphasize obedience and discipline to prepare them for subordinate roles in the division of labor. The idea has been criticized because:

- much more goes on in schools than just preparation for work
- if the correspondence is so good, how does change in education come about?
- it relies, at the most basic level, on some sort of conspiracy between employers and teachers.

corroboration: information that lends support to or confirms existing information. For example, in *questionnaire* design, researchers sometimes include questions whose answers are checked for consistency with answers given previously. Similarly, in *interviews* with people who are or have been in the same situation (such as in the same work group) one person's version of an event or situation can be checked against the answers of another member of the group. Differences do not, of course, mean that either person is lying; they may simply be reporting the situation as it seems to them.

cosmology: the study of the fundamental nature of the universe and people's place within it.

cosmopolitan opinion leaders: those who stand between the media and their contacts and who are oriented toward world affairs and international news. They are often relative newcomers to a local community and tend to rely on national sources for their political information. Opinion leaders are usually asked questions about foreign affairs rather than local issues. (See *local opinion leaders.*)

cosmopolites: a concept developed by Gans to describe those inhabitants of the inner city who may be relatively poor, but who are not otherwise disadvantaged. These might include students, artists of all kinds, intellectuals, etc.

cottage industry: a *mode of production* typical of preindustrial societies, where the home was the main locus for the manufacture of goods needed in society. Such industry is small-scale and produces a limited range of goods. In modern societies, cottage industries continue to exist with some craft workers, but there is also a variation termed *outworking*.

counterculture: a general term for any subcultural form of ideas, beliefs, or practices that is distinct from and often hostile to the dominant *culture* in society. Countercultures can emerge from a common interest or from *ideology* or from social experiences that differ from the normal ones in society as a whole. It is often associated with alternative cultures such as the hippie movement of the 1960s, but can also be organized around political principles such as the environmental, or "green" movement.

countervailing power: the ability to resist dominant loci of *power* through the organization of solidaristic groups beyond the reach of the dominant culture, and the creation of alternative sources of strength to oppose official agencies. The classic example of countervailing power is *labor unions*, who provide alternative careers for the working class outside of, but in relationship to, the dominant industrial and political forces of capitalist society.

coupe epistemologique: literally the epistemological break, a term used to describe the belief that there is a fundamental difference between the early work of *Karl Marx*, represented by *Grundisse*, and his later work, especially *Das Kapital*. Proposed by Althusser, the epistemological break defines Marx's rejection of the romanticism of his youth for the hard science of his later years. The crucial difference was his abandonment of the concept of *alienation* and all its romantic allusions to a fundamental human nature.

coursework: work done by a student during a course of study, the mark for which usually forms part of the final grade awarded for the course. Most pieces of coursework take the form of an independent investigation carried out by the student, or an artifact produced during the course.

couvade: rituals that involve husbands simulating the experience of childbirth during the pregnancy, or most usually the childbirth, of their wives. Generally associated with simple societies, the custom also existed among the Basque people of southern Europe until the middle of the 19th century, and involved the husband taking to his bed with the new baby after the birth, and being visited and complimented by neighbors, while his wife went about her normal domestic tasks. The wearing by some *"new man"* expectant fathers of water-filled harnesses to experience the sensation of the advanced stages of pregnancy may also be seen as a new Western form of couvade, albeit only practiced by a few.

covert participant observation: see *participant observation*

covert research: research in which those being studied are unaware of it. (See *participant observation*.)

cow sociology: a term of derision applied to the type of sociology that puts itself at the service of capitalist enterprises. The concept was developed about the sociology of work, where some sociologists were employed by industrial enterprises to develop work enrichment programs so that workers would produce more at no extra cost. The implication of the term was that the task of the sociologist was to produce contented "cows" who would produce more "milk," thus denying the human qualities of workers.

craft industry: a form of production in which the work is carried out by skilled workers, fashioning the product from start to finish. Products tend to be individual or made through *batch production*. As the worker carries out a large number of varied tasks with some skill, it is said to be a less alienating form of production than others.

craft unions: *labor union* organizations for those workers who exercise a particular skill that is the result of long years of apprenticeship. An example might be the unions representing carpenters or bricklayers. (See *industrial unions*.)

credential inflation: a process in which higher and higher qualifications are demanded by employers, leading to a situation where many employees are significantly overqualified in terms of the demands of their actual job. (See *credentialism*.)

credentialism: a tactic of *social closure*, in which an occupational group seeks to close off rewards from other social groups by emphasizing the qualifications needed to practice. The claim to higher rewards therefore rests on the skills represented by the certificates that members of the occupation need in order to carry out the duties of the job. (See *exclusion; solidarism*.)

crime: behavior that breaks the law of the land. Sociological interest in crime has tended to focus on the social context in which it occurs and the consequences of lawbreaking for both criminal and victim. Recently, sociological interest has begun to focus on the process of lawmaking, as well as lawbreaking, with sociologists such as Foucault looking at the way that the law acts as a *discourse* to criminalize or decriminalize activities.

crime control industry: the security sector of industry, increasingly seen as a major part of the postmodern economy. Based on the idea that we are now all more afraid of crime than in the past, the industry includes elements such as the private patrol industry, the burglar alarm and house protection sector, closed-circuit TV, personal alarms, etc.

crime statistics: a range of official figures encompassing a number of different measurements of criminal activity. These might include reported crime broken down into constituent elements like detection rates, clearup rates, conviction rates, and so on. Crime statistics are *soft statistics* in that they are subject to social negotiation at every stage of their collection and compilation.

crimes of the powerful: a phrase used to describe the criminal activity of those at the top of society. While such crimes are not highly visible in the way that working-class crime is, Pearce argues that they account for the greatest proportion of crime in terms of material *wealth*. Thus, for example, tax evasion by the powerful is estimated to cost the country much more than welfare benefit fraud.

crimes without victims: a term used to describe those actions that have been criminalized by the *state*, but in which none of the consenting participants suffers any loss. The concept includes prostitution, homosexuality, drug-taking, and so on. Such crimes are important sociologically because they represent the frontiers of the state's activities in policing the private actions of individuals and thus represent the struggle between the ideologies of individualism and stateism.

criminalization: the process of making activities unlawful, often in order to serve the interests of some powerful group in society, frequently identified as the *ruling* *class.* Thus criminal law categories are used to control sections of the population and sometimes to eliminate them as a social problem. Criminalization may also be aimed at individuals or groups who threaten the legitimized activities of society, such as gay people, or at those who threaten the secrecy of the activities of the state.

critical criminology: a Marxist view of *crime* that argues that capitalism is itself the cause of crime, through its cultivation of the ethic of possessive materialism. Only by the rejection of *capitalism* and the establishment of a socialist society can the prerequisites for a crimefree society be established. However, critical criminology is criticized for being vague regarding how a crimefree society would emerge in socialism, and for sidestepping the examples of the Soviet Union and eastern Europe by arguing that they were not truly socialist societies. (See *National Deviancy Conference.*)

critical Marxism: that variant of *Marxism* that looks for the ways in which human history is the product of the hidden potency of people. It is humanistic in its approach and takes into account the individuals who make up social classes. As such it differs from other types of Marxism in privileging the roles of individuals in the sweep of history. The critical school was represented by such Marxists as Gramsci, Sartre, and the *Frankfurt School.* (See *scientific Marxism.*)

critical pedagogy: a postmodernist school of teaching based on the idea that teaching should be about the possibilities in children's lives and getting children to recognize that we live in a fragmented and no longer certain world. This type of *pedagogy* does not accept that there is only one truth to be taught, but rather that there is a variety of ways of looking at the world depending on the position of the viewer.

cross-class families: families in which the husband and wife are both in paid employment, but in different occupations, in different social classes. The implication of this formation is that when classifying *families* into social classes it is not sufficient to use only the husband's occupation as traditional *stratification* theorists have done. Feminists in particular have pointed out the importance of cross-class families when calculating the social classes of individuals.

cross-class voting: where members of a particular social class vote against the party that is seen as representing their class interests.

cross-cultural comparison: a classical sociological method, rooted deep in the history of sociology, that examines two or more societies to see their similarities and differences. From these comparisons sociologists hope to establish universals in human societies as well as laying bare the possible variations.

cross-sectional studies: studies of a varied *population* that divide that population into representative subgroups with different characteristics to get a picture of the overall group. For example, a study of a multiracial inner-city area might divide the population into different *ethnic groups*, different age groups, different types of *family structure*, and so on. The aim is to make the cross-section as representative as possible of the population as a whole.

cross-tabulation: a simple statistical presentation that contrasts the proportions of different *variables* in a direct way. An example might be to cross-tabulate the proportion of the population of two towns engaged in mining and fishing:

	Town A	Town B
Percentage in mining	30	60
Percentage in fishing	20	2

Cross-tabulation allows the direct comparison and contrasting of social variables to arrive at similarities and differences.

cult: either the beliefs and *rituals* associated with a particular god, as in the cult of Isis, or a type of religious group. Cults are often characterized as being relatively short-lived, having a charismatic leader and possibly having no acts of collective worship, but promising their followers access to spiritual or supernatural powers. In practice it is often difficult to distinguish clearly between cults and *sects*.

cultivation analysis: an approach in the study of the media that emphasizes the central importance of television in representing the world to its audience. It concludes that for many individuals the distorted and partial reality portrayed on television represents what the world is "really" like. The extent of the portrayal of sex and violence on television, therefore, influences the way that such individuals actually see the world, which is as a mediated reality.

cultural accumulation: a process by which new cultural traits are added to a society, and become an accepted part of the *culture*. These additional cultural traits are often the result of borrowing from another cultural group that may live in close proximity, as with an ethnic minority within the society, or from a culture that is greatly admired, as in the case of the spread of aspects of rock culture, dress, and dance forms from the US and Europe to other parts of the world.

cultural capital: those desired *competences,* such as forms of language and expression and valued social skills, that the middle classes are able to confer on their children, together with economic capital. The concept was introduced by the Marxist writer Bourdieu, who argued that success in the education system is largely based on having and displaying these skills, which are much more difficult for working-class children to acquire, thus making it easier for middle-class children to succeed. Critics of the concept accuse Bourdieu of *cultural determinism,* i.e. belief in the inevitability of class cultures being transmitted from one generation to the next, and also of ignoring the significance of other factors in educational success or failure. (See *cultural reproduction.*)

cultural deprivation: the notion that the failure of certain groups of children within the education system is a result of their culturally deprived home background. The idea received widespread support in the 1960s, when a number of programs of *compensatory education* were developed to make up for this supposed deficiency in the child's home background. Critics of the idea argue that it is a contradiction in terms, i.e. by definition, all social groups have a *culture,* and what was actually being preferred was a white middle-class notion of desirable cultural forms such as particular kinds of literature and music. It was emphasized that children who were failing in the system, particularly black children, had a very rich culture that was ignored or misunderstood by the largely white teachers, educational psychologists, and administrators. It was suggested by many that blaming educational failure on the child's home background was a way of avoiding the real issues of *poverty* and *discrimination.*

cultural determinism: a belief that the dominant *culture* or way of life of a society or group exerts a determining influence on other aspects of behavior.

cultural difference theory: in the sociology of education, the theory that much working-class *underachievement* is caused by the mismatch between the culture of the working class and the middle-class *culture* of the school. In contrast to *cultural deprivation* theory, this therefore accepts that the responsibility for failure is at least in part to do with what happens in school. (See *black box view.*)

cultural dopes: a term in criticism of determinist theories that see individuals as unable to affect their own lives through their actions. It is often used as a critique of Marxist theories that suggest that individuals blindly follow the dictates of economics without *agency* of their own. Interactionists argue that, on the contrary, individuals do have real choices and are not determined by their social or economic position.

cultural drift: the notion that a society changes over time as a result of the largely unconscious, small changes to aspects of *culture*. It is believed that these changes will lead the society in a particular direction, e.g. becoming more Westernized.

cultural effects theory: a theory of the influence of the media, which suggests the media have long-term effects on the audience, mainly through the promotion of cultural *stereotypes*. The *audience* of these images is itself differentiated into social groups so that members receive and interpret the messages of the stereotypes according to the social position in which they find themselves. (See *drip effect.*)

cultural imperialism: the imposition by one group of its cultural forms on another group, particularly members of a different society. The term is often used in the context of the *mass media* to refer to the export of particular kinds of mass media and mass entertainment, and the products allied to them, such as certain styles of dress. With the growth of *media conglomerates* which now operate across different continents, it is alleged that cultural imperialism is increasing, and posing a real threat to indigenous forms of *culture*.

cultural pluralism: an approach to *race* relations that acknowledges the cultural diversity of modern society and accepts the legitimacy of *ethnic minority* cultures. One of the implications of this is to introduce strong elements of ethnic minority culture into the *curriculum* of schools. (See *assimilation; integrative race relations.*)

cultural relativism: the view that there are no universal beliefs, but that each *culture* must be understood in its own terms, because cultures cannot be translated into terms that are accessible everywhere. The implication of cultural relativism is that no one society is superior to another; they are merely different.

cultural reproduction: associated with Marxist theory, a term for the process whereby social relationships of superordination and subordination in the class structure are recreated *generation* by generation. Cultural reproduction in capitalist societies is therefore associated with the establishment of *ideological hegemony* in each generation, so that working-class children end up in working-class jobs and middle-class children in middle-class jobs. The conditions of cultural reproduction are the result of pervasive effort by the *ideological state apparatus*. It is never complete, as there are always changes in the *occupational structure* that create opportunities for *social* *mobility*, but the control of the *bourgeoisie* is made more secure through cultural repro-duction.

cultural taboos: aspects of social life that are considered forbidden by the *norms* of society. In methodological terms, these create some difficulty in using historical or cross-cultural documents as evidence for sociological research, as the existence of cultural taboos may cause the omission of important material. For example, if talk-ing about sexual matters were a cultural taboo, it is unlikely that surviving documents would contain information about this important area of social life.

cultural transmission theory: a basic idea of the *Chicago School* that, in cities, natural areas emerge that, because of immigration patterns, are isolated from the mainstream of the rest of society. As a consequence the inhabitants develop their own knowledge, beliefs, and forms of behavior that make possible specific forms of deviant behavior. Within each of these natural areas the cultures are transmitted to the next generation even if this is composed of a new set of immigrants. Thus it is areas of the *city*, not their populations, that demonstrate stable patterns of deviant behavior. As populations move out into the suburbs the transmission of the deviant *subculture* is broken.

culture: a term used in sociology to denote the way of life of a society. It covers all the folk-ways of a society, such as language, customs, and dress, as well as the symbols and artifacts that people develop. The concept of culture became a central organiz-ing theme of much sociology in the 1980s and 1990s, as postmodernists moved away from a focus on structure to look at cultural forms. There are different forms of culture that sociologists have identified, such as *high culture* and *popular culture*.

culture industry: a term developed by the *Frankfurt School* to denote that the pro-ducers of cultural material are embedded in economic processes, and therefore that to understand the media, sociologists need to look at processes of profit and loss, resourcing, etc. associated with any capitalist enterprise. The importance of this insight is that it is not enough just to look at the communication processes in media organizations, but at the economic basis underpinning these processes must also be examined.

culture of contentment: a concept devised by Galbraith to describe the 40% of the population who are relatively well-off and will block electorally any attempt to increase taxes to pay for more welfare services for the less well-off and the poor. The term arose after the success of the Republicans in the US and the Conservatives in Britain in the 1980s in creating the expectation of tax cuts among the electorate. The culture of contentment therefore represents an alternative to the postwar *consensus* that a strong *welfare state* is important for social stability.

culture of poverty: attitudes and patterns of behavior allegedly characteristic of the poor, which are transmitted from generation to generation and which serve to perpetuate the state of *poverty*. These attitudes include fatalism, dependency, apathy, and despair. The concept is particularly associated with the anthropologist Oscar Lewis, who carried out research into poor families in Mexico and Puerto Rico. The concept is often used in a negative sense to imply that poverty is largely the result of these negative characteristics, i.e. is the fault of the poor themselves. However, Lewis saw these attitudes as at least partly a response to an existing situation, and argued that poverty was particularly likely to flourish in a low-wage, profit-oriented economy with minimal assistance for the poor. Some critics of the "culture of poverty" explanation of poverty argue that the real causes of poverty lie not in the attitudes and behavior of the poor, but in the inbuilt inequalities of *wealth, income,* and *power* particularly associated with capitalist societies. (See *dependency culture; underclass.*)

culture of service: an ethos associated with the *New Right* sociologists, defining the appropriate way for public services to operate in relation to their *clients.* It implies that the main purpose of welfare organizations should be to serve client needs. This is in contrast to traditional ways of seeing welfare organizations as delivering state-defined services to those in need. The culture of service will be, according to the *New Right,* a result of the introduction of market principles into such services as the education system.

culture shock: the feeling of disruption that individuals might feel when confronted with a different and seemingly alien *culture,* which challenges the taken-for-granted assumptions of their own perspective. There is a tension between the unsettling effect that contact with the strange can have and the enlightenment that an alternative culture can provide.

culture structure: a term developed by Merton as a way of describing the relationship between means and ends in society. One half of the culture structure is the goals defined by the culture of society as the proper aims for people. The other half is the ways that individuals may legitimately pursue those goals. Where the relationship between these two is imbalanced, either because of the escalation of goals beyond the ability of many individuals to achieve them or through the blocking of legitimate means, then *deviance* is likely to result. Thus strain between ways and means leads to a state of *anomie,* to which individuals can respond in a variety of different ways. However, the idea of a culture structure has been criticized, because it takes societal goals for granted and does not ask who defines the proper aims for society or who decides which means are legitimate. The idea is therefore based on an acceptance of existing society as the best possible one. (See *innovation; institutionalized means; rebellion; retreatism; ritualistic deviance.*)

curriculum: the subjects and courses offered in educational institutions that form the basic program of study. These are also referred to as the "overt curriculum." (See *hidden curriculum.*)

custom: an established and traditional pattern of behavior, which may or may not have lost its efficacy through time. Customs can provide integrative activity for a society and are often taken for granted by those who share them.

cyber-ethnography refers both to a specific kind of research situation, in which researchers are examining types of interaction and communication between groups on the Internet, and also to the use of the Internet to gain access to a sample of respondents for the purposes of conducting real or virtual surveys or interviews.

cybernation school: a school of thought based on a theory about automation, which suggests that as it develops it will fundamentally alter society. Proponents of the cybernation school, such as Michael, suggest that:

- automation is a radical break from previous technological developments
- that the pace of automation is accelerating
- that it will lead to chronic and continuous high levels of unemployment.

Critics argue that the extent of automation has been exaggerated and that there is little evidence for an accelerating rate. Moreover, new technologies create jobs as well as destroy them, so there is little evidence for continued high levels of unemployment.

cybernetic analogy: an analogy developed from the work of Spencer that compares society to a machine. The basic idea is that communication is essential for the system of the machine or society to hold together. Communication is provided by specialist parts of the machine that provide feedback for the system to adapt its arrangements and prevent disintegration. (See *biological analogy*.)

cycle of deprivation: see *poverty cycle*

cycle of poverty: see *poverty cycle*

death: the cessation of existence. Sociologists have been interested in the rituals that surround it as one of the *rites de passage* and more recently, in the ways that death can be defined. Whereas death might seem to be an obvious state, the development of *medical technology* has complicated the definition so that the concept of brain death has been become central to the medical profession. However, the existence of life support machines can lead to emotional complications for those who are left behind.

death of the family: a widely expressed argument, found at all levels of society, that the *family* as an institution is "dying." Evidence given for this includes the high rates of *divorce* and *cohabitation* and the increase in the number of *single-parent families*. Many argue that the root cause of the perceived rising *underclass* in society is the breakdown of the family. Critics of the "death of the family" argument suggest that the family as an institution should be viewed as changing, rather than dying, pointing out for example that more couples remain married than get divorced, that many cohabitants later marry and that a high proportion of divorced people later remarry. Many single-parent families are only temporarily in that state. Critics also argue that the family continues to provide a wide range of essential welfare and support services for its members. (See *loss of family functions.*)

death of the subject: a phrase used in connection with *structuralism*, to indicate that structuralism tends to reduce the individual to an automaton with little ability to make free choices outside of the forces of the structures he or she inhabits. (See *bearers of the mode of production.*)

death rate: a calculation of the rate at which individuals die within a given population. The crude death rate is expressed as the number of deaths per thousand of the live population per year. It takes no account of the *age profile of the population.* The standardized death rate gives rates for males and females, and people in different age groups. The major cause of death in developed countries has changed from infectious diseases to degenerative illnesses, with circulatory disease, cancer, and respiratory diseases now causing the greatest number of deaths for men and women of all ages. (See *infant mortality rate; life expectancy.*)

decapitalization: the process whereby the natural assets of *third-world* countries are exported to the *first world*, thus depriving the third-world countries of the means to invest in their own development. While much decapitalization takes the form of the export of third-world goods, especially food produce, to the first world, there are also direct processes of decapitalization occurring. For example, the *patriation of profits* from the activities of *transnational companies* in the third world back to countries of origin is a major form of decapitalization. The term is usually employed by *underdevelopment* theorists when explaining the causes of *poverty* in the third world. New Right theorists have been critical of this process, arguing that capital flows between the first and third worlds are two-way, with the third world the beneficiary of capital injections from the first world through infrastructure projects, etc. (See *aid.*)

decarceration policies: the move away from prisons as the main form of punishment for wrongdoers. Such policies include electronic tagging measures, probation orders, community service work, halfway houses, etc.

decentering: a term used by postmodernists to indicate a moving away from traditional ways of looking at issues toward a more fragmented and oblique approach to social problems and *discourses.*

decentralization: the dispersal of *power* away from the center toward outlying areas. In politics, it is used when central governments give more power to regional governments or to county or town councils. In the sociology of work it is used when managements devolve responsibility for the quality of their work to the workers themselves rather than keeping power and responsibility only within management.

dechristianization: the process whereby modern Western societies, especially in urban areas, are turning away from Christianity, toward secular existence, non-standard Christian-inspired cults, or non-Christian religions. (See *secularization.*)

decoding: used by semiological analysts to indicate the process whereby the messages encoded by the producers of texts have to be interpreted by the "reader." The problem for analysis is that *audiences* do not always decode the messages in the way that the producer of the message intended. There is therefore always a gap between intention and effect. (See *encoding; text.*)

decomposition of capital: a term developed by Dahrendorf to describe how the capitalist class dissolves from a monolithic unity into separate and competing interests. Dahrendorf was writing particularly about the emergence of a distinct group of managers, separate from the owners of large corporations. (See *managerial revolution.*)

decomposition of labor: a term developed by Dahrendorf to describe the breaking up of a class-conscious working class into smaller groupings with different interests. The crucial part of the process was the development of different levels of *skill* among the working class, which led to differentials between them, and also the emergence of groups within the working class who saw themselves as distinct from other working-class groups. (See *aristocracy of labor.*)

deconstruction: associated with Derrida, the analysis of texts to demonstrate their ultimate ambiguity and *situatedness.* Derrida rejects the idea that any *text* contains some transcendental truth or meaning in favor of the idea that any meaning exists in relationship to other texts through their intertextuality. Meaning is established by social institutionalization which privileges one interpretation of a text over others. The idea of deconstruction has been criticized as an ultimately relativist one, in which one person's interpretation becomes as valid as any other.

deference: a social attitude that accords reverence to social superiors, on account of their *ascribed status.* Deference is demanded and given to social superiors by those who are in established and traditional relations of inferiority with them. It is linked to the idea of *paternalism,* which describes the sense of duty superiors have toward those who give them deference.

deferential workers: those in employment situations where there is a personal relationship between the employer and the workforce based on workers' respect for the superior employer and the employer's care for the deferential workforce. In its most extreme manifestation, deferential workers were taken care of by the employer in much wider areas of social life than just work. Deference was therefore expected from the workforce in the wider social world.

deferred gratification: the postponing of immediate satisfaction or rewards to enhance or increase those that will follow later. An example would be a child's decision not to watch television in order to prepare for a test the following day. It is argued that teaching children to defer gratification in this way enables middle-class parents to bring about the greater success in the education system of their children compared with working-class children, as the practice is often viewed as a particularly middle-class characteristic. The concept is not, however, restricted to use in an educational context. *Weber* saw it as an important feature of the *Protestant ethic.*

deficit explanations: see *cultural deprivation*

definition of the situation: a phrase identified with W.I. Thomas, who said, "If men define their situations as real, they are real in their consequences." Despite the implicit *sexism*, which was a product of the age in which Thomas was writing, the concept of the "definition of the situation" has been one of the most fundamental tenets of sociology. It indicates the power of the subjective in forging social relationships and influencing events.

deindustrialization: the process whereby a society loses its manufacturing capacity and concentrates on the service industries rather than a traditional manufacturing base. The loss of manufacturing is associated with the increased globalization of industry, with a growth in the service industries seen as partly compensating for this. In terms of *gender,* the loss of manufacturing has implications for *gender codes*, as it was within heavy industries that traditional "macho" notions of the male worker were forged.

deinstitutionalization: see *community care*

delayering: the process whereby organizations remove levels of the hierarchy to produce much flatter hierarchical structures. Delayering is an important part of creating a system of *lean production*, but it has been responsible in part for the phenomenon of middle-class unemployment.

delinquency: antisocial actions ranging from the criminal, such as vandalism, to the disruptive but legal, such as messing around in the classroom. Sociological focus has been largely on rates of criminal delinquency, mostly with respect to teenagers.

delinquent drift: see *drift*

demedicalization: the process whereby sections of society turn away from traditional medicine and toward alternative medical treatment, such as acupuncture. (See *alternative medicine.*)

democracy: a system of *government* that involves some form of election of the government by the people. The emergence of modern democracies has produced a large number of different ways in which elections might be conducted, from *representative democracy* to *direct democracy*. Democracy also has an ideological aspect, in that it is seen as a valued feature of societies. Some sociologists argue that modern *capitalism* necessitates the emergence of democracy if it is to function efficiently.

democratic elitism: a *power* situation, in which there are formal electoral arrangements for the people to cast their vote, but where real power rests with opposing factions of the *elite*, who compete for electoral support from subordinate groups. Thus while retaining the outward form of a democratic system, the rulers of society are able to concentrate power into their hands and rule for their own benefit. The establishment of hegemonic social relationships is important in establishing the legitimacy of this arrangement. (See *hegemony.*)

democratic pluralist model: an approach to *psephology* that focuses on the statistics of voting and the correlations between particular voting habits and certain social characteristics. It is thus an empirical approach to the study of voting behavior and uses statistical analysis to identify trends in elections.

democratic socialism: a philosophy of the collectivist left that favors the electoral process for achieving the socialist society, as opposed to the revolutionary instincts of the Communists.

demographic transition: the change in the balance of *birth rates* and *death rates* that is associated with the *Industrial Revolution* and thus with the different population dynamic associated with industrialized societies. The main factors in the demographic transition were firstly a fall in the death rate, which led to an increase in population. This was followed by a fall in the birth rate, which led to a stabilization of the population at a much higher level than at the start of the process.

demography: the study of populations, with particular reference to their size and structure and how and why these change over time. This means that demographers study *birth, death* and *marriage rates*, patterns of *migration*, and other important factors that affect population growth or decline, such as climate, food supply, and the availability of employment.

demystification: the process by which explanations based on *magic, religion*, and the *supernatural* are replaced by other explanations based on logic, science, and rational thought. (See *desacrilization; disenchantment.*)

denomination: a Christian religious organization usually thought to lie midway between a *church* and a *sect* in terms of its characteristics. Some denominations, such as Methodists, developed from sects. Denominations characteristically accept as members all who wish to join, and are tolerant of other religious groups, not claiming that only they know the true path to salvation. Most denominations have a professional body of ministers, but also make use of many lay (i.e. nonordained) people as preachers. Denominations can only exist in societies with a reasonably high level of religious tolerance.

denotation: used in *semiotics* to indicate the actual description of a *signifier* – what is actually seen. For example, the denotation of the signifier "torch" might be "a piece of wood with flames at one end." (See *connotation.*)

density: in urban sociology, the concentration of a large number of individuals in a relatively small area, characteristically the city. This was one of the features of *urbanism* defined by Wirth and its importance lay in the fact that as the density of people increased, the possibility of meaningful relationships decreased.

density of membership: with reference to *labor unions,* density is the actual number of members, divided by the potential number of members multiplied by 100 to gain a percentage. This can be represented thus:

$$\text{FORMULA:} \quad \text{Density} = \frac{\text{Actual number of members}}{\text{Potential number of members}} \times 100$$

The reason for calculating the density is that it provides a measure of how powerful a union is in relation to the employers. The higher the density the greater the union's power. A *closed shop* has 100% density. Density therefore represents the potential effectiveness of a labor union.

dependency culture: a term associated with the *New Right,* based on the idea that universal welfare provision has led people to expect the *state* to look after and provide for them, thus robbing them of self-reliance and social responsibility. The benefits of the *welfare state* are thought to be overgenerous and too readily available, leading to incentives for remaining unemployed rather than seeking work. Holders of these New Right views, such as David Marsland, also believe that the culture of dependency is a cause of family breakdown, rising levels of crime, and economic decline. They suggest that help should be given only to those in genuine need and that the welfare needs of the majority (e.g. education, health, pensions) should be largely met by private and voluntary organizations rather than by the state. Critics of the concept of dependency culture argue that there is no evidence to suggest that people would rather remain unemployed than be in paid work, and point out that no account is taken of the actual availability of jobs. Others point out the significance of the *poverty trap* in keeping people in *poverty,* and blame the structured inequality of a capitalist society. (See *culture of poverty.*)

dependency ratio: the ratio within a population of those under 15 and over 65 as compared to those between those years, i.e. of working age. Those under 15 make up the "young dependants," and those over 65 the "elderly dependants," and together they are referred to as the "dependent population." The dependency ratio is a very important factor in the economy of a country, as it provides a measure of the proportion of people to be supported by the labor of others. Nonindustrial and *newly industrializing countries,* with high *birth rates* and a relatively low *life expectancy,* typically have a high proportion of young dependants, while the low birth rates and low *death rates* of advanced industrial countries mean that these are all experiencing *aging populations.* World population statistics show that in 1990, for every 100 people of working age there were 53 people under 15 and 10 over 65, while projections for 2025 suggest that there will be 38 under 15 and 15 over 65. (See *age profile of the population.*)

dependency theory: an explanation for the continued lack of *development* throughout the *third world* and for the relationship of dependency between the third world and the developed capitalist societies of the West. The principal architect of dependency theory is André Gunder Frank. Though emerging from a Marxist perspective and concerned with the exploitation of the *third world* by the first world, Frank was not himself a Marxist, because he defined *capitalism* primarily as a market system, rather than in terms of ownership (as traditional Marxists would). Frank argued that the *undeveloped* state of the third world was a consequence of *first-world* policy toward the third world. He argued that first-world countries had "enclaves" in the third world, usually in the capital cities, to which he gave the name "*metropolis*." The role of the metropolis was to exploit the *hinterland* of the third-world countries, concentrating capital in the metropolis. In turn, first-world countries exploited the metropolis, so that capital was transferred to the capitalist countries of the West. This *decapitalization* was, according to Frank, the prime reason for the *underdevelopment* of the third world.

Frank has been criticized from many different angles:

- Some Marxists, such as Brenner, argue that it is the exploitation of the *working class* in the first world that should be the focus of analysis, not the relationship between the first and third worlds.
- Other Marxists, such as Warren, argue that Frank ignores the development that is going on in the third world, because capitalism has a positive role to play in the third world in destroying traditional patterns of behavior that could hinder development.
- *New Right* theorists, such as Bauer, argue that Frank gives too much attention to economic forces and ignores the importance of *culture* in promoting or hindering development.

Process of underdevelopment according to Frank

dependent elderly: a term used to describe those old people, usually over 75, who are in need of some sort of care. The increase in the dependent elderly is argued to be one of the main reasons for the crisis in the *welfare state,* as the resources needed to target the dependent elderly have to be raised from taxpayers. (See *aging population.*)

dependent population: see *dependency ratio*

dependent variable: that which changes as a result of changes in something else, known as the *independent variable.* For example, if the ability of women with children to take paid employment depended on the availability of affordable child care, then an increase in low-cost day-care centers and nursery schools (the independent variable) should result in an increase in mothers taking employment (the dependent variable). This could, of course, be tested, although since there are many other variables, it would be difficult to claim that an increase in child-care facilities was the only reason for the increase in working mothers.

deprofessionalization: the process whereby professionals lose their unique status in society and become like other occupational groups. Various factors are said to be involved in this process:

- The loss of monopoly of knowledge, as other forms of service grow up. For example, *alternative medicine* offers a different route to health from that offered by the medical profession.

- A loss of public faith in the service ethic of the professionals.
- A loss of *autonomy* as professionals increasingly work in large bureaucracies.

Many sociologists dispute that deprofessionalization is happening, but argue that the form of professionalism is changing under the impact of large-scale *bureaucratization* of the service industries.

depth interview: see *unstructured interview*

desacrilization: a decline in belief in the *sacred*. It is argued that this process is taking place and is part of the overall process of *secularization*. (See *resacrilization*.)

descent group: members of a society who can all trace their lineage back to the same ancestor.

deschooling: a process suggested by Ivan Illich by which the formal education system would be abolished, as it is damaging to students. Illich argues that schools indoctrinate students into accepting the views and interests of the *ruling class*, stifle creativity and nonconformity, and train children to become mindless consumers.

deskilling: a term used to denote the stripping away from workers of traditional skills, through the implementation of the principles of *scientific management*. Braverman argued that increasing specialization in modern industry results in a reduction in the skills workers can exercise. He argued that this was a deliberate policy introduced by management to increase the control they can exercise over the workers and as a result increase profits. Deskilled workers have little *power* as they are easily replaced. However, some sociologists dispute the view that the deskilling process takes place as a matter of policy, but argue rather that technological innovation (a central part of the deskilling process according to Braverman) both destroys old skills and creates new skills at the same time. (See *Taylorism*.)

detailed division of labor: the breaking down of a work task into its smallest and most detailed constituent parts. The term was devised as a contrast to *specialization*. (See *social division of labor*.)

determinant level: a term used by Althusser to describe the economic forces in society that determine whether the political and ideological levels have *relative autonomy* or not. Economic conditions therefore determine the rest of society, including whether other spheres of social life might be dominant. (See *dominant level*.)

determinism: the belief that individuals' activities are forged by their situations and environment and that they have little free will or choice in how they behave. Different theorists have identified different forces that determine individuals. Functionalists argue that common *values* are the prime determinants of individual behavior, while Marxists identify economics. (See *voluntarism*.)

development: usually a reference to the process whereby societies move from an agricultural base to an industrial state. The term is associated with *evolutionary theory* and is linked to the idea of progress from an undeveloped state to a superior, developed one. Sociological concern with the issue of development has been present from the very beginnings of the sociological enterprise. The *classical sociologists* were primarily concerned with explaining the immense changes that Western societies were experiencing during *industrialization* and it was on this development process that they focused in their theories. The term itself is controversial, in that sociologists often disagree about what constitutes development. Some sociologists see development as part of an inevitable convergence of all industrializing societies to an American-type society, while others see more than one way to develop a modern industrial economy. (See *convergence theory*; *underdevelopment*.)

deviance: on the simple level, behavior that goes against the dominant *norms* of the specific society or group in which it occurs. The problem with the concept from the sociological point of view is that deviance is socially constructed – that is, there are no actions that are in themselves inherently abnormal or universally condemned by all societies at all times. Deviance is thus situational and contextual. For example, killing another human being is seen as deviant in peacetime, but may be a requirement of a soldier in wartime. All social actions are governed by rules but the rules themselves are subject to change over time. Therefore, even to suggest that there are dominant norms in a society is to beg the questions: "Who says they are dominant and how does the sociologist know that they are?" Ultimately, sociologists tend to give specific examples of deviant behavior, which are then subject to qualification or amendment if circumstances change. There is also a further problem in that individuals who engage in what is seen as deviant behavior are not necessarily known or labeled as deviant, because the circumstances in which they engage in the behavior may exempt them from the label. (See *secret deviant*.)

deviance disavowal: the process whereby an individual or group comes to reject the label that is being pinned on them. While this often has an individual dimension, in that individuals may engage in a self-negating prophecy, there is also a group phenomenon, where socially "deviant" groups reject the labels that "straight" society attaches to them and seek to forge their own *identity*.

deviancy amplification: see *amplification of deviance*

deviant career: the process whereby an individual comes to accept a deviant lifestyle as a way of life, through the acceptance of the deviant label and the adoption of subcultural behavior and values. It implies that the labeled deviant has a choice of whether to accept the label and thus embrace a deviant lifestyle or reject it. (See *deviant disavowal*; *labeling theory*.)

deviant case: in *methodology*, the one example that does not fit the general circumstances that have been established. It may be seen as the exception that "proves" (i.e. tests) the rule.

deviant voter: one who votes for a political party that is said not to express his or her class membership. It includes the manual worker who supports a right-wing or conservative party and the middle-class professional who supports a left-wing or workers' party.

dharma: in *Hinduism*, a belief that everything in the universe has its proper place in an overall ranking system, with purity at one end and pollution at the other. The principles of dharma were used to rank the various *castes*, and the *rituals*, observances, and avoidances that were proper to each.

dialectic: a central idea of Marxism that argues that everything that exists is in a contradictory existence with its opposite, and the tension between the two produces a new situation, which also exists in contradiction to its opposite. It is thus an explanation of how *social change* occurs in society and history is produced. It can be represented as:

$$\underset{(\text{thing})}{\text{thesis}} + \underset{(\text{opposite})}{\text{antithesis}} = \underset{(\text{new thing})}{\text{synthesis}}$$

Dialectic

dialectic of control: a term used by *Giddens* to suggest that all citizens have some power to influence the course of events, even if very limited. The classic case is the prisoner, whose very dependence on the authorities to clothe and feed him or her confers some power over his or her situation. In conflict situations, the prisoner can go on hunger strike, refuse to work in prison workshops, etc., thus demonstrating a limited range of opportunity even in a tightly controlled environment.

dialectical materialism: the process identified by Marxists as the fundamental principle of history, which suggests that the *contradiction* and resolution of economic forces in society is the main way that change is accomplished. The actual material forces that are in a dialectical relationship are social classes, and it is the conflict between these that produces social progress.

diaries: written accounts of events as experienced and interpreted by the author. Diaries are a source of *secondary data* that can be of great use to the sociologist. One of the most well-known large-scale use of diaries is the Mass Observation studies of the 1930s, in which large numbers of people in Great Britain were asked to keep diaries. Supplemented by *interviews* and *questionnaires*, the Mass Observation diaries provide a rich account of life in Britain in the 1930s and 1940s. Obviously, it needs to be acknowledged that diaries are subjective documents, but they provide a rich source of information if used with care, particularly for research into the past. (See *documents*.)

dichotomous models: representations of social formations, in which opposites are used to compare the "before" and "after" situations. For example, the move from an agricultural to an industrial society is often shown in dichotomous terms, with agricultural societies displaying one characteristic (such as *ascription*) and industrial societies the opposite (such as *achievement*). Critics of dichotomous models argue that they inevitably oversimplify what are very complex situations. An example of a dichotomous model is shown below.

Traditional societies	Modern societies
ascription	achievement
role diffuseness	role specificity
particularism	universalism
affectivity	affective-neutrality
collective orientation	self-orientation

Parsons' pattern variables

differential association: a theory of *deviance* developed by Sutherland, which suggests that everyone comes into contact with attitudes toward the law that are favorable or unfavorable, and the deviant is one whose unfavorable contacts outweigh the favorable. The implication of this is that those areas of the city where unfavorable attitudes to the law are rife are likely to be high-crime areas. Critics argue that this theory reduces individuals to slaves of their environment, without any choice as to whether they commit deviant acts or not.

differential fertility: a term to indicate the differences among social groups in the average number of children per family. The differences are usually examined among varying social classes or ethnic groups. Social class differences in *fertility* were used as an explanation for *upward social mobility*, as it was argued that those in the upper and middle classes did not produce enough children, especially sons, to fill all the available white-collar, professional, and managerial jobs, thereby necessitating recruitment from the working class. With the advent of more reliable and easily available birth control and a rising standard of living for many, rates of differential fertility among the social classes have declined.

differentiation: ways in which the teaching and learning process can be adapted to cater for students of different abilities. There are two ways in which this can happen. "Differentiation by input" refers to ways in which the materials used in the classroom are adapted to match broad-ability bands of students, or where more able students are expected to tackle more tasks. "Differentiation by outcome" refers to a situation in which all students are given the same work, and then graded on the basis of their results.

diffusion: the process whereby social practices and *beliefs* are transferred from one group to another, so that similar cultural traits can be found in many different societies and levels of society. (See *stratified diffusion*.)

DINKY: an acronym for "double income, no kids yet." The term is used particularly in marketing to refer to a young or fairly young couple, both members of which are in well-paid employment, and who consequently have a high disposable income available to spend primarily on themselves and their home.

diploma disease: a term used by Dore to describe the way in which qualifications are becoming more and more important in securing employment and a decent standard of living. (See *credential inflation*.)

direct democracy: the political situation where every citizen is involved in decision-making through the casting of a ballot. The original model of direct democracy was ancient Athens, where men who were not slaves and who held citizenship gathered together in assemblies to decide the great issues of the day. A modern equivalent would be the Swiss system of referenda for making important decisions about the direction of the country.

direct instruction: a system of *pedagogy* that is highly traditional and is focused on basic skills. It has been criticized because it allegedly creates dependency and a lack of initiative among students.

direct taxation: the levying of taxes directly on a person's *income* or *wealth*, e.g. income tax or inheritance tax. (See *indirect taxation*; *progressive taxation*.)

disability: a term used to cover a range of health problems that incapacitate the individual in some way. The term has fallen into disuse, as many have challenged the implied contrast with being able to do things, which suggests a passivity and helplessness among those labeled "disabled." (See *handicap.*)

disciplinary drill: any widely accepted ritual that results in the docility of those subjected to it. The classic example of a disciplinary drill is large-scale drugs testing that occurs routinely in sports and work. Despite its intrusion into the personal lives of citizens, it is generally accepted without protest.

disciplinary technology: the techniques and practices identified by Foucault as central to the control of the bodies of citizens in modern societies. Disciplinary technology can be obvious, such as "electronic tagging," but much of it is mundane and everyday, such as school uniform or examinations.

discipline: a central concept of Foucault that refers to the processes by which societies control the bodies of their citizens through the "swarming" of *disciplinary technology* into all aspects of their lives. The aim of the discipline techniques, which are based on work, training, exercise, and surveillance (as though in a prison), is to produce docile bodies and thus manageable groups of citizens, without recourse to the violence of earlier societies.

discourse: a term developed by Foucault to explain how human beings attempt to bring order out of the chaos of social life. A discourse is a collection of related statements or events that defines relationships among elements of the social world. The establishment of these relationships involves the use and establishment of *power* to create knowledge. To Foucault, all knowledge establishes power over others, because discourses are used to control and channel behavior. Those who control the discourse have the power to define the position of others.

discourse of derision: the process whereby a phenomenon is discredited through establishing ways of thinking about it that inevitably lead to negative feelings about it. It is not just constant criticism, but a way of framing problems and issues so that whatever approach is made to something, a negative result is obtained.

discovery learning: a pedagogical method based on the belief that children learn faster and better if they are given the opportunity to solve problems and find out information for themselves, rather than having knowledge imparted by the teacher. The method, although very successful when used by good teachers, has its critics, who argue that children need more structure and guidance in their learning. Discovery learning is often contrasted with "*chalk-and-talk*" as an example of a progressive rather than traditional teaching method. Some critics have attributed what they see as the decline in educational standards to the widespread use of discovery learning in schools, particularly by teachers who were trained in the 1960s and 1970s. However, research has consistently shown that most teachers use a variety of teaching methods, with a bias toward the traditional. (See *experiential teaching.*)

discrimination: treating a person or group unfairly, usually because of a negative view of certain of their characteristics. Discrimination is suffered in a variety of spheres of life by certain groups, including those with disabilities, women, the poor, the elderly, and members of ethnic minority groups. (See *positive discrimination.*)

discursive consciousness: the ability to explain why we do what we do. We are being discursive when we offer reasons for our actions, and these may be bound up in formal discourse, or in humor, irony, etc. (See *practical consciousness; unconscious motivation.*)

disembedding: the process by which social relations are no longer contained within local settings, but can be lifted out to a global context. The use of email and the Internet as a means of swift contact with other parts of the globe is a good example. (See *space–time distanciation.*)

disempowerment: the process whereby marginal groups in society are robbed of the ability to influence decisions because of the control by the powerful. This may occur through legislation or through *discourses of derision.*

disenchantment: a process described by *Weber* in which, as a result of the development of *science* and rational modes of thought, the explanations for natural phenomena provided by beliefs in *magic,* miracles, and the *supernatural* are displaced. The process of disenchantment is one of the factors thought to lead to increasing *secularization.*

disengagement: the process by which the *state* and the church become increasingly separate and distinct entities, with a corresponding loss of *power* and influence of the church over the state. Disengagement is alleged to be one of the factors in the increasing *secularization* of society.

disintegrative shaming: the expression of disapproval by society regarding the criminal actions of individuals, which has the effect of labeling them as outcasts with no hope of being accepted back into the group. The effect of such shaming is to create, outside of the mainstream, *subcultures* of those who have been shamed in this way. (See *reintegrative shaming.*)

disorganized capitalism: the tendency in contemporary capitalist societies for structures to become increasingly fragmented and disorganized, through a variety of processes. Associated with Lash and Urry, the concept can be applied in a number of ways, but refers to three main developments in particular:

- The increasing *globalization* of industry, which reduces the ability of any capitalist society or company to control its own destiny. It may therefore operate in conditions of permanent insecurity.
- The constant development of new *technologies* that transform production and make all investment risky.
- The continual cultural transformation and fragmentation associated with the growth of *new social movements* and the decline of traditional class-based politics.

dispensability: an expression that refers to the ease with which certain employees can be removed from work, either voluntarily or through involuntary separation. Sociologists have suggested that the young, the old, women, and the disabled are more dispensable than male members of the *internal labor market.* Part of the reasons for dispensability are related to the absence of union organization among these groups and partly to the ease with which such workers can be dismissed without legal recourse. For example, older workers are more likely to be persuaded to retire early than workers in middle age.

dispersed extended family: where members of the same kinship group reside in distant places from each other. While relationships may remain close, they are conducted mainly through communication technology, with members meeting up only at certain times in the *life cycle*, such as weddings or funerals. (See *local extended family.*)

displacement effect: a term for the notion that television has taken over from other forms of entertainment to become a central part of many peoples' lives.

displacement of goals: a term used by Merton to describe the situation where individuals in organizations no longer focus on the overall aims of the *organization*, but only on the immediate task at hand. Organizational goals are displaced by immediate goals. This leads, he argues, to *formalism* by bureaucrats, in which adherence to the rules becomes more important than fulfilling the aims of the organization. (See *ritualism.*)

disrepute: the negative status associated with criminal activity. It can have a twofold effect, leading either to rejection of the individual by mainstream society or to individual feelings of excitement and pride in having a "dangerous reputation."

disrupting normalcy: a methodological technique associated with the ethno-methodologists. It consists of deliberately upsetting the normal, taken-for-granted rules that operate in everyday situations, in order to expose and explore them. The technique illuminates ordinary life in an interesting way, but it has been criticized for a lack of ethical consideration for those whose lives are being disrupted. It can be psychologically unsettling to be in a situation where the normal rules are not being applied.

diversification: the process whereby an *organization*, originally concerned with one area of production, buys stakes in other areas of production to produce conglomer-ates. The process is of particular interest to sociologists of the media, who have studied the way that certain companies have diversified their interests into several areas of the media. There are many examples of diversification in today's global economy, with huge international conglomorates having a wide range of financial interests across many types of business. (See *conglomeration.*)

dividing practices: the ways in which populations are classified and categorized to create groups that are segregated from the rest of society, such as lepers or criminals. Foucault argued that although the categories claim to have a scientific basis, they are more to do with the exercise of *biopower* than with scientific knowledge.

divine right of kings: a concept based on the belief that monarchs are placed on earth by God to rule and that any challenge to that rule is rebellion against God, worthy of eternal damnation. It is therefore an ideological device to legitimate monarchical rule and dissuade those ruled from revolting against the privileges of the monarch. (See *legitimation.*)

division of labor: where *specialization* occurs, so that individuals carry out only part of the activities needed for survival and sustenance. The basic *social division of labor* is where occupations emerge, so that needs are met by a variety of people carrying out specific jobs. This creates problems for society, specifically that the division of labor creates interdependence among individuals, while reducing the similarity of experiences they have. This can lead to problems of *integration* in a society, as more complex divisions of labor emerge. The chains of interdependence grow, while the *impersonality* of participants increases. More complex formations of the division of labor lead to problems of coordination between individuals and increase the need for constraint over individual behavior to achieve that coordination. (See *calculability*; *detailed division of labor*.)

divorce: the legal termination of a marriage. Divorce has been the subject of much sociological study, both to determine its causes and to understand the reasons for variations in divorce rates across geographical, cultural, age, and other divides. (See *divorce rate*; *single-parent families*.)

divorce inheritance: a concept of inheritance for children of divorce. It is based on the view that the children of divorced parents are more likely in later life to commit more crime, do less well in school, and have unstable relationships than are the children who experience childhood with parents who remain together.

divorce rate: a statistical measure of the number of divorces, usually expressed as the number of divorces in any one year per thousand married couples in the population.

documents: any written or printed material; in sociology, an important source of *secondary data* for sociologists. However, documents need to be used with caution. John Scott suggests that four appraisal criteria should be used when deciding whether, and how, to use documents in sociological research. These are:

- Authenticity – is the document "genuine," i.e. what it purports to be? Is it complete? Was it actually written by the alleged author?
- Credibility – did the author act from sincere motives when producing the document or was there some kind of pressure applied? To what extent is the material in the document accurate?
- Representativeness – is the document and its evidence typical of its kind, or if not, can the degree of its atypicality be judged? What other documents might exist of the same kind, and are these available for scrutiny?
- Meaning – is the document clear? Is the document written in shorthand, a foreign language, or archaic language, and if so, can it be accurately translated? What kind of interpretation needs to be placed on the document to render its meaning clear?

Scott does not suggest that negative answers to any of these questions render the document unusable, simply that the researcher has to recognize actual or potential problems and make corresponding allowances.

domestic division of labor: the division of household and child-care tasks among the members of a *family*, particularly between the adult male and female partners. Despite the prediction by Willmott and Young that families would become more "symmetrical," with a more equitable division of domestic labor between men and women, and despite the alleged appearance of the "*new man*," research suggests that, while attitudes toward the sharing of domestic tasks have shifted, in practice women still perform a disproportionate share.

domestic economy: a term that describes the system by which each member of the *family* makes contributions to the maintenance and survival of the family as a whole, through labor carried out at home. In preindustrial societies parents and children tended to work in the home or the fields, directly producing what the family needed. The domestic economy was therefore crucial for survival. In industrial societies the domestic economy has declined, with work in outside agencies replacing work at home.

domestic labor: an alternative name for *housework* and *child care*. The term is used by sociologists to indicate that it is a *social construction* and not some natural phenomenon. Sociologists have argued that domestic labor emerged with the *Industrial Revolution,* when surplus *wealth* allowed households to keep the female head at home engaged in running the house rather than contributing to the *household economy*, as previously.

domestic labor theory: an approach to *housework* and childbearing that seeks to establish their importance to the maintenance and continuation of capitalist *relations of production*. Rather than dismissing housework as nonwork, Marxist feminists argue that domestic labor is central to the survival of *capitalism*. Domestic labor is therefore seen as productive in itself, reproducing labor-power, both on a daily basis through the provision of food and opportunities for recuperation and generationally through the provision of the next generation of laborers.

domestic violence: usually a reference to physical abuse at the hands of a spouse or partner, although it may also include the physical abuse of children by parents/step-parents. Most adult victims of domestic violence are women, and many towns and cities now have women's refuges where the victims of domestic violence and their children may stay in safety. Domestic violence is one of the most widely underreported crimes, and even when the police are alerted they are often reluctant to become involved. Feminists argue that domestic violence against women arises out of the patriarchal system in which men are assumed to have *power* over women, who are expected, and who often themselves expect, to play a subordinate role.

domestication: one of the ideological ways in which oppositional *subcultures* can be neutralized in capitalist society, by reducing the "threat" seemingly posed through making the subcultural style seem "normal." This has been described in the phrase "otherness is reduced to sameness." (See *trivialization.*)

domesticity (ideology of): a set of ideas concerning women's role in society, which is seen as primarily wife, mother, and homemaker. Even today, when so many women are in the employed labor force, the *ideology* of domesticity is widely propagated, particularly through the advertising of household products. (See *dual role of women*; *housework.*)

dominance: see *dominant level*

dominant level: a term used by Althusser to describe a situation where politics or *ideology* are allowed by the economic *determinant level* to be the most important aspect of society, with a real freedom to act independently of economic imperatives.

dominant value system: the construct of ideas and viewpoints that, taken together, form the leading set of *values* in a society. The dominant value system is usually composed of the ideas that serve the interests of the *ruling class*, and through the effort of various agencies such as the media, they are also accepted as legitimate by large numbers of the subordinate groups in society. Where members of the *working class* accept the dominant value system, it is usually because they are either deferential or aspirational. The dominant value system therefore legitimizes society and contributes to *social order*. However it is difficult to show that the dominant value system actually exists and, if it does, that it is accepted uncritically by subordinate groups. Postmodernists point to the plurality of ideas and viewpoints in society, rather than the existence of a single dominant set. (See *radical value system; subordinate value system*.)

domination: in *Weber*'s meaning, a form of control illustrated by the likelihood that an order, once given, will be obeyed. It is thus a form of *power*, which is logically distinct from the imposition of one person's will on another. There are aspects of *legitimation* involved in domination.

double burden: a term used to indicate the oppression experienced by black women as a result of both sexism and racism. (See *dual systems theory; three systems theory*.)

double hermeneutic: an idea put forward by *Giddens*, that in order to understand meaningful *action*, we need to understand both the everyday knowledge of the individuals engaging in the action and the more technical language employed by sociologists to describe and explain it. Understanding therefore occurs on two levels.

downshifting: a process in which people (usually middle class) voluntarily opt for a simpler, more frugal lifestyle. The ultimate aim is being able to opt out of the "rat race" and take a less demanding job or voluntary work to allow more time for the things that one really wants to do. The American Trends Research Institute predicted that by the year 2000, 15% of people in their 30s and 40s would have chosen a less consumer-oriented lifestyle, preferring to buy simple, durable products. A random sample of 800 Americans carried out in 1995 showed that 28% had "downshifted."

downward social mobility: where an individual or group moves from a superordinate to a lower position in society. The causes of downward mobility are many, but poor health is perhaps the major one. Bad investments or a tough business environment can also lead to bankruptcy and downward mobility. The amount of downward mobility in society is variable, but since World War II, changes in the occupational structure (especially a shrinkage in working-class jobs) have reduced the opportunities for downward movement. (See *upward social mobility*.)

dramaturgy: the sociology of copresence developed by Goffman, using the *analogy* of social life as theater. The focus is on what happens when people are in the presence of each other and the way that they act out roles in their social life. As an *action theory*, it starts with the individual and looks at the way that individuals foster and maintain specific images of the self in different situations. The manipulation of image is a central part of the dramaturgical approach. It has been criticized for being ahistorical and episodic, focusing on the now, rather than on structures and the past.

drapetomania: literally, "running away madness," defined by doctors in the slave-owning southern states as the medical reason for runaways. Despite the lack of any biological evidence of its existence, the term functioned as an ideological device to legitimize the harsh measures taken by the owners to prevent their slaves absconding.

drift: a term developed by Matza as a theory of *deviance,* in which individuals do not engage in subcultural deviant activity, but move into deviance gradually by neutralizing ordinarily accepted moral objections to deviant activity through providing some justification for the action. The focus in the theory of drift is on the type of deviance that is mundane and trivial – the everyday deviant act. Thus, there is no commitment to a *deviant career,* and juvenile delinquents may drift back into normal society as they grow older. The idea has been criticized for trivializing much seriously deviant behavior.

drip effect: a term for the cumulative effects of the media on the individual, through continuous exposure to similar media messages. (See *sleeper effect.*)

dual career families: where both parents in a *nuclear family* situation are employed in occupations in which advancement is possible. The appearance of significant numbers of dual career families has been a significant development in the postwar period, with consequences for the way that *conjugal roles* are envisaged and child care planned.

dual consciousness: a term developed by Mann to describe the attitudes of the *working class* toward society, in which they accept the dominant values of the *middle class* while at the same time developing their own oppositional attitudes. This holding of two sets of attitudes at the same time is a normative feature of the *proletariat* and should be seen as resolving the *contradiction* that workers generally agree that individuals are free to withdraw their labor but should not strike. (See *normative ambivalence.*)

dual economy thesis: an argument that, in *third-world* countries, there are two economies operating, one a technologically advanced and urban-centered economy, the other a less sophisticated rural economy. The thesis was developed by Boeke as an alternative to *underdevelopment theory,* which saw the relationships between these two economies as one where the urban *metropolis* exploits the rural *hinterland.* Boeke argued that these two economies, while operating in the same national and cultural space, are economically separate, inhabiting a different economic reality. The relationship between the two economies is minimal, rather than exploitative.

dual labor market: the idea that there are two separate sectors of work in the economy, between which there is little movement. One part of the *labor market* is secure and provides full-time work for permanent workers while the other is composed of temporary and part-time workers. (See *external labor market; internal labor market.*)

dual role of women: a term to embrace the two major roles undertaken by an increasingly large proportion of women, namely those of wage-earner and housewife. Feminists such as Oakley point out that even though the majority of women of working age are now in *paid employment,* they are still expected to play the traditional role of the person primarily responsible for domestic tasks and *child care*. Though there is evidence that the partners of women in full-time employment take a greater share of domestic tasks and child care than the partners of women in part-time employment, most women still take the major share of the burden. One result of this is that women, on average, have less leisure time than men. (See *domestic division of labor; housework; new man.*)

dual systems theory: a theory developed by feminists to emphasize that both class and gender need to be taken into account when investigating the situation of women. It is an attempt to move beyond the debate of whether *capitalism* or *patriarchy* is more responsible for the oppression of women. (See *three systems theory.*)

duopoly: the situation where *political power* alternates between two dominant parties, so that they share the government between them and effectively squeeze out any third force. The situation in the US is an effective duopoly, shared by the Republican and Democratic Parties.

durée: the stream of experience that constitutes our everyday lives. It is the unbroken series of events that, unthinkingly, we perform and experience as our social lives. The importance of the durée is that it is broken when we stop to reflect on what is happening to us.

Durkheim, Emile: a French sociologist writing in the latter part of the 19th and the early part of the 20th centuries. Durkheim devoted much of his writing to his search for an understanding of what held societies together and what caused change. Like many others writing at that time he was influenced by the enormity of the social changes wrought by the *Industrial Revolution*. Durkheim was influential in the development of *functionalism*, and also introduced the important concept of *anomie*. His study of *suicide* was undertaken to demonstrate his belief that even what appear to be individual acts are, in fact, governed by *society*. The suicide rate was thus an example of a *social fact*. Durkheim also published important works on the *division of labor* and *religion*.

dysfunction: where a part of the social structure does not positively contribute to the maintenance of society, but causes disharmony and *conflict* rather than coherence and *integration*. The term was used by Merton to produce a more flexible *functionalism*, by doing away with the necessity for everything that existed in society to have a positive function for the maintenance of society. The term is often employed by sociologists to explain how an organizational feature, though generally functional (helping the organization to survive) may under certain circumstances become dysfunctional and even *pathological* for the organization. (See *organizational rules.*)

eating disorder: a general term for conditions such as anorexia nervosa and bulimia, in which an individual becomes progressively unable to maintain a normal, healthy diet as a result of psychological, rather than medical, causes. Eating disorders mainly affect girls and young women and are thought to be a response to low self-esteem and the desire to achieve a "model" figure. Recently, doctors have reported a rise in the number of boys and young men suffering from anorexia nervosa.

ecclesia: another term for *church*. More specifically, it is used for a universal or all-encompassing church, such as the Roman Catholic church in medieval Europe.

echelon authority: authority according to position. The term describes a situation where all the members in a particular organizational position have *power* over all members in a subordinate organizational position, regardless of any other social distinctions between them. For example, warders in a prison have echelon authority over all prisoners, even those who might have had high *status* outside prison.

ecological fallacy: a methodological error, in which the characteristics of a population as a whole are attributed to groups within that population, without any real connection between them being demonstrated. For example, if we take three areas and find the following results:

Areas	Number of smokers	Number of cases of lung cancer
A	500,000	1,000
B	250,000	500
C	100,000	200

There seems to be a strong correlation between smoking and lung cancer, but we would be committing the ecological fallacy if we concluded that. What we do not know is whether the lung cancer cases are smokers. We cannot just assume that they are.

ecology: see *environmentalism*

economic power: a term that includes a number of capabilities stemming from control of material resources, such as the right to hire and fire, the ability to locate industry in particular areas, and the influence that this can give over other areas of social life, such as politics. While ownership is a crucial dimension of economic power, it is not the only aspect of it. Economic power can also operate at the micro-level, for example between husband and wife, where control over domestic resources can lead to power of one over the other. (See *consumer power, institutional power, political power.*)

ecumenicalism: a process in which different Christian organizations, particularly *churches* and *denominations*, work together cooperatively, emphasizing their shared characteristics. This might mean that joint church services are held, with worshippers gathering alternately at, for example, the Anglican, Roman Catholic, and Methodist churches to engage in collective worship.

education: the acquisition of knowledge and skills, both formally and informally. Although education is a lifelong process that takes place in a wide variety of settings, sociologists have tended to focus on the formal education process and the specialist institutions in which this takes place.

educational vouchers: educational certificates with a nominal cash value of public funds to be "spent" to buy education. The parents of students can in theory use their vouchers to exercise a degree of choice in selecting education for their children, instead of seeing tax funds go automatically into the public school system. Proposals for educational vouchers have sparked great controversy, especially since President George Bush's endorsement of the idea in the early 1990s.

effectiveness: a term applied to *organizations*, that is a measure of success of an organization in achieving its goal. It is not the same as *efficiency*, though they are usually connected. A company might be efficient but if the organizational goals are wider than just making profits, it may not necessarily be effective if other goals are not being met.

efficiency: an economic concept that, when related to industry, is measured by the amount of resources needed to produce one unit. Efficiency is a central concept for *New Right* sociologists in the sociology of industry. The aim of industry is said to be the most efficient production possible – that is, maximum production at minimum cost. In this way profits can be maximized. (See *effectiveness*.)

egalitarianism: a philosophy that focuses on social policies that introduce greater *equality* into society. It is one of the sources of inspiration for the *welfare state* and *progressive taxation* and thus is attacked by philosophers of the *New Right* as the politics of envy.

egoism: self-interest. The term may be used to define the cult of the individual, or a situation in society where individual appetites are subject to little or no social control.

egoistic suicide: self-destruction that stems from the lack of integrating social contexts in society. *Durkheim* argued that individuals needed to be integrated into groups in order to be stable. Contexts that provided such integration were the *family* and *religion*. Where individuals were cut off from such contexts the possibility of suicide increased. It was therefore this type of suicide that Durkheim saw as differentiating Catholic low-suicide and Protestant high-suicide societies. (See *coefficient of aggravation*.)

elaborated code: a form of speech identified by Bernstein. It refers to a pattern of speech commonly used on formal occasions, in lectures, and between strangers. It is characterized by grammatically complex sentence structures, can describe abstract concepts (such as "freedom"), and is context-free, i.e. does not have to be tied in to a specific situation. The elaborated code is used extensively in education and while middle-class children come to school able to use both the elaborated code and less formal ways of speaking (which Bernstein called the *restricted code*), working-class children tend to prefer the latter, putting them at an initial disadvantage in school. (See *language codes*.)

electability: the calculation of a candidate's chance of attracting votes according to his or her social characteristics. For example, candidates are deemed to be more electable if they are male, married with children, good-looking, and so on.

elective affinity: a term used by *Weber* to describe the causal relationship between the ideas of ascetic Calvinism and the *spirit of capitalism.* The two meaning-systems were therefore congruent and through a variety of stages the ideas translated into the practices of *capitalism.* (See *asceticism.*)

elite: a small group at the top of an area of social life. It is often used to refer to the *power elite,* but elites can exist in any walk of life. For example, an important elite in postmodern societies would be the entertainment elite, who have the capacity to generate total devotion among fans. There are also elites within elites, so that the Hollywood star elite would be seen as the apex of movie elites.

elite-engineered model: an approach to *moral panics* that suggests that such panics are created by those in power to distract the population from other "real" problems in society. Moral panics, therefore, act as a diversionary tactic in the interests of the powerful. (See *grassroots model; interest-group model.*)

elite theory: see *unitary elite theory*

embourgeoisement: the process by which the affluent working class are said to become like the middle class in economic standing, lifestyle, and attitudes, while the middle class accepts them as their social equals. The theory first arose in Britain in the 1950s, largely as a result of the victories of the Conservative Party, which seemed to succeed in bringing *affluence* to a significant section of the working class. The hypothesis was tested by Goldthorpe, Lockwood, *et al.,* who found little evidence that embourgeoisement was taking place. While the weekly wages of the affluent workers and *white-collar workers* were similar, lifetime earnings were much in favor of the white-collar worker. Also, the affluent workers were becoming privatized, but beyond this, there was little similarity in lifestyle between them and the white-collar worker. Lastly, there was little evidence that affluent workers were seen as socially equal by white-collar workers. (See *socially aspiring worker.*)

emigration: see *migration*

emotions: feelings such as hate and love, which constitute the affective dimension of social life and which the *rationality* of sociology is often accused of neglecting. Emotions are an important factor in motivation, which *interactionism* in particular sees as the basis of social life.

empathy: the ability to understand the attitudes and behavior of another person by relating these to one's own experiences. Interactionists in particular believe that the use of *qualitative methods* of research allows the researcher to benefit from such an understanding of those being studied. *Weber* used the word *"verstehen,"* meaning to understand, to express, the same idea. However critics of qualitative research methods argue that empathy between the researcher and those being studied leads to loss of *objectivity.*

empirical studies: those studies that are based on research yielding actual data, such as statistics, or transcripts of interviews, rather than works of theory.

empiricism: an approach to *knowledge* that argues that the only basis for knowing anything is experience itself. It is an approach that rejects the idea that sociology, for example, can proceed through untested theorizing, maintaining that progress can be made only through the collection of empirical observations. This approach has been criticized for denying the importance of *theory* in sociological work and relying on the collection of a vast number of often unrelated facts.

employment: the exchange of labor for wages or a salary, which is unequal in both economic and power terms. It is thus a logically distinct category to the wider concept of *work*.

empowerment: a term originally associated with the *New Right*, but now widely used. It concerns the dispersion of *power* to individuals, so that they begin to take responsibility for their own decisions and their own lives. It began as an attempt to roll back the power of the *state* by taking areas of decision-making traditionally associated with government and giving them to groups or individuals. Elements of empowering political programs might be the sale of government housing, the devolving of power to local housing associations, local school boards, etc. There is a much wider use of the term in, for example, education, where students are empowered through taking responsibility for charting and planning their own courses.

empty bucket theory: a crude type of explanation for the effects of the mass media, which assumes that people approach media content with no prior beliefs or opinions, but just wait to be filled up with the ideas that the media put across. It tends to rely on a *conspiracy theory* of the media, which holds that those in power seek to control subordinates in society by using the media to control what they think. Critics point out that the *audience* for media content is not "empty" but approaches media messages with the ability to choose and interpret material intelligently and with its own predispositions. (See *selective interpretation*.)

empty nest families: families in which the offspring have grown up and moved out of the parental home, leaving the adult partners as a couple. The rise in *life expectancy* and the tendency for young adults to establish their own household as soon as possible has resulted in the creation of a large and growing group of middle-aged couples with few family responsibilities and, in many cases, relatively high incomes, particularly if both of them are in employment. The rise in the average age at which women bear their first child also means that, for many of these "empty nest couples," their services as grandparents will not be needed for some time after their last child has left home. There is considerable interest in this group by advertisers, who increasingly target such couples as potential buyers of a wide range of leisure and financial products. (See *family structure*.)

empty shell marriages: where a married couple continue to live together but are only going through the motions of married life, often for the sake of the children. In all other respects the marriage has broken down. (See *marital breakdown*.)

enclave development: a concept suggesting how *third-world* countries are developed through the activities of *first-world* agencies, such as the *transnational companies*. The idea of enclave development was put forward by opponents of *underdevelopment theory* which, they argued, took far too negative a view of the first world. The process involves the creation of areas of high technology in countries of the third world, which then act as spurs to the development of the rest of the third-world country's economy, as skills and *capital* are transferred from these pockets to the less-developed sectors.

encoding: the process by which producers of media texts weave their messages into the images or words that they use. Producers' intentions are important here because they wish to get across particular messages to their *audience*. However, audiences do not necessarily decode the messages in the same way that the producer intended. (See *polysemic; text.*)

enculturation: a type of *socialization* in which the young absorb the *culture* of a society holistically, through experiencing it directly. There are thus no specific mechanisms such as the *family* that engage in socialization. (See *acculturation; impulse control; role-training.*)

end of history: the idea that with the collapse of the communist regimes of Europe and the Soviet Union, the motor of history, which was competition between the two great ideological blocs of *capitalism* and *communism*, has stopped with the complete victory of capitalism. This suggests that there is now no serious alternative to capitalism as a way of achieving the "good life." Critics of the idea argue that this is to ignore a whole number of other possible motors, such the rise of *fundamentalism*, the rise of *Islam*, or the competition between first and third worlds. (See *Cold War.*)

end of ideology: a concept associated with Daniel Bell, who argued that as societies become *mass societies,* there develops a *value consensus* about what constitutes the "good life," so that competing *ideologies* die out in the face of this agreement. Bell was writing in a time of optimism during the 1950s in the US and has been criticized for being time-bound. Ideologies continued to be powerful during the Cold War period. (See *end of history.*)

endogamy: literally meaning "marrying inside" and referring to rules that prevent a person from marrying outside his or her designated group. In Africa it used to be the rule among many tribes to marry from within one's own tribe, and Indians under the caste system had to marry someone from the same caste as themselves. Under the apartheid system in South Africa, the Prohibition of Mixed Marriages Act of 1949 meant that marriage could not legally take place between a white and a "nonwhite" person. Endogamy is sometimes used by a group as an attempt to keep itself "pure" by preventing children born of "mixed blood." However, there may also be economic reasons such as helping to keep the *wealth* of a tribe or clan within the group. (See *exogamy.*)

Enlightenment: a philosophical movement that flourished in Europe and North America during the 18th century, characterized by a belief in progress and a desire to challenge traditional modes of thought through *rationality*. The Enlightenment is associated with *modernity* and the project associated with it is challenged in its turn by *postmodernism*, which denies the possibility of a teleological progress to a better society.

enterprise culture: a term developed by *New Right* theorists to describe a society in which individuals are encouraged by the social arrangements to enter business for themselves. The idea is that the *dependency culture* has reduced the capacity of the people to control their own destinies. The future should be concerned with creating the conditions, especially through taxation and *welfare*, that encourage many citizens to take entrepreneurial risks and so increase employment opportunities for others.

environment: the surroundings of an individual or society. With the growth of interest in ecological issues, the term has gained a new emphasis in sociology by being associated with the natural world that human societies inhabit. The impact of human activity, especially productive activity, on the natural world has been enormous and issues such as pollution, loss of natural landscapes, and the invasion of commercial development have become objects of sociological investigation.

environmentalism: a *new social movement* that concerns itself with the protection of the natural and built surroundings that form the backdrop for human society. It is multifaceted in its concerns and ranges from projects to clean up rivers to the heritage movement, which aims to protect historical monuments and buildings. Issues such as pollution and conservation have been brought to the top of the political agenda by environmentalists and altered the political programs of many major parties in Europe, for example. The success of environmentalist movements such as Greenpeace has spawned a whole range of copycat organizations each seeking to emulate its success. While mainstream environmentalists focus on peaceful and lawful process, there is a wing of the movement that is involved in more direct action and which can sometimes move into unlawful activity. The membership and organizational structures of environmental groups are often fluid and changing.

epidemiology: the study of the nature, amount, and spread of disease. It is a way of understanding the causes of particular diseases in order to develop an appropriate approach to prevention and cure. One of the earliest applications of epidemiology was the discovery in the 19th century of the link between cholera and infected drinking water, while one of the most recent is the attempt to understand *AIDS*.

episodic characterization: an approach to the study of society that is used as a contrast to the idea of historical progress, which sees history as one continuous story of improvement. It is the idea of *social change* as discontinuous – that is, as comprised of events that are forged in their own circumstances rather than in response to an overarching *meta-narrative*. A chief exponent is British sociologist *Anthony Giddens*, who rejects all ideas such as *historical materialism* and argues that social change must be studied taking due account of accidental and contingent factors.

episteme: a term used by Foucault to indicate the way in which *knowledge* is structured or organized and influences the way in which we view the world around us. It is therefore similar to a *paradigm*, but with a wider application to any *discourse*, not just scientific ones.

epistemology: the philosophical study of the nature of *knowledge*. For sociologists, the term is used to refer to the sociology of knowledge.

epoché: a method in which the sociologist suspends the natural attitude, suggested by Husserl as a means of understanding the social world. That is, epoché involves putting the world in parentheses or "brackets," and approaching the *durée* or the stream of experience that constitutes our life as if it were an alien culture. The sociologist therefore treats the world as if he or she had never seen it before, putting aside all previous beliefs and understandings.

equality: the state of being the same, or having things of equal value. The concept has been attached to several notions that have formed the basis of sociological investigation. It is part of the *nature versus nurture debate*, which considers that there are clear biological differences between individuals, but also social differences that do not flow from these biological differences, thus resulting in inequality.

equality of opportunity: the principle that all people should be provided with an equal opportunity to succeed, irrespective of their sex, age, ethnic or religious group, physical abilities, or sexual orientation. The principle is often used in the context of education, but has a much wider application, including in the workplace. (See *positive discrimination*.)

equality of outcome: a measure of *underachievement* that compares different groups in terms of their qualifications gained, percentage of university acceptances, etc. Inequality of outcome can coexist with *equality of opportunity* for a variety of reasons.

equilibrium: a state of balance among parts of the *social system*. Particularly in the context of *functionalism*, the structures in society are said to tend toward a state of equilibrium – that is, when there is a change in the social environment that alters the balance among the subsystems, there is an automatic process that restores the lost equilibrium. The notion is especially associated with those who adopt the *biological* or *mechanical analogy* in their depictions of society. (See *homeostasis*.)

erklären: literally "explanation." It is used as a contrast to *verstehen*, and is associated with the mode of studying the external objective world by employing the principles of science. As an objective methodology it is sufficient for explaining the external phenomena of society, but cannot access the subjective dimension.

eros: the erotic instinct identified by Marcuse as the object of *surplus repression*.

eroticism: the various social constructions that appear in every age associated with sexual desire. Foucault in particular investigated the changes in erotic formulations that have political as well as personal implications. For example, Foucault documented the ways in which the medicalization of sexuality shaped definitions of acceptable eroticism.

essentialism: where every occurrence of a phenomenon is assumed to have the same universal characteristics. An essentialist view of gender, for example, attributes the same emotional aspects to all women and a different set of emotional components to all men.

established church: a *church* that is likely to have national *status* in a society, e.g. the Church of England, the *Roman Catholic church*, the Greek Orthodox church.

establishment: a general term for the ruling class. It encompasses a number of *elites*, from the political rulers to the social elite. The term is often used to describe the traditional sources of *prestige* and *power* in society, and reflects a deferential attitude toward these.

estate stratification: a social structure found in *feudal* societies that are hier-archically organized according to an individual's inheritance and ownership of land, with the landless occupying the lowest stratum in society. Such societies are "closed," in that it is very difficult for an individual to change the estate into which he or she has been born. The crucial *social status* in estate societies is that of the monarch, who owns all of the land under his or her control. It is the granting of land by the monarch to feudal lords that creates obligations of duty by those below to those above.

esteem: see *social status*

estheticization: the process whereby everyday features of social life become open to artistic and esthetic influences, such as the principles of design and art appreci-ation. This has had the effect of countering the notion that art is somehow the prerogative of an *elite*, and has shown instead that artistic considerations are both social and political, with the ability to create environments that are either brutal or appealing.

ethical constraints: factors that prevent a particular method or research study from being used because of a belief that it would be morally wrong. Ethical con-straints provide one of the main reasons why very few *laboratory experiments* are carried out in sociological research. Some would argue that certain kinds of *covert participant observation* are unethical, since with this method the sociologist has to deceive those who are being studied.

ethical issues: issues that have a moral dimension, such as the debates over euthanasia and *abortion*.

ethnic group: a collection of people who share common history, customs, and identity as well as, in most cases, language and *religion*, and who see themselves as a distinct unit. It thus constitutes an identity for members and forms a basis for social action. Members usually seek to preserve their identity through a variety of closure tactics, for example, through *marriage* that tends to be *endogamous*. Where they form a minority within the population, increased emphasis on tradition and custom help to maintain boundaries.

ethnic minorities: groups of people in a population who are from a different ethnic group from the indigenous population. It is an imprecise term, and can vary according to whether or not certain members of the population describe themselves as belonging to an ethnic minority group.

ethnic plurality: a term used to describe the condition of postmodern societies that have more than one cultural group within them. This state of society is associ-ated with the dissolving of traditional national boundaries and the appearance of significant minorities in most societies.

ethnic underachievement: the condition of relatively low educational attain-ments by students from some ethnic minority groups when compared with average results of other children. Some sociologists, such as Mabey, argue that the focus on ethnic group obscures the real underlying factor, namely that of *social class*. It is likely that a number of factors adversely affect the performance of children from some ethnic minority groups, particularly *racism*, both in and out of school, and *poverty*.

ethnic vote: the concentrated electoral power of ethnic minorities that gives them political influence in certain urban areas. The ethnic vote is high in inner-city areas and most candidates in these areas must take account of their interests if they wish to be elected. The power of the ethnic vote has according to some sociologists been exaggerated because:

- independent candidates claiming to directly represent ethnic minorities have been unsuccessful in attracting votes
- ethnic minorities are themselves divided according to *religion* and politics and therefore do not represent a bloc vote.

ethnicity: a characteristic of social groups that relies upon a shared *identity*, whether this is perceived or real, based on common cultural, religious, or traditional factors. Ethnicity can involve a racial dimension, although this is not strictly necessary, as ethnic groups are usually based on narrower characteristics than those attributed to racial groupings.

ethnocentric: looking at an issue from the viewpoint of a particular cultural background and therefore obtaining a biased opinion of it. In sociology it is largely white sociologists who are said to be ethnocentric, though the term can be applied to any sociologist steeped in a particular cultural tradition.

ethnography: the study of the *culture* and way of life (or aspects of these) of a group of people by direct observation. The term is particularly used with reference to studies in anthropology, but ethnography is also widely practiced by sociologists. *Participant observation* studies form the most common type of ethnographic study in sociological research.

ethnomethodology: an approach developed by Garfinkel as a challenge to orthodox sociology. The ethnomethodologist's fundamental approach is to stress the infinite ambiguity of *language* and *action*. Rather than assume that we understand what another person means when he or she says or does something, "ethnos" argue that we have to struggle for their meaning, and that every situation is characterized by the search for common understandings. The social world is therefore built up of arbitrary rules, made up of a dense and often contradictory set of tacit understandings about what is going on. (See *glossing; indexicality; practical theorists*.)

ethnoscapes: the flow of people throughout the world that is a key feature of *globalization*. The flow consists of migrants, business people, tourists, guest workers, etc.

ethos: the particular social and cultural characteristics and norms of a group, organization, or society. Being socialized into accepting and adopting the prevailing ethos is usually an important part of becoming a member of a group or institution, such as a religious group or public school.

etiology: the science of determining causes. The doctrine of specific etiology states that specific germs cause specific diseases. It thus tends to ignore other factors, such as psychological and environmental, that may have an influence on the causes and nature of disease. (See *germ theory of disease*.)

eugenics: the science of breeding, which has become associated with plans for racial purity put forward by the Nazis in interwar Germany. It is based on the supposed links, far from proven, between genetic inheritance and various social and personal characteristics.

evangelism: religious activity characteristic of some Christian religious organizations, particularly *denominations* and *sects*, that places emphasis on preaching, especially with messages derived from the Bible, and on the notion of salvation through personal conversion.

evangelistic bureaucrats: a term devised by Davies to describe the attitude of many planners about their role in local communities, where they believed they could reform society through their work. They used their expertise to redesign the environment and saw themselves as consequently changing human behavior. These planners tended to overcome the resistance of local councillors by deploying "feel-good" words such as "community" in putting forward their plans.

everyday knowledge: a phenomenological term that describes the common sense that exists in society. It is the knowledge that we employ in our everyday, routine lives in order to effect social actions. Schutz argued that we build up our stock of everyday knowledge from our unique biographies. The contrast is with theoretical knowledge, which is rational and thought-out. Everyday knowledge is the taken-for-granted knowledge that underlies our normal way of thinking. (See *common-sense world.*)

evolutionary theories: in sociology, explanations that were heavily influenced by the theory of evolution put forward by the biologist Charles Darwin. The implication of evolutionary theory is that societies have been constantly progressing from a primitive past to a sophisticated future, not as a result of planned change, but as a natural order of things. The assumption was that societies followed much the same evolutionary rules as biological species and that there was a "natural selection" at work, in which successful societies displaced unsuccessful ones. Critics of these theories argue that they are ideological justifications for the developed world's exploitation of the undeveloped world, because such thinking allows this exploitation to be seen as a superior culture displacing an inferior one.

exchange theory: a sociological approach that stresses that the basis of social life is calculation by individuals. The idea is that social action is carried out when the individual has worked out the likely consequence of the action and what he or she may be likely to obtain from it. Relationships between individuals are therefore based on an exchange of benefits, with each calculating the best way of achieving what he or she wants with a minimum cost in terms of what the other in the relationship needs. It is a concept drawn from economics and has been criticized for assigning too much *rationality* and deviousness to individuals in their everyday lives.

exclusion: a tactic of *social closure* in which an occupational group seeks to prevent other groups from obtaining the same rewards. This has the effect of emphasizing the uniqueness of the occupational group, usually through some form of *credentialism.* (See *solidarism.*)

exclusivist definitions of religion: definitions that portray *religion* as a system of beliefs focusing on the *supernatural*, and relying on faith. (See *inclusivist definitions of religion*.)

existential sociology: sociological study that rejects most other sociology as too concerned with *rationality*, and starts from the idea that individuals are fundamentally situational (or existential). That is, people are like the world they inhabit, which is chaotic, uncertain, arbitrary, and changing. People can only survive in this world by becoming like the world itself. They are therefore, at bottom, varied, changeable, contradictory, and, most of all, irrational. To the existentialists then, sociology must concern itself with the irrational – the emotional and affective side of motivation and action – because this is the ultimately real. (See *brute being*.)

exogamy: literally means "marrying outside" and refers to the rules that exist in every society regarding the categories of people (usually kin) that a person may not marry. In most modern Western societies, this covers a fairly narrow range of relatives, but in many African societies whole *clans* are exogamous – that is, a person has to marry someone from a different clan. Exogamy is seen as a way of reducing conflict between groups, as a group is less likely to engage in hostilities with another group if it contains members of one's own family. (See *endogamy*.)

expectancy theory: the principle that work behavior can be predicted on the basis of what individuals will subjectively expect they will achieve in taking up particular modes of behavior in an occupation. The implication of the theory was that an individual will be motivated to work where the expectancy of work balances with the monetary values and *work satisfaction* actually received. As a *work motivation theory* it was criticized for assigning too much *rationality* to the individual in approaching work.

expectation of life: see *life expectancy*

experiential teaching: a style of teaching that provides the framework for students to become actively involved in what they learn and how they learn it, rather than being the passive recipients of knowledge handed down by the teacher. With experiential teaching, the teacher is viewed as one of a number of classroom resources, rather than as the sole repository of knowledge. (See *chalk-and-talk*; *discovery learning*.)

experiment: see *hypothetico-deductive method*; *laboratory experiment*

experimental group: in sociological research, a group within an *experiment* matched as closely as possible to another group, the *control group*. The main difference between the two groups is that only the experimental group is exposed to the *independent variable*, i.e. that which is controlled by the researcher and thought to be the cause of whatever changes are being investigated.

experimental method: see *hypothetico-deductive method*

expert society: see *postindustrial society*

explanation: an account of a phenomenon that is made understandable by identification of its causes. The search for explanations of social phenomena is a central feature of sociology, yet it is fraught with difficulty because of the complexity of social life and the capability of humans to exercise their free will to change the causes of things.

exploitation: see *appropriation*

expressive deviants: used by new deviancy theorists (NDTs) to describe those deviant groups at the margins of society, such as gays, drug-takers, and prostitutes, who were the focus of much of their work. These groups were seen by NDTs as representing goodness at the margins, in contrast to mainstream society where the real criminals were located.

expressive role: the role that *Parsons* suggested is played by females within a *marriage*. The expressive role is the caring, nurturing, supportive role that many functionalists believe women perform naturally, as a result of "biology." The expressive role complements the *instrumental role* of the male breadwinner. Parsons suggested that children need to grow up in a family where these roles are performed by the respective parents if the children are to develop "stable adult personalities." Feminists disagree that "expressive" tasks performed by women are somehow natural to them. Eichler accuses Parsons of *androcentricity*, and says that men are able to interpret the housewife role in this way because they are rarely present when *housework* and *child-care* tasks are being performed. (See *dual role*.)

extended family: see *family structure*

extension leisure: a situation where leisure is seen as linked to work, or leisure activities function to support work relationships. In the case of the former, an example would be teachers reading around their subject. The latter is usually found among higher executives, such as playing golf with clients or entertaining colleagues. (See *complementary leisure, oppositional leisure*.)

external labor market: refers to jobs where the pay is low and working conditions poor, with the characteristic of part-time, temporary contracts. There is both little chance of advancement and a high turnover of the labor force. The members of the external labor market move in and out of the *internal labor market*, according to supply and demand. (See *dual labor market*.)

extrinsic satisfaction: in work, satisfaction achieved through the monetary rewards that the employee receives. Workers who are interested only in extrinsic satisfaction are said to have a very *instrumental* attitude to their work, with home more likely to be their *central life interest*. (See *intrinsic satisfaction*.)

factory system: the process of production that emerged during the *Industrial Revolution*, when larger and larger groups of workers were brought under a single roof to carry out their work activities. The development of the factory system meant great changes for the way that people lived their lives, for example, introducing the concept of "going to work." It also allowed a huge increase in production, which eventually brought material benefits to many in capitalist societies, not just in terms of wages but also in terms of the products that became available to people. However, factory production has also been identified as a cause of increased *alienation* in society.

fallacy of misplaced concreteness: see *reification*

false consciousness: a term used by Marxists to describe ways of thinking that are the product not of the real material conditions the thinker inhabits, but of the ideological forces of other social groups. It is usually associated with the *working class*, who are said to show false consciousness when their thoughts are alienated from their real social being. Marxists use false consciousness to explain why the working class do not revolt against their subordination, but accept the legitimacy of the power structures that oppress them.

falsely accused: a term used by Becker to describe "one who does not engage in rule-breaking behavior but who has been publicly perceived or labeled as a deviant." Such people therefore suffer the consequences of being known as deviant without having committed any action that would warrant this. (See *pure deviant; secret deviant.*)

falsification: a principle of scientific procedure, whereby the scientist attempts to disprove a hypothesis rather than seek to verify it. The logic behind this principle is that scientists are human beings, and are tempted to find support for their hypothesis and ignore results that disprove it. By concentrating on the falsification of hypotheses, scientists can work on the assumption that their theories are provisionally true until disproved. (See *verifiability.*)

family: a group of people related by blood or marriage. Sociologically the definition is less obvious, with ambiguities surrounding the differences among family, kinship, and *household*. There is a difference between the family living together in the same household at any one moment in time and those whom we think of as our families in the wider sense. The family is also intimately connected to moral issues, because the family is a biological as well as a social formation. (See *core functions of the family; family structure.*)

family fit: a term to express the functionalist belief that the dominant *family structure* of a society will take that form because it best meets the needs of that society at that particular time. Thus functionalists such as *Parsons* claim that the *nuclear family* replaced the *extended family* as the dominant form in industrial societies because it provided a better "fit" than the extended family, which was better suited to the needs of a predominantly agricultural society. It is suggested that the nuclear family, being small, allowed its members to be geographically mobile and more easily able to move to where work could be found, such as in the new factories.

family of origin: a term used to describe the family into which an individual is born. (See *family of procreation.*)

family of procreation: a term used to describe the family in which an individual is a parent. (See *family of origin.*)

family size: usually refers to the number of children born to a couple. Family size is affected not only by the availability of reliable and affordable contraception, but by social *norms* governing the "ideal" family size and by economic decisions regarding the cost of rearing children against an improved standard of living for the family. (See *birth rate.*)

family structure: the composition of a group of people living together as a family. The two basic family structures are nuclear and extended. A nuclear family is regarded as an adult couple and their dependent children. An extended family is one in which the basic nuclear structure has been added to, or extended, either vertically (e.g. grandparents, parents, children) or horizontally (e.g. two or more brothers living together with their respective spouses and children). While there have always been variations on these basic structures, a number of social changes have resulted in a growing diversity of family structures. (See *empty nest families; reconstituted families; single-parent families.*)

fascism: a political movement of the right, which draws strongly on military imagery and organization in its aim to represent the will of the nation. It demands absolute obedience from subordinates to superiors and has a tendency toward militaristic expansion into neighboring countries. As an authoritarian movement, fascism appeals to nationalistic sentiment and is antidemocratic. It also tends toward racial exclusion in its definition of the nation.

fatalism: an attitude whereby the holder believes that there is nothing he or she can do about his or her circumstances. Fatalistic attitudes are usually associated with the *working class* and express a certain pessimism about life chances. Fatalism tends to lead to political inactivity, as the holders accept their present position as the only possible one.

fatalistic suicide: self-destruction that stems from overregulation of the individual by the collectivity. The classic example is the concentration camp prisoner who throws him or herself on the electrified fence rather than continue to suffer the total control of the camp guards.

favelas: an alternative term for the rather old-fashioned "shanty town," used to describe those areas of *third-world* cities where the conditions of life are harsh and basic amenities lacking. The use of "shanty town" fell into disrepute because it suggested a disorganized and haphazard urban development. While there are haphazard features in any urban development, research in Latin America suggested that the people of the "barrios" or favelas were more organized than was immediately obvious. They banded together to protect their homes and arranged what few services could be provided. The favelas can therefore be described as poor areas of third-world cities, often with the inhabitants squatting illegally on other people's land, with limited employment opportunities and poor housing materials. There can also be vibrant political and cultural features of the favelas, with a culture of resistance and improvement predominating.

fecundity: the ability to give birth to live-born children. (See *fertility*.)

female crime: lawbreaking by women, and an increasing focus for sociological investigation after having been neglected for many years. Early sociological approaches to female crime tended to see women who broke the law as somehow like men, or engaging in "typically" feminine crimes such as shoplifting or child-battering. More recent work has focused on female criminals in their own right and the emergence of "untypical" activity such as female gangs.

female gaze: in the sociology of culture, the way in which visual texts are viewed from the standpoint of a woman, which contrasts with the usually dominant "male gaze," associated with Western culture and generally employed to objectify women as sex objects.

female underachievement: a tendency for girls to perform less well at school than boys, particularly in mathematics and the sciences, and to be less likely to enter higher education. However, although there is still evidence of gendered subjects, girls now outperform boys at all levels of education up to college level, giving rise to concern about male underachievement.

femininity: the possession of those characteristics associated with being a woman. There is a traditional conception of being feminine that has been under attack by the feminist movement for limiting the possibilities of women, constraining them to act out defenseless and helpless roles. Conceptions of femininity are constantly being negotiated and renegotiated as women take more and more control over their own lives and seek to find ways of expressing themselves in traditional and nontraditional ways. Femininity according to sociologists is therefore socially negotiated.

feminism: the sociological (and philosophical) perspective from which social phenomena are evaluated with the interests of women in mind. Feminist critiques of the *classical sociologists* argued that they viewed social processes only from the view-point of males and that the traditional invisibility of women in society was repro-duced in sociology. The feminist movement in sociology therefore has two main aims:

- To redress the balance and examine society sociologically from a female point of view, laying bare the ways in which men dominate social relation-ships and restrict opportunities for women.
- To explore women's lives, which had been neglected by traditional socio-logy, and open up the lives of women to sociological scrutiny.

(See *black feminism*; *liberal feminism*; *Marxist feminism*; *radical feminism*.)

feminization of labor: the spread of those aspects of work typically associated with women (i.e. low-pay, part-time, and insecure) to sectors of the labor market tra-ditionally dominated by men.

feminization of poverty: a term to describe the fact that a growing proportion of those in *poverty* are women. Reasons for this include:

- Most heads of *single-parent families* are women, and such families are at risk from poverty.
- Women have a longer average life expectancy than men, and the elderly are at risk from poverty.
- Women's average earnings are less than those of men and many women are in very low-paid jobs.

(See *black feminism; liberal feminism; Marxist feminism; radical feminism.*)

feminization of work: the process whereby certain categories of work, especially clerical work, have become dominated by female workers. The process is accentuated by the fragmentation of clerical work, which has reduced the skill levels of these occupations and made them susceptible to colonization by female workers.

fertility: a reference to the number of children born to a woman. (See *fertility rate.*)

fertility rate: the number of live births in a population per 1,000 women of child-bearing age (usually figured as 15–45 years). The figure is often broken down still further into an age-specific fertility rate. Another measure of fertility is the Total Fertility Rate (TFR), which is the average number of children that a woman bears in her lifetime. The World Health Organization estimates that a TFR of 2.1 is necessary to keep population levels in a society stable (ignoring any possible effects of *migration*). (See *birth rate, death rate, fecundity.*)

fetish: an object that is worshipped or venerated because it is believed to have magical powers. Such objects often form an important part of religious or magical *rituals*.

feudal society: a society in which people exist in a strict *hierarchy*, depending on their relationship to the possession or nonpossession of land. In theory, all land is owned by the monarch, who gives grants to the nobles or *aristocracy*, who, in their turn, rent or lease land to others further down the hierarchy. The landless have very limited rights in society, but owe loyalty to their feudal lords. Relationships in a feudal society are therefore based on obligations to superiors in the hierarchy. Feudal societies tend to be closed, with little chance of *social mobility*. Production in feudal societies is largely agricultural, with *wealth* being made from the farming of land. Feudalism broke down in western Europe under the impact of the growth of the commercial class located in towns and the rise in *capitalist relations of production*.

field experiment: an experiment carried out in a natural setting rather than in a laboratory. The method is not widely used in sociology owing to the difficulty of controlling the *variables*. (See *comparative method.*)

fieldwork: a general term used to cover a variety of sociological research activities in which the sociologist is actively engaged in the real social world in a direct way. It stands in contrast to work that is carried in a laboratory or a library. (See *laboratory experiments.*)

finance capitalists: members of a group within the capitalist class, who are concerned with banking and the movement of money around the *global market*. Aaronovitch identifies the finance capitalists as the new *ruling class* in late capitalist societies. Critics argue that members of this smaller group within the capitalist class have competing interests and do not act in concert. Moreover, individual finance capitalists are subject to the same impersonal forces of *capitalism* and can just as easily fall prey to as make a great deal of wealth from them.

finanscapes: sites for the flow of capital and money through the world, claimed to be a central feature of a globalized economy. It is made possible by the development of new information and communication technologies. (Also see *technoscapes*.)

first world: a term to describe those areas of the world that are most highly developed industrially. The first world usually includes the economies and societies of western Europe, the US and Canada, Australia, New Zealand, and Japan. The criteria for inclusion in the category include technological sophistication, an advanced service sector, and a commitment to free enterprise. (See *second world*; *third world*.)

fiscal crisis: the result of the contradiction in *late capitalism* between the need to reduce state expenditure to maintain profitability in a global economy and the need to increase expenditure of welfare benefits to maintain legitimacy for the capitalist system. The fiscal crisis is discussed politically between those advocating a minimalist state and therefore a reduction in *direct taxation* and those who argue for an interventionist state and therefore continued public expenditure.

five stages of economic growth: an idea developed by Rostow to describe the steps that undeveloped countries need to go through to achieve a developed state:

1. traditional society, characterized by agricultural dominance and a low technological state
2. preconditions for "takeoff," where agriculture is reorganized to produce surplus food and national transportation systems are developed
3. takeoff, where society is transformed through increasing investment in advanced technology in the leading sectors of the economy
4. maturity, where industry is diversified into many areas of activity, and investment increases to produce a dynamic industrial sector
5. developed status, where there is a growth of the *tertiary sector*, combined with high national consumption.

fixation: a situation where a worker experiences frustration at work, and thus develops a compulsion to act in a certain way. The worker then becomes resistant to any change that might threaten the fixation.

flexible production methods: ways in which a company may switch from manufacturing one product to manufacturing another with little disruption of the production line and with use of much of the same sophisticated machinery. This is a key element of post-Fordist production, which seeks to meet the consumer needs of *niche markets*. The ability to respond to rapid changes in demand is important for the survival of industrial organizations in the situation of postmodernity.

folk devils: a term to denote a group with a particular common interest or activity that becomes stigmatized by society at large and thus the target for adverse comment and activity. (See *moral panics*.)

folk society: a term devised by the *Chicago School* to denote rural societies in which everyone knows everyone else. Such societies have a number of folk characteristics, such as oral traditions, their own style of music and dance, and a tendency to keep themselves to themselves, while preserving traditions of hospitality. (See *Gemeinschaft*.)

food: substances eaten to maintain life. In sociology, food is more than this, having symbolic as well as physical significance. The sociology of food examines the ways in which food is produced and marketed, the ways in which it is used as a medium of *status* and exchange, and the ways in which there are class and ethnic differences in the attitudes toward and use of food products.

forced mobility: where movement in the *class structure* is the result of changes in the *occupational structure* rather than an increase in the choices of individuals. The major cause of forced mobility in recent times has been the decline in manufacturing jobs and the increase in white-collar and service occupations. This has resulted in enforced upward mobility.

forces of production: a Marxist term that describes the raw materials needed to manufacture goods, the tools and machinery needed to work those materials, and the *detailed division of labor* that is organized around that production. It is similar to the *means of production*, which includes division of labor under its umbrella. (See *relations of production*.)

Fordism: a type of industrial production associated with modernity, based on a strict *division of labor*, with workers performing low-skill repetitive tasks to produce mass standardized goods for undifferentiated markets. Fordist production is associated with Taylorist methods of management, where the crucial issue is control over the minute-by-minute actions of the workers to maximize production. Sociologists have argued that Fordist conditions are likely to lead to an alienated or at least instrumental workforce. (See *post-Fordism*.)

formal economy: the part of the economy composed of paid jobs, either in manufacturing, extraction, or the service industries. A feature of jobs in the formal economy is that they are recorded by the *state* and therefore taxable. (See *black economy*; *informal economy*.)

formal interviews: see *structured interviews*

formal organization: a term used to describe the *structure* of an *organization* and the ways that communication, decision-making, and control are supposed to flow within it. Most formal organizations are hierarchical in nature – that is, the formal structure concentrates *power* and decision-making at the top of a pyramid of organizational positions. Those at the top control the activities of those below them, while those at the bottom are expected to obey the orders. Therefore, most formal organizations are "top-down" organizations. (See *informal organization*.)

formal rationality: associated with economic actions, and indicating the quantitative calculation of the effects of particular actions in strictly logical terms, often expressed as "maximum production at minimum cost."

formalism: a term applied to organizational behavior that indicates an overadherence to the formal procedures of the organization, often at the expense of overall goals. By focusing on the fulfillment of formal procedures, bureaucrats are said to produce organizations that are rigid and unresponsive to *clients*' needs. (See *displacement of goals*.)

formalization: the process whereby enthusiastic *sects* adopt more ritualistic and routinized practices as members age and settle down. It is contrasted with inspirational forces within sects.

fourth world: a term sometimes used in the sociology of development to indicate those countries in Africa and Asia that are the poorest in the world and stand out from the rest of the *third world* because of their lack of *development*.

foxes: a term used by Machiavelli to describe those who gain and maintain *power* in society through cunning and deviousness. (See *lions*.)

fragmentation theories: explanations for the development in class structures that argue that the traditional classes of working and middle class have split into a larger number of divisions of class, which disrupt the formation of class solidarity. The factors involved in fragmentation are:

- Growth in affluence, reducing external differences between the classes.
- Growth in occupational specialization, resulting in the proliferation of middle-class occupations.
- *Social mobility*, resulting in members of the fast-growing middle-class sector being recruited from diverse backgrounds.

Fragmentation theories suggest that all classes are split, with the modern *upper class* divided into four segments: the *elite*, the old professional class, *organization men*, and the *intelligentsia*. The *intermediate class* is highly fragmented through low-level non-manual workers, independent artisans to supervisors. The traditional working class has also contracted and fragmented into various levels of skill and particularly the employed and unemployed. (See *persistence theories; realignment theories*.)

frame of reference: used to indicate a particular way in which an individual comes to view the world, built up through his or her own experience of it. In looking at social phenomena, individuals do not do so objectively, but through the filter of their own experiences and understandings. The basic assumptions and preexisting attitudes of the individual constitute a frame of reference through which individuals will view new events as they seek to establish their meaning. Though highly variable, frames of reference do have a collective existence, since members, for example, of the same social class are likely to have similar experiences. They tend to be built up as images of other social groups and experiences, which may or may not be accurate accounts.

Frankfurt School: a group of radical sociologists associated with the Frankfurt Institute of Social Research, who moved away from the Marxist assumptions of its founders to develop a critical theory that was critical of both Western *capitalism* and Soviet-style *socialism*. Though it has many variations within it, the Frankfurt School tended to view most progress as illusory, with science and reason seen as tools for the perfection of tyranny rather than for liberating society. In particular, their concern with society's relationship with nature preceded much ecologically minded sociology.

free-floating intelligentsia: a term used by Mannheim to indicate the social group he believed could stand outside its own social interests when carrying out its work on ideas and thus avoid ideologies such as *fascism* or *communism*. The intelligentsia could therefore avoid the pitfalls of *relativism* and put forward ideas that were more truthful than ideological.

free will: see *voluntarism*

friendship: a relationship among people that is based on mutual respect and liking, and encompasses bonds of trust and loyalty. Though it is a central part of many people's lives, the importance of friendship in society has been little investigated by mainstream sociology.

fringe benefits: the wider monetary and nonmonetary rewards that are given to workers outside of the main wage or salary. These may cover overtime payments, vacation entitlements, flexibility of work hours, and other benefits. Sociologists have been interested in the way that fringe benefits systematically differ among various groups of workers, with nonmanual workers usually gaining greater fringe benefits than manual workers.

frustrated instrumentalism: a condition where voters increasingly vote against the party of government because of the decline in the material welfare that its policies has brought them. It is thus the lack of economic success that leads the electorate to make a protest vote against the government party. It is a feature of much democratic politics in the postmodern world.

frustration: where incentives other than money are not offered in work, and psychological feelings of blocked desires and goals build up. These may be released in aggression, but can also have other outlets, such as regression. (See *fixation*; *resignation*.)

frustration–aggression theory: drawn from the psychological work of Dollard, a theory used in the sociology of *deviance* to suggest that aggressive behavior is a result of the frustration of individual needs. For example, in the sociology of *suicide*, Henry and Short suggested that the frustration of blocked *goals* in times of business depression could lead to increased aggression against the self and therefore higher rates of suicide.

function: the job that an activity or institution does for wider *social structures,* and in particular its contribution to the maintenance and continuation of social arrangements. (See *latent functions*; *manifest functions*.)

functional equivalent: a structure in society that can carry out the same job as a different structure in another society with equal efficiency.

functional indispensability: the principle in *functionalism* that existing institutions are essential for society to continue to exist. This has been criticized because it leads to inherent conservatism, with change being seen as somehow threatening to the continuation of society. Merton also showed that there were functional alternatives.

functional prerequisites: the basic needs that *society* must have fulfilled if it is to continue to exist. The assumption of the functionalists was that existing social arrangements must meet some functional prerequisite; otherwise society would not exist. *Parsons* argued that societies had four basic needs, *Adaptation, Goal-attainment, Integration,* and *Latency* (the *AGIL* or *GAIL* needs). (See *functionalism*.)

functional rationality: a term used by Mannheim to indicate a situation where the *division of labor* results in efficient production. Mannheim argued that functional rationality was often achieved at the expense of *substantial rationality*, with a consequent increase in the *alienation* of workers.

functional rebel: an individual who, according to *Durkheim*, protests that the existing social arrangements are unjust, because they do not accord with the distribution of talents. While the functional rebels oppose the existing political realities, they are called deviant by those who benefit from them.

functional unity: the principle in *functionalism* that everything that exists in society contributes to the maintenance of everything else. It is criticized because social institutions could be shown to have a high degree of *autonomy*.

functionalism: that approach in sociology that seeks to explain the existence of *social structures* by the role they perform for *society* as a whole. It is thus a structural theory, beginning its analysis at the level of society rather than the individual. The focus of analysis is the interrelationship of interdependent parts and how the functioning of the parts is essential for the well-being of the whole. However, critics suggest that it:

- is a conservative approach, stressing order at the expense of conflict
- ignores individuals in focusing only on the structural elements
- is ahistorical, focusing on the present without any sense of the past.

functionaries: in Althusserian terms, the people who staff the *ideological* and *repressive state apparatus* and act as agents of capital, sometimes consciously, sometimes unwittingly.

fundamentalism: a religious belief (and any practices following from it) that there is a need to return to and follow the basic texts of that religion in order to gain salvation. Fundamentalist groups and movements exist in *Christianity*, *Judaism*, and *Islam*. While it is an essentially religious belief, fundamentalism is often involved with overtly political issues, as its views can bring it into conflict with the *state* over how society should be run.

fusionism: a theory in the sociology of *leisure*, which argues that work and leisure are becoming increasingly similar. Work takes on many of the attributes of leisure, such as piped music on the shop floor, and leisure takes on some of the organizational aspects of work. (See *leisure industry*.)

G

GAIL: see *AGIL*

gambles with death: a term used by Taylor to denote that most *suicidal acts* are Janus-faced – that is, oriented toward both death and life. Taylor argues that there is a continuum of suicidal acts from the trivial to the deadly serious. Most, however, are gambles with death in which the *actor* creates situations in which the suicidal act is more or less likely to be detected and stopped. The less likely the detection, the more serious the attempt to die. (See *attempted suicide.*)

games theory: a theory developed from economics that attempts to apply mathematical values to decision-making situations, where there are limited choices and participants have different interests in outcomes, which might be expressed numerically. It has been criticized for attaching mathematical values to what are essentially nonmathematical, complex social situations.

gang: any grouping (usually youthful, urban, and male) that seeks to control a "territory" and operates on the margins of legality. Gangs have been a particular focus for sociologists of *deviance*, who are interested in the way that gangs have subcultural rules and *status* systems and who have studied the relationship between members of gangs and "normal" society. Though often associated with violence, a distinguishing characteristic of youthful gangs is boredom. More organized and older gangs can move into more criminal activities, with an associated rise in disorderly behavior.

gated communities: middle-class residential areas surrounded by physical barriers to prevent unauthorized access, and usually monitored and patroled by security guards. Gated communities are increasingly found in the US, and are a response to their inhabitants' fear of rising levels of crime. (See *underclass.*)

gatekeepers: sociologically, those who control access to a valuable resource or outlet, by virtue of occupying a particular position. In the sociology of the media, the term gatekeeper refers to editors of journals and newspapers, whose decisions control what does and does not get published. They are therefore in powerful positions to shape what the public thinks about particular issues. The influence of the gatekeepers' *ideology* and interests is thus promoted through their ability to deny access to alternative ideas. In urban sociology, the *urban managers* act as gatekeepers, having the ability to open or close doors to valuable resources such as public housing, social security benefits, etc. (See *agenda-setting.*)

gay rights: part of the *new social movements*, and the focus of the campaign for equal treatment for lesbians and homosexual men. Much gay rights agitation concerns discrimination experienced by gay people in society, such as homophobic violence, negative portrayals in the media, and government policy toward *AIDS*.

Geisteswissenschaften: a term used by Dilthey to indicate the social sciences as distinct from the natural sciences. The crucial difference is that the social sciences have to be explored internally, in terms of the mind or spirit, as well as externally. (See *Naturwissenschaften.*)

Gemeinschaft: a term developed by Tönnies to describe the types of relationship found in *communities,* and in particular rural communities, of the preindustrial age. These sorts of relationship were close and intimate, because each individual understood where he or she was in relation to all others with whom they interacted. There is therefore a strong sense of position associated with *Gemeinschaft* relationships. *Gemeinschaft* relationships are *holistic* – that is, they involve the whole of a person's being, and are likely to be intimate and face-to-face. (See *Gesellschaft.*)

gender: the term used by sociologists to describe the cultural and social attributes of men and women that are manifested in appropriate masculinity and femininity. Sociologists use gender as distinct from the anatomical divisions of sex because although the two are connected, they are not necessarily coterminous. For example, the anatomically male can adopt feminine behavior patterns. In the case of transsexuals, gender behavior can be transformed into an anatomical reality through surgery. Postmodernists suggest that this illustrates the way in which individuals can reconstruct very basic aspects of their identity in fundamental ways. The relationship between anatomical sex and gendered behavior is thus complex and varied. (See *sex.*)

gender codes: hidden, unspoken assumptions about the proper roles of men and women that are transmitted through the *socialization* process and are negotiated by each new *generation.* Gender codes are not uniform but vary with location. Traditional gender codes tend to be stronger in the *working class* than the *middle class,* but all people have access to both conservative and radical gender codes and negotiate their way through to their own balance.

gender regime: a term used to describe the ways in which an institution is enveloped in messages concerning what is appropriate or inappropriate masculine or feminine behavior. For example, the term has been used in the study of schooling to examine the *hidden curriculum* messages about male and female behavior.

gender stereotyping: see *femininity, masculinity, stereotyping*

genderquake: a term used by Wilkinson to describe the fundamental change in attitudes toward women's role in society that has taken place since the impact of modern *feminism.* Crucial to this genderquake is a change in female attitudes toward education and work. Women are now more likely to see themselves in terms of career than housewife aspirations and therefore have much more positive attitudes toward education as a means of achieving a good career.

generalizations: propositions derived from studying a *sample* of people with specific characteristics that are applied to all people who have those characteristics. The ability to generalize is based on the representativeness of the sample being studied. It is important because it allows the cost-effective study of society as a whole.

generalized other: in *symbolic interactionism,* the ability of an individual to place himself or herself in the position of other people involved in a situation and calculate the effects of an action upon the individual. The capacity for *action* in society rests upon the ability to envisage the generalized other.

generation: all members of a society born in the same period and regarded as a collectivity, such as the "prewar generation" or the "sixties generation." It can also mean the members of a family descended by the same number of degrees from a common ancestor, or the time span between a group of contemporaries and the birth of their children, usually thought to be 30 years. It is often assumed that the generations in a society, having shared similar experiences, also share similar views and feelings.

generational unit: a term developed by Mannheim to describe those subdivisions of a *generation* that share something substantial, as against all other members of the generation, who may share little except age. Generational units are likely to be identified through class, *gender*, or *ethnicity*.

genetics: the study of biological inheritance, and an important counterbalance to the sociological enterprise. In part, genetics explores the extent to which individuals are the product of their parental DNA and therefore the extent to which people are determined as individuals. Sociologists, while accepting that people are to an extent determined, are more interested in the way that *culture* predisposes individuals to particular courses of action. Both genetics and sociology accept that there is a limited area of free will operating in society, though they may differ over the extent of this. The contradiction between genetics and sociology is sometimes expressed as the *nature versus nurture debate.*

genre: in the sociology of culture, a type of *text,* such as detective fiction or science fiction, that has associated informal rules and literary conventions. Sociologists have widened the definition to include all types of text, not just written ones.

geographical mobility: the movement of people around the country, usually in pursuit of jobs. In sociology, the importance of geographical mobility is linked to the degree of openness of a society. Societies with very limited geographical mobility tend to have closed social *stratification* systems, with little movement among different *social classes.* Geographically mobile societies also tend to be socially mobile.

germ theory of disease: a view that disease occurs through the action of invisible microorganisms. The work of Louis Pasteur in France and Robert Koch in Germany in the late 19th century led to an understanding of the nature of infection. The result of viewing disease in this way is that the emphasis tends to be on drugs-related treatment, with a corresponding lack of emphasis on disease prevention, and the focus is on the site of the disease in the patient, rather than a wider view encompassing the patient's subjective feelings and whole environment. A criticism of the germ theory of disease is its failure to explain why although many people are exposed to infectious organisms, relatively few develop the disease. (See *biomechanical model of health.*)

gerontocracy: a society in which the old have *power* and are the rulers. Such social arrangements are often associated with *traditional societies* and in particular with those societies where the social stratification system is one of *age sets.*

gerontology: the study of the old and the aging process, which has become a contemporary focus for much sociological research. Sociologists are interested in the way that different categories of old people have different experiences of aging and the way that the old have different *status* in different societies.

Gesellschaft: meaning "association," a concept developed by Tönnies to describe those relationships most likely to be found in urban areas. These were impersonal and calculative, based on the interrelationship between one segment of a person's being with that of another person. An example might be the fleeting contact between shopper and sales assistant during the purchase of goods. Such relationships are superficial and based on a lack of knowledge of the respondent's background and social standing. (See *Gemeinschaft.*)

Gestalt: the idea that the whole is greater than the sum of the parts. Sometimes referred to as the group mind, gestalt theory implies that individuals, when grouped together, create an entity that has an existence of its own. The criticism of this is that it is very difficult to show the existence of the gestalt without a leap of faith. (See *reification.*)

ghettos: in sociology, a term used to describe those areas of cities that are characterized by very poor housing, few amenities, and often a high concentration of ethnic minorities. The term was originally applied to areas of European cities in which the Jewish population was segregated from the rest of the population.

ghost dancers: members of a *millenarian movement* that existed among the Teton Native American tribe toward the end of the 19th century. Members believed that performing a "ghost dance" would reverse the social and economic upheavals that had afflicted the tribe since the coming of the white settlers. The movement died out after a massacre of ghost dancers by American troops.

Giddens, Anthony: the foremost contemporary British sociologist, who has been responsible for the development of *structuration* theory as an original theoretical contribution. He began his career as a reinterpreter of the classical sociologists and then as a contributor to the debate over the importance of class in contemporary capitalism. He has most recently been concerned with developing an understanding of the relationship between the global and the local.

gift: a term focused on by Bell and Newby as an important aspect of the *hegemony* of men over women in marriage. The giving of gifts by husbands to wives is seen symbolically as a means of establishing the superiority of the male in marriage. It also has the effect of creating obligation and dependence in the woman toward the man.

girl-friendly science: a term to describe attempts to devise ways of teaching and presenting science to girls to enable them to overcome their traditional reluctance to study areas such as physics and to improve their achievements in science. Various methods have been used, including girls-only teaching groups, lunchtime sessions to enable girls to acquire confidence in handling particular kinds of equipment in advance of the lessons in which they will be used, the use of textbooks that use examples likely to be meaningful and interesting to girls, and using female role-models to persuade girls to take up careers in science and engineering.

glasnost: a term meaning openness, used to describe the attempt by Mikhail Gorbachev to open up the political system of the Soviet Union to fresh, non-communist influences, which ultimately led to the collapse of the Soviet system. (See *perestroika.*)

glass ceiling: a term to describe the barrier experienced by women at work, who have difficulty in achieving promotion to a higher level. It is suggested that, above a certain level, an invisible barrier acts to prevent women from easily achieving the same levels of authority as their male colleagues. (See *feminization of labor, glass walls.*)

glass walls: a term to describe invisible barriers that have the effect of segregating men and women into different types of employment – i.e. vertical segregation. For example, women form the greater proportion of nurses, school cooks, secretaries, and elementary school teachers, while men with the same respective educational qualifications are more likely to be found in different types of employment. (See *feminization of labor, glass ceiling.*)

global markets: a term expressing the belief that the demand and supply of goods is now a worldwide undertaking in which the level of trade among countries has dramatically increased. The existence of a global market for goods and services is largely based on the information revolution that computer technology has delivered. The implications are enormous, as developments in industrial production in one part of the world can have effects in widely separated and completely different countries. The global market is so vast that it cannot be controlled by any individual nation, nor, some would argue, by any international agencies. The global market is serviced by vast *conglomerates* of *transnational companies*. Some sociologists have argued that the idea of a global market is exaggerated and that there has been a small increase in world trade that does not justify the idea of a revolution in the way the world operates.

global village: a term to express the idea that *mass communication*, particularly through film and television, has been able to transcend national boundaries to the extent where the world has become like one village. It is argued that particularly with the rise of *media conglomerates* and the development of cable and satellite television, people around the world are exposed to the same messages. Many are concerned by the potential for the misuse of such *power.*

globalization: the process of increasing *interdependence* of societies on a worldwide scale. This interdependence can take a variety of forms, but sociologists have focused mainly on the globalization of the economy and the globalization of *culture.*

- In terms of the economy, the activities of the *transnational companies* are seen as central to the globalization of production. Decisions about where to locate industry are taken with the whole world as a possibility, rather than within the confines of the *nation-state*. The financial markets of the world are now connected through fast *information technology*, so that *capital* and resources can be switched around the world constantly, without any limits of time or space. Much of this type of globalization is invisible to the individual, but the consequences are very real. Individuals may lose or gain jobs as a consequence of decisions reached by others thousands of miles away, who are operating with a global perspective. The implication of this view is that the nation-state is no longer the most important unit in the world's economy.
- More visible is the globalization of culture, as media images, increasingly drawn from a worldwide arena, are transmitted into people's homes through satellite or cable. Cultural products are increasingly dominated by media companies whose activities are spread throughout the world.

Critics of the concept of globalization have argued that the process has been much exaggerated. It assumes that some individuals at the head of transnational companies have almost superhuman powers of control and *rationality* which, in reality, individuals do not have. Sociologists such as Paul Hirst argue that, rather than a withering away of the national state as globalization theorists have argued, there has been an internationalization of the economy and of culture, based on the increased relationships among national states, which continue to be the most important source of *identity* in the world.

glossing: a term used by ethnomethodologists to suggest that everyone, in conversation and action, ignores possible misunderstandings by filling in understanding, without exploring it deeply. The need to gloss arises from the *indexicality* of language, which can only be understood in its context. As teasing out the context would be enormously time-consuming, people gloss in order to create meanings in the situations in which they find themselves. (See *ethnomethodology*.)

go-slow: a tactic in *industrial conflict*, in which workers carry out their tasks as slowly as possible in order to cut down production. The trick is to go slowly enough to disrupt without going so slowly that the supervisor can legitimately complain about the pace the worker is setting. Safety procedures are often called upon by workers to justify the slower speed they adopt.

goal: an aim or target, usually associated with an *organization*. Organizations are set up to achieve particular goals and these are therefore important motivators for members of the organization. (See *goal-model*.)

goal-attainment: one of *Parsons' functional prerequisites* that relates to the achieving of the system's aims, and in practical terms refers to political institutions. Congress would therefore be an institution that would contribute to goal-attainment. (See *adaptation*; *integration*; *latency*.)

goal displacement: see *displacement of goals*

goal-model: a traditional way of conceiving of *organizations* as devices for achieving aims. The importance of the goals in the goal-model is that they provide a measure of the *effectiveness* of any organization – that is, how far it achieves its goals.

gods of the gaps: a term used to describe the ideas that exist beyond formal religions, but which fulfill the spiritual and mystical needs of people in a secular society. Belief in astrology is usually found to be the main god of the gap.

going native: a process sometimes experienced by sociologists carrying out *participant observation*, particularly covert, in which they identify with the group under study so much that they lose their academic detachment and *objectivity*.

golden age of religion: an era presumed to have existed at some time in the past when members of society were far more "religious" than they are today. This era is used to represent a stage from which we have since declined. However, writers such as Hill call the whole concept into question, arguing that historical evidence shows that the clergy always found it difficult to persuade the mass of the population to attend church regularly and to follow the various religious observances on "holy days." In other words, it is argued by some that the golden age of religion is a myth.

golden age of senescence: a mythical time in the past, when all old people were cared for by their families and were not placed in homes. It is mythical because not everyone lived in extended families or had the resources to care for the old in the family. Yet it is a powerful idea that contemporary society has somehow lost its capacity to look after its old people in the caring environment of the family. On the one hand, old people in the past were not immune from abuse and distress within the family, and on the other, the neglect by the modern family of its elderly relatives is exaggerated.

golden age of tranquility: a presumed time in the past when the young were respectful to their elders and did not engage in *juvenile delinquency*. This was a myth-ical time, as in each *generation* the old see younger people as threatening the old order and a peaceful way of life. In each generation, there is created a *folk devil* who repre-sents the freedom and the threat of youth. The threat of the young is therefore not in reality new but appears new in every generation.

government: the political and administrative organs of the *state,* composed in the US of the executive, the legislative, and the judicial branches – i.e. the President and his Cabinet, Congress, and the courts.

grand theory: see *high theory*

grassroots model: an approach in the study of *moral panics* that emphasizes the real nature of public concerns about an issue as a source of moral panics. It there-fore rejects the view that moral panics are somehow created by elites, politicians, or moral entrepreneurs for their own purposes. (See *elite-engineered model; interest-group model.*)

Great Transformation: the combination of economic, social, political, and cultural changes that led to *modernity*. It refers to a specific but unbounded period of time during which Western societies fundamentally moved to recognizably rational and modern social practices.

green movement: a political and social movement that places the *environment* at the top of its priorities. In several countries in Europe, green parties have managed to place issues such as pollution, animal rights, and the environment onto the political agenda of all parties. The German Green Party in particular is a significant force outside the two main political parties.

green revolution: the scientific advances in agriculture made since World War II that have changed the way that crops are grown. Scientific progress in agriculture since this time has had two main elements. Firstly, selective breeding produced higher yielding crops, which were more resistant to disease and therefore more likely to end up as food. Secondly, the use of more sophisticated fertilizers and more effective pesticides reduced damage to crops and encouraged strong growth. The immediate results of the green revolution have been to stimulate food production throughout the world. However, sociologists have also examined the social con-sequences of this revolution, looking for both positive and negative, and intended and *unintended consequences*.

- The first and major social consequence is that starvation has been reduced throughout the world. This at first may seem strange, given the high profile of famine in the media's reporting of events in the *third world*. However, the green revolution has allowed the sustenance of larger populations than was previously possible.

- Some sociologists have suggested that the green revolution has led to enormous social dislocation, by encouraging peasant farmers in the third world to take on credit they could not afford to buy the expensive fertilizers on which higher yields depend. One bad year can often mean that the indebted farmers are forced to sell their land and migrate to already overcrowded cities in search of scarce work. The result of this is increased poverty for the migrant workers.
- Environmental sociologists highlight the increased toxins that enter the food chain through the intensive use of fertilizers and pesticides. The long-term effects of toxin buildup are not yet known.

It is also suggested that we are entering a period of "new green revolution," as bio-engineering manipulates the genes of food crops to produce vegetables and fruit with all kinds of desirable (and perhaps some undesirable) characteristics.

gross national product: a measure of the value of the production of a country, usually referred to as GNP. While economists are interested in the calculation of GNP, sociologists are more interested in the way that it represents the prosperity of a country and whether such a country is getting richer or poorer. It also provides a measure, when expressed as an amount per head of population, of the relative wealth of different countries.

gross volatility: the total amount of vote-switching between one election and the next, both voluntarily and involuntarily. Some of the gross volatility will occur because of the death of registered electors before the register runs out. (See *net volatility*.)

group: a collection of individuals who interact with each other on the basis of formal or informal contexts. For example, a friendship group would have informal rules for meeting and for carrying out activities, while an organized group of enthusiasts would have formal ways of coming together and interacting with each other. The concept stands in contrast to a category of people, such as "working class," who may have limited interaction.

group theory of democracy: the idea that a functioning *democracy* is one in which natural collectivities, such as the family or the workplace, stand between the *state* and the individual. The interests of individuals are protected from the *power* of the state by these intervening groups, who form the natural focus of *identity* for the individual. Representations to the state are made through these groups rather than by individuals' futile attempts to make the state notice.

guest workers: a term drawn from the German *Gastarbeiter*, which defines immigrant workers as temporary residents rather than granting them full rights of *citizenship*. Members of the Turkish immigrant community in Germany were the original focus of the concept, but as they have settled and had children who know little else except Germany, they have begun to agitate for more permanent rights. The term also distinguishes those non-German workers in Germany who have European Union rights from those who do not.

habitus: a term used by Bordieu to describe the distinctive sets of meanings that each social class passes on through the generations and that shape the thought and actions of individual class members. The habitus is thus the cultural context into which individuals are socialized and is influential in determining taste, perception, and aesthetic judgment. It is used by Bordieu in relation to the process whereby the culture of a particular class can come to dominate schooling so that its children are more likely to succeed in the education system than children from other social classes.

Halévy thesis: the argument that the hold of Methodism over the *working class* in 18th- and 19th-century Britain prevented the revolutionary upheavals that the rest of Europe experienced. It was the opportunity for independent organization that Methodism provided that channeled the energies of the leaders of the working class into agitation for peaceful change rather than violent *revolution.*

Hall-Jones scale: a method of classifying occupations into seven main groups, with professionals and senior managers at the top and unskilled manual workers at the bottom. A modified version of this scale was used by Goldthorpe in the *Oxford mobility study.* (See *occupational scale.*)

halo effect: where the *respondent* gives the answer that he or she thinks that the researcher wants to hear rather than what she or he really thinks. The phrase is also used to refer to the tendency to reward those of whom we approve in an overly positive manner. For example, students perceived as bright may be awarded higher marks than those perceived as less bright for similar pieces of work. (See *Hawthorne effect; self-fulfilling prophecy.*)

handicap: as distinct from *disability,* a term to describe the difficulties a disabled person faces arising from the social reaction to his or her disability.

hara-kiri: ritual disemboweling as a form of *suicide* among Japanese. It is often referred to as a way to demonstrate that actions such as suicide can have different social meanings in different contexts. Rather than being the shameful, sinful act that suicide is seen as in Catholic countries, hara-kiri is an honorable way of wiping out social shame.

hard statistics: those statistics relatively immune to the processes of *subjectivity* and manipulation in their collection. Examples are demographic statistics, such as those relating to births, marriages, deaths, and divorce, and those detailing the number of graduates with particular qualifications. (See *soft statistics.*)

Hawthorne effect: the unintended effects of the researcher's presence, or the knowledge that the subjects of sociological research are taking part in a research study, which may lead them to alter their behavior or responses. While particularly applicable to most kinds of *experiment,* the Hawthorne effect may also be present in all methods of *primary data* collection. (See *Hawthorne experiments.*)

Hawthorne experiments: research carried out for the Western Electric Company of Chicago between 1927 and 1932, interpreted and publicized by Elton Mayo. The experiments, looking into factors influencing employee productivity, were important for two main reasons. One is that they were one of the earliest attempts to investigate employees using the *human relations*, rather than the *scientific management*, theory of work. The other is their conclusion that both the presence of researchers, and the involvement of subjects in the research process, can influence the results. (See *Hawthorne effect*.)

Head Start: a cultural enrichment program, funded by the US federal government, that provides advantages such as day care and preschool instruction to disadvantaged children. (See *compensatory education*.)

headlining: where the media give prominence to a particular news story, thus insuring that it becomes a matter for public debate. (See *agenda-setting*.)

health: "not merely the absence of disease and infirmity, but complete physical, mental and social well-being" (World Health Organization). Sociologists recognize the problematic nature of the concepts of both health and *illness*, and emphasize that these are socially and culturally defined. In many countries there are still significant variations in health and health care among different *social classes* and between males and females. (See *biomechanical model of health; inverse care law*.)

health gap: the difference in health among members of different *social classes*. Health statistics in many countries show this gap clearly, as there are measurable class differences in virtually every indicator of health, including *life expectancy*.

hedonism: often put forward as a value held by the *working class,* the belief that a person should live for today, gaining present pleasure as against future gain. (See *deferred gratification*.)

hegemony: the dominant group in society, supported by the supposedly "spontaneous" consent given by the masses, who accept the type of society imposed upon them. It is held in place by the agreement of the masses to a set of *values* that are not theirs, but arise from the material interests of the *ruling class.* Though this may appear to be similar to *value consensus*, it is different, because hegemony is never absolute like the value consensus; it is economically determined and not genuinely spontaneous, but the result of a pervasive effort by the ruling class and its functionaries.

heredity: the genetic transmission of physiological characteristics from one generation to another. The concept is often discussed in the context of the *nature versus nurture debate* regarding *intelligence*. It also appears in discussions regarding the reasons for antisocial behavior or criminal activity. Originally associated with Lombroso, ideas that a propensity to criminal behavior can be predicted by an examination of characteristics such as skull size have recently resurfaced, e.g. in Rushton's work in Canada. (See *eugenics*.)

hermeneutics: a way of understanding *action* by analyzing the text (or action) within the larger framework of the world view that produced it. The method was derived from attempts to understand authentic biblical texts, which had become distorted in translation. True meaning was obtained by looking at the context in which the text was written. Similarly with social actions, the sociologist needs to place an event in its overall context and interpret the meaning of the event from this. The technique has been criticized because it is difficult to authenticate any one reading of an event compared to another person's reading.

Herrschaft: literally "power over man," a concept used by *Weber* to indicate domination, or the probability that orders, once given, will actually be carried out. Weber was concerned to describe the different types of domination associated with premodern and modern societies because he believed that there had been a fundamental change in typical types of *action* between the two forms of society.

heterogeneity: differences in many or all of the characteristics of a group. For example, a group of people present at any one time in a department store or a commuter train are likely to have so many differences from one another that they would form a heterogeneous population. Depending on the nature of their research, sociologists may or may not wish their subjects to form a heterogeneous group. (See *homogeneity.*)

heterosexuality: where an individual's sexual drive is oriented toward the opposite sex. The forms that heterosexuality may take are immensely varied, but the officially sanctioned arena for heterosexual activity is marriage. (See *homosexuality.*)

heuristic device: a model or an idea that aids our understanding. Though it is usually applied to concepts such as the *ideal type*, sociology itself can act as a heuristic device, as Giddens argues, because it aids our understanding of the social world.

hidden curriculum: all those things taught and learned in education that do not form part of the overt program of subjects and courses. In particular, the hidden curriculum refers to the *values, beliefs,* and attitudes that students learn alongside the knowledge and skills of the formal, *overt curriculum.* The messages derived from the hidden curriculum have a powerful influence on students' behavior and on their progress, or lack of it, at school. (See *ethos; labeling.*)

hidden economy: a term used to describe those economic activities that never come to the attention of the taxation agencies of the *state.* (See *informal economy.*)

hierarchies of credibility: these reflect a view of the world typically held by journalists and editors, in which the opinions and statements of those in positions of power, such as government ministers, senior civil servants, and high-ranking police officers are considered more "legitimate" and therefore more credible than the views of those in organizations such as pressure groups and labor unions. (See *primary definers.*)

hierarchies of oppression: a term to describe the social structure wherein different groups experience different levels of *discrimination,* depending on the mix of characteristics they might have. So, while white middle-class women face gender discrimination, their black counterparts experience further discrimination on account of their ethnicity. Black lesbian women experience yet another form of discrimination in the hierarchy of oppression on account of their sexuality.

hierarchy: a central concept in *stratification,* signifying the ordering of social positions in a structure of superiority and inferiority. Most hierarchies can be depicted as a triangle, with fewer superior positions at the top of the hierarchy than subordinate positions at the bottom.

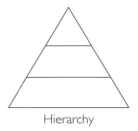

Hierarchy

Most *organizations* are hierarchical, with management, or sometimes just an individual, at the top of the command triangle. There can be more or fewer middle management positions, depending on how hierarchical the organization is.

hierarchy fetishism: a Marxist term used to describe the splitting-up of social groups into more and more levels of subordination and superordination, and the obsession with *status* and position that emerges from this. It is seen as a factor in the *false consciousness* of the *proletariat*, who, rather than uniting to combat the power of the *bourgeoisie*, are distracted by petty squabbles over positions much lower down society's hierarchy. The subdivision of levels thus acts to create the illusion of movement upward for individual members of the working class while leaving intact the monopoly of *power* enjoyed by the bourgeoisie.

hierarchy of needs: identified by Maslow as the rank order of the individual's needs, from the very basic to the more sophisticated. They are:

- physiological needs, such as food and shelter
- safety and security
- love, companionship, and affection
- self-esteem and the esteem of others
- self-actualization (i.e. realizing one's potential to the fullest).

The hierarchy was criticized as representing the hierarchy of needs for the academics who developed it rather than for all people. In particular, the hierarchy does not represent the needs of women, for whom social needs may be more important than the self-esteem needs suggested by Maslow.

hierarchy of the sciences: a concept associated with *Comte*, based on the belief that the natural and social sciences could be placed in a relationship of superiority and inferiority according to the complexity of their subject matter. Comte placed sociology at the top as the "queen of the sciences."

high culture: a term describing the arts usually patronized by the elite in society, such as opera, ballet, sculpture, etc. It stands in contrast to *popular culture*. Sociologists use the concept when examining the media and in particular the policies adopted by broadcasters to reach different *audiences*.

high-tech: a term used to describe businesses and activities based on technologies that are innovative and revolutionary. They usually involve a great deal of investment capital to be developed, are computer-based, and increasingly complex. The development of high-tech industries such as bioengineering has led to a questioning of the moral implications of such power being used in society and on individuals.

High-tech industries can be leisure-based and trivial or deal with fundamental issues concerned with life and death. (See *reproductive technologies*.)

high theory: attempts at explaining the large questions in sociology, such as "why do societies persist?" High theory is aimed beyond the merely empirical toward more philosophical areas. (See *theories of the middle range*.)

Hinduism: a polytheistic *religion* that predates *Christianity* by some three thousand years and forms the main religious belief system in India. One of the fundamental features of Hinduism is the belief in reincarnation, which views a person as having an unbroken succession of lives, not all human. The *caste* system provides the social embodiment of the main beliefs of Hinduism.

hinterland: the area in developing countries that provides the surplus wealth for the *metropolis* to exploit and appropriate. The hinterland is normally the least developed part of a *third-world* country and receives the least benefits from the *development* process.

historical documents: a wide range of *documents* from the recent or distant past, the study of which provides information for sociologists. Historical documents such as church registers have been used in the study of populations and population movements; wills have provided information on the extent of personal wealth of certain groups of people; and medical records have been used to trace the nature, extent, and treatment of disease at particular periods. There is a vast range of historical documents available to sociologists, although, as with all forms of *secondary data*, they have to be used with care.

historical materialism: the basic concept of *Marxism*, which describes how societies progress through history by the operation of economic forces. The motor of social change in historical materialism is the class conflict between the owners of the *means of production* in any society and the nonowning class. The fundamental

	Asiatic stage	Slave stage	Feudal stage	Capitalist stage
Owners	State	Slave-masters	Land-owners	Bourgeoisie
Non-owners	Villagers	Slaves	Landless	Proletariat
Mode of production	Self-sufficiency, reliant on irrigation	Slavery	Agriculture	Industry

Historical materialism

conflict of interests between these two groups insures that out of their struggle, new economic conditions emerge.

holism: a term used in sociology when referring to the whole of a thing. Theories that stress the importance of *social structures* are said to be holistic in their approach, in that they focus on the whole of the social structure as the most important area of study for sociologists.

holistic leisure: a theory in the sociology of *leisure* that argues that work and leisure should be seen as subject to the same forces in modern societies. Holists argue that both work and leisure are subject to the same growing exploitation of human resources, so that the problems of work are the problems of leisure. (See *fusionism*; *segmentalism*.)

home background: one of the explanations put forward by some sociologists and politicians to explain the different levels of achievement in education by different groups of students, particularly differences based on *social class* and *ethnic group*. A number of sociological studies have revealed aspects of a child's home background that appear to influence the level of academic achievement. J.W.B. Douglas' *longitudinal study* in Britain showed the importance both of *parental aspirations* and the educational background of the parents to whether or not a child was offered a place in a selective school, while Bernstein argued that progress was affected by the *language codes* learned in the home. Bourdieu developed the concept of *cultural capital* to explain the relative success of middle-class children. Critics have argued that too much emphasis on home background diverts attention away from other explanations, such as inequalities in *wealth* and *income* and the structure and organization of schools. (See *compensatory education.*)

homelessness: the lack of either a fixed address or adequate shelter. Homelessness is a growing problem in many advanced societies, and accurate statistics are difficult to obtain.

homeopathic medicine: treatment of disease and illness based on the administering of minute doses of substances (usually plant extracts) that mimic or reproduce the same symptoms as the disease or illness. While frequently used in many countries of the world, until recently this type of treatment has been largely ignored or even ridiculed by the medical profession in Western countries. However, growing concerns about the side-effects of some drugs, or about the effects of their long-term use, have led to a renewed interest in homeopathic medicine. (See *allopathic medicine.*)

homeostasis: the tendency for interdependent elements to move toward a state of relatively stable equilibrium. While the concept originates from the sciences, it is used by some functionalist sociologists to refer to their belief that the "natural" state of societies is one of harmony and *equilibrium*, and that conflict is therefore pathological, or abnormal. They argue that when this natural harmony is disturbed, mechanisms come into play to restore the equilibrium.

homeworking: the carrying out of occupational tasks by employees at home, not usually as additional to, but instead of, working in a workplace. Traditionally this kind of work has been low-status, low-paid work carried out by women, such as finishing garments, labeling envelopes, or performing simple assembly tasks. However, the advent of the computer has meant that increasing numbers of white-collar and professional workers are also spending some or all of their time working from home. While some people focus on the benefits of this (such as flexible working hours, the ability to combine paid work with *child care*, reducing the number of commuters and the time spent commuting) others are concerned about the isolation that home-working brings. (See *outworking*.)

homogeneity: the presence of a range of common characteristics within a group. A group of people of the same sex, age, social class, ethnic group, educational and occupational background, and political views would form a homogeneous group. Depending on the nature of their research, sociologists may or may not wish their subjects to form a homogeneous group. (See *heterogeneity*.)

homosexuality: where an individual's sexual drive is oriented toward a person of the same sex. The term encompasses both lesbianism and gay male orientation. Sociologists such as Foucault have focused on the ways in which homosexuality has come to be seen as a distinctive attribute of certain individuals, associated with a particular lifestyle and capable of "treatment." The creation of a medical *discourse* for homosexuality had the effect of marginalizing and criminalizing certain homosexual activities.

honest broker: a term to describe the *state* as viewed by pluralists, who see the role of the *government* as neutral between competing *interests groups*. Because the state is a referee between opposing ideas, the theory goes, it can make decisions in the best interests of all. The idea has been criticized for offering an idealistic view of the workings of the state, which in reality not only favors certain groups systematically, but has its own interests to promote in its decision-making.

honor: a term denoting the standing of an individual in society and the subjective feelings of esteem that stem from that standing. Social honor has been an important dimension in most societies. It is bound up with ideas concerning proper behavior and the regard that the group has for the individual. It has been of interest to sociologists of suicide as one cause of *altruistic suicide*, in which individuals are compelled by the duty of honor to kill themselves for the sake of their good name in the community.

horizontal segregation: the distribution of social groups (such as men and women or ethnic groups) differentially among various occupations. High degrees of horizontal segregation can be found between men and women, with females concentrated in administrative and nonmanual work, and men concentrated in heavy manual work. (See *core workers; glass ceiling; vertical segregation*.)

household: a term for the living situation of a person living alone or a group of people who have the same address and share one meal a day and/or the living accommodation. This differs from a *family*, which is defined as a married or cohabiting couple, with or without children, or a single parent with children. Thus, most families live in households, but not all households are families. A group of students sharing a house, for example, comprise a household but not a family. (See *family structure*.)

household economy: a term used generally to describe the circulation of goods and services within the *household* and more specifically the jobs done by the members of the household that might otherwise have been done by workers in the *formal economy*. The term has become more prominent as home-improvement becomes an important element in the economy as a whole.

housework: work undertaken to support the running of a *household*. It includes a wide range of domestic chores and is often extended to include child care and out-of-home activities such as shopping. It tends to be seen as "women's work," and has relatively low status. However, anthropological studies have shown a wide variation regarding which sex should perform what type of domestic task, and in some cultures what we regard as housework tasks are shared or done interchangeably by men and women. Housework was not a topic that received much attention from sociologists (an aspect of *malestream sociology*) until Oakley's 1971 study of 40 working-class and middle-class housewives. This showed that the women spent an average of 77 hours a week on domestic tasks. They also reported feelings of isolation, boredom, loneliness and frustration, and described their work in terms similar to those used by male assembly line workers, such as monotony, fragmentation, repetition and pressure from working at excessive speed. The women got little pleasure from their work, 70% being "dissatisfied" with the role. Medical evidence shows that full-time housewives are more prone to physical and mental illness, including depression, than women in paid employment or men. Although it was widely believed that labor-saving domestic appliances would free women from housework, evidence shows that women still spend between 40 and 70 hours per week (depending on their circumstances) in domestic and child care tasks. (See *dual role of women*.)

housing classes: a term devised by Rex and Moore to describe those groups in the housing market who compete with each other for access to different types of housing. They argued that housing classes were important in determining with whom a person associated, their interests and lifestyles. Housing classes were distinguished by their ability to satisfy the rules of various local government and financial institutions, which were biased toward the middle class and the *respectable working class*. Rex and Moore identified seven housing classes in their study. Critics argue that Rex and Moore take the concept of "desirable" for granted and that the seven classes are open to constant amendment and refinement. Moreover, the theory hides the most basic distinction in the housing market, which is between public and private housing provision.

housing segregation: a concept developed by Rex and Moore to describe the separation of different ethnic minorities into particular residential areas, and in particular the process by which black immigrants end up in the old, run-down housing of the *zone of transition*. While *racism* and low incomes play their part, the rules of the housing market also operate against ethnic minorities. For example, ethnic minorities have found it more difficult to obtain mortgages, or gain priority on housing lists. The result of the operation of the housing market has been that different ethnic groups are to be found in separate residential areas. Though the segregation is never total, it has been sufficient to produce concentrations of ethnic minorities in the worst housing in the city.

human capital theory: a theory of education that sees schooling for individuals as an investment in the future of society. The idea focuses on the way in which individuals can be trained through education, and society reaps the rewards later on in the development of technological applications.

human ecology theory: a theory developed by Park and Burgess of the *Chicago School* that likened the city to a social organism, with a life of its own. The city was made alive by the constant tension between the individual's need for freedom and society's need for social control. Heavily influenced by *evolutionary theory*, human ecology theory argued that there was a constant struggle for existence in the city, where the richest and strongest seized the most favorable urban locations and resisted attempts by other groups to displace them. Each urban area developed a distinctive lifestyle that characterized the location. Critics of the theory argue that too much was taken for granted, such as what made a particular urban area attractive, what was the process whereby one social group was displaced by another, what was the nature of the power used to seize the best locations, etc.

human relations school: developed in reaction to *scientific management,* and emphasizing the human dimension of work by recognizing workers' need to be involved in their work, rather than just interested only in money. Originally, the human relations school was associated with Elton Mayo and the experiments carried out at the Hawthorne factory of Western Electric. The human relations school was often held as a contrast to the impersonality of scientific management and was presented as a less exploitative form of management, or "management with a human face." However, critics of Human Relations dismiss it as *cow sociology,* and argue that it represents just a different way of intensifying the *exploitation* of workers. Postmodernists have been interested in human relations as one of the ways in which postmodern workers become accepting of their own exploitation and actively involve themselves in self-surveillance – that is, in increasing their workrate as they accept responsibility for their own work.

hydraulic society: a term to describe ancient cultures in which power was related to the control over access to water. Hydraulic societies were identified in Egypt and in the Tigris–Euphrates basin, where survival depended on appropriate irrigation. Such societies tended to develop bureaucratic or theocratic control of the waterways.

hypergamy: marriage to a person of higher *social status* than oneself. In practice most marriages occur between people of broadly similar social status.

hyperghetto: an area of the inner city that exhibits an extreme concentration of poverty. Typically it will contain more than 40% of the population in poverty and only loose attachments to the labor market. Hyperghettos often display high levels of ethnic segregation.

hyperreality: a term used by Baudrillard to suggest that our knowledge of the world is drawn from media images of reality rather than direct experience of it. The signs contained in media images constitute hyperreality and in the postmodern world are our main source of knowledge.

hypodermic syringe approach: an early approach to the study of the effects of the media on behavior, taking the view that the media "injected" its content into the audience's lives in a fairly direct way and subsequently influenced their behavior. It has therefore been criticized for seeing individuals as passive in the process. (See *empty bucket theory.*)

hypothesis: one of the steps in the scientific method consisting of the unverified assumptions that might possibly explain an observed phenomenon. In short, an hypothesis is an untested *theory*, or a possible explanation. The hypothesis is important to the scientific method because it provides direction for the research and shapes the experiments that the scientist designs. The hypothesis is also an exercise in creativity, because scientists must use their imaginations in devising possible explanations of events. (See *hypothetico-deductive method; laboratory experiments.*)

hypothetico-deductive method: the process involved in *positivism,* in which certain logical steps are taken in order to try to arrive at the truth. The method is usually conceptualized as consisting of a series of stages:

1 observation: the researcher observes a phenomenon considered worthy of investigation
2 conjecture: the researcher thinks of a plausible explanation
3 hypothesis formation: the conjecture is put in the form of a predictive statement that can be empirically tested
4 testing: a rigorous empiral test is designed and carried out under controlled conditions, with all observations and measurements accurately recorded
5 data analysis: the resulting data are carefully analyzed, using applied logical reasoning
6 final stage: in the light of the results, the researcher decides whether the hypothesis is confirmed, rejected, or is in need of modification and further testing.

I

iatrogenesis: a concept meaning doctor-induced illness, used by sociologists to indicate that medical intervention can at times lead to negative outcomes.

icons: in sociology, *signs*, usually pictures, whose meanings are transmitted through their similarity to the thing being represented, such as the Cross standing for Christianity. (See *index; signs proper.*)

ideal type: a typification of a phenomenon built up by extracting the essential characteristics of many empirical examples of it. The purpose of an ideal type is not to produce a perfect example, but to provide a measure against which real examples may be compared. For example, the most famous ideal type is *Weber's bureaucracy,* which is used to answer the question: "How bureaucratic is this or that organization?" Ideal types do not therefore exist in the real world, but are a sociological construction.

identity: the sense of *self* that develops as a child grows up and establishes himself or herself as an independent individual. More recently, identity has come to be an important concept in sociology, under the influence of postmodern ideas. It has come to mean the sense of self associated with the identification the individual has with certain social formations. Postmodernists therefore see identity as a shifting situational aspect of the individual, in which an individual may have a certain identity and may identify with others because of a similar ethnic background, or may have an identity influenced by particular religious ideas. The importance of the concept of identity is that it allows a person some element of choice, freed from the determinism of, for example, much class-based analysis.

identity construction: the ways in which conceptions of the *self* are forged in relationships with others and with regard to existing notions of the self. For example, the construction of a sexual identity such as masculinity is carried out in terms of relationships with women and with current notions of what it is to be a man. Identity construction can lead to the reinforcement of traditional conceptions or to negotiated versions of them.

identity politics: campaigns and struggles based on issues concerned with self-expression, rather than class-based activity. Environmentalists engage in a prominent form of identity politics.

ideological form of incorporation: the way that oppositional *subcultures* are neutralized by capitalist society through the redefinition of deviant behavior by the police or media. This is done either through *trivialization* or *domestication*. (See *commodity form of incorporation.*)

ideological state apparatus (ISA): an Althusserian term used to describe those agencies of the *state* whose prime function is to secure the compliance of subordinates with the established capitalist order. Thus ideological *hegemony* is the result of pervasive effort by the state to establish legitimacy. The term has been criticized because it assumes something of a conspiracy among the functionaries of the ISA. The major ISA in modern societies is the education system. (See *repressive state apparatus.*)

ideology: a systematic set of beliefs that serves the interest of some social group in society. Studied in particular by Marxist sociologists, ideologies are associated with *power* and the ability of those at the top of society to put forward their own ideas as right and natural for everyone else in society. In some senses, the term ideology is also used to indicate the falseness of a set of ideas, or at least a distortion of the truth. There is a distinction drawn here between "ideology," which as the ideas of a particular social group is necessarily partial, and "truth," which is universally applicable. Perhaps the best way of describing ideology is as ideas that are put forward for a purpose – to fulfill the aims of a social group in society and which may or may not be true in some more fundamental sense.

ideoscapes: sites for the global flow of political ideas and ideologies, which is said to lead to increasing similarities in political arrangements throughout the world.

illegitimacy: see *births outside marriage*

illness: a physical or mental state that is seen as abnormal and undesirable and in need of treatment. Sociologists emphasize the culturally defined nature of the concept, and how illness is defined and treated differently in different societies and contexts. (See *epidemiology; etiology; health; mental illness.*)

immigration: see *migration*

immigration controls: rules that are applied in order to define who has (and, often more importantly, who has not) the right of settlement in a country. Concern in some quarters about the number of immigrants to wealthy Western societies has led to increased debate about immigration. The issue is occasionally fueled by stories in tabloid newspapers about the supposedly large number of "illegal" immigrants entering a country. Controls are also imposed on those seeking not to migrate but to obtain political asylum. (See *migration.*)

immiseration: the process whereby the *proletariat* become poorer and more miserable, as their *exploitation* by the *bourgeoisie* is intensified. Marxists argue that this process is inevitable under a capitalist *mode of production* and can lead to widespread *poverty* and discontent. Critics point out that for many sections of society, including large parts of the *working class, capitalism* has produced a higher standard of living than previously enjoyed, and therefore that immiseration has not occurred. (See *polarization.*)

imperialism: the process of empire-building through acquisition of colonies and territories, associated particularly with the Western powers in the 19th century.

impersonality: the requirement in an *organization* that *clients* should be dealt with impartially, without fear or favor. Merton argued that the pressure to deal with clients impersonally could be harmful to the interests of clients seeking help from the *bureaucracy*, as they were reduced to a number or a cipher. (See *particularism; universalism.*)

impression management: according to Goffman, the manipulation of image by the social *actor* in order to convey particular messages to the *audience* of the action. The idea is that in interaction, individuals seek to convey favorable impressions to others, as part of a dramaturgical role. (See *dramaturgy.*)

imprisonment: the incarceration of those convicted of certain types of crime. Also in prison are those held "on remand," – i.e. accused of a serious crime and awaiting a trial. Different societies hold different views regarding the purpose of imprisonment, with the result that the proportion of the population in prison at any one time varies widely among different societies. (See *universities of crime.*)

impulse control: a type of *socialization*, in which the antisocial drives of children are limited and controlled, either through the application of restraint or through their sublimation into other legitimate activities. For example, violent tendencies may be channeled into soldiering. It is thus a control theory of socialization. (See *enculturation; role-training.*)

incapacitation theory: an approach to crime that argues that crime rates will only fall by locking up offenders so that they cannot reoffend while they are imprisoned. Incapacitation theorists reject all policy aimed at rehabilitation or changing individual criminals. Only the removal of perpetrators to prison will have an impact on levels of crime.

incentive theory: a *work motivation theory* that argues that individuals will work harder when faced with a specific reward for doing so. It was the basis for piecework schemes in which individuals were paid more if they produced more within a specific time scale. *Taylorism* took up incentive theory and made it into a whole scheme of management.

inclusivist definitions of religion: those definitions of *religion* that consider it as any system of thought that attempts to make sense of the world and form a "universe of meaning." This kind of definition, used by Berger and Luckman, is much broader than that conventionally used to define "religion," and could include, for example, ideologies such as *Marxism.* (See *exclusivist definitions of religion.*)

income: an inward flow of money over time. Many people's main income is wages from employment, but other sources of income include benefits, pensions, interest on savings, and dividends from shares. (See *wealth.*)

incorporation of the working class: the way in which members of the *working class* are wedded to *capitalism* and come to accept their position within it. The incorporation of the working class is the result of effort by the *state* to engage the working class in the material and ideological arrangements of capitalism. The *welfare state* is seen as one of the major ways in which incorporation is achieved, as it provides the working class with security and a stake in the system. Incorporation is not a permanent state and consent, once given, can also be withdrawn. The crucial factor in insuring incorporation is the establishment of sufficient material welfare for the working class so that it has too much to lose by changing the system.

independent variable: the variable chosen by a researcher to be controlled or manipulated during an *experiment* to observe its effects on other variables. In sociological research, where it is often difficult or impossible to control variables, the effects of an independent variable are often gauged by a retrospective examination of the available evidence. For example, a study of the effects of youth unemployment on the staying-on rate in school would need to look at the possible correlation between the two. In this case, the level of youth unemployment would be the independent variable, and the attendance rate of youths of school-leaving age the *dependent variable.*

index: a term for a sign that derives its meaning from some causal relationship associated with it. For example, dark clouds can signify rain. (See *icons; signs proper.*)

index of deprivation: a list of aspects of material and social life the lack of which was used by Townsend as an indication of social deprivation. Townsend compiled the index for his 1979 research study, "Poverty in the United Kingdom." Using the concept of *relative poverty*, he attempted to define a style of living that met with people's general approval. The index of deprivation covered material goods, household amenities, social activities, and nutrition. Using this index, Townsend showed that the lower the household *income*, the greater the extent of the deprivation. (See *consensual view of need.*)

indexicality: a term used by ethnomethodologists to indicate that all events, whether physical actions or the spoken word, are dependent for their meaning on the context in which they occur. Events can only be understood by reference to context, so the actual event is only a pointer to the meaning of the situation. In order to understand what is going on, actors need to grasp the context through *glossing*, or explore the indexicality of the event through further interaction. (See *ethnomethodology.*)

indicators of class: various pointers used by sociologists to determine a person's position in the *hierarchy* of unequal rewards. The concept of class combines a whole range of elements, both objective and subjective, so that it is difficult to pinpoint an individual's exact class position. However in research sociologists need to be able to use accessible clues to a person's class position. These indicators are not chosen arbitrarily, but are related to the distribution of rewards in society, which is an important element in the class structure. The most commonly used indicator of class is occupation. (See *Hall-Jones scale.*)

indirect taxation: taxes levied on the purchase of goods and services (e.g. sales tax). Unlike *direct taxation*, indirect taxation is regressive – that is, it takes a greater proportion of the income of poorer than of wealthier people. (See *progressive taxation.*)

individuality: the condition of the individual's uniqueness in the social world. Individuality constitutes one half of the central dichotomy of sociology, which may be defined as the relationship between the individual on one hand and *society* on the other. Sociologists are interested in the way that individuality is affected by *social forces*, and in the way that in many respects it is socially *constructed.*

individualized learning: a type of *pedagogy* where the tasks set in the classroom are geared toward the individual child's needs and abilities, rather than to a whole class.

individuation: the process whereby religious institutions become less important in the individual's search for meaning. As industrial societies have developed so has the proliferation of religious forms, as groups and individuals reject traditional forms of religious experience and search out their own salvation.

inducement–contribution equilibrium: a term developed by Simon to describe the calculation that an individual makes before deciding to join an organization or not. The inducement aspect consists of the rewards that the individual is offered, which are then balanced against the contribution, or effort, the individual will have to make in return. Where the rewards (not just money) are balanced by the contribution, the individual is likely to participate in the organization effectively.

industrial conflict: a term that encompasses a number of strategies whereby workers may seek to pursue their own interests against management. These might include *work-to-rules, go-slows, strikes, industrial sabotage,* and *absenteeism.*

industrial democracy: a term to describe a variety of situations where workers have some *power* in the workplace and therefore some control over working practices. There are a number of different ways in which industrial democracy can be accomplished, from direct control to shareholding by the workers.

industrial relations: the network of rules that govern how managers and workers respond to each other in situations of *conflict.* Industrial relations have been a main focus for sociologists of industry, who have often taken a remedial approach, studying industrial relations in order to resolve industrial conflict problems.

industrial relations systems theory: an approach to *industrial conflict* that focuses on the industrial company as a unified system binding managers and workers. It emphasizes the fundamental community of interest between management and workers, and therefore holds that any conflict should be resolved through negotiation. Industrial conflict is seen as *pathological* to the *equilibrium* of the system. Sociologists who concentrate on industrial relations systems have been criticized for taking a conservative approach, assuming that all problems can be resolved through appropriate rule-making. They are also criticized for assuming that managers and workers have identical interests in the success of the company. Workers have their own separate interests from management and cannot be assumed to share common values with them.

Industrial Revolution: that period of time in the 18th and 19th centuries in western Europe, and later in other countries, when societies were transformed from being agricultural to ones in which production was based on the factory system. (See *industrialization.*)

industrial sabotage: when workers cause a breakdown in production by damaging machinery. Industrial sabotage is sometimes caused by the pace of work being so high that workers take matters into their own hands, to force a rest period. At other times it may be the result of individual disgruntlement with conditions in the factory or a sense of grievance against the company. As lost production means less profits, industrial sabotage is taken very seriously by management and usually leads to dismissal if the perpetrator is caught.

industrial societies: a term to describe those societies where the goods and services needed for social living are produced primarily in factories, and where the majority of the population is engaged in servicing the needs of industry and manufacturing. The contrast here is with those societies that are mainly agricultural. The *wealth* of an industrial society is therefore found in the *secondary* and *tertiary sectors* rather than the *primary sector.*

industrial unions: labor union organizations of skilled and unskilled workers in a single industry regardless of skill or grade differences. An example might be a union representing workers in the automobile industry. (See *craft unions.*)

industrialization: the process whereby a society moves from a predominantly agricultural base to one where the economy is dominated by manufacturing. Industrialization is associated with dislocation as a society adapts to the massive social changes that industrialization creates. *Urbanization* and the growth in standards of living are just two of the consequences of industrialization, which transform the way that people live their lives. Features of early industrialization were the development of transportation systems in canals, road and rail, the emergence of a banking system, and the concentration of production in factories. In one sense, industrialization created sociology, as the *classical sociologists* were primarily motivated by the need to understand the huge transformation that had occurred as western Europe industrialized. (See *Industrial Revolution.*)

inequality: see *social inequality*

infant mortality rate: the number of deaths in a population of infants under one year of age per thousand births. The Infant Mortality Rate (IMR) of a society is often taken as an indicator of general prosperity, and there are wide variations among different countries and different regions in the same country. (See *death rate, neonatal mortality rate, perinatal mortality rate.*)

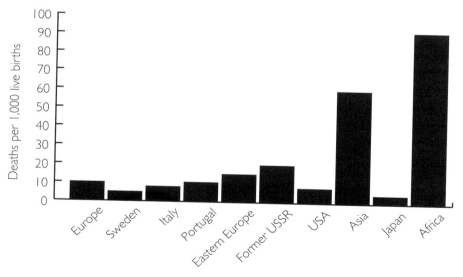

Infant mortality rates in selected countries/areas 1990–95

infantilization: the process whereby *childhood* is perceived as getting longer and longer, as adolescents are forced to remain at home, usually for economic reasons.

inflation: the increase in prices in a given economy over the course of time. As a central target of economic policy, the control of inflation also has social effects in which sociologists are interested. In particular the relationship of inflation to the wage demands of the labor unions has been a source of sociological investigation.

informal carers: those who take responsibility for the care of others (often relatives) who are unable through disability to care for themselves. The term "informal" is used to show that these carers, though providing a crucially important service, are operating outside the formal, paid system of care. Most informal carers are women, but a significant number of children provide vital care for disabled parents. (See *community care*.)

informal economy: a term used in contrast to the *formal economy* to indicate economic activity, more or less legal, that is carried out using cash-based transactions. Many self-employed workers and the unemployed may engage in the informal economy at times. While the cash earned in the informal economy is legally obtained, it is easier to avoid taxation in a situation where records of transactions may not be rigorously kept.

informal interviews: see *unstructured interviews*

informal organization: a term used to describe the actual workings of an organization, as opposed to the way the *formal organization* describes what is supposed to go on. Informal organizations grow up within the constraints of the formal *structure* of the *organization*, but they operate partially independent of it. Whereas formal organizations take no account of the human aspects of members, informal organizations show how members of an organization work together outside of the formal rules to pursue their own interests, to protect each other from management, or to gain some control over the activities they have to carry out within the formal organization. Thus, informal organizations represent the human dimension of participants in organizations and are a more valid description of what actually happens than the formal organization.

information overload: the situation in the modern world where individuals are bombarded with opinions and facts about the world, that are often contradictory. It arises as a consequence of the *globalization* of the media, which means that we can be subjected to enormous amounts of news and views at a fast rate. The pace of this information revolution is such that we cannot hope to deal with the amount of information we receive in any rational way. (See *babble of experts*.)

information technology (IT): the use of computers to store, manipulate, and transfer knowledge. In postmodern societies, the employment of information technology is a central part of the economy and constitutes an information revolution in which the manipulation of information creates *wealth* in itself. (See *information overload*.)

inheritance: the process whereby *wealth* is transferred from one *generation* to the next, upon the death of the older members. Systems of inheritance vary and are sociologically important for the distribution of wealth in society.

initiation: a *ritual* that allows and defines the passage of a person or group into membership of a defined group. Some societies mark the passage from one age group to another by initiation rituals, such as from youth to adulthood, while other initiation ceremonies are associated with particular occupations (e.g. military graduation parades), religious groups (e.g. becoming a nun or a priest) or special societies (e.g. fraternities).

inner city: as the name suggests, an area usually found near the center of large cities, but also associated with poor housing, deprivation, high *unemployment*, and, in some cities, a high concentration of ethnic minorities. Therefore, the inner city is a geographical, social, and economic concept. The inner city is often the target of urban programs, aimed at solving the associated long-term problems. Inner cities are thus often a *site of struggle* between national and local government and the inner-city community.

innovation: according to Merton, a form of *deviance* that occurs when individuals continue to accept the cultural *goals* of society but are denied the legitimated ways in which to achieve them. Innovation often takes the form of property crime, as individuals seek to achieve material wealth through illegitimate activity. However, innovation may also take the form of cheating in examinations, for example. (See *rebellion; retreatism; ritualistic deviance.*)

insight: the sociological ability to see into the workings of social life in a creative and revelatory way. The *sociological imagination* relies on insight for its most penetrating observations.

institution: a term used in a variety of ways in sociology that refers to established patterns of behavior, which make up a rule-constrained order within which individuals can act.

institutional barriers: obstacles to involvement in, for example, political activity, which are a consequence of the operation of *organizations*. For example, nomination procedures for political parties can form an institutional barrier to women who are seen by party members as being less electable than men. Women are therefore less likely to be nominated than men.

institutional power: the ability to get things done that emerges from holding a particular position in an *organization*. It is usually associated with the top decision-makers in large organizations, whose occupation of key positions legitimizes their ability to get their own way against opposition. The important feature about institutional power is that it is only given to an individual for as long as she or he occupies that position. It is therefore not personal but a feature of the organizational role itself. (See *economic power; political power.*)

institutional shareholding: where a company rather than an individual holds shares in another company's stock. Sociological interest has focused on three aspects of institutional shareholding:

- the way that links between companies are developed as the same people appear on the board of directors of several companies, because the institutional shareholder has nominated them
- the way that institutional shareholding makes the control of large companies invisible
- the way that the institutions represented in annual general meetings can act as a block to what individual, small shareholders may desire.

institutionalization of conflict: the process whereby *industrial conflict* between management and workers becomes governed by rules and therefore managed. Institutionalization requires the organization of opposing sides into *labor unions* and employers' representatives and the establishment of negotiating procedures between them. Further institutionalization takes place if procedures for *arbitration* are also established.

institutionalized means: used by Merton to describe the legitimate ways in which individuals may seek to fulfill their *goals* in society. For example, if an individual has a goal of a comfortable standard of living, then a job would be an institutionalized means, while stealing would not. (See *culture structure.*)

institutionalized racism: where the everyday practices and procedures of an organization lead to discrimination against ethnic minorities either intentionally or unintentionally. This type of racism is often unacknowledged and denied, so that it can become deeply ingrained as part of the culture of the organization, without members being aware of the consequences of their activities.

instrumental collectivism: a term put forward by Goldthorpe and Lockwood to describe the dominant consciousness of the *affluent worker*. It is an attitude toward work in which only the wages count, and any *labor union* involvement is on the basis of improving wages. It stands in contrast to more class-conscious modes of thought, which are associated with the *traditional working class*. (See *class consciousness; labor union consciousness.*)

instrumental role: a term used by *Parsons* to define the position men hold in family life, as the main breadwinner and provider. It stands in contrast to the *expressive role* of the wife. The implication is that men are less involved in the rearing of children and more concerned with the financial aspects of marriage. The instrumental role also means that men are more likely to be involved in the *public sphere* of work.

instrumental voting: voting for a party on the basis of calculations about financial benefit rather than for political or ideological reasons. (See *check-book voting.*)

integration: one of *Parsons' functional prerequisites,* a term that relates to the ways in which the system needs to bind its members together as a unified whole. The *church* is a good example of an integrating institution. (See *adaptation; goal-attainment; latency.*)

integrative race relations: an approach to immigrant communities that aims to involve and encourage "immigrant" children through the inclusion of elements of their *culture* in the *curriculum*. It has been criticized for being tokenist and for often being included on a piecemeal basis. (See *assimilation; cultural pluralism.*)

intelligence: a problematic concept usually associated with the ability to acquire and retain knowledge, to learn from experience and to adapt behavior to respond to changing circumstances. There is considerable controversy over whether human intelligence is hereditary and fixed at birth, or is much more flexible and capable of being developed with appropriate intellectual challenges and stimulation. This is often referred to as the "*nature versus nurture debate,*" and the evidence is still inconclusive.

intelligence quotient: see *IQ*

intelligentsia: a term to describe the collective *elites* of the arts, broadcasting, the universities, etc. The intelligentsia is seen by *fragmentation theory* to be an important component of the *modern upper class*. It is distinguished from other elements of the modern upper class by its relative lack of remuneration and the distinctive *style of life* members pursue. It tends to be more liberal in politics than other sectors.

interactionism: a term covering a wide range of different perspectives within sociology, which share the feature that they begin their analysis of society from the level of the individual and work up to *society*. The focus of interactionist analysis is therefore the day-to-day activities of millions of individuals, who, through the way that they act together, make up what we call society. Interactionists agree that there is no such thing as "society," apart from the individuals who constitute it, and therefore their research is based on the small-scale interactions of everyday life.

interdependence: where two individuals or social formations rely on each other for their basic *needs*. Interdependence is a feature of all societies, because even where there is only a basic *division of labor*, any one participant needs others to guarantee the fundamental means of life. For sociologists, the consequences of this interdependence create much of their field of study, as sociology can examine the ways in which societies resolve the contradictions of personal desires and the desires of others locked into *reciprocity*.

interdependency: a term used by sociologists to describe the reliance of one social formation on another. It is particularly associated with *functionalism*, where it is seen as a central feature of social structures. Thus, for example, the social structures of the family and education would be seen as interdependent, with schools relying on parental support for children's learning and families needing schools to educate the children in all the ways that families could not possibly do.

interest-group model: an approach to *moral panics* that sees their source in the activities of middle-level interest groups, such as social work professionals, the police, religious associations, etc. It is argued that these groups benefit from a moral panic, because dealing with it increases their status and levels of funding. (See *elite-engineered model*; *grassroots model*.)

interest groups: see *pressure groups*

intergenerational mobility: where movement in the *class structure* is measured by comparing the position of fathers (and occasionally mothers) against sons (and sometimes daughters). The opportunities for movement given to each *generation* are different and therefore the degree of mobility is likely to change. However it is difficult to measure this form of mobility accurately because the sons or daughters may not have reached the apex of their careers at the time of the study. (See *intragenerational mobility*.)

interlock: the degree of connectedness among companies, as illustrated by the same directors appearing on the boards of different companies. Sociologists are interested in the degree of interlock in societies, because it is used as an indicator of the existence of a *ruling class*. The idea is that the greater the interlock the more likely it is that members of company boards will act together to pursue their own interests. The problem with this approach is that it is difficult to show that, just because some people know each other and appear in the same arena, they then act together in this particular way. Interlock can be illustrated in the following way:

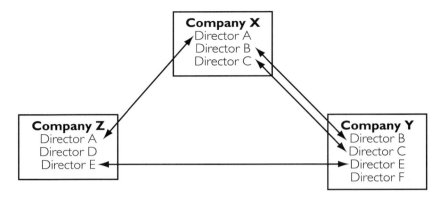

An illustration of the degree of connectedness among company directors

intermediate class: a term used by sociologists of *stratification* to describe the mass of people in occupations between the *modern upper class* and the *working class*. The intermediate class is very amorphous, being a middle way for those on their way up the stratification system and those on the way down. It also contains many individuals who will remain in the intermediate class for most of their careers. Employed in such diverse occupations as clerks and skilled artisans, its members exhibit little solidarity or ability to combine to pursue their own interests. (See *new middle class.*)

intermediate groups: see *group theory of democracy*

intermediate technology: technological processes based not on the capital-intensive technology of the developed nations, but on processes that, though efficient, still make use of human labor. Intermediate technology is thought particularly appropriate for use in developing countries, which need the application of technology to make production more efficient, but have limited *capital* and a large labor force to employ. Many of the systems that have been developed insure that they are sufficiently simple to be repaired quickly and easily, using readily available materials. As most of the applications of intermediate technology cause far less damage to the environment than much advanced technology it is increasingly suggested that intermediate technology is just as relevant in the *first world* as in the *third world.*

internal labor market: a term to describe those employed in permanent lifelong careers, with high pay, good working conditions, and chances for promotion. It is white males who have traditionally dominated the internal labor market. (See *dual labor market; external labor market.*)

internalization: the process whereby *values* and ideas are taken in by individuals as their own, so that they accept them as natural and normal. The *socialization* process is said to result in the internalization of values. However, some sociologists criticize the idea, suggesting that it is not an automatic process such as internalization implies.

international division of labor: see *new international division of labor*

interpretative sociology: see *interactionism*

intersubjectivity: a term used by Schutz to describe how we have conceptions of the world and therefore how we understand each other. It is a central concept of the sociology of the everyday world and suggests that we each have a unique stock of knowledge, some of which overlaps with those with whom we interact. This overlap constitutes our intersubjectivity. (See *everyday knowledge.*)

interview: a series of oral questions put by an interviewer (the questioner) to a *respondent*. Interviews are widely used in social research and are of two main types, *structured* and *unstructured interviews*, sometimes known as formal and informal interviews, or standardized and depth interviews. Questions used in an interview may be *closed* or *open-ended,* and interviews can produce *qualitative* or *quantitative data.*

interviewer bias: evidence of unrepresentative, inaccurate, or biased information given by a *respondent* as a result of the characteristics of an interviewer. Such *bias* may be conscious, but is usually unconscious, and may arise from reactions to different features of the interviewer – appearance, manner, sex, age, perceived class, accent, tone of voice, gestures, etc. For these reasons, many sociologists using *structured interviews* employ trained interviewers to lessen the amount of bias. The bias can also derive from the actions of the interviewer rather than the respondent. Interviewers may misunderstand or fail to follow instructions, use probes and prompts in an inconsistent manner, and make selective recording of responses. Attempts are sometimes made to distinguish between random errors and systematic errors in interviewing, but these distinctions are very difficult to make.

intragenerational mobility: where movement in the class structure is measured by comparing the first job of an individual with the current job. The advantage of this measurement is that it charts real individual movement. The problem with this approach is that, of necessity, it omits young people from the process.

intrinsic satisfaction: the pleasure obtained from work that comes from doing the work itself. It is a central concept in *self-actualizing theories,* which argue that individuals would work harder if the job itself were interesting and not reduced to boring, specialized routine. (See *work enrichment programs.*)

intuition: one basis of truth, the flash of insight that illuminates an issue or problem. Intuition is not a firm basis for truth, but it is a very powerful one. It is a useful technique in history, where the ability to visualize the *Zeitgeist* of another age is crucial.

inverse care law: a relationship suggested by J. Tudor Hart in which the need for good medical care varies inversely with its availability. In other words, those groups at or toward the bottom of the *class structure,* with generally poorer health than those in higher social groups, have less access, or less easy access, to appropriate medical resources. The concept may also be applied to make comparisons between people in the developed and the developing world.

inverted U-curve: a model devised by Blauner to explain the relationship between types of technology and levels of *alienation*. The argument is that, as technology developed away from its craft origins toward *assembly-line* production, alienation increased. However, as continuous process and automated technologies were developed, the level of alienation fell off. It is often illustrated in the following way:

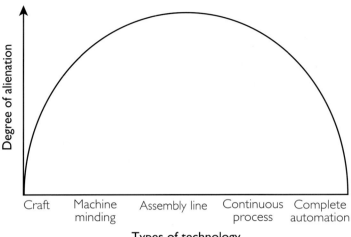

Inverted U-curve

invisibility of women: a term referring to the situation in which women's lives and female concerns have usually been neglected in traditional academic research, so that for example our notions of women's history are thin and *androcentric*. Sociology has to the same extent as other subjects treated women as invisible and has, until recently, been concerned mainly with men and male experiences. The growth of feminist sociology has to some extent redressed this imbalance. (See *malestream sociology*.)

invisible religion: a concept particularly associated with Luckmann based on the idea that certain features in contemporary society, while not obviously "religious," nevertheless contain elements of *religion* in that they give everyday life meaning and significance. These features, or "themes," are mainly concerned with individualism. Luckmann argues that the pursuit of individuality through self-expression and self-realization can be seen in *social mobility*, achievement motivation, sexuality, and the privatized family. Together, these form part of a "sacred cosmos" through which the individual constructs a sense of "self." Luckmann suggests that a new form of religion, based on consumerism, is emerging, so that what appears to some to be religious decline is in fact a shift from one form of religion to another, reflecting a different type of society.

involuntary minorities: a term developed by Gibson and Ogbu to describe those offspring of immigrants who are born in the host country and have already experienced a history of discrimination and exploitation there. Their *marginalization* in the host country produces a strong reaction and rejection of the educational system that discriminates against them. (See *voluntary minorities.*)

IQ: a measure of a person's *intelligence* based on performance in *IQ tests* and expressed as a number. The average (mean) is 100, and 95% of the population have an IQ that falls between 70 and 130.

IQ tests: cognitive tests that attempt to measure and define a person's *intelligence.* The first tests were devised by the French psychologist Binet at the start of the 20th century, when he was looking into the education of "retarded" children. The process was taken a stage further by dividing a child's mental age (as measured by the tests) by her/his chronological age and multiplying by 100 to give the IQ. Considerable controversy surrounds the issue of IQ tests, with disagreement over what is actually being measured. Many argue that the tests are not neutral, and have an inbuilt cultural *bias* that favors white middle-class children, while others claim that a gender bias also exists. The psychologist Arthur Jensen has argued that the poorer performance of black Americans in IQ tests when compared with white Americans is evidence of the intellectual inferiority of black people, a view that has sparked considerable debate and controversy. Sociologists tend to focus on the tests as social constructs and look at how they have been used to categorize certain groups as intellectually inferior, rather than accepting the tests as objective measurements.

iron cage: a term used by *Weber* to describe the condition of modern societies, in which *bureaucracies* control the actions of individuals, so that freedom is curtailed.

iron law of oligarchy: a principle developed by Michels that states that all *organizations* eventually end up being ruled by a few individuals. His argument is that however democratic the intention of the founders of organizations, as these grow larger there is an inevitable tendency for *power* to be concentrated in the hands of fewer and fewer people. By virtue of their smaller numbers, those at the top of organizations are able to monopolize information and therefore power in their own hands. This pessimistic view of the possibility of *democracy* has been attacked from various positions:

- Some sociologists argue that Michels underestimates the democratic forces in organizations, and that for every concentration of power there are others struggling to bring power back to the ordinary members of an organization.
- Others argue that there are empirical examples of long-standing democratic organizations that have defied Michels' "iron law."
- Still others argue that oligarchic organizations are unstable, as *autocracy* leads to resistance by those subject to arbitrary power.

Islam: a monotheistic religion dating from the 7th century AD based on the teachings of the prophet Mohammed. Moses and Jesus are recognized by Muslims as prophets, but Mohammed is seen as God's supreme prophet. Islam is one of the great world religions, with at least one billion followers worldwide. The followers of Islam can be divided into those who wish to see it coexisting in harmony with Western social and political values and those who believe that there is a need for Muslims to return to what they see as the basic teachings of the 7th century. These latter are often referred to as "Islamic fundamentalists." One of the areas of disagreement between the two groups concerns the role and status of women, as the fundamentalists have views concerning the status and clothing of women which are at variance with modern Western ideas.

isolation: a condition of alienation identified by Blauner to indicate the worker's lack of membership in any industrial community. This results in the worker having no commitment to work and being subject to administration by impersonal management. (See *meaninglessness; powerlessness; self-estrangement.*)

J

job enlargement: a reversal of *specialization,* in which workers are given more tasks to do so that they have varied work experiences rather than boring repetitive routines. Job enlargement is claimed to interest workers much more in their work and thus increase their productivity.

job enrichment: see *work enrichment programs*

joint conjugal roles: role relationships between spouses in which there is relatively little *domestic division of labor* by sex, and in which household tasks, *child care,* and *leisure* activities are likely to be shared. (See *conjugal roles; new man; segregated conjugal roles.*)

joking relationship: a relationship between two people or two groups in which one is permitted, or even obliged, to tease or make fun of the other, who must not take offense. Joking relationships are often found in situations containing the possibility of *conflict,* but where both sides are anxious that conflict should not occur. Under such conditions, the joking relationship thus becomes a ritualized form of the expression of antagonism under controlled conditions.

Judaism: a monotheistic *religion* of the Jewish people. It is the root religion of both Christianity and Islam.

just-in-time system: a type of production associated with *post-Fordism* that uses computer control of stock to avoid the need for large-scale stockpiling of parts in warehouses, but instead delivers parts to the appropriate place in the production process just as they are needed. It is an example of the way that the control afforded by computer technology can assist industries to reduce their costs considerably.

justice: a term synonymous with fairness. Sociologists are interested in the way that the concept is translated into a system that dispenses judgment, punishes wrong-doers, and protects those in need. The term is a contested one, in that what might seem to be an accepted definition of justice is open to challenge from different parts of the social structure. Because justice often concerns the resolution of *conflict,* it is argued that it is a basic requirement of a civilized society.

juvenile crime: lawbreaking by the young, often argued to be a distinctive feature of urban living. The existence of juvenile crime is supposed to develop with urbanization, where the lack of *community* loosens the social controls that society has over the young, with the result that they exploit the increased opportunities for lawbreaking that urban areas present. However, juvenile crime is also found in rural areas. (See *juvenile delinquency.*)

juvenile delinquency: a wider term than *juvenile crime,* used to describe the disorder and disruption caused by the young in society, which is the focus for much of the policing activity of the *state.* While the term includes much serious activity, such as urban rioting and burglary, it encompasses less serious crimes such as graffiti, drunkenness, public disorder, etc. It also includes noncriminal activity such as rebellious behavior, skipping school, and so on. Young people have always been the focus of *social control* activity, as they are responsible for much of the high spirits of society as well as much of the crime. However, there is usually a sense among nonyoung society that things are getting worse than when they were themselves young. (See *golden age of tranquility.*)

karma: the effects of all the actions of a person's current and previous existences, which will influence all future existence. Karma is allied to the Hindu belief in reincarnation. The term is also used more generally to mean "fate." (See *dharma.*)

kinship networks: networks of people related by blood or marriage that provide a support system for members of the group. The extent to which these networks are formalized, acknowledged, and used varies from society to society and over time. In many industrialized societies, particularly before the need for formal qualifications to obtain work and the introduction of the *welfare state,* kinship networks were very important, especially to the *working class.* Even today, when it is argued that the importance of networks has declined, many people find them an invaluable source of support. Despite the importance of formal qualifications, some members of the upper social classes still rely on these networks for career opportunities and advancement.

knowledge: the body of beliefs that is thought to be true. In sociology, knowledge is a multifaceted concept, encompassing a number of issues. In epistemology, sociologists examine the grounds for believing that specific items of knowledge are true or false. Sociological interest in knowledge has also been focused on the relationship between the *social structure* and the form of knowledge in a society. For example, sociologists have examined the ability of those in power to define what passes for knowledge in society. In the sociology of education, sociologists are interested in what is passed on as knowledge in schools and colleges. In the sociology of religion, sociologists have focused on the nature of religious belief and its status as knowledge or otherwise. (See *knowledge-as-fact*; *knowledge-as-practice.*)

knowledge-as-fact: where what is learned in schools is presented as the objective truth, waiting "out there" and being revealed to the students by the expert teacher. This recognizes that there is a canon of wisdom and knowledge to which all members of a society should have access. (See *knowledge-as-practice.*)

knowledge-as-practice: where what is learned in schools is the result of exploration by the students, who discover knowledge through their own educational activities, guided by the facilitating teacher. This recognizes that knowledge is a social product created through human activity and without an objective existence. (See *experiential teaching*; *knowledge-as-fact.*)

knowledgeability: the idea that human agents can draw upon different types of knowledge in carrying out their actions. (See *discursive consciousness*; *practical consciousness*; *unconscious motivation.*)

knowledgeable society: see *postindustrial society*

L

labeling theory: an approach in the sociology of education and the sociology of *deviance* that focuses on the ways in which the agents of *social control* attach stigmatizing *stereotypes* to particular groups and the ways in which the stigmatized change their behavior, once labeled. Labeling theory is associated with the work of Becker and is a reaction to sociological theories that examined only the characteristics of the deviants or underachievers, rather than the agencies that controlled them. The central feature of the labeling theory is the *self-fulfilling prophecy*, in which the labeled correspond to the label, either in terms of delinquent behavior or educational achievement. It has been criticized for ignoring the capacity of the individual to resist labeling and for assuming that it is an automatic process.

labor aristocracy: see *aristocracy of labor*

labor market: the supply and demand of workers in the economy. The existence of a highly competitive labor market, in which more workers are seeking jobs than there are jobs available, can result from the *automation* of productive and clerical processes. This in turn can lead to high levels of *unemployment*. However, a generally competitive labor market can coexist with shortages of labor requiring specific *skills*.

labor power: a term used to denote the productive capacity of a worker's work. In Marxist terminology, workers are employed by the capitalist, not for their whole personality, but purely for their labor power, which is the capacity they have for making profit through their effort.

labor process: the means by which products are manufactured to satisfy human *needs,* through the application of *labor power*. The elements of the labor process consist of the work of the laborer, the tools of production, and the raw materials that are transformed by the labor process.

labor relations: see *industrial relations*

labor theory of value: the argument that the worth of a good is calculated by the labor that is put into its creation, and that the price should therefore be determined by the amount of work on the good and not by other considerations. The term is associated with *Marxism,* which privileges labor over all other components of production. Thus *capital* is seen by Marxists as only the outcome of past labor.

labor turnover: the rate at which workers leave employment with a specific company. The majority of labor turnover is accounted for by retirement or dismissal, which is involuntary turnover. However, increases in voluntary turnover are argued to indicate dissatisfaction with the company.

labor union: an organization of workers set up to defend and promote their interests and improve the condition of their working lives. Sociological interest in labor unions has largely been focused on their expression of the consciousness of workers and their role in *industrial relations*. However, much of the work on unions in sociology has been criticized for taking a managerialist view, seeing unions as problems for companies to deal with. Another important aspect of labor unions that has been studied is the extent to which they can truly be said to represent the interests of their members. Different types of occupation show differences in the extent of union membership. Labor union membership in the private sector has fallen in the US since the 1970s, but is increasing in the public sector.

labor union consciousness: the awareness by individual workers in a factory or industry of their common interests, and their joining together to form collectivities to promote them. This form of consciousness leads to union struggles. As a form of collective consciousness, it is to be distinguished from *class consciousness.* (See *status consciousness.*)

laboratory control: the ability of a researcher, in a laboratory environment, to control all the *variables* in an experiment. This ability is regarded as one of the main advantages of the experimental method, but critics argue that such control is far less absolute than is often thought. (See *hypothetico-deductive method*; *laboratory experiment.*)

laboratory experiments: the classic method of research in the *natural sciences*, but very seldom used by sociologists, although sometimes by psychologists. The main constraints on sociologists' use of experiments are both practical and ethical. (See *field experiments*; *hypothetico-deductive method.*)

laicization: the process by which *organizations* once controlled by religious groups pass to the control of secular (nonreligious) authorities. An example would be the national education system of France since the Revolution. (See *disengagement*; *secularization.*)

laissez-faire: literally meaning "leave to do," a term used as shorthand for a particular philosophy of society, in which *government* has only a minimal role. Most recently associated with *New Right* sociology, principles of laissez-faire suggest that the most efficient and free society is one in which the *state* provides only the most basic of society's *needs*, in the form of law and the defense of the nation. In particular, they are applied to the economic system, where the New Right argues that governments should not interfere in the market at all, but allow the free market to produce the fairest form of society.

language: a way of communication that involves symbolic representation. Language is possibly the distinguishing characteristic of humanity and enables the transmission of *culture* from one generation to another. It exists as an objective reality, in a structural form that individuals draw upon to make sense of each other. Language is therefore not just descriptive, but is in itself *action*.

language codes: patterns of speech identified by Bernstein, who argued that children from different social classes were socialized into using language in different ways. Bernstein argued that there were two main speech codes, the *"elaborated"* and the *"restricted."* He believed that as education is delivered in the elaborated code used mainly by the middle class, middle-class children are given an advantage over their working-class counterparts at school. Bernstein's ideas have been criticized, often by those who mistakenly thought him to have been claiming that middle-class speech patterns are somehow superior to those of the working class.

latch-key children: a journalistic term referring to the children of working mothers left unsupervised after school until their parents return from work. The term refers to the fact that many such children used to have their front-door key hung on a string around their necks. It is still a widely used term in the debate, originally sparked by the psychologist John Bowlby in the immediate postwar period, about the possible damage to children caused by the absence of their mothers from the home. Bowlby firmly believed that mothers should stay at home, and linked what he saw as *maternal deprivation* to the development of *juvenile crime* and psychopathic personalities. Such views have led to many working mothers, then and now, experiencing strong guilt feelings, as well as social disapproval.

late capitalism: a term devised by Mandel to describe the situation developing in Western societies in the latter part of the 20th century. The features associated with late capitalism are increasing *automation* of production, increasing *exploitation* of workers, and the development of larger but fewer worldwide companies. (See *contestation.*)

late modernity: a term used by *Giddens* as an alternative to postmodernity to signify that modernity has changed under the impact of *globalization*, but that there has not been a postmodern turn in society.

latency: also known as pattern-maintenance and tension-management, one of *Parsons' functional prerequisites* that relates to the ways societies seek to insure commitment to the *values* of the system and to control those who might challenge those values. (See *adaptation; goal-attainment; integration.*)

latent functions: the hidden or unacknowledged outcomes of people's actions. For example, while churchgoing may have the *manifest function* of worshipping God, it may have the latent function of integrating individuals into society.

law of science: a principle, usually derived from the results of a number of scientific experiments, that attempts to be both universal (i.e. holds good for all similar situations) and predictive (i.e. can accurately state the outcome of a given set of circumstances). *Natural sciences* are based on the belief that a number of laws exist that govern matter (e.g. the law of gravity), and the task of the scientist, by experiment and logical reasoning, is to discover these laws. As the equipment used in the natural sciences has become more sophisticated, allowing scientists to research phenomena hitherto impossible, such as subatomic particles, or faraway galaxies, the notion of universal laws has begun to be questioned, and many scientists now talk more cautiously of probabilities, rather than laws. Some scientists have developed the notion of "chaos," which suggests that the universe does not, after all, conform to the previous theories of order, but rather that scientific events, including the development of life, occur randomly. (See *chaos theory.*)

law of the three stages: see *three stages of human development*

lean production: where the manufacture of goods to meet demand is carried out with a minimum of waste and with the least number of workers needed. It is usually associated with high-tech industries, with large levels of investment in computerized controls. (See *just-in-time system; outsourcing.*)

leap of consciousness: a term used by phenomenologists to describe a jump to a different way of thinking, when we move from the fundamental world of everyday *knowledge* to another reality. (See *multiple realities.*)

Lebenswelt: literally the life-world, a term used to describe the everyday activities of people in society, in which individuals take the social world for granted as the natural order of things.

left idealism: an approach to *deviance* from the 1960s onward that focused on marginal groups in society, seeing them as the prototype for a new revolutionary movement against capitalist injustice. This approach saw protest against society's *norms* whether political or deviant as a rational response to the injustices within *capitalism*, and to the coercion that is used to insure *conformity*. Deviance was therefore *voluntarism* breaking through the complacency of capitalist society. The idea was criticized because it played down the extent of working-class crime against the working class and the sheer antisocial nature of much deviant activity. It therefore represented a romantic view of deviant activity. (See *new left realism.*)

left-wing: in the political spectrum, a term to describe those ideas and organizations that tend to be critical of existing social arrangements. These encompass democratic parties such as the US Democratic Party and authoritarian antidemocratic parties such as the Communist Party. (See *center*; *right-wing.*)

legal-rational organization: an *organization* based on strict rules limiting the *power* of superiors to order the lives of subordinates in the organization. Legal-rational organizations have agreed procedures for carrying out tasks that define each individual's role. The term is often used as a contrast to *charismatic* organizations, in which the whims of the leader determine the actions of subordinates. (See *bureaucracy.*)

legitimation: the process whereby control by the dominant group in society is consolidated with the acceptance by subordinate groups of the superordinate group's right to rule. Legitimation is important because societies based on *coercion* rather than consent are unstable. Legitimation is the result of effort, in which the dominant group uses state power to obtain the consent of those ruled through a variety of ideological agencies such as schools and the media. The ideological basis of legitimation varies from the *divine right of kings* to *meritocracy*. Legitimation is always conditional, in that changing circumstances can lead to the withdrawal of consent.

leisure: time during which there is an element of freedom for the individual to choose what to do. Sociologists find it difficult to define exactly what leisure is, because different people will view similar activities carried out in similar circumstances in different ways. For example, two people watching a football game may have different views about the activity if one is a commentator and the other a spectator. As a result, sociologists such as Kelly have broken down leisure into different categories:

	Freely chosen	Determined by work
Independent of work	Ideal or pure leisure	Complementary leisure
Related to work	Spillover leisure	Recuperative leisure

Types of leisure

leisure class: a social class identified by Veblen as the outcome of a capitalist society that has produced sufficient surplus *wealth* for some individuals never to need to work again. Within society they therefore form a distinctive group, whose prime activity is the pursuit of leisure. The purpose of such activity is not to be idle but, in the absence of war and opportunities to plunder, to allow the leisure class to display its wealth in an ostentatious manner and thus to establish its *honor* in society. (See *conspicuous consumption.*)

leisure industry: the commercial provision of *leisure* facilities, indicating the increasing tendency for leisure to be carried out in *organizations* where individuals pay for access. In the past, leisure tended to be centered on the family and was not paid for. However, as *industrialization* proceeded, leisure opportunities increasingly came to be provided by outside agencies. These organizations are not just providers of leisure, but are a major part of the modern capitalist system, with huge global interests. (See *globalization.*)

leisure-poor: a term for groups of people who, for a variety of reasons, are unable to take full advantage of *leisure* activities. They include those who have the time but not the money, such as the unemployed, the money but not the time, such as successful but overworked business people, and those with neither the time nor the money, such as mothers with young children from the lowest income groups.

leisure-rich: a term for those people with both the time and the money to indulge in their preferred *leisure* activities.

leisure society: a vision of the future, in which the main focus of people's lives will be their pastimes and hobbies. The development of the leisure society is predicated on the advance of *automation,* which will not only reduce the necessity for everyone to carry out a 40-hour week at work, but will also produce enough surplus *wealth* to enable the majority of society to enjoy *leisure* activities as their *central life interest.* The idea has been criticized for ignoring the social inequality in society, which may produce increasing polarization and the provision of leisure opportunities for only a small minority of society, while the rest have more limited resources to pursue their interests. (See *lifestyle enhancement.*)

lesbianism: where the *sexual orientation* of a woman is toward other women. It is to be distinguished from male *homosexual* orientation, which has a different history and culture from that of lesbianism. (See *heterosexuality.*)

letters: a form of personal *document* that may be used in sociological research. As with all *secondary data,* letters have to be used cautiously. While some letters are intended only for the recipient, others are written with the expectation that, sooner or later, they will reach a wider audience (e.g. by politicians and authors). (See *diaries.*)

liberal feminism: a feminist perspective concerned to demonstrate that women suffer discrimination in many areas of life. It is sometimes referred to as reformist *feminism.* Liberal feminists actively campaign for laws and policies that guarantee equal rights for women. They are often criticized by other feminists, who argue that liberal feminists fail to challenge and to try to change the underlying social or economic structures that lead to women's oppression in the first place. (See *black feminism; Marxist feminism; radical feminism.*)

liberation theology: a belief that people have a duty to free themselves from social, economic, and political oppression in this world, rather than waiting for wrongs to be righted in the next. The doctrine of liberation theology is particularly associated with a number of radical groups that emerged within the *Roman Catholic church* in South America in the 1960s.

life chances: a term used in sociology to indicate the statistical chances of specific opportunities or disadvantages within different groups in society. For example, the life chances of a member of the *working class* are very different from those of a member of the *upper class*. The working-class individual has statistically more chance of dying young than the upper-class person. If that upper-class person is also female her life expectancy is increased again. However, it is important to note that life chances are group phenomena and cannot tell us what will happen to any specific individual. Other aspects of life chances concern education received, income earned, housing acquired, degrees of *health* and *illness*, and so on.

life course: a term to describe the many varied experiences that individuals go through during their existence, which are unique to those individuals. It stands in contrast to the *life cycle*, which suggests a more predictable set of experiences for the individual.

life cycle: a term denoting the cycle of development that most people in a society go through as they move from birth to death. A typical life cycle might be as pictured below. The concept is important in sociology, not just for the similarities it indicates, but also for the differences that might be examined. For example, women can have different life cycles from men.

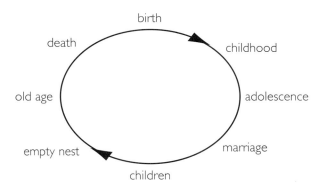

Example of a life cycle

life expectancy: the average number of years a newborn baby can be expected to live. The correct term for this is actually "expectation of life at birth," as life expectancy can be calculated at any age (e.g. "expectation of life at 21"). In 1900, the average expectation of life at birth in the US was 47 years. American babies born in 1990 could expect to live until 75 years of age. The expectation of life in the US has been rising steadily since the 1960s, though there are still significant variations between advantaged and disadvantaged groups. The increase in longevity is largely due to improvements in nutrition, housing, and health care. The lack of such improvements in some countries leads to wide variations in life expectancy rates throughout the world. (See *aging population*; *death rate*.)

life history: an autobiographical account usually obtained by *unstructured interviews* and often supplemented by personal *documents* such as letters and photographs. Life histories can be used to obtain an account of people's lives in the present, but also to obtain information about the past, such as from people who have lived through significant events like World War II, or mass emigration, or who represent a disappearing way of life, such as peasants in an industrializing economy. While providing very useful information that might be difficult to obtain by any other method, life histories need, of course, to be treated with caution, as they rely on people's memories and personal interpretations of the past.

life-world: see *Lebenswelt*

lifestyle: see *styles of life*

lifestyle enhancement: associated with the idea of the *leisure society*, the provision of increased opportunities for individuals, usually in the area of leisure, that leads to greater enjoyment.

lineage: see *descent group*

lions: a term used by Machiavelli to describe those who gain and maintain *power* in society through bold and courageous actions. (See *foxes*.)

local extended family: a social grouping characterized by large numbers of the same kinship group residing in a small area. Relationships are likely to be close and personal, with many face-to-face interactions. (See *dispersed extended family*.)

local labor market: the supply and demand for different types of worker within a locality. Each part of the country has its own labor profile, which is shaped by the type and variety of industry that is present within an area.

local opinion leaders: those who mediate information between the *mass media* and their contacts, and who concentrate on local affairs and issues. They are usually prominent members of the local community, well respected and asked for their opinions on a large number of local issues. (See *cosmopolitan opinion leaders*.)

locality: a term for a limited geographical or social area, which is much used in sociology to describe local space. A locality may, for example, be a small town or a defined area of a city if it is being used geographically. However, it might also be used to describe a social position, such as "factory worker." The concept is therefore a flexible one, which can unite either those in a particular geography or those dispersed geographically but bound by similar social positions.

location: see *structural location*

logic of industrialism: a theory developed in the 1950s that suggested that all industrializing countries would be forced by the needs of *industrialization* to adopt similar social, political, and economic arrangements. The "imperatives" of industrialism are:

- a mobile work force
- an education system with a technological emphasis
- an urban society, with developed transportation
- high levels of government intervention
- a complex *division of labor.*

The logic of industrialism also suggested that *capitalism* provided the social arrangements that could best provide these imperatives and therefore that alternative industrial societies such as *socialist* societies were *pathological* and would wither away. Critics of the theory argued that there were alternative ways that society could industrialize and that these imperatives could be met by social arrangements that were not capitalist. The critics also argued that the logic of industrialism ignored the very different histories and *cultures* of industrializing societies that could lead them to very different social arrangements. Although associated with *functionalism* and conservative sociologists, *New Right* sociologists are critical of the imperative that suggests that high levels of government intervention are necessary in an industrial society. The New Right argue that the workings of the market are the only imperatives for an efficient society. (See *convergence theory; three roads to modernity.*)

logics-in-use: a term used by Kaplan to describe the actual process of research, as against the account presented in the formal report of the work. There is a gap between the *reconstructed logics* and the logics-in-use, which represents the difference between the idealized account of science and the mistakes and false starts of the real process.

lonely crowd: a term developed by Reisman to describe the conditions of modern living, in which individuals are crammed together in large *urban areas,* but have few intimate relationships with others. Thus, in the midst of plenty, individuals do not have interactions other than the transitory and superficial.

longitudinal studies: a research study of a *sample* of people who are investigated, usually by *questionnaires* or *interviews* or a combination of both, not only at the time of the original selection but also at regular intervals afterward. While overcoming the problem of most sociological research as being a "snapshot" taken at a particular time, the longitudinal study also has problems. One is persuading the original group to remain within the study over what is sometimes a long period of time; another is managing to keep track of the group; and a further concern is the extent to which the group remains representative. Simply being part of a study may make the participants more aware of aspects of their life that others might take for granted. This last point poses more or less of a problem depending on what kind of information is being gathered. (See *Hawthorne effect; panel studies.*)

longue durée: the passage of time measured by the fall and rise of institutions, which have a life span of their own.

looking-glass self: a term used by Cooley to suggest the image each of us has of a "social self" that is built up by our reflections on the opinions that others have of us. It is to see ourselves as we think others see us. (See *generalized other; self; symbolic interactionism.*)

loss of community thesis: the idea that in the transition from rural to urban living, people have lost the sense of identity with one another, and with it, security and certainty. The assumption behind the idea is that *rural communities* were somehow more authentic ways of living than are urban ways of life. The contrast in the theory is between an idyllic sense of place and the crime and loneliness of urban environments. However, the loss of community thesis has been interpreted in different ways:

Emphasis on relationships	The loss of identity and affection, based on personal knowledge, through the growth of scientific advances.
Emphasis on locality	The loss of the village as a locus for identity as it loses its economic self-sufficiency and becomes dependent on towns.
Emphasis on neighborhood	The loss of local neighborhoods in urban areas as developers destroy the traditional urban communities of the working class.

Versions of the loss of community thesis

Critics of the thesis argue that it is based on unsubstantiated views of rural living as somehow "good" and urban living as "bad." It therefore simplifies what is a very complex process, relying on *stereotypes* of urban and rural lifestyles. For example, there is much research to suggest that *alienation* exists in rural communities and that communities exist in urban areas. (See *urbs in rure.*)

loss of family functions: the notion that, as institutions in society become more specialized, the *family* has lost many of its former functions, such as production. This view is particularly associated with *Talcott Parsons*, who argues that the loss of some functions does not, however, make the family less important to society. Other writers agree, claiming that the physical and emotional care and support provided by most families forms an essential buffer against the increasingly impersonal and stressful world outside of the home. (See *core functions of the family; death of the family.*)

loss of functions: a part of the structural differentiation process wherein a social structure has certain of its activities taken away from it, often by bureaucratic organizations.

lumpenproletariat: a term used by *Marx* to identify the unorganized working class who stood outside the *labor union* and political organizations identified with proletarian culture and politics. The lumpenproletariat have become associated with the *underclass,* the petty criminal (often unemployed), and the *culture* of the *inner city.* The lumpenproletariat have little faith in political activity as a means of bettering their lot.

McDonaldization: a term used to describe the penetration of American cultural and economic products throughout the world. It is used symbolically and is drawn from the market and ideological success of the McDonald's franchises all over the world. It is a central process in the *globalization* of *culture* and the economy, and relies on the worldwide marketing of a recognizable logo and the provision of a standardized product. It is seen by some sociologists as an aspect of the neoimperialism of American *capitalism*. (See *coca-colonization*.)

machine-minding technology: a form of technology developed during the *Industrial Revolution* consisting of mechanical devices, driven by some form of power, in which the worker's main task was to insure that the machines were running smoothly. The worker's function was to restart any machine that became stuck. This type of technology was usually associated with the textile industries.

macrosociology: sociology that focuses on the large-scale and structural in society. Associated with *functionalism*, it emphasizes the way that individuals are constrained by *social facts* and how society imposes particular courses of action onto individuals. (See *microsociology*.)

madness: the disruption of "normal" mental conditions, so that the individuals affected become unpredictable or *pathological* in their behavior patterns. The study of madness has a sociological as well as a psychological aspect, as sociologists have examined the ways in which madness is socially negotiated and defined in different societies. (See *mental illness*.)

magic: the use of *ritual* to call upon *supernatural* powers to intervene in the natural world to effect a desired end. Sociologists have been interested in the way that magic is able to hold the faith of individuals even in a world that is supposed to be rational and secular. However, the manifestation of magic in the modern world tends to take less supernatural forms, such as astrology, belief in luck, and so forth. (See *disenchantment*.)

magic bullet: a popular term for the messages aimed by the *mass media* at their *audiences*. It suggests that media messages are aimed at, and penetrate, an essentially passive audience who receives these messages uncritically. (See *hypodermic syringe approach*.)

magnet schools: schools that have a considerable emphasis on one specialist area of the *curriculum*, and aim to attract the most able students in that particular field. Magnet schools have been developed since the 1970s for curriculum areas such as the performing arts, literature, and science.

mail questionnaires: see *postal questionnaires*

majority control: a term used by managerial revolutionists to describe the situation in which a small group, usually from the same family, owns the majority of shares and controls a company directly. (See *minority control*.)

male chauvinism: see *chauvinism*

male gaze: a term used in the sociology of *culture* to describe the way that movies and other mass-media products are often made with the viewpoint of men in mind, so that women are objectified as sex objects rather than being represented as full human beings.

male underachievement: a growing phenomenon in education, in which boys at all ages are showing poorer levels of achievement than girls. A number of reasons have been put forward to explain this, including the fact that in some areas it is difficult for young males to find work, particularly those with relatively few qualifications. Such jobs as are available are increasingly aimed at females, as they are mainly retail, clerical work, and jobs in catering and accommodation. It is suggested that the knowledge of low chances of employment acts as a demotivating influence on boys. A problem with this explanation is that boys in areas with a more buoyant job market are also performing, on average, less well than girls. (See *female underachievement*.)

malestream sociology: a concept developed by feminists to describe the origin and shaping of sociology by male sociologists and male concerns. Because the *classical sociologists* were all men living in patriarchal societies, the initial questions asked in sociological research reflected male perspectives. Similarly the domination of sociology by men has also had the effect of marginalizing female interests and areas of concern. Feminist sociology was developed partly in response to this situation.

management: a term to describe the positions in an *organization* that are concerned with the control of subordinates, so that coordination of activity is achieved for the efficient functioning of the organization to achieve goals. Management has been treated as a distinct category within work organizations, with its own interests and social processes. (See *managerial revolution*.)

managerial revolution: a term developed by Burnham, among others, to indicate that the individual control of industrial companies by capitalists in the 19th century has now given way to control by teams of managers. The important part of this separation of ownership from control is the development of joint stock companies, where shareholders buy a stake in a company and thus dilute the control of the individual capitalist. Thus, the predominant ownership pattern has moved from the "family firm" of the 19th century to the managerial control of the 21st century. The ideological impact of this development is that managers are able to take a more objective view of the company and, for example, favor long-term investment over immediate profit. Critics of this theory have taken several positions:

- Some sociologists argue that the extent of shareholding has been exaggerated, with the majority of large companies still being controlled by a very small group of people.
- Others argue that wider share ownership allows the capitalist to control larger amounts of capital, while retaining individual control over the actions of the company.
- Another view is that while managers may have *operational control* over the day-to-day activities of the company, the large shareholders still retain *allocative control*, in which decisions about where to invest and place resources in an industrial company remain in the hands of the owners.

manifest functions: the intended consequences of *actions*, – that is, what the actions are intended to achieve. (See *latent functions*.)

manual work: a term to describe those occupations that involve fairly hard physical effort, though it literally means work with the hands. Manual work is traditionally seen as *working class* and is part of one of the fundamental ways of classifying *social class* groupings.

margin of error: the range within which a given value is likely to fall. For example, it might be said in an opinion poll that 35% of people intend to vote Republican at the next election, "plus or minus 3%." This means that the likely correct figure is between 32% and 38%. (See *sampling error*.)

marginalization: the process by which certain individuals or groups are pushed to the periphery of, and sometimes excluded from, mainstream society. Disabled people are at risk of marginalization, and so, it is argued, are the poor, whose *poverty* forces them to lead a *lifestyle* increasingly at variance with that of the more fortunate.

marital breakdown: a situation in which the relationship in a marriage has broken down, and one or both partners believe that it has lost its meaning for them. Often, this breakdown will lead to *divorce*, but sometimes couples will continue to stay together "for the sake of the children," and exist in an *empty shell marriage*. Other couples actively seek help by attending counseling sessions to try to repair the relationship. The term indicates the end of a marriage, not legally, but in the reality of everyday living. It is claimed that the rate of marital breakdown is increasing, often due to the financial pressures of *unemployment* or low income.

market economy: where production and distribution are determined by the free activities of buyers and sellers, rather than there being any direction by the *state*. The market economy also functions as an ideological device for the *New Right*.

market forces: the balance of supply and demand for goods and services, unhindered by any artificial restraint. The *New Right* sociologists believe strongly that market forces should not be distorted by government intervention. By leaving the market free, they believe that the best of all possible societies will result. It is the exercise of individual choice in the market place that the New Right sees as the fundamental freedom. Critics of market forces argue that they are inherently unfair, since everyone is not equal in the market place, and many have limited resources with which to make individual choices. (See *laissez-faire*.)

market research: research into the attitudes and buying and spending habits of consumers. While many of the methods used in market research are identical to those used in sociological research, market research focuses on the consumer market, resulting in differences, both in the nature of the information gained and in the use to which is put, from sociological research.

market situation: a term used by Lockwood to describe the degree of employment security for clerks and other occupational groups. In the examination of the *proletarianization* thesis, the market situation of clerks was said to have changed from one of relative security to one of insecurity. The main reason for this change was the growth of universal literacy, which allowed the easy replacement of clerks. (See *status situation*; *work situation*.)

marketization: the process by which market principles and practices are introduced into areas previously immune to the workings of the market. The claim is that marketization can produce a system more responsive to client needs. Critics have argued that it has more to do with saving money for government than with any possible efficiency effects.

marriage: the legal union of a man and a woman. In many industrialized countries, the institution of marriage is undergoing some radical changes, particularly in evidence since the end of World War II. Some people claim that the falling rate of marriage indicates a declining belief in the value of marriage as an institution. However, the number of cohabiting couples who are in stable, long-term relationships, together with changes in the law giving certain rights to "partners" that were once available only to spouses, suggest that perhaps what we mean by "marriage" is changing, rather than it being in a state of decline. (See *cohabitation; divorce.*)

Marx, Karl: one of the world's leading philosophers and economists, also recognized as a classical sociologist. He is notable for the enormous influence he had on the world of politics, so that, from 1917, followers of his theory seized political power throughout a third of the world until the collapse of Soviet communism in the late 1980s. His influence on sociology has been to provide the methods of a critique of conventional sociology and capitalist society, by using the techniques of dialectical analysis. The main impact of his work in sociological terms has been in the areas of industrial sociology and class analysis. (See *dialectic; historical materialism; Marxism.*)

Marxism: a sociological perspective that emerged from the work of *Karl Marx* and stresses the role of conflict in society. The key concepts associated with Marxism are the *dialectic, historical materialism, class struggle,* and *revolution.* The basic argument of Marxism is that economics is at the base of social life and progress is made through the struggle between different *social classes.* The *ruling class* in any society is based on the ownership of particular productive capacities and control of economic resources also gives the ruling class political and cultural control. Marxist sociologists have been influential across a number of areas of social life, particularly in the study of stratification, work, and politics. There are different variations within Marxism, and they are often as divided from each other as they are from their political opponents. Critics of Marxism argue that:

- it is a determinist theory, giving little freedom to individuals
- it is wrong to give primacy to economics in the way that Marxists do
- emphasis on *conflict* denies the *social order* that is characteristic of most societies.

Marxist feminism: a branch of feminist thought that attempts to explain the particular place of women in capitalist societies on the basis of *Marxism.* While recognizing the inequalities between men and women, Marxist feminists focus their attention on the *class struggle,* seeing women's oppression arising not only from *patriarchy* but from *capitalism.* Women form part of the *reserve army of labor,* often being excluded from the *labor market,* and they also provide unpaid labor, nurturing the current generation of workers and raising the next. The main source of their oppression, then, is seen as the capitalist system.

masculinity: the possession of those characteristics associated with being a man. There is a traditional conception of being masculine that has been investigated by sociologists for its effects on male behavior, both in regard to women and in the way that this limits the possibilities of men expressing themselves fully. Conceptions of masculinity are constantly being negotiated and renegotiated as men seek to find other aspects to their character than the traditionally "macho" ones. There has been a resurgence in sociological interest in masculinity with the growth of *postmodernism* and its emphasis on the construction of identities. (See *femininity.*)

mass communication: the transmission of messages to a large number of people simultaneously. It is associated with the development of technologies that widen the reach of the communication device. The improvement in media technologies is a crucial part of the *globalization* process.

mass culture: a collective term referring to cultural products and experiences aimed at a mass market. Many of these products and experiences are geared toward entertainment. Mass culture, also referred to as *popular culture*, is often contrasted with *high culture*, usually taken to mean those forms of *culture* appealing to a relatively small number of people, such as opera, classical music, "serious" literature, and art. Mass culture is usually designed to be accessible to a much larger group. It is traditional to view mass culture as somehow inferior to high culture, though sociologists have found that the study of mass culture yields a rich source of information about cultural forms and changing tastes.

mass leisure: a concept developed by Marxists to describe modern *leisure* that is provided for people in large numbers. A crucial part of mass leisure is provided by the media industries of newspapers, television, and movies that have grown into global conglomerations. (See *leisure industry.*)

mass media: those means of communication that reach large numbers of people at the same time. Sociologists have always been interested in mass media, but as their importance in society has grown, so has sociological study of them. The mass media began with the development of newspapers and magazines. Modern mass media grew out of developments in the latter part of the 19th century, such as the telegraph, and the early part of the 20th century, such as radio and television. The term now includes a whole range of different technologies, including the computer, video, and the telephone. Developments in the mass media are accelerating, with fiber technology, satellite television, and the Internet, and the impact on individual lives is enormous. What that impact is forms the object of study of sociologists of the media.

mass observation: see *diaries*

mass production: a process in which goods are manufactured in large numbers, usually through a form of *assembly line,* and supplied in a standardized form to the market. It is particularly associated with the first half of the 20th century and is said to be a characteristic of *modernity.* (See *Fordism.*)

mass society: a concept developed by Kornhauser to describe a society where individuals are atomized, attached to hardly any intermediate groups that might stand between them and the power of the *state.* The idea has a negative moral connotation, in that it is used to describe a modern society that has lost the intimacy and authenticity of societies in the past. It is an expression of the fear of the totalitarianism that was experienced in the 1930s in Nazi Germany and Soviet Russia. The mass society is said to develop as local traditions and culture dissolve under the impact of *mass media* influences, and the usual support for individuals, in the form of families and local associations, are weakened.

mass unemployment: where the numbers of the unemployed exist at high levels for a relatively long period of time. The classic period of mass unemployment was the 1930s during the Great Depression. Sociologists are interested in the effects of mass unemployment on individuals, their families, and society as a whole. They recognize that there are differences between the 1930s and the present, in particular that the *welfare state* now provides a safety net for the long-term unemployed.

material activity: economic actions in the widest sense – all the building, production, artistic, and cultural artifacts that human beings produce. From a Marxist perspective, material activity leads to *consciousness.*

material control: a type of *power*, usually exercised in work *organizations*, in which money operates as an incentive and therefore a control over the activities of employees. (See *physical control; symbolic control.*)

material deprivation: in the sociology of education, underachievement by the *working class* and some ethnic minorities has often been linked with the conditions of *poverty.* Factors such as poor diet, overcrowding, and lack of homework facilities have been cited as factors that limit the achievement of deprived groups. However, it is difficult to show a direct causal relationship between material deprivation and educational attainment. (See *clash of cultures; cultural reproduction.*)

maternal deprivation: negative consequences allegedly resulting from the absence of full-time care by a mother for her young child or children. In the 1950s the British psychoanalyst John Bowlby argued that children denied such full-time care, as in the case of "working mothers," might later suffer from *delinquency* or *mental illness.* Feminists in particular disagree with this viewpoint, arguing that it was used to persuade women to stay at home as full-time housewives and mothers at a time when women were not needed in large numbers in the labor force. Subsequent research has shown that, provided there are alternative, stable child care arrangements, young children actually benefit from short periods away from their mother. (See *child care; domesticity; latch-key children.*)

matriarchy: a form of society in which women are rulers and leaders. As there is little empirical evidence for the existence of such societies, the term is widely used to refer to situations in which the mother is, or is regarded as, the head of the household, and has authority over other family members, especially children. (See *patriarchy.*)

matrilineal: a form of kinship in which descent is traced only through females.

maturity: a stage at which physical development is complete. However, in many societies the term refers to the stage at which a young person is recognized as being able to take part in adult activities and *rituals.* The age at which this takes place shows considerable variation among different societies.

maximum security society: a metaphor for the situation of postmodernity, where techniques of *surveillance* are so widespread that they provide the context for a major part of an individual's existence.

meaning: an important aspect of all *action theories*, referring to the beliefs, intentions, purposes, or motives that *actors* attach to their actions. In *phenomenology*, meaning is created only by self-conscious thought – that is, when the *durée* is broken by reflection and the actor engages in looking back on or projecting forward about his/her actions.

meaninglessness: a condition of *alienation* identified by Blauner as the "lack of a sense of purpose in work." The feeling is connected to the worker's inability to see a link between his or her own work and the overall production process. (See *functional rationality; substantial rationality*.)

means of production: used in *Marxist* sociology to describe the factories, tools, and machinery that are needed to produce the goods and services that individuals need. According to the Marxists, it is the ownership or nonownership of these that is the determinant of an individual's position in the *class structure*. (See *forces of production; relations of production*.)

means-tested benefits: *social benefits* that are delivered only when the claimant is able to show "need," according to however this is defined. Supporters of means-tested benefits argue that the system allows benefits to be targeted toward those in greatest need. Others argue that the process by which a claimant must by definition prove to a bureaucrat that a genuine need exists, is unnecessarily demeaning, and that the complexity of the means-tested benefits system deters some of the genuinely needy from even applying. (See *universal benefits*.)

mechanical solidarity: the way in which traditional agricultural societies remain integrated, through individuals identifying with other people because they fundamentally experience the same things in life. This identity of sameness was argued by *Durkheim* to be the way that social life was made possible in stable rural societies. (See *organic solidarity*.)

mechanistic organization: a term used by Burns and Stalker to denote a rigid, hierarchical, bureaucratic *organization*, in which individuals have very specific and specialized tasks, coordinated by a dedicated management structure. Burns and Stalker argued that mechanistic organizations develop in a situation of industrial stability, where demand for mass-produced standardized goods is constant. Mechanistic organizations are therefore efficient at meeting this stable demand, through routinizing manufacturing processes. (See *niche markets; organismic organizations*.)

mechanization: the process whereby industrial production is no longer carried out through the manual skills of *craft* workers, but increasingly by machines. Mechanization was a central process in *industrialization,* which allowed the development of *mass production* techniques. More specifically, mechanization has come to represent a particular era of industrial development, distinct from the era of *automation* which we are now going through. It is therefore associated with *Fordist* modes of production.

media conglomerates: see *conglomeration*

media effects: a collective term referring to the different effects exerted by the mass media on their *audiences*. (See *hypodermic syringe approach; magic bullet; two-step flow model; uses and gratification approach.*)

media industry: a term to describe centralized media organizations in postmodern economies and the global and national companies that dominate the *mass media.* The importance of the mass media industry can be defined in terms of the influence it has over patterns of behavior that transcend national boundaries, and also in the wealth that it generates for those who own media companies. The economic importance of the mass media industry in society is therefore a focus for sociological investigation.

media representations: those images of our *culture* and society that are relayed by the *mass media.* Both sociologists and psychologists have studied media representations, and have particularly focused on those representations that lead to or draw on *stereotypes.* In this respect, women, blacks, homosexuals, single mothers, and members of various minority groups have provided good examples of victims of negative media representations. It is possible, of course, for the reverse process to take place, and for positive representations to be used, such as in the case of leading politicians who wish to improve their "image" with the general public.

mediascapes: sites in the flow of information, images, and texts through the world, which is said to lead to a global culture.

mediation: the process whereby individuals negotiate or alter their lived conditions of existence, so that they are transformed in some way into a different experience. In the media the mediation process is connected with the way that *ideologies* are transformed into news content through the operation of the news-values held by journalists. The argument is that *ruling-class* ideologies appear not in a raw form, but in a mediated way, so that they are absorbed without the recipients even knowing they have been exposed to them.

medical gaze: a term used by Foucault to indicate the important power of modern medicine to define our bodies. The categorization by medical practitioners of individuals as healthy/unhealthy or behavior as appropriate/inappropriate is a central feature of the *surveillance* society.

medical model of health: a view of *health* and *illness* that sees the body as primarily a machine, and the role of the medical profession to cure rather than to prevent illness, and to focus treatment on individuals, rather than exploring the relationship between individuals and their social and physical environment. (See *biomechanical model.*)

medical technology: a term to describe the increasingly sophisticated and expensive technologically based equipment, including drugs, used by the medical profession. While some of this undoubtedly helps to save lives, concern is expressed over the fact that the equipment may be used simply because it is there, while other, less interventionist forms of treatment are ignored. Childbirth is often cited as a prime example of the use of medical technology, with childbirth increasingly treated as though it were an illness, rather than a natural process. Women wishing to have their babies at home using more natural methods of childbirth have often faced strong opposition from the medical profession.

medicalization: the tendency for an increasing number of areas of social life to become subject to medical classification and treatment. The classic example of this is the way that childbirth has become the province of male doctors as opposed to female midwives. Other areas that have become medicalized include sexuality, in its many different facets. This was an area of particular interest to Foucault, who saw the medicalization of sexuality as part of a process of increasing *surveillance* in society, where the development of new *discourses* of power marginalized and stigmatized different groups. (See *demedicalization.*)

membership involvement ratio: an indicator of *strike* activity that calculates the sum of all workers involved in all strikes during a year divided by the average number of union members during that year. It was used by Ross and Hartman to compare the strike rates of different countries.

mental health: a term to indicate the degree to which someone exhibits "normal" patterns of thought and behavior. The term is in a way very misleading, because it is often used in the context of exactly the reverse, i.e. mental illness. Therefore various "mental health" provisions are, in fact, dealing with "mental illness." It is important to note that what are considered "normal" patterns of thought and, especially, behavior are capable of a very wide interpretation that differs over time in different societies and according to the context in which the behavior occurs. Interpretations also reflect the social characteristics of both the labeled person and the person doing the *labeling*.

mental illness: the supposed disturbance of "normal" patterns of thought and behavior. The concept is a very controversial one, as it rests on a definition of what is a "normal" mental state. Sociologists such as Goffman have investigated mental illness in terms of *social control* and *labeling*, and it has also been studied in relation to *deviance*. The label can also be used as a form of social control. This was shown clearly in several of the show trials in the Soviet Union in the 1930s, when many intellectuals, especially those critical of the system, were deemed to be mentally ill and placed in psychiatric hospitals.

mercantilism: a belief that the economic prosperity of a society can only be secured by the state regulation of trade. (See *laissez-faire.*)

meritocracy: a social system in which rewards and occupational positions are allocated justly on the basis of merit, rather than on ascriptive factors such as class, gender, ethnic group, or wealth. It is often claimed that modern *industrial societies* are more meritocratic than in the past, and that the education systems in such societies are also meritocratic. However, there is much evidence to show that ascriptive features like those listed above exert a considerable influence on an individual's *life chances*. (See *ascription.*)

Mertonian functionalism: that branch of *functionalism* that does not accept that everything that exists in society has a positive function to perform within it, but that some existing structures have dysfunctional effects. That is, it is a type of functionalism that moves away from a conservative emphasis on order, toward an interest in *social change*. (See *dysfunction; structural-functionalism.*)

messianic movements: see *millenarian movements*

meta-narrative: a term developed by Lyotard to describe those theories and ideas that attempt to explain the whole of the social totality. Lyotard argues that these are *myths* or stories encompassing the whole of the natural and social worlds within their reach. Such meta-narratives may be religion, science, sociology itself, or the idea of progress, and Lyotard argues that, in a postmodern world, we no longer accept meta-narratives as being capable of explaining anything. Social life is so fractured and disjointed in postmodern conditions that no one theory can hope to explain everything. As a result, the project of the *Enlightenment*, which was to understand and control the world through the application of rational principles and the continuous progress of science, has been abandoned.

metaphysical stage: one of *Comte's* three stages of human development, where the *theological stage* was broken down as people speculated about the nature of the natural world rather than taking religious authority for granted. (See *positive stage*.)

methodology: the study of the types of method used by researchers, the reasons for their choice of method, and how they collect, select, interpret and analyze their data. The term is often used instead of "method," e.g. a reference might be made to the "methodology" of a particular piece of research, when what the writer/speaker is actually referring to is the method(s) used.

metropolis: a term used by *underdevelopment theorists* to describe the position of large cities in the *third world*. These are seen as outposts of the *first world* in the *hinterlands* of underdeveloped societies. In the metropolis, local *elites* are dominant, both politically and economically. These local elites may be foreigners, the indigenous capitalist class, traditional feudal leaders, or in some cases the military. The role of these elites is to act as the representatives of the first world in the third world, mediating between capitalist interests in the first world and their own populations. (See *enclave development*.)

micropower: a term used by Foucault to describe the way that, in postmodern societies, the body is trained and supervised through *disciplinary drills, surveillance,* and examinations. Foucault argued that postmodern societies were not characterized by the gross power of the physical punishments of previous years, but by the small-scale exercise of power, hardly noticed by those who experienced it. Power was no longer grand and awesome, but mundane, modest, and routine.

microsociology: sociology with a focus on the small scale and individual within society and usually associated with *interactionist* sociologists. The emphasis is on the way that millions of everyday events build up to make *society* and produce patterns of behavior. (See *macrosociology*.)

middle class: the traditional *social class* grouping that stands between the upper and working classes, and is usually associated with nonmanual work, such as clerical work or the traditional *professions*. (See *working class*.)

migration: the movement of people to another region (internal migration) or another country (external migration). Migration is one of the factors, together with *birth rates* and *death rates*, that determine the population level of a country. (See *immigration controls*.)

militancy: a fighting attitude; in industrial terms, an extremist position held by workers in which strong *labor union* stances are taken and industrial action of various descriptions is encouraged. Sociologists are interested in why certain groups of workers are more militant than others, and what conditions encourage militant attitudes. *New Right* sociologists in Britain, for example, argue that militancy has been decreasing since the powers of the unions to create industrial strife were diminished during the 1980s under the government of Margaret Thatcher.

military–industrial complex: a term used by Mills to describe the domination of US society in the 1960s by an alliance of manufacturers who supplied goods to the armed forces and key military personnel, who in turn wanted larger and larger budgets. Critics of the idea suggest that there are no formal or informal mechanisms by which such an alliance could be maintained, and that if there was a community of interest between them, it was unconscious.

millenarian movements: religious movements that expect the world to be transformed by *supernatural* intervention in the near future. Many millenarian movements involve their members practicing particular *rituals* that often borrow elements from other cultures or religions. It has been noted that millenarian movements often emerge among groups who are undergoing rapid *social change*, often accompanied by economic and/or political upheaval. (See *cargo cults*; *ghost dancers*.)

mind–body dualism: a belief that the mind and the body are independent of each other. It is a view associated with the 17th-century French philosopher Descartes, whose views on mind–body dualism were counter to the prevailing Christian orthodoxy that the body and the soul were indivisible, and that unless the body were preserved intact the soul would be unable to ascend to heaven. Following the acceptance of Descartes' views in the West, it became possible to undertake the detailed study of human anatomy by dissection, opening the way for the development of medical science. (See *biomechanical model of health*.)

minority control: used by managerial revolutionists to describe the situation where between 20% and 50% of shares in a company are owned by a small group of shareholders, which gives them great influence, because the rest of the shares are dispersed among a large number of others.

mixed economy: an economy in which there is no dominance by either the *public* or *private sector* in producing the goods and services that people need. The actual mix will vary from one society to another and political parties differ on how much of one or the other there should be.

mob: an unorganized, unruly mass of people engaged in some type of public disorder. The mob was symbolic in the 19th century of everything that the *upper class* feared – the first *folk devil*. After the French Revolution, the mob came to represent the disrespect of the lower orders for their upper-class "betters" and revealed the fear of the upper class that their privileges could be taken away from them in an upsurge of violence.

mode of production: the way in which relations between the owners and nonowners of the means of production, as well as the *forces of production* themselves, are organized, which distinguishes one type of society from another. In Marxist terms, the mode of production is central to understanding the nature of a particular society. In feudal societies, for example, the feudal aristocracy did not control the forces of production directly, which remained under the direction of the peasantry, but through their monopoly of physical force they were able to appropriate the produce of those forces of production and distribute them as the aristocracy saw fit. (See *relations of production*.)

models: intellectual devices that represent social phenomena in some way, usually through an *analogy*. There can also be diagrammatic models of the social and more recently mathematical models, where very complex relationships are manipulated by computers to depict patterns of social relationship.

modern upper class: a term used by stratification sociologists to differentiate the traditional aristocratic *upper class* from the superordinate groups who dominate contemporary capitalist societies. The necessity for this concept arises from the growth of complex divisions at the top of society, in which the traditional upper class has been subsumed. The dominant sections of society that make up the modern upper class are the business *elite*, the professionals, the *intelligentsia*, and the top management of large corporations.

modernism: a movement in the arts, culture, and architecture that accepts the progress of the *Enlightenment* project and is particularly concerned with functionality in form, where a preference for "modern" functional design is always stated. It stands in contrast to postmodern forms of culture.

modernity: used to describe the condition of society from the *Enlightenment* of the 18th century to the middle of the 20th. It encompasses a rational outlook on social issues and an attempt to shape social arrangements according to scientific and logical principles. Modernity can be seen as the belief in certainty and knowledge that are solid. There was little room for doubt in the modernist enterprise, as in various disciplines theorists tried to establish the rational principles by which subjects might be controlled and progress forged. (See *postmodernity*.)

modernization: the process whereby societies move from being traditional to being characterized by rational action. Modernization, as used by sociologists, has an ideological dimension, in that the process is imbued with positive feelings. The modern, in contrast to the traditional, is associated with being bright, exciting, up-to-date, and attractive. In more recent times however, modernization has come to have more negative connotations. Some sociologists see modernization as destroying much of value in *traditional societies*. Other postmodernists see modernization as producing soulless, uniform, and ultimately inhuman social formations, such as apartment blocks, urban decay, and increased crime.

modernization theory: the dominant approach to *development* issues in the 1950s and 1960s, characterized by the search for those factors that undeveloped countries lacked and were presumed to be the cause of their lack of development. This involved modernization theorists such as Rostow in a comparison of developed countries with undeveloped countries to identify the differences between them. These differences were put forward as the reason for the *third world's* lack of development. Different theorists put forward different factors as the main causes of undevelopment:

- a lack of technology
- a lack of capital
- overpopulation
- a lack of entrepreneurs
- inappropriate values for development.

However, modernization theories have been criticized for the following reasons:

- that they view the experiences of the third world from a Western point of view
- that they lack a historical perspective, lumping all third-world societies together, ignoring their individual *cultures* and histories
- that they assume that many of the features of third-world societies that were actually imported there by the colonial powers are "native" to the third world
- that all the third world has to do to develop is to repeat the experience of the *first world*. This is difficult, because the first world developed without any competition from other societies, while the third world has now to compete with the first world.

(See *five stages of economic growth.*)

modified extended family: a term used to denote the continuing importance of wider kinship networks, even when most people live in nuclear families or on their own. It is made possible by the development of modern communications, which have allowed families to keep in touch with each other even when they live at a distance. It implies that the wider family is still an important locus for *identity*, even where *geographical mobility* is high. (See *family structure.*)

monogamy: a pattern of *marriage* in which people may have only one legal spouse at a time. It is the form of marriage found in most Western societies. The growing pattern in many industrial societies of marriage, *divorce*, and remarriage (possibly continuing through more than one divorce/remarriage) is referred to as *serial monogamy*. (See *polygamy.*)

monotheism: religious belief based on the notion of a single, omnipotent god. *Christianity, Judaism,* and *Islam* are examples of monotheistic religions. (See *polytheism.*)

moral entrepreneurs: individuals and groups that claim and are recognized by society as having a particular interest in issues of morality. They include religious leaders, media *gatekeepers* (such as the editors of newspapers), and politicians. They are often active in moral panics, and are important in the process of *agenda-setting*.

moral involvement: the way in which individuals are committed to a society if there is a *value consensus*. Because individuals share common *values*, they are likely to be committed in a way that engages their moral senses. Such an involvement is likely to be deep-seated and lead to strong feelings of loyalty from individual members of society.

moral panic: a situation in which media reporting has created a *folk devil* out of a particular social group, and the public demands that the authorities do something about it. This expression of concern is described as a moral panic, because it is based on an outraged sense of offense to public standards of behavior, though the information that prompts it is often limited and inaccurate.

morbidity data: information relating to the nature and extent of *illness* in a population. It is usually measured by the number of hospital admissions and doctor–patient consultations, statistics relating to time off from work as a result of sickness, and self-reported illness data from health surveys.

mores (pronounced "more-rays"): preferred and socially sanctioned ways of behaving in any given society. These are a stronger form of *norms,* in which more fundamental habits of behavior are involved.

mortality rate: the number of deaths per thousand of the population per year. These rates are often broken down to show differences by age, gender, and social class. The *infant mortality rate* is considered a particularly important indicator of economic prosperity or the lack of it. (See *death rate.*)

mortification of self: the process by which, on entering a *total institution,* the individual is stripped of all social supports and individual *identity.* The process involves many different aspects:

- humiliation by staff
- abuse from staff and other inmates
- allocation of a number
- allocation of a uniform
- issue of standardized equipment
- cutting of career occupational contacts
- restriction of family access.

motivator-hygiene theory: a theory developed by Herzberg, among others, to try to explain *work satisfaction* and work dissatisfaction. The theory suggests that the factors leading to satisfaction in work are not the same as those leading to dissatisfaction. Satisfaction factors were motivators and included achievement, recognition from superiors, and responsibility. Dissatisfaction factors were more associated with "hygiene" and included working conditions, as well as job security and type of supervision.

mugging: generally a term for street robbery with violence, although the importance of the term sociologically is that there is no actual offense of mugging, just a vague and undefined category of offenses. Sociologists have therefore been interested in mugging as a *social construction* and in particular in the way that the *mass media,* police, and judiciary can shape public attitudes toward phenomena and create *moral panics.* It is the apparent appearance of a crime wave of mugging that set sociologists to investigate the reality behind the statistics. They were able to show that the statistics were less important in creating a moral panic than the official reaction to the statistics.

multicultural education: education that teaches students about the *culture* of other groups, particularly other *ethnic groups.* This has led to controversy, as some parents have argued that they wish their children to learn only what they see as the indigenous culture, rather than the food, customs, and religious beliefs of other cultural groups, particularly immigrant ethnic groups. (See *antiracist education.*)

multinational companies: a term used to describe capitalist companies that carry out their business operations in more than one country. The term has been attacked for hiding the central issues of who owns these companies and in whose interest they operate. "Multinational" seems to imply that these companies are operating outside of national interests, and are not owned by individuals of any nation in particular. While there is some evidence of a dispersion of large companies' shares throughout the world, most of the large companies operating on a global level are still dominated by people from one particular country. It is thus possible to identify multinational companies (MNCs) primarily owned by Japanese or American capitalists. For this reason, the term has fallen into disuse. (See *transnational companies.*)

multiple realities: a term used by Schutz to suggest that every individual exists on a variety of levels, each of which is real for as long as the individual inhabits it. The basic reality is the *Lebenswelt*, the world of everyday knowledge, which exists at the level of the unconscious and which we inhabit without reflection. However other realities also exist when we pause in the everyday world and engage in other forms of thinking such as speculation, rational calculation, religious devotion, or thinking sociologically. These other realities exist as long as we are thinking this way. To reach these states of thought, we perform a *leap of consciousness.*

multiple roles: the adoption of different *roles* in different circumstances as we move through different parts of our lives. For example, during the course of a day we may be parent, workmate, boss, customer, lover, etc. We switch from one role to another with relative ease, though there is potential for *role conflict* within these multiple roles.

multistage sampling: a *sampling* technique in which an initial (usually random) sample is selected (for example of high schools in the US), and then a further sample is drawn (say of groups of students within those schools). Multistage sampling can go through more than two stages, providing that the sample at the end of the process is large enough to generate useful data.

myth: a sacred tale that usually relates events of great significance to a particular society, such as the origin of its people, or tales about its gods or past heroes. This is the anthropological definition of myths, and they were studied by Malinowski, who used them to try to uncover the dominant *values* of a society, and by Levi-Strauss, who argued that all myths expressed ideas about certain fundamental "binary oppositions," such as male/female, friend/enemy, and nature/society. However, more recently Barthes has examined myths as a system of communication, namely the signs through which *culture* is expressed. For Barthes, myths can be found not only in oral or written *discourses*, but in all forms of *popular culture*, such as sports, movies, fashion, advertising, etc.

narcotization: the process by which the *mass media* reduce individuals to a state of mindless existence. The term was developed as a contrast to the notion that the media provide an opportunity to educate and entertain the masses. The idea of narcotization is a response to the power of the media in totalitarian societies, where absolute control over the radio and newspapers can be seen to insure the domination of nations by particular ideologies. It is argued that, by being provided with endless diversions, the masses lose the capacity for independent political thought.

nation-state: the political unit that covers a particular geographical area, but more importantly, encompasses all those who identify with each other as sharing a common history, *culture*, and language. The growth of the nation-state was characteristic of Europe in the 19th century, although the process is still continuing in the areas of the former Soviet Union and Yugoslavia. *Globalization* theorists argue that the importance of the nation-state is in decline, under the impact of the twin processes of globalization and localization.

National Deviancy Conference: a group of British sociologists who challenged the orthodoxies of criminology in the 1970s, by focusing on the deviants' own accounts of themselves and the political dimension of crime and criminality. The offshoots of the NDC developed radical alternatives to conceptions of *deviance*, which shifted the focus away from the criminal and toward the forces of law and order. The increase in crime in Britain during the 1980s and the reality of violence as an aspect of criminal activity led several of the NDC theorists to turn to alternative ways of conceptualizing crime, associated with a realist approach.

nationalism: in general usage, the belief in the *nation-state* as the prime political unit, usually based on linguistic or cultural similarities. More specifically, it can apply to activism in the cause of national independence from a larger authority.

nationalization: the policy and practice of taking industries into public ownership. Usually associated with socialist politics, it has fallen out of favor in many modern industrialized societies, as the policy of *privatization* has increasingly taken hold.

natural history of professionalism: a concept developed by Wilensky that suggests that there are certain logical and historical steps through which an occupational group must go before it can become a *profession*. Critics of this approach to the professions are of two types:

- Some sociologists argue that the existing professions emerged at a particular historical time, when governments were infused with an *ideology* of handing over powers to occupational groups. That time is now past and governments are unlikely to hand over any more power to non-professional groups.
- Other sociologists argue that history shows that the existing professions did not follow through a particular set of procedures in order to become professions, but took a wide range of routes.

natural science: specifically, the disciplines of biology, chemistry, and physics, but more generally, a way of looking at the natural world that is systematic, objective, and capable of generating universal laws. The exact nature of natural science is in much dispute, with some philosophers of science arguing for only one strict way of approaching natural science and others arguing that there is no one way of approaching natural science. The latter argue that natural science, just like any human endeavor, is open to social construction. The term "natural science" is misleading because it presumes that there is a single science, whereas in fact it is more accurate to talk about the natural sciences in the plural. Many of the assumptions regarding the methods and the degree of *objectivity* in science have been challenged, particularly by interactionist sociologists, and also by philosophers such as Popper and Kuhn. (See *falsification; hypothetico-deductive method; scientific revolution.*)

natural selection: see *evolutionary theories*

natural world: a term used in contrast to the *social world* to describe the world that exists, regardless of human perception of it. It is the world of plants, animals, matter, atoms, stars and space, etc. It is sometimes referred to as the objective world, because it would exist whether we subjectively experienced it or not. We do experience the natural world as external to us, but action theorists suggest that it only becomes meaningful when human beings impose their understanding onto it.

nature versus nurture debate: the controversy over whether human *intelligence* and behavior is primarily determined by heredity and genetic makeup, or by the process of *socialization*. The extreme positions in the debate are taken by those who argue in favor of the former view, such as Eysenck, and the cultural determinists, who support the latter. It is difficult to find really conclusive evidence either way, and many people adopt the position that both genetics and socialization play their part in shaping human attitudes and behavior; the question is one of emphasis. A concern expressed regarding the genetics view is that beliefs in the purely biological determinants of human character could be, and indeed have been, used to justify discriminatory treatment of particular groups, such as racial minorities. It also implies that there is little point in trying to "cure" or "rehabilitate" criminals, as it is in their "nature" to offend.

Naturwissenschaften: a term used by Dilthey for the "natural sciences" to distinguish them from the social sciences. (See *Geisteswissenschaften; natural science.*)

need-achievement: a term developed by McLelland to suggest that all individuals, as a basic part of their human nature, have a basic desire to make something of themselves. However, the drive to achieve will vary from individual to individual, depending upon childhood experiences and the extent to which parental warmth supported competitive encouragement.

needs: what is required by individuals to survive. According to sociologists, definitions of need are socially constructed, so that they will vary from one society to another and from one era to the next.

negative abstention: where electors fail to vote because they cannot be bothered to or have no interest in politics. Negative abstention is therefore a feature of indifference to politics. (See *positive abstention.*)

negative correlation: see *correlation*

negotiated order: a term developed by Strauss as an alternative conceptualization of society to the reified view of the functionalists to suggest that society is constantly being worked and reworked by those who live in it. Society does not therefore exist independently of the individuals who create it on a day-to-day basis, through their interactions with each other. This negotiation of the social order is not conscious, but an effect of the everyday activities of individuals.

neighborhood: a term used to describe localities in *urban areas* that are characterized by a common sense of identity and usually a common lifestyle. Neighborhoods are usually class-based and particularly in working-class neighborhoods they have a developed sense of *community*. To sociologists, the importance of neighborhoods is that they demonstrate the existence of a sense of community in urban areas, contrary to the soulless stereotype often put forward. (See *loss of community thesis*.)

neocolonialism: a term to describe the situation in which former colonial powers continue to dominate the affairs of former colonies through a variety of means. Although formal control of the colonies was given up at the time of political independence, the former colonizers tend to retain important influences over economic and even cultural affairs. Such ties between former colonies and their former imperial powers are partly the result of shared history, sentiment, and language, but also operate through the dominance of trading and industrial organizations from the original colonial power. The terms of trade between former colonizers and colonized tend to operate in favor of the imperial power, which can control crucial sectors of the former colony's economy. Former colonies have often tried to break the dominance of the former colonizer's industrial giants through policies such as *nationalization,* or by restricting the amount of profits that can be patriated to the former imperial power. However, it is also argued that through *globalization* the power of *transnational companies* has grown so much that the interests of the former colonies and imperial powers can be ignored.

neofunctionalism: sociological theory that draws upon and extends traditional functional analysis and seeks to apply its principles to the changed conditions of the contemporary world. In particular, the neofunctionalist examines the problems of *integration* in an increasingly fractured world.

neo-Marxism: in sociology, an approach that updates the insights of *Marx* and applies the basic principles of *Marxism* to the conditions of the contemporary world. In particular, the neo-Marxist perspective attempts to take into account the growth of sources of identity other than social class.

neonatal mortality rate: the number of deaths of infants under four weeks of age per thousand live births. (See *infant mortality rate, perinatal mortality rate.*)

nepotism: a form of *power* in which key positions in *organizations,* whether political, administrative, or economic, are allocated to relatives of those already in positions of power. The importance of nepotism is that it allows autocratic rulers to control societies through particularistic relationships. The regime of Saddam Hussein of Iraq would be an example of a nepotistic government.

nesting: within *hierarchies of oppression*, the way in which one level of oppression may be contained within another, so that there is more than one set of disadvantages associated with a particular characteristic. So, for example, for black women ethnic disadvantage may be nested within gender discrimination.

net volatility: the change in the proportion of the parties' votes between one election and the next. While net volatility may be low, such that the percentage change is small, there may still be a high degree of *gross volatility.* The result may be very similar, but large numbers of people have changed their minds both ways. (See *volatility.*)

networking: the process by which people establish business and personal contacts that they believe will be useful to them. It is argued that, at least in the business world, this is easier for men than for women, as many of these contacts are made through membership of golf clubs and other associations run mainly or exclusively for men. As many networking activities take place outside normal working hours, it is also difficult for those women who have *child care* responsibilities.

neutralization: an important part of the process of *drift,* where those committing deviant acts minimize the importance of their actions and provide justifications for them.

new Christian right: a term used to refer to those Christian groups taking a right-wing approach to matters of social policy. Such groups are exerting an increasingly strong influence in American politics in particular, where members of Christian right-wing groups form a numerically very strong group of voters. They are opposed to many actual and proposed social welfare policies, including the right to abortion, welfare payments to the poor, attempts at greater racial integration and the extension of certain civil rights to homosexuals, such as their acceptance in the armed forces.

new class: a term developed by Djilas to describe the group of high communist officials who held *power* in the Soviet bloc and who used that power to further their own interests and those of their children. Djilas argued that this new class used their control of the *state* and also the industrial enterprises run by the state to establish their total control in society. They, to all intents and purposes, operated as a *ruling class,* just like the *bourgeoisie.*

new criminology: see *critical criminology*

new deviancy theory: an approach to *deviance* that attempts to do away with assumptions about criminal types or criminal *subcultures.* It begins with the idea that everyone is potentially deviant, with deviant impulses, and the creation of a deviant is through the intolerance of the powerful, who stigmatize and label the relatively powerless in society. The *working class* do not therefore have greater criminality *per se,* but just have less *power* to resist the labels of the powerful forces of the social control agencies. True goodness therefore appears only on the margins of society among *expressive deviants.* This idea has been criticized as representing a hopelessly romantic view of humankind, whose natural goodness is brutalized by official society. (See *National Deviancy Conference.*)

new international division of labor: the shake-up in the world's economy in which manufacturing jobs have been moved to the developing countries of the Southern Hemisphere while countries of the Northern Hemisphere have retained high-tech industries. The move of manufacturing jobs to the *Pacific rim* has occurred because they are labor-intensive industries and the labor force is cheaper there. High-tech industries employ relatively few workers who are mainly highly skilled and well-paid. The consequence is increasing *unemployment* in the developed countries of the West.

new left realism: a left-wing analysis of crime that acknowledges that inner-city crime is a reality, and cannot be explained away simply by reference to policing policies, a biased judiciary, media-led *moral panics,* or the oppression of the *working class,* even if these are factors. Writers such as Lea and Young view some Marxist writing on crime as overromantic and recognize that the victims of working-class crime are usually working-class people. They refer to themselves as left realists, rather than left idealists. Critics of the view argue that, by focusing on working-class crime, the new left realists are ignoring the *crimes of the powerful,* which pose a much greater threat to the working class.

new man: a term applied to those men who have allegedly moved away from the stereotyped image of the "macho" male, in order to allow their natures to be more expressive, and who also take a larger share of domestic and *child care* tasks. Despite many references to the new man in the media, and the increasing participation of many men in some domestic and child care tasks, some research has shown that reports of "new manism" have been greatly exaggerated. (See *domestic division of labor.*)

new middle class: a term used to describe the postwar growth, particularly in Britain, of certain nonmanual occupations such as the salaried office workers, managers, and professionals employed by large bureaucracies. The distinguishing characteristic of this group compared to the *old middle class* is that it is unpropertied.

new poor: groups of people in *poverty* who fall into groups other than the traditional groups of the sick, the disabled, and the elderly. While these groups are still found among the poor, other categories now make up a growing proportion of those in poverty. They are low-paid workers, *single-parent families* (especially those headed by a woman), the unemployed, and the young homeless. Many of these groups receive all or part of their income from social benefits.

new professions: see *personal service professions; semiprofessions*

new rabble: a term coined by Murray to describe members of the *underclass* inhabiting *inner-city* areas and causing businesses and the middle class to move out.

new racism: a form of discrimination against ethnic groups on the basis of cultural rather than biological differences. The central process of new racism is to define ethnic minorities as the *other,* in contrast to an overall national identity, on the basis of them holding values perceived to be unassimilable with the norm. Through this exclusionary process, ethnic minorities are characterized as different from, and inferior to, those who belong.

new religious movements (NRMs): a collective term applied to the numerous religious groups, not necessarily Christian, that have emerged in increasing numbers, particularly in Western societies, in the last few decades. These groups are so diverse in character that Wallis has attempted to classify them with regard to their view on, and interaction with, mainstream society. Wallis suggests three main categories, as follows:

- World-rejecting – groups that expect their members to withdraw from the world, reject its values, and live a life based on the principles of the group. Examples would be the Unification Church of Sun Myung Moon (the "Moonies") or the cult of Hare Krishna.
- World-accommodating – groups that have relatively little impact on the way members live their lives; members are told to be more "religious," according to how that is interpreted by the particular group. The main focus of religious experience tends to be acts of collective worship. Examples would be the house-church movement or Neo-Pentecostalism.
- World-affirming – groups whose values actively embrace the values of mainstream society, and claim to be able to make their members achieve greater success within it. Examples are scientology and transcendental meditation.

Even apparently "mainstream" religious groups, however, can display characteristics of new religious movements, such as some Christian churches that try to appeal to young people, and show a willingness to adopt methods more usually associated with mass youth culture in order to bring young people to the church. Many new religious movements are regarded with great suspicion, and even hostility on the part of the public at large. (See *sects.*)

New Right: a perspective in sociology that draws upon conservative traditions and insists on the freedom of the individual and the primacy of the free market in all social and economic arrangements. Supporters of the New Right in Britain were influential in shaping social and economic policies in the 1980s and 1990s, introducing market principles into large areas of public life. There are various strands within the New Right, from the libertarians, who wish to reduce the power of the *state* to the bare minimum, to the traditionalists, who seek the return of a more respectful and deferential social order. New Right ideas and policies have been criticized for, among other things:

- overseeing a centralization of *power* in the *state* while claiming to do the opposite
- replacing public monopolies with private ones
- destroying any sense of *community* through the introduction of market relationships as the basis of social life.

new social movements (NSMs): an umbrella term for a whole range of organizations that are expressions of the *identity* of individuals in a postmodern world. They therefore are organized around interests and identities such as gender, ethnicity, sexuality, religious feeling, etc. They may also express political identities in the broadest sense such as in the case of *environmentalism.* They stand in contrast to traditional political movements that were class-based.

new working class: a term devised by Crewe to describe a new class of manual workers in Britain, who live in the south rather than the industrial north, work in the private sector, and own their own homes. It is argued by Crewe and others, that this section of the working class can be attracted to Conservatism as a political force, as it accords with their material interests. (See *old working class; sectoral cleavages.*)

newly industrializing countries (NICs): those nations in the Southern Hemisphere that do not easily fall into the category of *third world*, because they are relatively affluent or relatively developed. First, oil-rich nations like Saudi Arabia have a great deal of wealth, so cannot be seen as "in poverty." Second, countries like Brazil have high rates of growth and large *gross national products*, which makes it difficult to describe them as undeveloped. (See *Pacific rim; tiger economies.*)

news-values: the ideas and beliefs held by those involved in news-gathering regarding what constitutes good copy. It is argued that there is a professional *socialization* process for new reporters that inducts them into these news-values and shapes the way that they go out to look for news. Typical news-values emphasize the dramatic, prominent personalities, and "close to home" stories.

niche markets: a term used to describe markets where demand for particular goods is contained within identifiable and often small segments of the population, each requiring variations in a product. Niche markets can be defined by such social characteristics as age group, gender, class, ethnic origin, or sexuality, or by considerations of style. Some sociologists would argue that niche markets are heavily influenced by the *advertising industry*, which constantly absorbs, creates and molds cultural and stylistic trends. (See *pink economy.*)

NIMBY: an acronym for "not in my back yard," used to describe an attitude of disapproval toward developments such as new housing or a home for disturbed children that might encroach on private property or living space.

nomenclatura: the list of those in communist societies who were candidates for official positions through their membership of the Communist Party. They constituted a powerful block against reform, as their interests were tied up in the perpetuation of the bureaucratic communist system. The overthrow of the communist system in the late 1980s meant that many of the nomenclatura moved into positions of power in the newly privatized industries.

nonmanual work: occupations that do not involve heavy physical labor. It stands in contrast to *manual work*, and the difference between the two constitutes a basic cleavage in industrial societies. Nonmanual work is usually seen as *middle class* and would include both *white-collar work* and *professional* work.

nonresponse: in sociological research, the problem when members of a selected *sample* fail to participate fully in the research process. The term is usually applied to those who fail to complete *questionnaires,* particularly *postal questionnaires.* The degree of nonresponse has an important effect on the *reliability* of the final data, as the greater the degree of nonresponse, the less representative the sample.

nonstatutory services: a range of services available to citizens, the provision of which is not laid down by law, and which are consequently provided largely by voluntary agencies. Examples of valuable but nonstatutory services would be those provided by the Citizen's Advice Bureau, the NSPCC, and the Salvation Army. (See *statutory services.*)

nonvoters: the widest category of those who do not cast their ballots in elections. It includes those who are registered to vote and do not and those who were never registered in the first place. Though it is a legal requirement that people register, certain groups are systematically omitted from the *voting register*, such as the homeless, and those who object to voting on religious grounds such as the Jehovah's Witnesses.

nonwork: a general term that covers all the different types of activity an individual may engage in outside of *paid employment*. The concept is used because time out of work is not just *leisure* time, but can consist of *work-related time*, *obligated time*, and so on. The area of pure leisure is not therefore equatable with nonwork. (See *nonwork obligations*.)

nonwork obligations: activities outside of paid work that individuals are under some pressure to carry out, but which retain an element of choice. For example, *housework* is a nonwork obligation that is carried out to varying degrees by different individuals. (See *semileisure*.)

nonzero-sum relationship: a situation of *power* between two individuals or social formations, in which all participants benefit from the outcome of the struggle. This view of power is interested in how parties to a struggle maneuver to attract support for their position and build up power through the consent of others. The aim of such relationships is the achievement of collective objectives, so that there are no outright winners or losers. Rather, all benefit to a greater or lesser extent. (See *zero-sum relationship*.)

normal science: a term used by Kuhn to describe the position where science has a dominant *paradigm*, which privileges a particular way of looking at the world and suggests ways of looking for solutions to problems in science. (See *scientific revolution*.)

normalizing judgments: a term used by Foucault to indicate the exercise of disciplinary power in postmodern societies by "experts" who judge the individual's actions against a standard in order to find them "normal" or "abnormal." The abnormal individual then becomes subject to *discipline*, aimed at producing a more "normal" result from examination.

normative ambivalence: a term used to describe the usual state of the consciousness of the *proletariat*, where the workers accept the dominant middle-class values of society at one level, but do not uphold them in any meaningful sense in their everyday work lives. This concept is used to explain the fact that many workers respond to opinion poll questions in terms of dominant values, such as rejecting strikes, but then act very differently in their own workplace, as they "negotiate" their exception from the no-strike belief.

normative order: the system of rules of behavior that operates in a given situation. These rules appear as normal to participants and become taken for granted.

normative power: a type of control that relies on the giving or denial of *status* and acceptance to equals or subordinates. This is a very powerful form of control because it relies on the willing participation of those wishing to be accepted. (See *coercion*; *utilitarian power*.)

normative reference: a value or set of *values* that individuals or groups acknowledge as their source of inspiration for the way that they ought to behave. It is often the dominant value system that acts as a normative reference, but for the *working class* it might also be negotiated forms of it.

normlessness: see *anomie*

norms: social rules that define what is expected of individuals in certain situations. They are measures of what is seen as normal in society. Norms operate at several levels, from regulations concerning etiquette at the table to moral norms relating to the prior discharging of duties. (See *values*.)

north–south: an alternative term to express the division of the world into rich and poor countries. It emerged out of the fact that the richest countries in the world tend to be concentrated in the Northern Hemisphere, while the poorest are to be found mainly in the Southern. Although this division has never been an absolute one – for example, Australia has never fitted this model – developments in the last part of the 20th century made the term virtually obsolete. In particular, the emergence of the *tiger economies* of Southeast Asia have made such a neat division impossible to sustain.

noumenon: the "thing-in-itself," or, a presumed essence of a phenomenon that lies beneath the surface of reality. The search for the noumenon involves looking for deeper meanings and structures in society and is in contrast to *phenomenology*.

nuclear family: a family unit consisting of an adult male and female and their dependent offspring. It is regarded by some sociologists (in particular functionalists) as the basic universal form of *family structure*. Functionalists such as *Parsons* also suggest that the nuclear family replaced the *extended family* as the dominant form in industrial societies because it provided a better fit, i.e. more closely matched the *needs* of society. The (white) nuclear family is sometimes referred to as the cereal box family, because of its frequent portrayal by advertisers as the norm. Despite the fact that research shows that nuclear family households are far from universal, the notion of the nuclear family remains central to family *ideology*. Sociologists and particularly politicians of the *New Right* frequently express the view that many social problems stem from the fact that not enough children are being brought up in stable, two-parent families.

object: see *subject–object dualism*

objective social class: position in the social *hierarchy* as indicated by some characteristic external to the individual, for example occupation or income. Sociologists usually employ occupational scales to indicate objective social class. (See *Hall-Jones scale*.)

objectivity: a lack of *bias*, preconceptions, or prejudice. Objectivity is a central concept in the discussion about sociology and science, both as to whether sociology as a discipline and sociologists as researchers can be objective, and also as to what extent research in the *natural sciences* is as objective as is claimed. Scientists are not agreed over what it actually means to be objective. Some claim that following the procedures of the scientific method results in objectivity. Others argue that because scientists are subject to the values and prejudices of all humans, it is very difficult to be truly objective, and therefore values and prejudices ought to be declared publicly. It is often argued that the replication of scientific work acts as a self-righting mechanism that eliminates experimental work that is subjectively tainted. Objectivity then can be applied both to the researcher, along with the values and attitudes brought to the research process, and to the method(s) used and the extent to which they are themselves neutral. (See *positivism*.)

obligated time: see *nonwork obligations*

occupation: the job that a person does. Occupations are organized by sociologists into categories, based on their relationship to prestige, income, and wealth. They are thus often used by sociologists as indicators of *social class*.

occupational scale: the ranking of occupations to divide the working population into mutually exclusive groups. Occupational scales can be set up in a number of ways, and they are generally used in sociological research into *social mobility*. (See *Hall-Jones scale*; *Surrey occupational scale*.)

occupational structure: the distribution of different types of occupations in a society. The occupational structure is usually conceived in terms of three types of jobs: the primary sector, the secondary sector, and the tertiary sector. Changes in the distribution of these have consequences for the stratification systems of modern societies. In particular, sociologists have focused on the decline of the primary and secondary sectors and the rise in the tertiary sector as influencing the class structure of society, so that the *middle class* is expanding and the *working class* declining.

occupational transition: the change in *occupational structure* since World War II, which has involved the expansion of nonmanual work and the contraction of manual jobs. The implications of the occupational transition are enormous and sociologists have been particularly interested in effects on *class structure,* with the development of a diamond-shaped distribution rather than the traditional hierarchical structure.

official documents: *documents* produced by official bodies such as government agencies, and records such as those of court proceedings and company operations. While providing a rich source of information for sociologists, official documents can themselves be the object of research, i.e. can be examined as the products of various social processes to see the ways in which they reflect particular political or economic interests or viewpoints. As with all sources of *secondary data*, such documents need to be treated with caution.

official goals: the aims of an *organization* set out in its founding charter, annual reports, etc. These are usually vague and general, rather than descriptive of the day-to-day functions of the organization. (See *operative goals*.)

official statistics: statistical data produced by central and local governments and government agencies. Official statistics are produced in vast quantities, and provide a rich source of information for sociologists, much of it impossible for researchers to gather themselves, e.g. statistics on the *birth rate*, or *census* data. The critical examination of official statistics as the product of social processes has played a significant part in much sociological writing, in particular statistics relating to crime, poverty, and unemployment. (See *hard statistics*; *soft statistics*.)

old-boy network: a term to describe the continuation of friendship groupings made in exclusive colleges, particularly the "Ivy League" universities, and into later careers. The existence of an old-boy network is argued to be a major factor in the perpetuation of traditional *elites* in society and the reason why *social mobility* into the top echelons of society is limited. Whether the old-boy network exists or not is very difficult to prove. While clearly friendship does survive graduation from exclusive schools, there is limited evidence to suggest that these friendships operate to exclude non-Ivy League graduates, for instance, from important positions in later careers.

old middle class: a term encompassing members of the traditional *professions*, such as lawyers and doctors, and the owners of small and the managers of large businesses. The distinguishing characteristic of the old middle class was either property ownership or self-employment. The old middle class is now said by fragmentation theorists to be subsumed in the *modern upper class* and is distinguishable from the occupations that make up the *new middle class*.

old working class: a division of the *working class* in Britain proposed by Crewe. It is composed of manual workers who share certain characteristics, namely living in the north of England or Scotland, living in rented government-provided accommodation, and belonging to a labor union (known as trade union). The significance of this group for Crewe was that it represented the traditional Labour Party supporters, unlike the members of the *new working class*, who were more disposed to vote Conservative. Given that the members of the old working class are declining in number, it has been suggested that the Labour Party may continue to win a declining share of the overall working-class vote. (See *traditional working class*.)

oligarchy: see *iron law of oligarchy*

one-parent families: see *single-parent families*

one-party state: where political control rests in the hands of a single party, with all other political expressions of opinion, organized or unorganized, made illegal. The form of one-party states can take many guises, from the apparent plurality of many communist societies, to attempts to force every individual into the ruling party.

one-way convergence: a type of *convergence theory* that argues that all industrializing societies will end up like the US. One-way convergence theories have been boosted by the collapse of Soviet-style communism in eastern Europe and the acceptance of the free market in those societies.

ontological security: a term used by *Giddens* to describe the basic human need for the social and natural worlds that people inhabit to exhibit some recognizable pattern, which they can then understand and within which they can operate with some degree of confidence. It is thus the search for some sort of order and predictability in an uncertain and often changing world.

open-ended questions: in sociological research, questions that allow the *respondent* to reply freely rather than choosing from a provided set of answers. An example of an open-ended question is, "What are your views regarding the changes to your working hours currently being considered by your management?" While allowing the collection of much useful and interesting information, open-ended questions pose a problem in their analysis, particularly if a large amount of information has been gathered. One way of dealing with this is to construct broad categories, and to put answers into one or more of these, although if several researchers are involved in this process, there is considerable room for inconsistency, and therefore *bias*. (See *closed questions*; *coding*; *unstructured interviews*.)

open societies: those societies in which there is a great deal of *social mobility* in the *class structure*. Openness is associated with modern, capitalist societies, which are said to be characterized by *meritocracy*. It is usually through education and certification that individuals can move upward in the social structure. (See *closed societies*.)

operational control: power over the day-to-day running of a company. Enough power is devolved to the managers of large companies to insure the smooth running of the organization. However, the *goals* of the organization, which all activities are tailored to meet, are set by those with *allocative control*. Therefore, while powerful in itself – for example, operational control would include the power to hire and fire workers – it is a secondary form of power.

operational definitions of suicide: the rules-of-thumb used by the appropriate authorities in deciding what is a *suicide*. In the case of coroners, there are several verdicts open to them, and they need to use operational definitions when deciding which verdict to record for any individual case. The problem is that different coroners are likely to use different operational definitions. Some might record suicide only if a note is left, while others might more readily accept circumstantial evidence. This suggests that suicide statistics are *socially constructed* through these operational definitions.

operationalization: the process whereby a theory or concept is translated into a practical instrument when the sociologist is carrying out research. For example, if sociologists ask people whether they are alienated or not, the sociologist could not guarantee that all *respondents* understood the same thing by this concept. Therefore, sociologists break the concept down into more understandable elements, in order to gain more meaningful data.

operative goals: what an organization actually does and achieves, as opposed to what the *official goals* might say is the aim. Perrow argued that the operative goals are the more important ones and that they are shaped by the dominant group in the organization. However, subordinate individuals and groups also bring their own operative goals into the organization, which may undermine or support its effectiveness. (See *goal-model.*)

opiate of the people: a term used by *Marx* to describe *religion*, particularly in capitalist society, where it is used by the oppressed classes to dull the pain of their exploitation. Religion forms part of the *ideological state apparatus*, and has, according to Marx, an important role in justifying the status quo and reducing the threat of revolution by making inequalities appear to be God-given.

opinion leaders: influential groups of people who access information from the *mass media*, digest it, and pass it on to members of their circle. They are seen as a crucial part of the process of communication between the media and the mass of people in society. They expose themselves to mass media campaigns by the political parties and use media-supplied information to influence others around them. They are also opinion-formers, but are not in positions of power within the media itself. Rather they become leaders through the confidence of the group around them. (See *two-step hypothesis of the flow of information.*)

opinion poll: the collection of the public's attitudes by telephone or through *questionnaires* from a carefully controlled *sample* of the population. The main use of opinion polls is to collect voting intentions. They are criticized because they are not always accurate and can therefore give a misleading impression of the state of political opinion.

oppositional leisure: leisure characteristic of a situation where there is sharp distinction made between work and *leisure*. It is usually associated with hard manual work such as mining and leads to leisure activities that are focused on the pub, sport or the home. The point of such leisure is to take participants' minds away from the arduous and sometimes dangerous nature of their work. (See *complementary leisure, extension leisure.*)

oppositional orientation: associated with the *working class*, a term to describe attitudes opposed to the dominant bourgeois values in society. They have a physical manifestation in working-class organizations such as *labor unions* and are composed of radical ideas that stress collectivism against individualism and the importance of state provision of *welfare* for those least able to defend themselves.

oral history: knowledge of the past gathered from information about a person's life obtained by direct questioning, usually by *unstructured interviews.* (See *life history.*)

organic analogy: see *biological analogy*

organic solidarity: the way in which industrial societies integrate, i.e. through the interdependence of all individuals. This solidarity of difference operates, according to *Durkheim*, because of the complexity of industrial societies, in which no one individual could hope to provide everything needed for life. Individuals are therefore bound together by their need for each other. (See *mechanical solidarity*.)

organismic organizations: a term used by Burns and Stalker to describe flexible, responsive organizational structures. This type of organization is in contrast to *mechanistic organizations*, and is distinguished by its ability to respond rapidly to conditions of change. The features that make such organizations responsive are said to be:

- a willingness by participants to contribute to solving problems according to their expertise
- a reflexive attitude by the organization, whose members constantly review performance
- a commitment by members to achieve the overall *organizational goals*
- a network structure rather than a *hierarchy* of control
- a communication system in which information flows freely, not just from the top down.

Burns and Stalker saw organismic organizations developing whenever markets were no longer secure, and wherever the demand was for individualized, customized goods. They were therefore more appropriate to the production conditions of *postmodernity*. (See *niche markets*.)

organization man: a term developed by Whyte to indicate executives who tend to develop similar personalities in their search for promotion. The features of organization man are conformity, loyalty to the company, dedication to work, and a preparedness to sacrifice family life for the good of the business.

organizational culture: the *values, beliefs*, and *norms* of a specific organization that shape the ways in which individual members of the organization interact with each other to achieve goals. The form of organizational culture varies, and sociologists are interested in the ways that these cultures affect the efficiency of the organization.

organizational goals: the formal aims of an organization when it is initially set up. Organizations have a purpose, expressed either formally in their charters, or more informally in the stated aims of members of the organization. Therefore, organizations are devices for achieving goals. The importance of organizational goals for sociologists is that they represent one way in which the efficiency of an organization can be measured, that is, by the extent to which it achieves its goals. However sociologists such as Etzioni argue that the formal goals of an organization should not be taken for granted. Organizations often have goals other than the formally stated ones. Individual members of the organization may pursue their own goals at the expense of the formally stated ones. Other sociologists such as Simon argue that there is no such thing as "the goal" of an organization, but that goals represent a constraint on the actions of individuals in organizations, which may or may not be referred to when they are justifying a particular course of action they have undertaken.

organizational rules: the regulations that govern the behavior of those who belong to an organization. Sociologists have been interested in organizational rules because they were originally identified by *Weber* as one of the main instruments for insuring the efficiency of organizations. In *legal-rational organizations*, there is a need for the coordination of activities to achieve maximum efficiency. Weber argued that one of the main ways coordination was achieved was through obedience to rules. However, this approach has been criticized by other sociologists:

- Blau suggests that rules can be *dysfunctional* for organizations, as well as functional. He argues that rules cannot cover all situations and the generation of new rules to meet challenges often creates contradictions and confusion. Moreover, rules can be employed by individuals in ways other than intended by those who created the rules and in pursuit of the individual's own goals, rather than *organizational goals*.

- Perrow argues that, although rules are devised by *management* to control the actions of workers through coordination, the rules are double-edged swords. While the rules may define what workers are supposed to do, they also create opportunities for workers not to do other things, which are beyond the remit of the rules. This allows, for example, workers to disrupt an organization by *working-to-rule* in a strict way.

- Ethnomethodologists, such as Zimmerman, argue that rules should be looked at situationally, that is, examined in the context in which they are actually employed. Only by so doing will sociologists understand how the rules actually operate in an organization. Rules are therefore a resource for members of an organization to be employed or not employed as it suits their purposes.

(See *situational rules*.)

organizations: bodies of people, persisting over time, that are set up to achieve specific aims, and are characterized by having a *structure* and a *culture*. The study of organizations is one of the central aspects of sociology, because individuals inhabit or deal with organizations throughout the whole of their lives. Organizations differ from random groups in various ways:

- Organizations survive the departure of individual members of the organization. That is, organizations have a history that can precede an individual member.

- Organizations have goals, often written into their founding charters, that guide the activities of members of the organization.

- Organizations have decision-making and enforcement procedures that seek to control the activities of members of the organization.

- Organizations are characterized by the allocation of formal *roles* and duties to participating members.

Organizations have their *formal* and their *informal* aspects. There are also many different types of organization. (See *bureaucracy*; *mechanistic organization*; *organismic organization*.)

organized crime: a term used to describe the activities of groups that make their living from breaking the law. It is usually associated with extortion, drug-dealing, and prostitution, and the groups are run through the use of violence and are often in conflict with other organized criminals. In the US, the term has been traditionally associated with the Mafia.

organized labor: see *labor unions*

ostracism: in industry, a sanction used by workers, in which offenders are ignored until they come into line with the wishes of the group.

other: a term developed by Foucault to indicate members of marginalized groups in society, who are characterized by mainstream society as somehow alien. This alienation is represented by the concept of the other. The others are pushed aside by powerful forces through processes such as *stigmatization* and *marginalization*.

other-worldly orientation: a term used by Pfautz to indicate individuals who focus on the after-life in dealing with the world around them. Social action is therefore shaped by belief in the *supernatural* and the continuation of life after death. (See *this-worldly orientation.*)

outing: a strategy employed by some militant gay groups of making public the homosexuality of prominent figures, who would otherwise have preferred their gayness to remain private. The tactic is controversial and has split the gay community as to the ethics of forcing unwilling gays into the open. Those in favor of outing argue that they only "out" those who have taken public stances against homosexuality.

outsourcing: the use by organizations of outside companies to carry out aspects of their operations that were previously carried out by employees. The subcontracting of cleaning duties to specialist companies is an example. Outsourcing is a key feature of *lean production.*

outworking: a system of production wherein certain processes are given out to low-paid workers working from home. The system is symbiotic, if exploitative. The outworker may be tied to the home because of *child care* commitments, while the employer is relieved of the need to provide factory space for workers. There is also a strong element of the *black economy* operative in outworking. (See *homeworking.*)

overt curriculum: see *curriculum*

overt participant observation: see *participant observation*

overt research: research in which both the identity of the researcher and something of the nature of the research are known to the objects of that research. The term is usually applied to overt *participant observation.*

overurbanization: the conditions of insecurity that affect many of the inhabitants of cities in the *third world.* The term does not mean overpopulation or overcrowding in these cities, although these may be aspects of insecurity. The insecurity stems from the circumstances of *migration* to third-world cities, where many peasants are forced off their land and have to seek work in urban areas. However, the economies of third world cities are geared to overseas, rather than local markets, with the result that there is "growth without development," and *unemployment* and *underemployment* in the cities is rife. As a consequence, adequate housing, sewage, and water supplies are absent from some areas as shanty towns or *favelas* develop.

ownership and control debate: see *separation of ownership and control*

Oxford mobility study: a large-scale survey of *social mobility* in Britain carried out by Goldthorpe and the Nuffield team, who claimed they found a considerable increase in rates of social mobility since World War II. The increase was largely the result of changes in the *occupational structure* and was leaving a self-recruiting, more *homogeneous* working class behind, as occupational change slowed down. The major feature of social mobility according to the Oxford study was that it was *forced mobility*.

P

Pacific rim: a term describing the geographical location of the expanding and dynamic economies of the world, which heralds a shift in the global balance of *power*. The center of world power has traditionally been Europe and the US, with the actual "center" of the power bloc somewhere in the Atlantic. However, it is argued that production is shifting globally to produce a new center of power somewhere in the Pacific, with the most dynamic economies of the world situated around the edge of the Pacific Ocean. This is partly to do with the move in US production from the traditional northeast to the more dynamic west and south, partly to do with the pre-dominance of Japan in the world economy, and partly to do with the most rapidly developing countries in the world, such as Taiwan and South Korea, being situated there. The big unknown in this apparent development is what will happen to the enormous market represented by Communist China. If China opens up fully to trade, or develops an effective industrial sector itself, then the Pacific rim is likely to form a powerful new focus for the world economy.

paid employment: a term to distinguish *work* in the *formal economy* from other types of work, such as domestic labor. One of the distinguishing characteristics of paid employment is the existence of an employer, although this does not take into account those who are self-employed.

panel studies: a form of *longitudinal study* usually associated with research into polit-ical attitudes and opinions. A selected group of people (the panel) is repeatedly tested for changes in their political views and opinions, often to judge the impact of political broadcasts or campaigns.

panopticon: a type of prison building that enables wardens to oversee every aspect of prisoners' lives. It is associated with a view of prison that seeks to survey the whole of the inmates' existence through organizational as well as architectural features. Foucault saw the panopticon as symptomatic of the increased *surveillance* in modern societies, aided by *rationality*.

paradigm: a set of ideas and beliefs (particularly in *natural science*) that provides a consensual framework or model, within which practitioners can operate. A paradigm defines existing knowledge, the nature of the problem or problems to be investi-gated, the appropriate methods of investigation, and the way in which the findings should be analyzed and interpreted. Alternative views of the world are rejected by the dominant paradigm, whose *gatekeepers* obstruct the promotion of alternatives. An example of a paradigm might be the Newtonian or Einsteinian conception of the universe. The concept of paradigms is particularly associated with Kuhn, who argued that scientific knowledge was neither objective nor cumulative, but developed through a series of paradigm shifts, during which existing paradigms were chal-lenged and eventually replaced. Some sociologists argue that sociology as a discipline is in a preparadigmatic stage, as there is no consensus regarding the nature of soci-ety and how it operates, nor a generally accepted model of how sociological research should be conducted. The concept has been criticized because Kuhn uses it in many different ways and it ends up being a relativistic concept. (See *scientific revolution*.)

parasuicide: see *attempted suicide*

Parent-Teacher Associations (PTAs): organized volunteer groups in schools with representation of both parents and teachers, found in elementary, middle, or junior high, and high schools. These associations are often involved in fund-raising activities, but can often take a more actively political role, with organized campaigns over various education issues.

parental aspirations: the hopes and expectations of parents for their children, particularly in terms of educational achievement. Research by Douglas found that those children whose parents hoped that they would go to selective schools in Britain and do well gained a higher proportion of school places than children of the same measured ability whose parents did not have such high aspirations. It is often assumed that working-class parents have lower aspirations for their children than do middle-class parents, but a considerable number of working-class parents are extremely eager for their children to do well at school, seeing it as a way out of the working class and a chance to have a "better life."

parentocracy: a term to describe both the increasing power given to parents within the education system and their willingness to exercise it. The shift to parent power has come with the enhanced powers of local organizations like citizens' advisory committees. Parental power is also claimed to emerge from the ability of parents to choose which schools their children attend. Critics argue that parental choice can in effect lead to greater imbalance in the public education system.

Parsons, Talcott: arguably the most influential American sociologist of the 20th century, and generally acknowledged as the founding father of *structural-functionalism*, the school of sociology that dominated American and to a certain extent British sociology during the 1940s and 1950s. Parsons' overall aim was a synthesis of the major ideas in sociology and the social sciences in general, from *Durkheim* through to *Weber*, into one complete theoretical framework that explained both the structure of society and the behavior of the individual. (See *functional prerequisites*.)

participant observation: a form of sociological research in which the researcher takes a *role* in the social situation under observation. The fact that the researcher is conducting research may be known to the other participants, in which case the participant observation is known as "overt," or the role of the researcher may be such that her/his true identity and motive may be kept secret, in which case the method is known as "covert participant observation." Both methods have their advantages. Overt research allows the researcher to ask questions, and no one would be surprised if s/he were seen taking notes. However, it can be argued that covert research allows the researcher even greater insight into the *values*, *meanings*, and behavior of those under study, as they are unaware that they are being studied. Participant observation also has its problems or, as critics would say, its weaknesses. Some of the main difficulties are:

- it is a relatively costly method, as most studies are conducted over a period of time
- it is impossible to say with certainty that members of the group studied are representative
- overt participant observation may lead to the *Hawthorne effect*
- covert participant observation leads to particular problems with regard to the keeping of accurate notes without being observed, and also of possibly having to remember lengthy conversations
- the stages of covert participant observation have been referred to as "getting in, staying in, and getting out," and all three of these can pose problems for the researcher
- the researcher may find it difficult to maintain *objectivity,* particularly after spending a considerable length of time with the group, and may risk "*going native.*"

Despite these problems, the method is a valuable one, and has given particular insight into groups that would have been difficult, if not impossible, to study any other way, such as religious *sects,* teenage gangs, drug-users, and juvenile delinquents.

participative groups: a term developed by Likert to denote a form of work organization based on production by groups of workers rather than by individuals on *assembly-line systems.* Likert argued that organizations should be made up of interlocking work groups, who take responsibility for producing goods from start to finish, as opposed to the specialization of the assembly line. He argued that such organization allows the self-actualization of individuals, and thus increases efficiency. (See *job enlargement.*)

participative leadership: a form of *management* in which the managers are prepared to involve themselves in the everyday activities of the workers. While they continue to manage, it is with a "hands-on" attitude, so that they know and understand the problems workers face. Similarly, workers are encouraged by participative leadership to become involved in the running of the company. This stands in contrast to impersonal leadership, which is separated from the workers in time and space.

participatory democracy: see *direct democracy*

particularism: a situation where personal relationships are important in social actions. Particularism was a feature of traditional societies, where in particular family relationships formed the basis of public life. In particularistic societies, relatives and personal friends gain preferment over strangers. (See *universalism.*)

partisan alignment: the situation where support for the major political parties in a society is stable and class-based, so that the *working class* largely supports left-wing or workers' parties and the *middle class* supports right-wing or traditionalist parties in the main. It is important to note that, even in a situation of partisan alignment, significant factions of a class will support a party that does not represent their supposed *class interest.* (See *duopoly.*)

partisan dealignment: the process whereby electoral support for the major political parties based on class alignment diminishes, and third parties in a *duopoly* consequently increase their electoral basis. (See *class dealignment*; *political identification*.)

parvenus: a term meaning newcomers, often used as term of abuse for rising moneyed groups in society, who did not have the breeding of the *aristocracy*. It is therefore associated with the lack of *status* in money-making in societies dominated by traditional *elites*.

passing: a situation in which a sociologist undertaking covert *participant observation* is successfully able to adopt a *role* within the group, and keep her/his identity as a researcher secret from the other members.

paternalism: a system of social relationships that takes as its analogy the protective care a father has for his children. It has both political and industrial forms. In the political manifestation, a paternalistic relationship between an authoritarian *elite* and subordinates is conceived as a type of "father-knows-best" situation, in which decisions are removed from subordinates and concentrated in the authority figure, who then exercises power in the interests of the subordinates. In the industrial form, employers take a wider interest in the welfare of their workers than just the wages they give them. In an advanced form, employer activity might extend to building workers' houses, providing education for their children, and supplying *leisure* opportunities for their families. Critics argue that even this benevolent form of paternalism is more about control than care, with only sanctioned leisure activities and particular forms of education being provided.

pathological: in sociology, a term used to describe any feature of social life that may be fatal to society's survival. The term was originally applied by functionalists for characteristics that undermined an assumed *value consensus* in society. To functionalists, anything that did not contribute to the integration of society was likely to lead to disintegration and was therefore defined as pathological. For example, one-parent families were often seen by functionalists as pathological.

pathology: the study of the causes and symptoms of disease, both physical and mental. *Durkheim* also applied the term "*pathological*" to any form of deviant behavior.

patriarchal ideology: a set of beliefs (and the practices stemming from them) that assumes that males are in some way superior to females, and that it is therefore natural and right that men should enjoy a more privileged position in society than women, particularly in terms of *power* and *prestige*. (See *patriarchy*.)

patriarchy: a form of society in which males are the rulers and leaders, and exercise power both at the level of society as a whole and within individual households. Feminists argue that the existence of a patriarchal system explains the multiple disadvantages experienced by women, since the supporting *ideology* leads to the assumption that male power and dominance are somehow "natural." Marxist feminists see patriarchy as inextricably linked with *capitalism*, because of the benefits patriarchy brings to a capitalist system. Women are used as a *reserve army of labor*. They produce the future workforce and, by their unpaid labor, nurture and support the male workers, deflecting a cost that would otherwise fall on *capital*, i.e. would need to be met in the form of higher wages.

patriation of profits: the process whereby profits made in the *third world* by *transnational companies* (TNCs) are transferred back to the TNC's country of origin. This is often achieved despite laws in the third-world country limiting the amount of profits that can be sent back. Creative accounting processes, which are legal but against the spirit of laws prohibiting excessive patriation, are used to effect the transfer. Often, the dependence of a third-world country on the activities of the transnational companies insures that patriation is achieved with little hindrance.

patrilineal: a term to describe a form of kinship system in which descent is traced through males. In the *aristocracy*, hereditary titles are passed through the male line, ignoring females, and in the succession to the throne, younger brothers take precedence over their sister(s).

pattern maintenance and tension management: see *latency*

pattern variables: the basic variables of "value orientation" in the formulation associated with comparative analysis, in which specific aspects of two societies are compared to see how similar or different they are. The way in which the similarities and differences pan out creates a pattern, which can be used as a basis for generalizations about the effects of social changes, such as *industrialization*. The technique is particularly associated with Parsonian *functionalism*, which attempted to establish the differences between traditional and modern societies through determining the pattern variables.

peasant economies: economic systems associated with preindustrial and undeveloped societies. These economies are dominated by small-scale agricultural production, in which a significant proportion of the population gains a living from the land, mainly from small plots inherited through the family. The productive capacity of such economies is limited, but traditional agriculture in peasant economies is often able to sustain large populations, because the people have worked out how to produce sufficient crops without causing long-term damage to the land.

pecuniary model: a *frame of reference* in which the holder sees society as differentiated into groups according to the money each possesses. Society is thus seen as a system of subordination and superordination in which money, rather than status or class, is the defining characteristic. (See *power model*; *prestige model*.)

pedagogy: the science (or art) of teaching. Pedagogy is often divided into two broad types, traditional/conservative and progressive/liberal. The former emphasizes structure and control, with the teacher as the fount of knowledge, while the latter puts greater emphasis on the active involvement and participation of students, with the teacher seen more as one who creates a framework within which learning can take place. (See *chalk-and-talk*; *discovery learning*; *experiential teaching*.)

peer group: a group of people sharing common characteristics – usually age, but also possibly gender, occupation, or ethnic group – who perceive themselves, and are perceived by others, as forming a distinct social group. In sociology the term is usually applied to adolescents, and studies of peer groups have focused particularly on schools and leisure-based groups, including gangs. Peer groups can exercise considerable control over their members, and this *peer group pressure* is often much stronger than pressure exercised by other people, such as parents or teachers.

peer group pressure: the control exercised by a *peer group* over its members to achieve conformity. The most powerful form of peer pressure is usually the threat of exclusion from the group.

penology: the study of prisons. In sociology, prisons are seen as an interesting *case study* of a *total institution*, and penology provides an arena where ideological struggles over the role of penal institutions are carried out.

perestroika: a term for "reconstruction," associated with the process of reform instituted by Mikhail Gorbachev in the Soviet Union during the 1980s, which ultimately led to the collapse of *communism*, and which focused on changing the economic principles that had governed Soviet industry since the 1917 revolution. (See *glasnost*.)

perinatal mortality rate: the number of stillbirths and deaths of infants under one week old per thousand births. (See *infant mortality rate*.)

periphery workers: in post-Fordist *modes of production*, those unskilled workers who are employed on a casual, often part-time basis to carry out nonessential parts of the production process. They might be involved, for example, in cleaning or catering work, often through a subcontracting or *self-employment* arrangement. They are low-paid and the company has little obligation to them, so that they can be employed and dismissed easily. (See *core workers*.)

permeability: in sociology, the extent to which the social distinctions that operate outside of an organization are maintained within a *total institution*. For example, in a prison, gender does not permeate at all, while in an army camp, differences between men and women might be maintained in the allocation of tasks.

persistence theories: theories concerning *stratification* that suggest that social changes such as *occupational structure* movements have not seriously altered the *class structure* of modern capitalist societies. In particular, these theories suggest that evidence concerning the distribution of *wealth, power,* and opportunity shows no significant long-term movement toward a more equal society. Instead, the important divisions in society, such as between owners and nonowners, and between manual and nonmanual workers, have continued to remain large in many capitalist societies. (See *fragmentation*; *realignment theories*.)

personal documents: a term referring to a wide variety of papers and other documentary material that can be used as a valuable source of *secondary data* in sociological study. Almost any personal document can be of interest to a sociologist, but among those most frequently used are letters, diaries, school reports, photographs, birth, marriage, and death certificates, *documents* relating to property, and wills. As with all secondary data, personal documents need to be treated with caution, but they can reveal significant insights, particularly into the past.

personal service professions: a term devised by Halmos to describe that group of occupations dealing with human beings and their social problems, in areas such as education, social work, and mental health. This group aspires to professional status, but does not have that claim recognized by others and has not been granted professional powers by the government. The practitioners sustain a professional self-image, which separates them from other lower occupational groups, but which does not guarantee them entry into the ranks of the traditional professions.

perspectives: ways of looking at things, such as social phenomena, from a particular viewpoint. A perspective is usually organized around a specific principle, which distinguishes it from other perspectives. Perspectives thus represent partial ways of looking at the social world. While perspectives are important in sociology, they are not all-encompassing because:

- it is frequently difficult to place an individual in a perspective, as sociologists often draw upon a number of perspectives in their work
- perspectives are continually changing as the world changes and as they are influenced by other perspectives
- individual sociologists can have long careers in which their view of the social world may change as they further develop their theories.

pervasiveness: the extent to which an organization seeks to control the lives of its participants. A *total institution* will be very pervasive, while a factory will be less pervasive. Some sociologists have argued that there are cultural differences among similar organizations throughout the world. For example, Japanese industrial organizations are more pervasive than their American equivalents.

petty bourgeoisie: in *Marx*'s formulation of social classes, the self-employed, or those who employ very few laborers in their economic activity. They are associated with the shopkeeping and independent artisan class, who form a buffer between the *bourgeoisie* and the *proletariat*. Because of their intermediary position, they were seen as being pulled in both directions, sometimes taking a revolutionary role and sometimes a conservative stance in the political questions of the day. They were thus economically determined, but ideologically and politically fluid. (See *dominant level*.)

phenomenology: a *perspective* drawn from the work of Husserl and popularized by Schutz that starts from the premise that sociology should be concerned with what appears to us on the surface of things and not with the hidden depths of society. Our knowledge of the social world should therefore be based on things as they are, not things as we would like them to be. Schutz argued that each individual had a unique biographical situation, which constituted a stock of knowledge known only to the individual. So while we all know things differently from anyone else, when we interact we assume that we can ignore these differences and act from our *common-sense* understandings – what we assume everybody knows. (See *everyday knowledge, multiple realities*.)

physical control: a type of *power* exercised by *organizations,* which includes force or the threat of coercion. In capitalist societies, it is government organization that keeps a monopoly over physical control. (See *material control; symbolic control*.)

pillarization: a term used to describe the division of a society vertically into groups, for example, different *ethnic groups*. Each section reproduces the usual social divisions to be found in society, but has an existence that is separate from other pillars. The classic example of a pillarized society is Belgium, which is divided into Flemish and Walloon sections, each having, for example, its own socialist and conservative parties.

pilot study: a small-scale test of a particular piece of research, usually a *social survey*, in order to test its design and the nature and quality of the data generated. Particular emphasis is placed on testing the method of *sampling* and the questions used in the *questionnaire* or interview plan, as flaws in the design of these are likely to seriously affect the quality of the research.

pink economy: a term used to describe the spending power represented by the lesbian and gay populations in liberal Western democracies. With the emergence of an overt gay and lesbian community from the 1970s onwards, industry has become increasingly aware of the purchasing power of a group of people who are often to be found in well-paid occupations and who usually have few children to support. The existence of a group with a large disposable income has made them a new target for industry, with the result that in the 1990s, positive gay and lesbian advertising images began to emerge. (See *niche markets.*)

playing it cool: a term to describe a reaction to being placed in a *total institution*, in which the inmate becomes indifferent to the organization. It was developed by Goffman to describe the inmate who just stays out of trouble and "does time." (See *situational withdrawal.*)

plural societies: societies in which there are distinct sections of the population that are distinguished by ethnic, linguistic, or cultural features.

pluralism: the view of *power* in society that sees it dispersed among many different groups and individuals. While there are several versions of pluralism, they are united in their rejection of any concentration of power in the hands of a single *elite.* Pluralists argue that decision-makers are acted upon by many different *interest groups*, whose activities often cancel each other out, but who are attempting to influence the political powers to make policy decisions in their favor. The *state* here acts as a referee among many different groups and makes decisions in the best interests of everyone in society rather than in the interests of any consistently favored group. The concept of pluralism has been criticized because:

- it has a very narrow definition of power, restricting it to political power
- it tends to see the operation of all interest groups as equally influential, when in reality some are more powerful than others
- it neglects the ability of powerful groups to prevent controversial issues being raised in the policy-making arena in the first place.

(See *unitary elite theory.*)

pluralist theory of industrial relations: an approach to industry that sees the company as a miniature democratic state in which the opposing "parties" of management and workers seek to pursue their own interests within the limits of the rules of *collective bargaining.* Industrial relations are therefore typified by shifting alliances among various different groups within the company, who constantly maneuver for position in pursuing their own *goals.* Critics suggest that this is to ignore the historic imbalance between management and workers, in which the former can usually rely on the power of the *state* and the media to support their case.

polarization: the process whereby opposites are driven further and further apart. It is particularly applied by Marxists to *social classes*, which they believe become more and more divided from each other by the logic of machine production. *Marx* believed that the owners of the *means of production* were forced by the logic of *capitalism* to increase the *exploitation* of the *proletariat* in order to maximize profits. The proletariat responds to this increase in expropriation by rejecting capitalism altogether and looking for revolutionary alternatives. (See *immiseration*.)

political correctness: a popular term for an attitude of mind focused on attempts to eliminate discrimination on the grounds of gender, ethnicity, ability, or sexuality in word and deed.

political culture: the ideas and beliefs that underpin and inform the political system in a society. Sociologists have distinguished among different types of political culture, from the authoritarian to the democratic. The development of political cultures is continuous, often taking long periods to emerge and under constant change. However, at certain times in a society's history, the political culture may change rapidly through revolutionary events.

political deference: an acceptance of the legitimacy of the government whatever its political complexion. The most common example of this type of deference is toward the President of the US, which declined under the unprecedented personal attacks on President Clinton. (See *ascriptive sociopolitical deference; sociocultural deference*.)

political identification: a term used to describe the situation where individuals strongly support a particular *political party*. When the political identification of a social group is strong (for example, such as when the working class identifies with left-wing parties and the middle class with right-wing parties) alignment is said to take place. (See *class dealignment; partisan dealignment*.)

political immunization: a term to explain the situation where the older generation is proportionately more conservative in politics, not simply because they are older but because of political influences when they were young. The theory suggests that political ideas formed in youth are held fairly constantly into old age, being immune to alternative influences. Therefore it is important in explaining any generation's political preferences to examine the situation that existed when they were young. (See *political senescence*.)

political participation: the involvement of individuals and groups in a number of electoral situations and organizations concerned with *power*. The level of participation is said to be lower among women and the young, as measured by the propensity to vote, join, be active in political organizations, and stand for election.

political party: an organization of individuals united in a common purpose of electing representatives to a *government* who will introduce policies that the party supports. Political parties are therefore organized "appetites for power" that encompass coalitions of individuals with different ideas, but who usually agree upon a principle of politics. These principles are often symbolic or encapsulated in vague concepts such as "freedom" or "socialism."

political power: decision-making capacity that is held by those occupying positions in the machinery of *government*, either at the national or the local level. (See *economic power; institutional power*.)

political senescence: a term to describe the phenomenon where as people become older, they become more conservative. This drift to the right is often associated with nostalgic longing for a supposed golden age in the past. The idea has been criticized as a static analysis of voting, which is based on the study of specific older generations rather than all old people through time. Analysis of voting behavior does, however, show different patterns among different age groups. (See *political immunization*.)

political socialization: the process whereby individuals are initiated into the dominant values and traditions of a society, including those values that define the legitimate processes of politics and the way that *power* is exercised. While the family is the main agent of political socialization, there is little overt indoctrination into political traditions. Rather, the traditions and *values* of a society are absorbed through the expression of general sentiments toward political symbols and personalities.

politics: is in a narrow sense the workings of the *state*, including the operation of national and local *government*. However, in a wider sense politics are concerned with *power* and the ways in which individuals, groups, and organizations are able to create history through the application of power.

polity: a political unit, usually the *state*. The term is taken from the Greek word for city-state, which was the important political unit in ancient Greece.

polyandry: a rare form of marriage in which women are legally permitted more than one husband at a time. (See *polygamy; polygyny*.)

polyarchy: where power is dispersed and political decisions are arrived at through the interaction of many formal and informal groupings and organizations. It is associated with *pluralism.*

polygamy: a form of marriage that allows more than one legal spouse at a time. (See *monogamy; polyandry; polygyny*.)

polygyny: a form of marriage in which men are legally allowed more than one wife at a time. This is the more usual form of *polygamy*. The balance between the sexes means that in polygynous societies few men have more than two wives and, of course, some men have none. (See *polyandry*.)

polysemic: a term used to denote that texts are open to many differing *audience* interpretations, and that their meaning also shifts over time. This is important, for example, where new producers reinterpret classic texts, such as the works of Shakespeare. Changing fashions and ideas constantly affect the *meanings* attached to the same words; for example, the line between pornography and eroticism is constantly shifting. (See *decoding; encoding*.)

polytheism: a religious belief that accepts the notion that there is not one, but many gods. *Hinduism* is an example of a polytheistic religion. (See *monotheism*.)

popular culture: a term used by sociologists to describe the mass features of culture, particularly as communicated by the media, in postmodern societies. It is often considered in contrast to *high culture*, which is generally supported by an *elite* and does not, unlike popular culture, appeal to the taste of the masses. The study of popular culture has been adopted by postmodernists, who have detached it from its reputation as an inferior form and made it an important focus for sociological study in its own right.

population: the number of residents of a defined geographical area. In 1790, the year of the first US census, the population of the US was about 4 million. By 2000, the estimated population was 275 million. (See *aging population*; *migration*; *survey population*.)

population theory: a theory that identifies population growth as the main cause of *third-world* poverty. Due to Western medical advances, the *death rate* is falling in the third world, while the *birth rate* remains relatively high. As a result, population theorists argue that the increase in population in the third world hinders *development*, as resources are channeled into *welfare* policies rather than development projects. Despite the diversion of resources into welfare, population growth is said to outstrip the ability of the third world to produce enough food to feed its population, with the result that starvation and occasional famine result. The policy implications of this approach are that birth-control measures are needed in the third world, regardless of cultural or moral objections. Critics of this theory come from both the *New Right* and the Left. New Right theorists argue that population growth is, by itself, not the problem. They suggest that history tells us that development reduces the rate of population growth, and therefore there should be a deregulation of *capitalism* in the third world to allow for rapid development. This would then solve the population problem. Such an approach is particularly to be found among the *new Christian right*, who are hostile to *abortion* and, in some cases, suspicious of artificial birth-control methods. From the Left, conflict theorists argue that it is not the size of the third-world population that is the problem, because it consumes a minority of the world's resources. Rather, it is the consumption patterns of the developed world, with its emphasis on environmentally costly meat, that leads to periodic shortages in the third world.

populism: a political philosophy that appeals to the mass of the people as the source of all authority. Populist movements oppose the status quo and the governing *elite* and are often nostalgic and nationalistic in approach.

positive abstention: a term to describe those who do not vote in elections because of a definite decision to withhold support. This may be because of dislike of a particular candidate, a protest against a particular policy, or a simple disenchantment with the whole democratic process. (See *negative abstention*.)

positive correlation: see *correlation*

positive discrimination: measures in society designed to boost the prospects of disadvantaged groups through, for example, special programs in employment, housing, or education. It has been the subject of great controversy, and has been criticized both by disgruntled members of the "majority" (such as white males) and by members of minority groups who find the notion of making special allowances demeaning and intrinsically unfair. (See *affirmative action*; *whitelash*.)

positive stage: the ultimate stage in *Comte*'s three stages of human development, characterized by ideas that the natural and social worlds could be explained through rational thought and the application of scientific principles. Comte believed that by knowing things positively, people could control and shape the world for the better. (See *metaphysical stage*; *theological stage*.)

positivism: the view that phenomena, of whatever description, should be studied in a scientific manner. The insistence on science stems from the attempt by thinkers to find out things for certain. The search for certainty comes from the desire to be able to change things for the better. Thus, sociological positivists argue that, by applying scientific principles of research to the study of society, sociologists will be able to put forward proposals for social change that will lead to a better society. Critics argue that this is untrue, because science cannot help with the moral choices that social change necessarily involves. Positivism has also been attacked from a number of other positions:

- that science itself is not as objective as it claims, and its "truths" are as ideologically tainted as other systems of thought
- that positivism has not lived up to its promise in sociology, in that universal laws have not been developed
- that positivism is not an appropriate vehicle for the study of human society, because humans have free will and are not subject to invariate laws.

postal questionnaires: printed *questionnaires* sent to *respondents* through the mail, as opposed to questions being asked directly by an interviewer. Postal questionnaires, or mail questionnaires, have the obvious advantage of being relatively cheap, and provide a useful method where the *sample* may be distributed over a very wide geographical area. They are also helpful if the answers need reflection, or if the information needs to be looked up. As there is no one asking the questions, there can be no question of interviewer *bias*. However, postal questionnaires also have significant drawbacks. The main ones are:

- There is generally a low *response rate*, sometimes as low as 20%; this, of course, significantly affects the randomness, and therefore the *reliability*, of the sample.
- There is often a long time span between the first and the last questionnaires received back; this again can introduce bias, as those completing their forms later will have been exposed to information and events not experienced by the early returners.
- There is no guarantee that the questions have been answered by the selected respondent; he or she may have consulted with others, or even given the questionnaire to someone else to complete.

Nevertheless, postal questionnaires can form a useful method of research, particularly in research studies among groups of people who may be difficult to reach by other methods, or who may not have the time to answer questions when an interviewer calls.

postcapitalism: an assumed development in the future in which a nonsocialist state will emerge, in which the historic conflict between capital and labor is put to one side and a new sense of unity, based upon the acceptance of the free market as the good society in action, will be the defining characteristic.

postcolonial pedagogy: in education, the idea that those who are victims of racist practices and ideology should be developing in an active way the teaching approaches to racist patterns of behavior in the classroom. This would empower disadvantaged groups by allowing them to speak with their own voice. It has been criticized for being at a high level of abstraction, with very little to offer in the way of practical strategies to challenge racist behavior and ideas.

postfeminism: the fragmenting of the feminist movement into strands divided by particular identities, either political (as with socialist feminists), cultural (as with black feminists), or sexual (as with lesbian feminists). Behind this fracturing is a rejection of the idea that there is only one way to be a feminist woman in postmodern societies. Rather, the emphasis in postfeminism is on the many different ways in which women can construct their identities drawing upon a whole range of *gender codes*.

post-Fordism: in contrast to *Fordism*, the organization of production in a flexible and responsive way, so that constantly changing consumer demands can be met swiftly. Post-Fordism relies on computer technologies to produce and therefore there is a change in the type of worker needed by industry. Workers in a post-Fordist factory need to be flexible and multiskilled, not resistant to changes in productive practice.

postimperialism: the situation that emerged after the liberation of the colonies of the West, in which the exploitative relationships between colonizer and colonized were replaced by the beneficial development activities of the *multinational companies*. The term postimperialism tends to be used in contrast to *dependency theory*, which sees the continuation of exploitation after colonialism by less direct means.

postindustrial society: a term developed by Bell to suggest a new type of society emerging from industrial societies, characterized by the *professionalization of everyone*. In Bell's view, industrial societies have been changing under the impact of new technologies, and a new society that is predominantly *white-collar* has been developing. An implication of a postindustrial society is the end of class-based *conflict* and the emergence of a more unified, status-differentiated society. Other terms associated with the postindustrial society are Lane's *knowledgeable society* and Etzioni's *active society*. These convey the prominent position given to the *professions* in the postindustrial society, which Bell also characterized as the "expert society."

postmodernism: an approach in sociology, as well as other disciplines, that stresses the uncertain nature of societies. It considers a world in which all certainties have been challenged and undermined, so that the conditions of lived existence occur in a global and fractured society where there are no absolute rules or explanations. Postmodernism stands in contrast to most other sociological theories in that it rejects *Enlightenment* ideas of seeking to understand and control society through the application of rational thought. To the postmodernist, societies cannot be understood in a rational way, because they are subject to constant change.

postmodernity: the condition of Western society at present, represented by the dissolving of all certainty in *social structures*, as the temporal and spatial boundaries that define modernity breakdown and are replaced by fluid and fractured social relationships. The growth of a global economy and culture are central to the postmodern condition, where global events have local effects and vice versa. (See *modernity*.)

postsocialist societies: a term referring to the former communist states in eastern Europe and the Soviet Union, who have abandoned socialist planning in favor of more capitalist economic practices. They are characterized by dismemberment of constituent nationalities into separate nation-states, for example the Czech Republic and Slovakia. Not all these societies have embraced capitalism and democracy with the same enthusiasm.

poststructuralism: theories that reject the idea of any underlying logic or structure in the social world. As far as the poststructuralists are concerned there is only the surface world, with no hidden depths. The proper study for sociology is therefore the world as it is experienced rather than some hypothetical underlying stratum. (See *structuralism.*)

potlatch: a form of ritual and competitive gift-exchange found among indigenous people of the North American Pacific, which developed to the stage where huge quantities of possessions were ceremonially destroyed as a demonstration of wealth before rivals. These would then reciprocate with displays of their own. The economic value of possessions was therefore considered less important than the pursuit of social *status*. It has been suggested that potlatch was a response to a period of rapid social and economic change among the participating peoples.

poverty: a state in which, for an individual or a family, there is either a lack of resources sufficient to maintain a healthy existence (i.e. *absolute poverty*) or a lack of resources sufficient to achieve a standard of living considered acceptable in that particular society (i.e. *relative poverty*). Poverty is a very controversial concept and sociologists fail to agree on either its definition or on how it should be measured.

poverty cycle: an explanation of how *poverty* may be transmitted from one generation to the next, suggesting that one aspect of poverty leads to another, with the cycle repeating itself in succeeding generations.

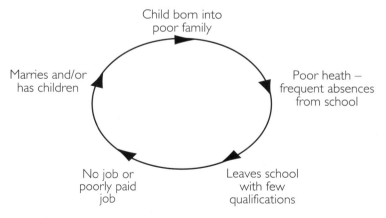

Representation of the poverty cycle

Some critics of this view regard it as overly deterministic, and point out that it is possible for children from poor households to escape from poverty, often through educational success. However, few would disagree that the material deprivations of poverty make it more difficult for such children to succeed at school and in the job market than it is for their peers from more privileged backgrounds. Supporters of the view argue that it shows clearly the need for more generous benefits for impoverished households, particularly those with young children. (See *poverty trap.*)

poverty line: a level of *income* below which an individual or household is deemed to be in poverty. The concept is a controversial one, as it is almost impossible to achieve a consensus regarding what the chosen level of income should be in various societies. In the US, the federal government defines the poverty line according to various needs such as housing, food, and medical care, that are required to achieve a basic standard of living. (See *consensual view of need; index of deprivation.*)

poverty of lifestyle: a way of defining and measuring poverty that tries to take into account the actual quality of life possible on a certain level of *income*, rather than simply taking the amount of money available. (See *consensual view of need; index of deprivation; poverty line; relative poverty.*)

poverty trap: a situation in which a number of factors combine to prevent a person or household from escaping from poverty. Such factors include:

- low-paid workers obtaining a pay raise may discover that this brings them into a new tax bracket, leaving them with the same income as before
- the lack of any sizable disposable income results in the poor buying goods in smaller quantities, losing the benefits of bulk-buying, and lack of transportation often prevents them from using cheaper out-of-town superstores
- it is very easy to fall into debt, and a fixed, low income makes it very difficult to clear the debt
- the poor often borrow their money from private "loan sharks," who may charge an exorbitant rate of interest
- poverty leads to ill-health, making it more difficult to find and keep employment.

power: the ability of an individual or group to achieve their own aims against opposition. There are many different forms of power, but it is a basic dimension of social *stratification*. The distribution of power in society is a matter of debate among sociologists, with some arguing that there is a concentration of power at the top of society and others arguing that there is a widespread distribution in society. Power is not just confined to the formal political arrangements but exists wherever there are relationships between individuals, for example between a cohabiting couple.

power elite: the group believed by unitary *elite* theorists to dominate society, through their ability to control the important institutional positions in society. The elite is composed of those at the top of the great institutions of society, such as the *government,* the military, universities, industry, etc. The power elite hold broadly similar views and share similar interests, so that policy decisions are made in their favor. They also have considerable influence over access to elite positions, so that they can pass on their privileges. The notion has been criticized by Marxists as denying the importance of economic power in society and by pluralists for assuming that there is some sort of gigantic conspiracy going on. (See *pluralism; ruling class.*)

power model: a *frame of reference* in which the holder views society in terms of "them" and "us." It is a dichotomous model of society often held by traditional proletarians in the *working class*. Oppositional in outlook, the power model is based on a view of society as primarily a class-divided society. (See *pecuniary model; prestige model*.)

powerlessness: one of the conditions of *alienation* identified by Blauner as the inability to control one's own work. This has several dimensions, including the inability to influence management decisions, to determine the conditions of work, or to control the pace of work. (See *isolation; meaningless; self-estrangement*.)

practical consciousness: our knowledge of social conventions and rules that we enact, even where we cannot articulate them. We thus speak grammatically without being able to explain the rules of grammar to one another, because of our practical consciousness. (See *discursive consciousness; unconscious motivation*.)

practical constraints: factors that may influence, or even prevent, the use of a particular sociological method. Practical constraints would include time, money, ease of access to those the researcher wishes to study, and the amount and source of funding. Gender and age can also act as constraints; in certain research situations a woman can go and ask questions in places a man could not, and vice versa. Some covert *participant observation*, such as that involving teenage gangs, would be difficult for an older sociologist to conduct, unless a suitable *role* could be found. (See *ethical constraints*.)

practical reasoning: a term used by ethnomethodologists in connection with scientific inquiry, to suggest that scientists do not just produce theories separate from their everyday practices, but within their own specific social contexts. Scientists are therefore said by ethnomethodologists to be nonobjective in their scientific work. Science is produced through the grounded experience of scientists and not as an objective process.

practical theorists: a term used by ethnomethodologists to indicate that everyone in society is essentially a sociologist in his or her everyday life, because we are constantly trying to understand and explain the social world that is going on around us. Because ethnomethodologists believe there are few, if any, common understandings among people, social life is a constant struggle to understand one another. It is this search for meaning that makes us all theorists of the practical world. (See *ethnomethodology; glossing; indexicality*.)

pragmatism theory: an explanation of *industrial relations* that looks for commonsense solutions to any problems. In identifying fair solutions to industrial problems it tends to draw upon management's perspectives, which are defined as:

- how to better utilize labor
- how to curb unofficial *strikes*
- how to control shop stewards.

praxis: in Marxist sociology, the unity of theory and practice. Marxists use praxis to describe the freedom of men and women to alter their real circumstances by the working through of ideas in the material world. Given the economic determinism of Marxism, however, priority is given in praxis to the real material circumstances that people find themselves in rather than to the ideas they hold. Attempts to change economic circumstances therefore come out of those economic circumstances. Ideas about change are not "free-floating" but socially constructed in the economic milieu that individuals inhabit.

preconditions for takeoff: a phrase used by Rostow to define the situation that *undeveloped societies* need to obtain before they can make the transformation to a developed state. The crucial elements of the preconditions relate to the agricultural sector, which must be reorganized to generate a surplus for investment in the industrial sector. A transportation system must also be developed, able to deal with the demands of an industrializing society. In some countries, this might be the development of a canal system, for instance, while in other societies it might be roads, rail, or river transportation. (See *five stages of economic growth*; *takeoff*.)

preindustrial societies: a general term for those societies that have not undergone an *Industrial Revolution* and remain agriculturally based, more specifically used to refer to societies in the past than to societies in the present day. Sociologists argue that the transformation that *industrialization* effected meant that there was a contrast between preindustrial and industrial societies in many areas of social life, which could be described by a series of dichotomies. Therefore the notion of a preindustrial society is important for the contrast it provides with an industrial one, rather than in its own right.

pressure group: an organization formed for the purpose of influencing the political process, either through the defense of members' interests or in the pursuit of particular policy. It thus represents sectional interests to the decision-making centers of government. Pressure groups are a central part of the democratic process, as they act as a channel of communication between the governed and the governors. The crucial difference between *political parties* and pressure groups is that the latter do not seek election. Rather, they seek to influence the outcome of elections by supplying information to the electorate and then trying to influence those elected through lobbying.

prestige: in sociology, a term usually attached to occupations and used to describe the honor attached by society to a particular job. Occupational prestige is associated with the functionalist perspective, which sees it as a basic dimension of *stratification* in highly specialized societies. The particular prestige attached to any job is determined by the *values* in society and by its functional importance in contributing to the maintenance of society as a whole. In operational terms, prestige is usually ascertained by asking *representative samples* of the population to place a list of occupations in rank order of importance. Those ranked most highly are given the highest prestige and those at the bottom the lowest. Critics of the concept suggest three problems with it:

- Prestige scales usually end up as a defense of the *status quo*, because people in the sample already have the existing rank order in their heads. This is why different groups produce very similar rank orders. It is not because there is some inherent merit in these occupations, but because they are already defined as worthy.
- The use of prestige is often vague and encompasses many other indicators of class, such as *income*.

- In building a prestige scale individuals tend to privilege their own and similar occupations, so that any sample bias is inevitably exaggerating the importance of particular groups of jobs.

prestige model: a *frame of reference* in which the holder sees society as divided into many layers of differentiated *status groups*. It is usually associated with the *middle class* and the attitude that sees society as relatively open, with those at the top of society deserving their positions on account of their merit or *talent*. (See *meritocracy; pecuniary model; power model.*)

primary data: in sociology, information collected by the sociologist at first hand, using any appropriate method.

primary definers: those individuals whose powerful position in society allows them better access to the media than those in other groups, and whose views, therefore, are more likely to be propagated by the media. (See *hierarchies of credibility.*)

primary deviance: identified by Lemert as the initial deviant act, which may or may not be noticed by others, and which may or may not be subsequently processed as a deviant act by the forces of formal or informal *social control.* (See *secondary deviance.*)

primary health care: health care delivered directly to the client in the community. The care is usually delivered by a physician who acts as "gatekeeper" to more specialized health care.

primary labor market: see *internal labor market*

primary poverty: see *Rowntree, Benjamin Seebohm*

primary sector: in the *occupational structure*, a term encompassing high-wage jobs with good job security, such as in unionized industries. (See *secondary sector; tertiary sector.*)

primary socialization: the learning of *values* and forms of behavior in the frontline agency of the family. It is usually associated with the acquisition of basic attitudes and social skills, which form the foundation of civilized living.

primogeniture: a system of inheritance in which the eldest male inherits the family property and title, if any. It is largely associated with the Salic laws of western Europe that were dominant in pre-20th-century Europe. More recent notions of inheritance have included all sons and daughters within their regulations.

private sector: a term to indicate those industrial and service activities that are funded for profit by private individuals or private organizations. (See *privatization.*)

private sphere: a term used by many feminists to indicate the world of domesticity, with which women have ideologically been identified. Feminists have used the concept to show how women have been marginalized in society, through their association with the private rather than the public domain. Though neither the private nor the *public sphere* is the sole domain of either gender, it is the ideological link that has led to the invisibility of women.

privatization: the process, usually as a result of government policy, of reducing the *public sector* as much as possible, through the transfer of industries, activities, and utilities to private ownership. The aim of the policy is to reduce the burden on public finances and introduce the disciplines of private enterprise into what were previously seen as public industries. Critics have argued that it can result in the creation of private monopolies, with price increases beyond those that might have been expected if industries and utilities had remained in public hands, and without any efficiency gains for the consumer. (See *nationalization.*)

privatized working class: a class identified by Goldthorpe and Lockwood as a distinct section of the *working class* in postwar affluent Britain, whose members had withdrawn from public political activity into home and child-centered activities. As work became less salient for the privatized working class, they retreated into their homes and were less likely to spend leisure time with their workmates. This shift toward the home was accompanied by an increase in home-improvement activities and an increase in the consumption of domestic goods. (See *affluent worker.*)

probability: a statistical term referring to the mathematically calculated chance of a particular event occurring.

probability sampling: a sampling technique in which every unit in the *survey population* has a known chance of being selected.

problem of consciousness: in Marxist sociology, the gap between the objective material conditions of the class and the subjective manifestations in the minds of members of the class. Though members of the *working class* exist in a state of exploitation, in which they are denied their basic humanity, this does not lead inevitably to a revolutionary outlook. *Marx* argued that there were several reasons why there is no inevitability of revolutionary consciousness among members of the working class:

- Within the working class, there are differences in objective material conditions, from the large impersonal factory to the small workshop, in which the worker has personal contact with the capitalist.
- The chances of individual *upward social mobility* drain off the most able of the working class, defusing their revolutionary potential.
- The *ruling class* uses ideological power to consolidate its rule.
- The working class can wrest concessions from the ruling class, which allows an acceptance of the system through an alleviation of *exploitation.*

problem of order: a philosophical problem that asks the question why people obey the state when their natural instinct is to gratify their own desires at any cost. The problem is that if individuals are interested only in themselves, why do they then form a society in which their individual passions are curbed by law and government force? (See *state of nature.*)

productivity: in economic terms, output produced per worker, but in sociological terms, a key *concept* underlying much of the work done in industrial sociology. Many industrial sociologists have been employed by industry to research ways of increasing productivity. For example, *work motivation theories* are based on the premise that if sociologists could uncover what makes workers happy, they could contribute to increasing productivity in the industry. (See *cow sociology.*)

profane: secular and nonsacred; in sociology, part of a dichotomy suggested by *Durkheim*, in which everything in a society can be viewed as either *sacred* or profane. Things deemed "set apart and forbidden" were defined by Durkheim as "sacred;"

everything else in society was therefore profane. This distinction has been criticized as overly simplistic.

professional associations: the organizations that govern and control those occupational groups that have been granted professional *autonomy*. Though the professional associations have very similar attributes to *labor unions*, in that they defend and promote their members' interests, Millerson argued that they are multifunctional compared to the single function of unions. In particular, professional associations have a different ideological basis from labor unions and adopt different tactics to pursue their aims. Thus, professional associations use *certification* to enhance prestige, while labor unions often use industrial action to achieve their goals. (See *social closure.*)

professional authority: authority based on the respect and acceptance that the public give to members of the *professions* on the basis of their superior knowledge and expertise in a particular area. Professional authority is the reason why professionals are listened to and their advice taken. Their knowledge-base is such that professional advice is more likely to be effective in solving problems than lay knowledge. This does not mean that professional authority is unchallengeable, but that professionals will usually be listened to with respect. *Clients* may challenge professional authority publicly through the professional body or by changing their practitioner.

professional crime: lawbreaking committed by individuals and gangs for whom crime is a way of life. Professional crime is actually responsible for a small percentage of total criminal activity, but represents one of the most visible and newsworthy aspects. (See *street crime.*)

professional employees: a term developed to describe the position of those members of the traditional *professions* who are also employed in bureaucracies. Sociologists suggest that this position creates problems for the traditional professional. For example, professional behavior is theoretically governed by the code of ethics of the profession. Yet, in a *bureaucracy* the professional is also subject to the rules and discipline of the employer. These can sometimes be in conflict.

professionalization: the process whereby an occupational group seeks to obtain professional powers for itself. Professionalization is one of the ways in which *upward social mobility* is sought, and along with it, increased earnings and *status*. The process is particularly used by those occupational groups that have an individual skill to offer society, or esoteric knowledge supported by a theoretical framework. (See *social closure.*)

professionalization of everyone: a term to describe a hypothetical future for work, in which all workers have the skills, training, and rewards associated with today's *professions*. Friedman, for example, argued that as the manual labor force declined through *automation*, there would be a growth in knowledge-based service industries. Manufacturing itself would be dependent on skilled engineers and scientists, rather than routinized manual labor. Friedman argued that the large professionalized sector would be the new power in *organizations* and challenge *management*. Because of their knowledge, these professions would be able to resist *bureaucratization* and would generate *organic solidarity*, ushering in a new era of prosperity and freedom. Critics argued that this was an optimistic view of the future and that *automation* does not leave the professions untouched. Indeed, the processes of *fragmentation* and *routinization* affect all occupational groups and will change the traditional professions as much as *deskilling* manual work. (See *deprofessionalization*.)

professions: types of occupation, such as law and medicine, that are self-governing, in that the representatives of the members of the occupation set the regulations governing the behavior of members. It is difficult to define a profession exactly as there is so much variation among different professions. However, most professions have the following characteristics:

- Their skills are supported by a systematic body of knowledge.
- Their possession of this knowledge gives them *authority* over clients, who do not possess the knowledge.
- The profession is given certain privileges by the community, such as the duty of confidentiality and the right to be judged only by other professionals.
- Their behavior is regulated by a code of ethics.
- There is also a professional *culture* in which the professional is given certain *status* and symbols of authority.

A crucial aspect of a profession, as against other occupations, is that it is granted powers not usually given to other jobs, such as the power to regulate entry to the profession, and to carry out the long training needed to give practitioners the knowledge they need to practice effectively. (See *semiprofessions*.)

progress: the movement toward a better existence in society. The idea of progress was a central feature of the work of the *classical sociologists* and of the sociological project. Progress was seen as the outcome of sociological examination of the social world, as people came to understand and therefore control the forces at work in society. The concept has come under attack by postmodernists for being based on a particular ideological view of history and for being hopelessly optimistic.

progressive taxation: *direct taxation*, such as income tax, based on the principle that the more *income* or *wealth* one has, the more tax one pays. Progressive taxation is one of the ways in which a society may achieve a greater equality of distribution of income and wealth. (See *regressive taxation*.)

progressive teaching: see *discovery learning*, *experiential teaching*, *pedagogy*

proletarianization: the process whereby *nonmanual work* comes increasingly to resemble *manual work*, and nonmanual workers adopt the attitudes of the *working class*. The concept is applied to a wide range of white-collar and professional occupations, but has specifically been employed in considering the changes in clerical work since the 19th century. The evidence used to support the idea of proletarianization includes the greater unionization of *white-collar workers* and their willingness to employ labor union tactics traditionally associated with manual workers. The causes of proletarianization are many and varied, and include greater *bureaucratization* of work, the *deskilling* of work through computerization, and the emergence of universal literacy, which has destroyed the esoteric nature of clerical work. The concept of proletarianization has been much criticized for oversimplifying social processes by equating changes in working conditions to changes in consciousness. It also denies the power of *status* considerations holding sway over white-collar workers.

proletarianization of the professional: a concept developed by Oppenheimer, who argued that the *bureaucratization* of work inevitably leads to a deterioration in working conditions for professionals, until they are subject to the same work discipline as manual workers. Features of bureaucracies that lead to proletarianization are:

- the replication of factory conditions for professionals, such as the imposition of hierarchy, the establishment of bureaucratic rules, and crucially, increased specialization of tasks
- control over work increasingly removed from the professional
- financial and status advantages eroded as bureaucracies operate within strict budgets
- bureaucrats rather than professionals increasingly determining treatment.

The main result of proletarianization is the increasing *unionization* of the professions. (See *deprofessionalization*.)

proletariat: one of *Marx*'s major classes in capitalist societies, technically including all those who do not own the *means of production*. Because this definition would also include some members of what is seen as the traditional *middle class*, it has been criticized for providing a very crude division of society. It is therefore used mainly to describe the *working class* (that is, manual workers), especially when it is used in a political sense. Marx believed that it would be members of the proletariat who would bring about revolutionary change in society, as they resolved the contradictions inherent in capitalist societies.

promotional pressure group: an organization formed to promote a particular interest or cause through political lobbying and informing the general public about the issue. These groups tend to be proactive and seek to effect change that they see as beneficial to their particular cause. (See *protective pressure group*.)

proportional representation: an electoral system in which the ratio of members of a legislature matches the percentage of the vote that each political party attracts. While this is said to be a fairer system than one of election by numerical majority, it tends to lead to a proliferation of smaller parties and to potentially unstable coalition governments.

protective pressure group: an organization formed to defend its members' interests in dealing with political organizations. Such groups would include *labor unions*, professional associations, and the like. They tend to be defensive organizations reacting to events rather than promoting a particular course of action. (See *promotional pressure group*.)

Protestant ethic: a term used in particular by *Weber* to refer to a set of beliefs especially associated with the Calvinist religious *sect* in the 17th century. Weber was interested in exploring the origins of the "ethic" of *capitalism*, and suggested that these lay in the beliefs of the Calvinists. According to these, worldly work was seen as a "calling," rather like a religious vocation, and it was therefore a duty to treat work as a way of honoring God. The Calvinists believed in predestination, that is, that from the point of creation, God had chosen those who would be "saved." As there was no way in which these decisions could be changed, and no way of knowing in this life whether or not one was among the chosen, Calvinists began to seek signs of God's favor in their lives. Worldly success was seen as a sign of "election" to the chosen. Emphasis was placed on a sober, thrifty lifestyle, and on the "stewardship" of goods rather than their use in displays of *conspicuous consumption*, thereby supporting a belief in *deferred gratification* in the form of the reinvestment of profit rather than expenditure on worldly goods. Weber argued that this particular set of beliefs, and the consequences stemming from them, provided the right social and economic climate for the development of what he called "modern capitalism." Weber used his argument about the relationship between the Protestant ethic and the "*spirit of capitalism*" to show that, under certain circumstances, religious belief could be instrumental in bringing about *social change*, and was not necessarily, as *Marx* had claimed, a conservative force in society. However, Weber's views have been criticized, and a 1959 study of the origins of Calvinism in the Zurich Reformation shows that modern capitalism appears to have already been in existence at the time. Nevertheless, Weber's views form an important part of the debate regarding the role of *religion* in society.

prototypicality: a methodological term, suggesting that the *sample* under study by the sociologist points the way to how similar groups will behave in the future. The most famous prototypical research was carried out in Britain on *affluent workers* by Goldthorpe and Lockwood. They argued that the workers in a large town were at the cutting edge of societal developments and that the consciousness they exhibited would be the consciousness that all affluent workers would eventually develop.

prudent sociability: according to Goffman the basis of morality. It is also known as "tact" and implies a calculation of the most careful course of action before an *actor* acts.

prudential interest theory: an answer to the *problem of order*, a theory that states that it is in people's self-interest to come into society for mutual protection against the cruelty of nature. It is thus a rational calculation of individuals to form social order. (See *competitive interest theory*.)

psephology: the study of voting behavior.

pseudopressure group: an organization that exerts political pressure on behalf of others, rather than in its own right. Political lobbying organizations are pseudo-pressure groups since they are paid by others to try to influence political outcomes regardless of their own particular beliefs.

public ownership: see *nationalization*

public sector: a term to describe those activities that are organized and funded by national and local governments. Apart from the direct activities of the *state*, such as welfare provision, the public sector can also include nationalized industries and an important section of the housing industry. *Privatization* of industries and utilities, a decline in government housing, and the tendering out of traditional state activities has led to a decline in the public sector in many modern societies. (See *private sector*.)

public sphere: a term used by feminists to indicate the world beyond the home, of paid employment, politics, religion, and other public activities. It is identified by feminists as a mainly gendered sphere, in which men dominate and in which women are tolerated at best. (See *private sphere.*)

pure deviant: a term used by Becker to define one who engages in rule-breaking activity and who is also publicly labeled as such. (See *falsely accused; secret deviant.*)

purposive action: doing something with an aim in mind, and the distinguishing feature of *action* as opposed to behavior. Action theory defines action strictly in this way so that instinctive behavior is not included. Interactionists believe that to understand action it is important to access the intentions of the person carrying out the action.

Pygmalion effect: the way in which expectations and consistent behavior by social actors can shape the behavior of others in social relationships to produce a new situation. The term refers to the play *Pygmalion*, by G.B. Shaw, in which a Cockney flower-seller is passed off as a duchess. Its use in education is taken from a study by Rosenthal and Jacobson of an American elementary school, entitled "Pygmalion in the Classroom." Having tested all the children's *IQs*, the researchers selected a *sample* of children at random, and informed the teachers that these were children of high academic potential. A year later, Rosenthal and Jacobsen returned and again tested the children's IQs, finding that those in the randomly selected sample had, on average, made greater gains in IQ score than the nonsample children. A similar interpretation of the importance of teachers' expectations can be placed on findings from Douglas' longitudinal study, in which children of the same measured IQ at 8 years of age showed improved scores at age 11 if they had been taught in upper streams, and lower scores at age 11 if they had been taught in lower streams. It was also used by Barnard in the sociology of the family to describe the reshaping of a woman's identity by the male, when she enters into marriage. She argued that this often leads to stress and depression as her aims are subordinated to those of her husband. (See *self-fulfilling prophecy.*)

qualitative data: data that express, usually in words, information about feelings, *values,* and attitudes. Such data are usually associated with qualitative research methods such as *participant observation, unstructured interviews,* and the use of certain kinds of *personal document,* but qualitative data may also result from *open-ended questions* used in *structured interviews* and *questionnaires.* Interactionist sociologists in particular favor the collection of qualitative data. In practice, much research contains both qualitative and *quantitative data.*

qualitative research methods: methods that will result in mainly *qualitative data.* They include *observation, participant observation,* and *unstructured interviews.* If using *secondary data,* the sociologist would be most likely to refer to *personal documents.* (See *quantitative research methods.*)

quality assurance systems: systems set up to insure that certain agreed standards of quality are met throughout an organization as a means of insuring client satisfaction.

quantitative data: data that can be expressed in numerical form, e.g. numbers, percentages, and tables. Positivist sociologists argue that the collection of quantitative data is less prone than qualitative data to *bias* arising from the subjective involvement or interpretation of the researcher. However, many interactionist sociologists claim that much quantitative data and the methods by which they are obtained, such as large-scale *social surveys* and *structured interviews,* contain both value judgments and subjective interpretations.

quantitative research methods: methods that will result in mainly *quantitative data.* They include *social surveys* and *structured interviews.* If using *secondary data,* the sociologist would be most likely to refer to *official statistics.* (See *qualitative research methods.*)

quantum theory of religion: the belief that everyone has religious feeling or a spiritual dimension that must be fulfilled by one means or another. The implication is that, if formal religions are rejected, then other *functional equivalents* are substituted. It allows no possibility that an individual might believe that no world other than the material one exists.

quasi-experimental method: see *comparative method*

questionnaire: a widely used tool in data collection, both in sociology and market research, that consists of lists of questions. The term is usually applied to formal, standardized questionnaires used in large-scale *social surveys.* The questions used may be *closed, open-ended,* or a combination of both. Where a large number of *respondents* is involved, the closed questions are likely to be precoded – that is, each possible response is given a code number, which makes it easier and quicker to process and analyze the replies. (See *coding.*)

quota sampling: a *sampling* method in which the researcher/interviewer has a list of characteristics required of *respondents,* and a given quota of each to select and interview. The usual characteristics include sex, age-bands, marital status, occupation, and/or social class, and may also include ethnic group. A researcher's quota, then, might be 50 males and 50 females; within each sex 20 manual workers, 20 white-collar workers, and 10 professional workers, and within each occupational group a given number of people in particular age-bands. Quota sampling is not properly random, and is not as reliable as *probability sampling*, particularly if the sample size is small. It is used quite widely in market research, and less so in sociology.

QWL: quality of working life. It is the focus of organizational theory in which the experiences of all participants are examined to develop more productive ways of engaging participants in fulfilling the goals of the organization. (See *job enrichment.*)

race: an imprecise term, the origins of which stemmed from a belief that it was possible to divide human populations into groups having distinct inherited physical characteristics. One view saw different racial populations as evidence of the process of evolution and natural selection, with some races being biologically more "advanced" than others. These beliefs led to the idea that biological differences were accompanied by other innate differences, such as in *intelligence* and behavior patterns. This view is now discredited, but sociologists are interested in how the concept of "race" is often used to justify the oppression of one group by another, such as the treatment of the Jews by the Nazis, or the system of apartheid in South Africa. (See *ethnicity*; *eugenics*; *racism.*)

race spies: a term used by the *New Right* to criticize teachers who adopt antiracist strategies in their classrooms, thus supposedly indicating a policing of thought and deed about racial issues that allows only the expression of *politically correct* ideas and behavior. The implication is that antiracist education is a totalitarian tool to impose a straightjacket of thought on young children.

racialization of poverty: the idea that, increasingly, ethnic minorities are over-represented among the poor in modern society, as processes such as the loss of capital investment in the inner city concentrates ethnic minorities in racially segregated areas, characterized by high levels of unemployment and poverty.

racism: beliefs or ideas about *race* that are often translated into negative feelings and discriminatory or hostile actions against members of the supposed racial group. Racism can be expressed as individual racism, such as the use of negative and abusive language or even physical assault, or institutional racism, whereby members of a group may be discriminated against, such as in access to housing or employment. (See *ethnicity*; *race.*)

radical: in politics, believing in the need for fundamental change in existing social arrangements. Though often associated with left-wing ideas, radical beliefs can be also right-wing. The former tend to support change in favor of the lower classes in society, such as redistribution measures, while the latter tend to be authoritarian and nationalistic, favoring a strong, uniform social order.

radical criminology: see *National Deviancy Conference*

radical feminism: a branch of *feminism* based on the belief that men, and the patriarchal system they have established, are the origin and perpetuators of women's oppression. Men are also seen as the main beneficiaries of this oppression, primarily through the institutions of *marriage* and the *family*. There are differences within the radical feminist perspective, ranging from a belief that women can coexist with men, provided that men are willing to overthrow *patriarchy*, to the belief that men are the "enemy" and that women can, and should, exist without them. (See *black feminism*; *liberal feminism*; *socialist feminism.*)

radical value system: that set of ideas associated with the *working class* that is oppositional to the capitalist system. The radical value system therefore seeks to change capitalism in fundamental ways and represents *class consciousness* in a traditional sense. (See *dominant value system; subordinate value system.*)

random sampling: a way of choosing a smaller number of "subjects" from a larger population, with each member of the population having an equal chance of being chosen, through the use of an unbiased selection method. Each subject in the population is given a number and then the sample is chosen by a random method. The sample is usually generated using random number tables, though picking names from a hat would also be effective. The point of using a random method is that it usually generates a group that is representative of the population as a whole. (See *survey population.*)

ranking: the placing of phenomena in a particular order; in sociology, most usually done with occupations. (See *prestige.*)

rapport: in sociological research, the feeling of identity between researcher and researched that allows for the collection of appropriate data. The ease that rapport brings to the interviewee helps the sociologist to obtain the needed information.

Rastafarians: followers of Ras Tafari Makonnen(the Emperor Haile Selassie of Ethiopia), who form an oppositional religious *subculture* that rejects white-dominated power structures, including mainstream Christianity. The outward style they adopt is distinctive both for its dreadlocks and for the use of "ganga" (cannabis), which is of religious significance to Rastafarians.

rational action: see *Zweckrational*

rational choice model: a theory of voting in which support for a party is likened to a consumer decision. The theory suggests that electors are open to rational argument, and shop around for the policies that best fit their particular interests. Parties therefore have to compete for the individual elector's vote rather than take their class-based loyalty for granted. The theory has been criticized because:

- it overemphasizes the decline of class as a predictor of voting behavior
- it overemphasizes the rationality of the electorate and underestimates their affective loyalty
- it ignores the long-term forces that shape political preferences.

(See *political participation.*)

rationality: a term used by sociologists to define a distinguishing characteristic of *modernity*, which is that actions in modern societies are governed by logic and order. So, in modern rational societies, actions are said to be governed by logical thought, in contrast to the traditional societies of the past, where actions were controlled by what had always been done. Rationality has been particularly associated with bureaucratic organizations, where the actions of members of the organization are coordinated and controlled through rules, to achieve *organizational goals* in a rational way. The analysis of rationality in sociology is particularly associated with the work of *Max Weber*, who distinguished between *Zweckrational action* and *Wertrational actions.*

rationalization: the process whereby modern societies increasingly use logic and rationality to address and solve social problems. The development of *Zweckrational* *actions* was, according to *Weber*, one of the hallmarks of modern societies, in contrast to traditional ones. Some sociologists argue that rationalization can be overstressed and that modern societies are also characterized by the irrational and affective, not just the rational.

reaction formation: a term used by Albert Cohen to explain working-class *delinquency* as a rejection of middle-class standards and the adoption of the opposite as a status game that they can win. Thus, delinquency is a reaction to the respectability and academic standing of the *middle class*, which does not allow many working-class people to succeed in mainstream society.

reaggregation of tasks: the process whereby *specialization* is reversed and routine work tasks are put back together to give more *craft* skills to workers. A group of workers therefore produces a product from start to finish, each employing many different skills. (See *detailed division of labor*.)

real rate of suicide: a term to indicate the actual number of suicides in a society rather than just the ones appearing in the *suicide* statistics. Given that we can never know whether an individual really intended to kill himself or herself, the real rate of suicide is unknowable. However, it does highlight the gap between the statistics and actual events in the real world, raising questions about the *validity* of all statistics. (See *gambles with death*.)

realignment theories: theories of social stratification based on the idea that the old class divisions are disappearing and are being replaced by new and stable divisions. For example, Rex and Moore argue that new "*housing classes*" are emerging. Others argue that consumption patterns, use of public-sector or private-sector services, or regional divisions are now more important than class divisions. (See *fragmentation*; *persistence theories*.)

realism: in sociology, the general approach that argues that social phenomena such as structures and institutions have an existence beyond the lives of the individuals that make them up. The basic premise is that social structures predate the existence of any one individual member and continue after any individual's death.

reality construction: in *phenomenology*, a term to suggest that most arenas in social life are composed of individuals seeking to understand what is going on, who therefore come to different conclusions about what is actually happening. For example, the classroom has been explored as an arena of reality-construction, with the teachers giving one account of reality and the students giving various other accounts, none of which accord with the teachers'. Each participant in the *interaction* has therefore constructed his or her own reality about it. While phenomenologists accept that there is a basic understanding among all participants, ethnomethodologists argue that there is little constancy of meaning or sharing of the same reality from one classroom situation to the next, or in the same classroom from one day to the next.

rebellion: according to Merton, a form of *deviance* that occurs when individuals reject either the cultural goals or the *institutionalized means* in society, or both. The focus of these deviants is the reconstruction of society on a different basis, substituting either new aims or means for the existing ones, or seeking to overthrow both means and goals. (See *innovation*; *retreatism*; *ritualism*.)

reception analysis: an approach to the study of the media that stresses the interpretation of media texts by those who receive them. This *active audience* does not just sit back and absorb media messages, but tries to make sense of what it sees and reads by interpreting the texts. This means that no one "receives" quite the same message from a specific text, and it cannot be guaranteed that anybody receives the message intended by those who made the media text in the first place. (See *decoding*; *encoding*.)

recession: a situation of deteriorating economic conditions, in which industrial production is in decline, *unemployment* is rising, and the economy as a whole is shrinking. Recession plays an important part in the politics of a nation, and sociologists among others have shown how the fortunes of governments are bound up with the performance of business.

reciprocity: a term closely associated with *consensus* theory to describe an interrelationship between two individuals or phenomena that involves the giving and taking of advantage and disadvantage. The classical example of reciprocity is the *gift*. Reciprocity is important in consensus theory because reciprocity involves mutual dependence, which helps to integrate individuals into the collectivity.

reconstituted family: a family in which one or both adults have been previously married, and therefore children are living with a step-parent and possibly stepbrothers and stepsisters. The relatively high rates of *divorce* and remarriage are leading to this kind of family becoming increasingly common.

reconstructed logics: a term used by Kaplan to describe the writing-up of scientific research, in which real events are squeezed into a formulaic structure of reporting. The problem of reconstructed logics is that they do not tell the whole truth about the process of scientific experimentation. They tend to ignore the things that go wrong and present a sanitized version of *methodology*. Moreover, reconstructed logics also tend to conform to the dominant way of writing scientific work at the time and therefore may vary with time. (See *logics-in-use*; *paradigm*.)

recruitment policies: policies used by companies in the process of recruiting personnel. Such policies have recently come under scrutiny, as it is alleged that many companies have a hidden recruitment policy that discriminates against certain groups. The most common forms of *discrimination* are allegedly against women, particularly mothers of young children, members of ethnic minority groups, the disabled, and those over a certain age, the last being referred to as victims of "*ageism*." Another area of concern regarding recruitment policies is the growing trend toward recruiting only part-time workers. One of the problems in investigating this area is the difficulty of proving that a company is operating a discriminatory policy.

redistribution: the process in which *income* and *wealth* are either taken from the rich through *progressive taxation* and given to the poor in the form of benefits, or taken from the poor in the form of *indirect taxation* and given to the rich, in the form of tax breaks. The issue of redistribution is a central political debate and lies at the heart of a fundamental philosophical division between those who believe in the *trickle-down effect* and those who argue for a welfare safety net.

reference group: the collectivity to which individuals or groups refer when making comparisons about their lives. Reference groups may be set up as models of behavior or as representing goals for attainment. They may be positive or negative, encompassing respectively behavior that is to be aspired to and behavior that is rejected as inappropriate. (See *relative deprivation*.)

reflexivity: also called self-reference, the ability for a subject to reflect on his/her own activities and knowledge. In sociology, reflexivity is used not just as a sociology of sociology, but also to describe the way in which individual *actors* in the social world are capable of reflecting on their own actions and ideas.

reformist feminism: see *liberal feminism*

refutation: the disproving of a *hypothesis* by the occurrence of a single event or piece of evidence. The term is closely associated with the philosopher Karl Popper, whose view of scientific knowledge was that it was always provisional – that is, it could only be counted as "true" until something occurred to show that it was not true, and it was the task of scientists to try to find evidence that would refute their hypotheses. In other words, we can only be sure of what is not true, rather than what is true. The example usually quoted in this context is that seeing one black swan refutes the hypothesis that all swans are white. (See *falsification*; *scientific revolution*.)

regression: a situation in which, as a result of frustration in work, the worker reverts to childish forms of behavior, such as pranks, to relieve the tension. On a more serious level, this can be expressed in temper tantrums or *industrial sabotage*. (See *resignation*.)

regressive taxation: taxation that, as a result of being a flat rate independent of a person's *wealth* or *income*, takes a greater proportion of the income of the poor than of the rich. (See *progressive taxation*.)

regularities: patterns of activity displayed by people carrying out their everyday activities. It is this patterned activity that is the basis of much social life and, for example, allows others to make assumptions about a person's behavior in any given situation. The existence of regularities is thus an important aspect of *calculability*.

reification: treating an abstract concept as if it had a real concrete existence. This is a common criticism of functionalist notions of society, because they argue that society has an existence "out there" beyond the sum of the individuals from which it is composed.

reinforcement theory: an approach to the media that argues that the effects of television cannot be separated from the social context of the *audience*. It rejects the view that media images directly affect the behavior of individuals. Rather, it claims that people try out what they learn from the media in their own lives and if it works, reinforcement of that behavior occurs. If the media model of behavior does not provide any satisfaction in a real situation, then it is rejected.

reintegrative shaming: the expression of disapproval of the actions of an individual by society, in such a way as to allow the labeled individual to be absorbed back into society. The end result of such shaming is a chastened deviant, who returns to the mainstream. (See *disintegrative shaming*.)

relations of production: in *Marxism*, the ways in which capitalists and workers interact with each other, in class terms. It is not usually used to describe how an individual capitalist deals with the workers he or she employs, but the ways that, for example, the *working class* reacts to the conditions of work that the employers impose on it generally. According to the Marxists, the relations between the owners and nonowners are essentially antagonistic. (See *forces of production.*)

relativ-naturliche Weltanshauung: a term used by Scheler to indicate the partial world view each individual has that is specific to them and also seems the natural way to view things. It therefore takes a leap of imagination to appreciate that another's point of view is equally natural to them. (See *Wissensociologie.*)

relative autonomy: a notion developed by Althusser to describe the relationship between the base and superstructure in Marxist thought. It suggests that political and cultural forces have some degree of freedom from economic forces, although in the last analysis, politics and *culture* serve the long-term interests of the owners of the *means of production.* The problem of base–superstructure has been a central problem in Marxist sociology. *Vulgar Marxism* had assumed that the social totality was an expressive totality, in that all superstructural phenomena, such as politics or culture, were determined directly by economic forces. Althusser rejected this and argued that economic reality might dictate that the political and cultural spheres of society could be given real freedom to act, for example, to insure the long-term survival of the capitalist system against the short-term economic interests of the capitalist class at any moment in time. However, the freedom of the political and cultural spheres was a qualified one. They were free to act, but only in the long-term interests of capitalism. The idea has been criticized for being contradictory, in that the freedom to act cannot be conditional upon acting in only one direction. Critics argue that this is not freedom at all, but just a more sophisticated version of *determinism.*

relative deprivation: a situation where, when people compare themselves with other imagined or real groups, they feel that they are less well-off than they ought to be. The importance of the concept is that feelings of deprivation are not always connected to absolute standards; comparatively well-off groups can still feel deprived if they compare their situation to other slightly better-off groups. For example, Glock and Stark suggest that feelings of relative deprivation may explain why some middle-class people join *sects*, and point out that feelings of relative deprivation are not necessarily confined to economic deprivation, but may also include social, ethical, or psychic deprivation. (See *reference group.*)

relative isolation of the family: a term to describe how the weakening of wider *kinship* ties and increased *geographical mobility* have led to many contemporary families becoming both socially and geographically isolated. *Talcott Parsons* argued that the isolated *nuclear family* is the typical form in modern industrial societies. This is largely the result of the family losing many of its wider functions to other agencies, and specializing in the rearing and *socialization* of children and the stabilization of adult personalities through a close husband-and-wife relationship. Goldthorpe and Lockwood, in their 1962 Affluent Worker study in Britain, noted that married couples spent most of their *leisure* time together, and that the husbands' activities were increasingly "home-centered." They referred to this type of family as *"privatized."* It is suggested by some that the emotional stresses that may result from this isolation, particularly for mothers at home with young children, may be a factor in the breakdown of marriage. However, there are cultural variations in the relative strength of kinship ties, and it is also suggested that modern methods of communication enable family members to keep in contact even though they may live at a considerable distance. (See *kinship networks*; *loss of family functions*.)

relative poverty: the state of being poor with reference to a real, or perceived, standard of living in a society. It is very difficult to define relative poverty precisely, as standards of living vary over time and from place to place, and it is also difficult to agree on what should be the standard of living used as a reference point, and how it should be measured. (See *absolute poverty*; *consensual view of need*; *index of deprivation*; *poverty line*.)

relative rate of mobility: the amount of movement in the *class structure*, taking into account changes in the *occupational structure*, that might provide greater or fewer opportunities in particular occupational groupings. Thus, while the *absolute rate of mobility* has been high since World War II, the shift from *primary* and *secondary sector* jobs to tertiary employment has meant that the relative chances of movement have remained much the same as before 1945.

relativism: in the sociology of knowledge, the belief that all knowledge is partial and related to the position the individual holds in the social structure. Therefore, there can be no such thing as "the absolute truth." Critics suggest that if that last statement is true, then relativism is by definition itself only partially true.

reliability: a term used in connection with research methods, particularly quantitative research. Research is said to be reliable if, when repeated using exactly the same methods, it produces the same results. Positivist sociologists argue that methods such as large-scale sample surveys, yielding *quantitative data*, are more reliable than interpretative methods such as *unstructured interviews* and *participant observation*. (See *interpretative sociology*; *positivism*.)

religion: an organized expression of the perceived relationship between the *natural* and *supernatural* worlds, which usually refers to a god. In sociology, the definition of religion is not agreed upon, with different types of sociologists offering alternative views. A Durkheimian view suggests that a religion should be defined by the functions that it performs in society, in particular, the function of creating social solidarity among members of society. The problem with this definition is that since there is no reference to any god, it could include many institutions that are not usually seen as religious, such as the Communist Party in the socialist societies of eastern Europe in the postwar period. A Weberian view suggests that religion should be defined by the belief in some other level of existence beyond the real world, and that religious ceremonies are therefore an expression of the relationships between the everyday world and this higher plane of existence. A problem with this definition is that it tends to exclude certain *common-sense* definitions of "religions." The Marxist definition of religion emphasizes the role of religion as a "cloak of respectability" for the *ruling class*, who use religion as a way of controlling subordinate groups in society, through the promise of a better life in the next world and threat of damnation if subordinates rebel in this world. A problem with this approach is that it depends on religion being a conspiracy and ignores any real religious feeling.

religiosity: the sense of the religious in the individual. Functionalist sociologists see every individual as having this religious sensibility, which needs to be fulfilled in some way. Marxists tend to see religiosity as a "false need" created by society as a means of *social control*. The importance of this difference is that, if religiosity is an essential part of the individual's makeup, then religion generally cannot decline, as there will always be a need for it. If, however, religious feeling is socially created, then theoretically societies could exist without religion.

reluctant militants: a term derived by Roberts to describe *white-collar workers* who go on strike. The concept conveys the fact that white-collar workers are often reluctant to strike, associating it with lower-status *manual workers*, but can be driven to it by what they see as unfair treatment. This can be either a depression of salaries, as the economics of *recession* means that all sectors of the workforce have to accept sacrifices, or a deterioration in conditions, usually in comparison with other groups in the workforce.

remunerative power: see *utilitarian power*

replication: the exact repetition of an experiment by someone else. This can show that the results of the experiment are not just random or a fluke, but can be reproduced by other scientists. Replication is a central principle of the scientific method, because it establishes the *objectivity* of the experiments, in that they are untainted by personal preconceptions or biases. (See *hypothetico-deductive method*.)

representative democracy: a political system in which the people elect representatives who will represent them in political decision-making. The representative can be seen as having the right to express their own views about political policies or as being mandated by the electorate to carry out their collective will.

representative sample: a *sample* whose members are representative of the whole *survey population* in terms of the characteristics considered important by the researchers, (e.g. sex, age, social class, ethnic group, occupation, or marital status). As a general principle, and provided that a suitable sampling method has been used, the larger the sample as a proportion of the population, the more representative it is likely to be. Thus, if the population under consideration contained 2,500 people, a sample of 250 (1 person in 10) would be more likely to be representative than a sample of 50 (1 person in 50).

representativeness: in sociological study, the degree to which a research study group is representative of other, similar kinds of group. In some studies great care is taken to insure that the group is representative, for example by carefully drawing a *representative sample*. This is likely to be the case with a large-scale *social survey*. In other studies, greater emphasis is placed on the degree to which a whole group can be studied in depth, such as a group of students, or a group of workers, or a tribe, or members of a religious *sect*. In such cases, even though the group studied may not be exactly typical of other such groups, the researcher believes that the depth of information gained is worth the possible loss of representativeness.

repressive state apparatus: a term used by the Marxist writer Althusser to refer to the joint authority of the army, the police, and the judicial system in a capitalist state. Althusser argues that, under *capitalism*, the *bourgeoisie* will attempt to rule with the compliance of the *proletariat*, who are led to believe that capitalism is the best system under which to live – indeed, they are discouraged from seriously considering any alternatives. The belief in capitalism as a system is spread by the institutions that make up what Althusser referred to as the *ideological state apparatus*, such as *education*, *religion*, and the *mass media*. However, this *consensus* sometimes breaks down, and there is opposition to capitalism. At this point, the power of the repressive state apparatus will be used against dissidents to maintain capitalist supremacy and the power of the *ruling class*.

reproductive technologies: a general term covering a whole range of developments in the area of birth and reproduction. These include *in vitro* fertilization, fertility drugs, and possible advances in cloning. While they have some importance for issues such as the genetic engineering of vegetables and animals, sociologists and particularly postmodernists are interested in the ways that these technologies intervene between nature and humanity, divorcing the reproductive act from the process of reproduction. Feminists are also interested in the way that male science has taken control of reproduction away from women and placed it in male hands through the development of reproductive technologies.

resacrilization: a term adopted by Greely to refer to the resurgence of religious beliefs in many Western societies, particularly the US. Greely referred to this process as the "re-establishment of the sacred realm," and it is used as an argument to counter allegations that *secularization* is taking place.

reserve army of labor: a term for those groups in society who move into and out of the *labor market*, according to the demand in the economy for workers. The term was originally used by *Marx* to refer to a permanent pool of unemployed people which, he argued, *capitalism* needed to operate profitably. In contemporary usage, it is more likely to be used to refer to unskilled workers, often carrying out part-time, seasonal and temporary work as and when they are needed by companies. The most prominent component of the reserve army of labor is married women, who may or may not prefer to have a full-time occupation. Many feminists argue that the prominence of women in the reserve army of labor reflects society's *patriarchal ideology*, which sees women as only subsidiary wage-earners. Marxists draw attention to the usefulness of the reserve army of labor to the functioning of capitalism. It allows industries to recruit labor when they need it, without any long-term commitment. The reserve army can also be used, according to Marxists, as a weapon to divide and rule the working class and to break strikes if necessary. *New Right* sociologists see the reserve army of labor as an important aspect of labor flexibility in a global economy, so that companies can respond swiftly to changes in demand by employing or releasing labor.

residential zone: a term for one of Burgess' zones of the city, usually composed of high-class apartments relatively close to the center, but far enough away to be seen as a separate area. (See *urban zones theory*.)

resignation: a response to *frustration* in work, consisting of apathy and escapism. It is a consequence of the individual believing that feelings of frustration are the result of his or her own inadequacy. (See *fixation*; *regression*.)

resistance: a term used by some sociologists of *youth culture* to explain the oppositional nature of many working-class youth cultures. It suggests that these *subcultures* are formed as an expression of working-class youth's rejection of the *alienation* of capitalist societies. The stress in this ideological opposition is not on political resistance, but on a resistance through *style*, in which dress, hostile behavior patterns, music, etc. are symbolic of their oppositional stance. Critics of this idea argue that:

- It is a romantic view of working-class youth culture. White gangs beating up members of ethnic minorities is not romantic.
- The resistance element is overemphasized, with many stylistic features adopted by youth subcultures being adaptations of mainstream society.
- It ignores the fact that most working-class youths are conformist, not oppositional.

respectable working class: a group said to be found within the manual *working class,* who are set apart from other groups of workers by their habits and lifestyles. They are usually influenced by *religion* in some way and are keen to see themselves as separate from the *rough working class.* Their patterns of life often mimic middle-class lifestyles in certain ways, with an emphasis on a good reputation in the community. (See *aristocracy of labor.*)

respondents: those who provide information for research purposes by answering questions. The term is usually applied to those taking part in *social surveys* and *interviews.* (See *response rate.*)

response rate: the proportion of responses obtained out of the *sample* in a piece of research. Different research methods vary in their likely response rates. Research using *questionnaires* conducted face-to-face by trained interviewers will have a fairly high response rate, while questionnaires sent by mail characteristically have a low response rate (sometimes as low as 20%), even though followup letters are used. Low response rates indicate that the findings of the research may be biased, as those who reply might differ significantly in their views from those who do not. When looking at the results of *social surveys,* it is always advisable to look for the response rate. This is sometimes expressed as a percentage of the whole sample, and sometimes as the number of completed questionnaires or interviews. In this case, the number should be compared with the total number in the sample, which is usually expressed as N (e.g. N = 1,500).

restricted code: a form of *language code* identified by Bernstein. It refers to a pattern of speech commonly used among close friends or members of a family, in which sentences are short and grammatically simple, and much of the meaning is implicit, i.e. understood by those taking part in the conversation without being expressed in words, or at least in detail. Bernstein argued that, while the restricted code is perfectly adequate for normal everyday conversations, another form of speech, which he called the *elaborated code,* is necessary to express more complex and abstract ideas, and is used extensively in education. While middle-class children learn both speech codes at home, working-class children tend to use only the restricted code, which puts them at a considerable disadvantage at school. Labov disagrees with Bernstein, arguing that the methods used to identify the two speech codes failed to recognize the richness and subtlety of working-class speech, which can and does express complex and abstract ideas.

restrictive practices: in industry, the use of particular modes of working by workers that limit the productive capacity of the company. They are usually concerned with traditional ways of working that rely upon strict demarcation of workers' jobs, with no crossover between different types of worker. They were evolved over many years by workers to provide themselves with some form of protection from the demands of employers and to increase the rewards they gained.

retreatism: according to Merton, a form of *deviance* that occurs when individuals reject both the accepted goals in society and the legitimate ways in which they may be obtained. As such, they become the "dropouts" of society, finding expression in alternative ways of living on the margins. This may take the form of drug-taking, homelessness, or alcoholism. (See *innovation; rebellion; ritualism.*)

revolution: a term to describe any radical restructuring, most often associated with the violent overthrow of an established political order by an opposing section of society. Sociologists are interested in revolution because it represents an extreme event in society, and sociological explanations have focused on the possible causes of revolutions and whether their outcomes involve any real change in the conditions of those for whom the revolution was intended. In a more general sense, revolution can refer to any social activity in which fundamental change occurs, usually swiftly, but also sometimes slowly. Thus, sociologists talk of the *Industrial Revolution* or *scientific revolution* in referring respectively to shifts in productive techniques and shifts in *paradigms.*

revolutionist sects: a type of *sect* identified by Wilson, the members of which believe that the world will be transformed by a single cataclysmic *supernatural* event, in which the existing order will be destroyed and a new divine order ushered in. Jehovah's Witnesses are an example of a revolutionist sect.

ribbon development: where towns and cities grow through housing being built along the major roads leading in and out of population centers. Development therefore takes on the appearance of spokes:

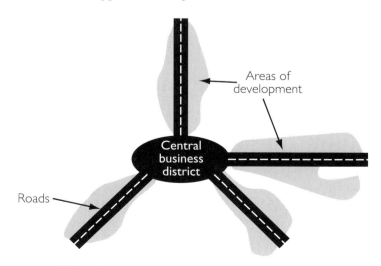

Representation of ribbon development

right to rule: a term to express the notion that the dominant group in society is naturally in charge of the political affairs of the *state*. It refers to some inherent quality, such as breeding, heredity, or *intelligence*, that legitimizes the power of the ruling group. (See *divine right of kings*.)

right-wing: along the political spectrum, a term to describe the ideas and organizations that tend to favor existing social arrangements and support traditional elitist values. The right encompasses democratic parties such as the Republican Party and authoritarian antidemocratic organizations such as the Fascist movement. (See *center*, *left-wing*.)

risk: a term used by postmodernists to indicate that postmodern societies are characterized by attempts to control and minimize levels of danger in the natural and social environment. It is not that such risks can be eliminated from society – as risks become global (global warming, for example) they are less open to rational solution – but that the degree of risk can be calculated and action taken on the balance of probability. (See *trust*.)

risk society: a term developed by Beck to indicate that in the postmodern world, life is experienced in many social areas with an increased sense of danger and challenge. Whereas the modern world offered some degree of certainty in social relations, with, for example, a class system to define an individual's social position, the postmodern world has seen the dissolving of such certainties, so that social life becomes more risky. (See *self-identity*.)

rites de passage: ceremonies or *rituals* that mark important transitions in an individual's life. Developed by anthropologists to describe in particular the traditions associated with becoming an adult, the term is used by sociologists in connection with important points in a *life cycle*, such as marriage, birth, and death.

ritualism: where members of an organization stick strictly to the rules, carrying them out as if they were the only justification for the existence of the *organization*. Blau argues that ritualism stems from the insecurity of individuals in organizations, who find some sort of security in formally keeping to the rules, regardless of whether they are actually helping *clients* or not. This ritualism often leads clients to complain about the red tape that stifles the ability of organizations to respond effectively to need. (See *formalism*.)

ritualistic deviance: according to Merton, a form of *deviance* that occurs when individuals reject the sanctioned cultural goals in society, but continue to follow the legitimized means of achieving them. The result is that these deviants continue to slavishly follow the rules to no apparent purpose. They may be often found in large *organizations*, insisting on a strict interpretation of the rules, regardless of whether goals are met or not. (See *innovation*; *rebellion*; *retreatism*.)

rituals: individual or collective actions that are designed to achieve some social end and have a repetitive element. Religious rituals, as expressed in ceremonies of all kinds, are perhaps the most obvious example. However, there are secular rituals as well, such as "coming-of-age" celebrations. Rituals usually have a symbolic content, in which *meaning* is expressed through traditional actions, such as facing Mecca when praying, or crossing oneself. *Durkheim* argued that rituals were a way of expressing social solidarity, because taking part in a collective service reaffirms the individual's commitment to the collectivity of which he or she is a part.

robotics: a term used to describe particular forms of new *technologies*. The usual representation of robotics is to be found in car assembly lines, where computer-controlled machines carry out the routine work of assembling the cars. Symbolically, therefore, robotics describes those new technologies that substitute for human labor in the production process.

role: the expected pattern of behavior associated with a particular social status under defined circumstances. The analogy is with roles in the theater, but, unlike the theater, these are not pretended roles. Roles allow individuals to predict how others will act in particular situations and to respond appropriately. They thus allow for a degree of *social order*, through their very predictability.

role conflict: a situation that arises when the demands of the different parts of our lives are contradictory. These demands can be trivial, such as needing to be in two places at the same time, or of a more fundamental nature, such as those associated with being a working mother. (See *role set.*)

role diffuseness: where an individual engages in relationships on the basis of various different aspects of individual personality and function. Role diffuseness is associated with traditional societies, where the activities of individuals are not specialized, and therefore when interaction occurs, it is on the basis of the whole person and not just one *role*. (See *role specificity.*)

role distance: the separation of an individual's deepest being from the *role* he or she is playing at the time. The concept is used to indicate the detachment or lack of engagement that many individuals feel in playing some of the roles they are required to act out.

role models: people whose behavior and attitudes we try, consciously or uncon-sciously, to copy. Parents are often important role models, especially for ideas about *gender*. Teachers, bosses, pop and sports stars, and those of a higher *social status* are also often used as role models.

role set: the total number of roles a person has to adopt when occupying a par-ticular *social status*. As a worker, the individual may have a number of roles, e.g. employer, workmate, boss, labor union member, taxpayer, etc.

role specificity: where individuals engage in relationships for specific purposes and on the basis of a particular aspect of their social being. It is associated with modern societies, where roles are specialized and individuals relate to each other in a less holistic way than in traditional societies. The dualism (with *role diffuseness*) was developed by *Parsons* as one of the *pattern variables* between traditional and modern societies.

role-training: a form of *socialization* in which the young acquire the skills and attitudes necessary for the fulfillment of institutionalized positions in their adult life. It is usually associated with *secondary socialization* agencies. (See *enculturation*; *impulse control.*)

Roman Catholic church: the largest of the Christian churches with a worldwide membership. The Roman Catholic church has an authoritarian and hierarchical structure, and the conservative views of the Pope on issues such as divorce, contraception, and abortion have caused controversy and the allegation that the church is out of touch with modern ways of thinking. However, not all the activities of the church can be labeled as conservative. In South America, Roman Catholics have taken an active stance on issues of human rights, and the church was a powerful force in some eastern European countries, particularly Poland, during the overthrow of *communism*. (See *liberation theology*.)

romance, ideology of: a term used by sociologists to suggest that what might be seen as a "natural" emotion is in fact a socially constructed *ideology*. The concept of romantic love has a historical origin, arising from notions such as "courtly love" and has not been a universal feature of all societies. The development of the ideology of romance is said to be part of an increase in self-surveillance in modern and postmodern societies, in which individuals in society need fewer and fewer external controls like force and punishment, but instead "police" their own actions through accepting and acting upon dominant ideologies. The ideology of romance is therefore an important support for the structure of the *nuclear family*.

rough working class: a section of the manual *working class*, distinguished by a particular lifestyle. Associated with a "drinking" culture and implicated in a criminal *subculture*, the "rough" elements of the working class were often stigmatized as a dangerous group in society. They were often concentrated in particular occupations, such as mining or fishing, and often had a "public" culture carried out outside the home, in bars, race tracks, and so on. There was also a tendency for the rough working class to be male-dominated, with women having a more domestic role. (See *respectable working class*.)

routine activities theory: an approach in the sociology of crime that examines the ways in which the everyday behavior of individuals exposes them to more or less risk of being a victim. The exploration of such routine activities allows the criminologist to identify "hot spots" where criminal activity is likely to be concentrated.

routinization: the process whereby previously skilled jobs become repetitive and boring through the introduction of standardized procedures. It is usually associated with the introduction of new *technology* that effectively deskills workers. Sociologists have used the concept with particular reference to office work, where the impact of firstly the typewriter and subsequently computer technology has allowed paperwork to become standardized, with low-level clerical grades of workers staffing the office. (See *deskilling*.)

Rowntree, Benjamin Seebohm: a wealthy British businessman and social researcher best known for his research into *poverty* in the city of York in 1897, 1936, and 1950. Rowntree used a subsistence definition of poverty, based on the lowest cost of the basic necessities of life. He also grouped poor families into two categories. Those in primary poverty lacked the earnings sufficient to obtain even the minimum necessities, while those deemed to be in secondary poverty had earnings that would have been sufficient, had not some part been diverted to other expenditure, either "useful" or "wasteful."

ruling class: the group at the top of the social order that governs the rest of society, either directly or indirectly. The term is usually associated with Marxist theory, in which the ruling class plays a central part. Marxists define membership of the ruling class by ownership of the *means of production*. Marxists argue that through owning wealth-creating assets the ruling class is able to control much of what goes on in society, including *government*. Though the precise relationship between the owners of the means of production and politicians, administrators, etc. is subject to much dispute, the Marxist view can be summarized in the phrase "an owning class is a ruling class." The ruling class does not just control government, but also, according to Marxists, influences what is produced in the media, what is taught in schools, and many other areas of social life. Some Marxists argue that the ruling class directly controls these other spheres of social life, while others suggest that institutions such as government are relatively autonomous. Non-Marxist sociologists deny that there is a ruling class in this sense at all. Their main point is that Marxists do not identify the precise ways in which the ruling class is supposed to rule. (See *relative autonomy*.)

rural community: a social community, such as a village, based in the countryside. The term embodies an important concept for early sociologists such as *Durkheim* and Tönnies, who believed that such communities played a vital part in instilling basic moral values in their members. They were concerned that the breakup of rural communities under *industrialization*, and the subsequent process of urbanization, would leave people rootless and unsatisfied, and lead to *anomie*. Tönnies used the term *Gemeinschaft* to refer to the notion of *community*. Empirical research by Wilmott and Young and Gans challenged the idea that "communities" could exist only in rural areas. Pahl also showed that it was a mistake to believe that the populations of rural areas were necessarily close-knit communities, showing that marked social divisions could exist between different groups of residents. One of the current debates in the sociology of community concerns the extent to which there are real differences between rural and *urban areas*. (See *Gesellschaft*.)

rural–urban continuum: a term to express the idea that there are few stark differences between city and countryside, but rather a gradation between the big city on the one hand and isolated farmsteads on the other, with a huge range of community sizes, lifestyles, and habitats in between. The idea was developed by Sorokin to counter simplistic dichotomies between the two types of location.

S

sacred: a term used by *Durkheim* to refer to those things in society that are regarded as set apart and forbidden, and not forming part of everyday life. All other phenomena could be labeled, according to Durkheim, as *profane*. He argued that every society makes the distinction between the sacred and the profane, and the study of religion should focus on those phenomena regarded as sacred.

sample: in sociological study, the group selected from the wider population to take part in research. Choosing an appropriate sample is an important stage in the research process. (See *sampling; sampling frame.*)

sampling: the selection of a part of a *survey population* to be studied rather than the entire population. Sampling is a widely used procedure both in sociological research and in industry, for example in checks on quality control. There are various methods that can be used to select a sample, but the overall aim is usually the same, i.e. to make the sample as representative of the whole population as possible. This allows any conclusions drawn about the sample to be broadly applicable to the whole population. (See *random sampling.*)

sampling error: in sociological study, the difference between data based on an entire *survey population* and data collected from a *sample* of that population. No sample can be relied on to be so representative that it is completely identical to the whole population. *Random sampling* methods can keep the sampling error to a small and calculable percentage.

sampling frame: in sociological study, the list of people (the *survey population*) from which a *sample* will be drawn. In sociological research, a common sampling frame is the *voting register*. Others, depending on the nature of the research, could include school lists, club or *pressure group* membership lists, a list of subscribers to a specialist magazine, or telephone books. It is not always easy to insure that the sampling frame is complete. For example, some people do not register as electors, and telephone books exclude not only those without telephones but those who have opted to have unlisted numbers. The omission of certain people from a sampling frame can affect the degree to which the sample, and therefore the findings, are representative of the population as a whole.

sampling interval: in sociological research, the randomly chosen number between 1 and the number representing the proportion of the population in the sample (e.g. 1 in 30), used to add to each selected name on the list from which a *systematic sample* is being drawn.

sampling unit: in sociological research, the level at which sampling takes place. While sampling units are usually the individual, if a sociologist is taking a sample of hospitals in the state of New York, then the sampling unit would be hospitals (not the individuals within the hospital).

sanction: the means whereby a social *norm* is enforced, either by a positive or negative device and either formally or informally. A formal negative sanction, for example, might be a law that leads to imprisonment of those who break it.

satellite towns: small *urban areas* located close to large cities that constitute a major source of housing for workers in the city. The economy of satellite towns is intimately connected to the city, with workers dependent on the city for employment and shopping.

science: see *natural science*

scientific management: a theory developed by F.W. Taylor that applied scientific principles to the management of workers in an industrial company. (See *Taylorism*.)

scientific Marxism: that variant of *Marxism* that searches for the invariate laws of history that exist independently of human free will and are therefore deterministic of it. It thus denies the importance of the individual in the sweep of history. The scientific school includes Marxists such as Althusser, Poulantzas, and Blackburn. (See *critical Marxism*.)

scientific revolution: a term given by Kuhn to the process in which a once-dominant scientific *paradigm* is successfully challenged, overthrown, and replaced by another. Kuhn's argument is that, at any time, in any branch of knowledge, including *natural science,* a particular set of ideas, beliefs, and practices (paradigm) is used to explain natural or social phenomena. The paradigm is defended by academics and practitioners, and is taught to those newly entering the field. However, according to Kuhn a paradigm, although it may be accepted for a very long time, is only temporary, as it will not be able to explain satisfactorily all the pheonomena in that discipline or branch of science. Alternative paradigms will begin to emerge to challenge the prevailing set of ideas, and eventually one will succeed and will replace the existing one, becoming in its turn the dominant paradigm. With the adoption of the new paradigm, a scientific revolution will have taken place, and the whole process will begin again. Kuhn is thus challenging the idea that "science" is a set of *laws* that represent the "truth." Kuhn's views have been challenged by those who claim that there is no evidence that scientific knowledge has developed in this way. Interactionists make use of Kuhn's ideas to challenge the positivist view that interactionist sociology is not "scientific," by arguing that positivists themselves have a mistaken view of the nature of science.

scientism: a term to suggest the dogmatic application of the principles of science to the social world, so that an inflexible and inappropriate sociology is developed.

scientist as human being: a term developed by interactionists to emphasize that science is not carried out by cold, objective, dispassionate robots, but by individuals with all the human foibles we might expect, such as pride, consciousness of status, and proneness to error. Thus, scientists operate in a situation of pressure, to publish, get results, bring in funds, and gain the recognition of their peers. Interactionists argue that these pressures create a predisposition for scientists to privilege evidence that proves their hypothesis and to explain away or ignore results that do not. (See *objectivity*.)

scope: in sociology, a term to define the number of activities in an institution that are carried out jointly by participants. The degree of scope will vary from one type of *total institution* to another, so that prisons will have a high degree of scope, and a hospital will have less scope. (See *pervasiveness*.)

second world: a term used in the sociology of development to distinguish the former socialist economies of eastern Europe and the Soviet Union from the capitalist economies of the *first world*. While second-world economies contained highly developed sectors, such as the space programs of the former Soviet Union, they also retained many out-of-date and unsophisticated technologies. They thus often had the surface appearance of advanced technological societies, while relying on an industrial base that was stagnant and undynamic. The collapse of *communism* in the second world at the end of the 1980s revealed the underlying weaknesses of their economies. One of the most startling revelations was the extent to which second-world economies had ignored environmental and safety issues in the running of their economies. (See *third world*.)

secondary data: in sociological study, information used by sociologists that has not been collected by them. Secondary data include *official statistics*, historical and personal *documents*, books, and movies. While providing a great deal of important information, all secondary data must be used with caution, as it is not always possible to know the criteria for either the collection or the selection of the information.

secondary deviance: a deviant act, as identified by Lemert, that has been publicly processed as a deviant act so that the perpetrator becomes labeled a deviant. The importance of the distinction between this and *primary deviance* is that everyone commits primary deviant acts from time to time, with few social consequences. More serious social consequences arise from secondary deviance, where the stigmatizing force of the label is likely to lead to changes in relationships between the labeled person and the people around her or him and perhaps a change in the attitude and behavior of those so labeled. (See *labeling*.)

secondary health care: patient health care, usually curative in nature, provided in hospitals. (See *primary health care, tertiary health care*.)

secondary labor market: see *external labor market*

secondary organizations: *organizations* that depend for their existence on a previously existing organization. *Labor unions* are the main type of secondary organization that exists.

secondary poverty: see *Rowntree, Benjamin Seebohm*

secondary sector: in the *occupational structure,* a term to describe low-wage jobs with low security, such as manufacturing jobs in factories, that are frequently nonunionized. (See *primary sector, tertiary sector*.)

secondary socialization: the learning of skills and attitudes outside of the main agency of the family. In modern societies, schools are the main agency for secondary socialization and are associated with the learning of specific occupational skills as well as attitudes which contribute to work discipline. (See *primary socialization*.)

secret deviant: defined by Becker as one who engages in rule-breaking behavior but who has not been perceived or labeled publicly as a deviant. The term does not just apply to a deviant who has not been caught, because the *labeling* process is not automatic. (See *falsely accused; pure deviant*.)

sect: a religious group with characteristics that distinguish it from either a *church* or a *denomination*. It has been suggested that common characteristics of sects include:

- membership by conversion
- usually a charismatic leader
- acceptance of members only if they are thought suitable
- the claim that only the sect has the "true" way to salvation.

However, sociologists such as Wilson have argued that an attempt to define sects by reference to common characteristics is unhelpful and indeed impossible, as sects take so many different forms. Wilson proposed a typology based on the sect's views of, and relationship to, the *values* of mainstream society, namely whether a sect was world-rejecting, world-accommodating, or world-affirming. Although precise figures are difficult to obtain, sect membership appears to be growing, casting doubt on the view that *secularization* is taking place in many Western industrial societies. (See *new religious movements; theodicy of disprivilege.*)

sectional interests: interests that determine the divisions of society into groupings of people who have something in common. An individual may have many sectional interests, ranging from a class interest in the broadest sense, to membership in occupational, religious, regional, or ethnic groupings. In political terms, sectional interests represent the basic unit of political appeal. The aims of the successful politician are usually rooted in a sectional interest.

sectoral cleavages: in *psephology,* a term to describe the various oppositional patterns of voting behavior based on differences in important social characteristics beyond *social class.* Psephologists have identified home ownership/public housing or private-/public-sector work as important factors in voting patterns. (See *new working class; old working class.*)

sectoral model of urban areas: developed by Hoyt as an alternative model to *urban zones theory,* with the growth of cities seen as occurring in wedges from the city center, rather than in concentric circles. This theory suggests that *ribbon development* is an important factor in the evolution of cities. This development looks like this:

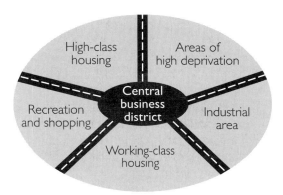

Sectoral model of urban areas as developed by Hoyt

secularization: usually defined as the process by which religious thinking, practices, and organizations lose their social significance. *Weber* argued that the development of scientific knowledge and rational thought would replace beliefs based on *magic*, superstition, and the *supernatural*. Evidence of secularization is usually presented as a decline in church attendance and religious observance in societies, and the declining power of the church and religious leaders in everyday life. However, this evidence is contested. It is argued that much religious practice goes unrecorded in the kind of statistics that are presented to show evidence of secularization – for example, statistics fail to take into account people worshipping in house churches, joining in religious programs on television, or becoming members of *sects*. It is also pointed out that, in many societies, the church remains a powerful political and economic, as well as religious influence, and that in industrial societies like the US membership of religious groups is increasing rather than decreasing. Weber's prediction of the decline of religion as a result of rational thought is questioned on the basis of evidence of beliefs in magic, superstition, and the supernatural. It is also pointed out that the "*golden age of religion*" is historically suspect. *Parsons* claimed that religious institutions, far from losing their influence, were becoming more highly specialized, and still had an important function. (See *differentiation*; *disenchantment*; *disengagement*.)

segmentalism: the theory in the sociology of *leisure* that modern life is carried out in two distinct spheres, *work* and leisure, which are largely independent of each other. Individuals choose which of the spheres is to be their *central life interest*. (See *holism*.)

segmented labor market: a market characterized by job differentiation according to levels of pay, skill, and prospects in a structured way, so that similar jobs in different companies will exhibit similar conditions, and different jobs within the same company will have different conditions. Skill levels, pay, and conditions are socially structured and tend to be associated with people in relation to different characteristics such as gender or ethnicity.

segregated conjugal roles: roles within a *marriage* in which the husband and wife perform separate and quite distinct tasks. Typically the male role is defined as that of "breadwinner" and major decision-maker, while the wife's role is that of "homemaker," with a sharp focus on *housework* and *child care*. In her 1957 research, Bott found that couples with segregated domestic roles also tended to spend their *leisure* time in separate activities. (See *conjugal roles*; *joint conjugal roles*.)

segregation: the separation of one ethnic group from another, both geographically and socially, by means of law, customs, and values. Segregation was an institutionalized system in the southern states of the US, where the black population was separated from the dominant white majority through force, intimidation, and ingrained habit. (See *busing*.)

selective exposure: the idea that individuals do not use the mass media haphazardly, but with purpose. Katz and Lazarsfeld, for example, argue that people tend to look for media experiences that reinforce their existing *beliefs*. They therefore seek out media content that coincides with their views and turn away from those media experiences that contradict long-cherished beliefs. This view is supported by the trend, for example, toward theme television devoted to niche media markets such as religious groups or sports fans. People also seek out newspapers whose views tend to reinforce their existing political beliefs. (See *selective interpretation*; *selective retention*.)

selective interpretation: the way in which individuals see media images in a particular way, so that such images are slotted into existing beliefs and attitudes, regardless of the intention of the producers of the media material. (See *selective exposure*; *selective retention*.)

selective retention: the way in which the media *audience* does not retain all the information it is given, but keeps only those aspects that conform to its existing beliefs. (See *selective exposure*; *selective interpretation*.)

self: in *symbolic interactionism*, the image that the individual constructs to see himself or herself as an external object. It is the result of our ability to step outside of ourselves and see the results of our actions as if we were someone else. It is the self that allows us to anticipate the effects of our future actions and gauge the outcomes of alternative courses of action. It is therefore the basis of *calculability* in social life. (See *generalized other*.)

self-actualizing theories: explanations for work motivation that assume that every individual has a *hierarchy of needs*, at the top of which is the need to fulfill personal potential. Associated with Maslow and Argyris, such theories imply that a particular form of work organization, i.e. one that offers opportunities for personal fulfillment, is the most efficient. Critics of these theories, such as Silverman, argue that the need for self-actualization is an assumption that cannot be proven. Rather, Silverman argues that needs are not unchanging and given, but vary according to the situation in which individuals find themselves. Therefore to base work organization on the assumption that individuals need self-actualization is mistaken. However, Argyris responded that Maslow had always recognized the changing nature of needs, and accepted that there was only a limited number of individuals for whom self-actualization was a necessity. (See *job enrichment*.)

self-assessed class: see *subjective social class*

self-employment: where workers work for themselves rather than for an employer. The self-employed sector is an important part of the economy, constituting a bloc between capital and labor. The ranks of the self-employed are fragmented, including small entrepreneurs such as plumbers and low-paid casual workers such as *outworkers*. The role of self-employment is argued to be increasingly important in postmodern societies, where the costs of employment are likely to increase. Therefore, more and more self-employed people, it is argued, are likely to be used by large-scale organizations as independent consultants, casual workers, and so on, creating a *hidden economy*.

self-estrangement: a condition of *alienation* identified by Blauner, characterized by workers feeling a depersonalized detachment from work. It is the denial of *self-actualization* in work. (See *isolation*; *meaninglessness*; *powerlessness*.)

self-fulfilling prophecy: a theory about predicted outcomes that states that the act of making a prediction helps to bring about the expected outcome. The concept is closely linked to that of *labeling*, and in sociology is used particularly in the contexts of *education* and *deviance*. It is argued that, by making a prediction (e.g. these students will all do well because they are the brightest in the class) those in positions of influence will act as though the prediction were already true (e.g. teachers will have high expectations of the students concerned). This also causes those about whom the prediction has been made to respond accordingly, and thus make the prediction come true. (See *Pygmalion effect.*)

self-identity: a term used by postmodernists to describe the individual's constant creation of an image of himself or herself to present to the public world in a reflexively self-conscious manner. Thus, individuals constantly recreate themselves through their everyday practice and rewrite their own biographies by choosing lifestyles. The implication of this is that individuals no longer have a single *self*, but reconstruct themselves in a series of selves throughout their lifetimes. *Giddens* believes that the creation of self-identities empowers us, in that we can be who we want, when we want. Beck believes that this self-identity is uncomfortable, because if it is an unsuccessful self, we have only ourselves to blame. (See *risk society.*)

self-orientation: one of *Parsons' pattern variables*, based on the idea that, in modern societies, *individualism* and personal success are more important than the interests of the collectivity. (See *collective orientation.*)

self-recruitment: the degree to which the sons and daughters of the members of a *social class* end up in the same social class themselves. The higher the degree of self-recruitment in a society, the more closed it is likely to be. Self-recruitment has been found to be highest among the top social classes, as members use their privileges and positions to insure advantages for their own children. There is also a significant amount of self-recruitment among members of the *working class*, though this is mitigated by the *occupational transition*. (See *social mobility.*)

self-referral: a situation in which a *client* himself or herself seeks the services of a professional, e.g. a social worker or psychiatrist.

self-report studies: surveys of the population that ask people to confess to crimes they have committed but for which they have not been caught. The studies are one of the ways in which the amount of criminal activity that never appears in crime statistics can be shown. They have been criticized because there is no way of knowing how true the reports are, nor how representative they are of society as a whole. (See *victim studies.*)

self-surveillance: a term used to describe the situation where individuals assume that their activities are being monitored in some way, whether they know it or not, and therefore modify their behavior to conform to what is seen as "normal." The concept was developed by Foucault from his study of the *panopticon*, where prisoners could be seen at all times and therefore had to assume that they were being watched, even though it was physically impossible to watch all of them all of the time. Such is the "swarming" of surveillance techniques in society that Foucault argued that we all engaged in self-surveillance – modifying our behavior because we might be being watched.

semiautonomous employees: a term for members of one of Wright's *contradictory class locations*, described as workers in nonowning occupational groups who sell their labor power, but have some control over their own work processes because they have valued skills. An example often used is airline pilots, who have many of the features of the *proletariat* in their job, but also have some independence in the execution of their work.

semileisure: a concept developed by Dumazedier to indicate those activities carried out outside of work that have an element of compulsion attached to them. Though they may be done in a person's own time they are not necessarily pleasurable, e.g. *housework*. (See *leisure, nonwork obligations*.)

semiology: see *semiotics*

semiotics: the study of the system of *signs* in society. In the beginning, semiotics was mainly concerned with *language*, but the subject has been developed under Barthes into a powerful analysis of the symbols employed by the media and the *myths* that are deployed in modern societies. (See *signifiers*.)

semiprofessions: a term describing those occupations that aspire to professional status, the practitioners of which may call themselves professional, but do not have the full range of professional powers. The semiprofessions are associated with "people-working" professions or what Bennet and Hokenstadt described as "full-time people workers." The knowledge base of the semiprofessions is less theoretical than that of the traditional *professions*, and professional training is more concerned with the transmission of methodological skills than with substantive knowledge. Teaching is a good example of a semiprofession. Another important difference between the traditional professions and semiprofessions is that the latter tend to function largely in bureaucratic settings and are less likely to be found in private practice. (See *personal service professions*.)

semiskilled labor: work in which there are some basic capabilities needed by the worker to perform the task. Training is likely to be minimal and rewards relatively limited. (See *skilled labor, unskilled labor*.)

separation of home and work: the process whereby, during the *Industrial Revolution*, the unity of family life and production was dissolved. Prior to *industrialization*, most families worked together on the land and produced other goods they needed at home. Therefore the family unit was also a production unit. With the development of widespread factory production, economic life was transferred to locations outside of the home and this was to have profound effects on *gender* roles. After the conversion of the peasantry into wage-laborers, the female tasks of childbearing and nursing could be less easily combined with productive work. Thus women were forced into a domestic role, with increased dependence on men. (See *cottage industry*.)

separation of ownership and control: a theory developed by Berle and Means based on the argument that, with the emergence of the joint stock company, direct control of large corporations has, in the main, moved from personal control by owners to a situation in which the owners have relinquished control to the managers. (See *managerial revolution*.)

serial monogamy: the recently developed pattern of *marriage* in which an individual can have several marriage partners over the course of his or her lifetime, with the majority of these marriages ending in *divorce*. The pattern is most apparent in the US and is a consequence of increased *life expectancy* and the increased span of a lifetime marriage.

service class: a term used by Goldthorpe to describe those jobs at the top of the *occupational structure*. It is composed of the professional groups, administrators and managers, and supervisors of nonmanual employees. In following a Weberian schema, Goldthorpe was concerned to use styles of life rather than ownership as the distinguishing feature of classes.

sex: either of the biological divisions between males and females (and very occasionally hermaphrodites). Sex is argued by sociologists to be distinct from *gender*. Though the two are clearly connected, they are not necessarily directly related. Sociologists debate with members of other disciplines such as biologists over the relative importance of biological forces such as sex, and social and cultural forces such as gender. Obviously, sociologists tend to give priority to social explanations in examining the differences between the sexes. However, there is some meeting of the disciplines of sociology and biology in this area, with various crosscutting and complex interactions between them.

sex ratio: the balance between the numbers of men and women in a population. A balance between the sexes is usually reached around the age of 40, when the greater number of males born, and their propensity to die earlier than women, equalizes. There are therefore more males in the population below the age of 40 and more females above the age of 40. In some societies, the practice of female infanticide and more recently selective *abortion* can lead to a greater imbalance in the sex ratio.

sex stereotyping: where ideas about the proper *roles* of men and women are given to oversimplification and near-caricature. The classic sex stereotype is the distribution of paid work and domestic chores according to sex, where women take prime responsibility for housework and men are the main breadwinners. This is stereotypical because there is a limited number of households that actually operate in this way, and yet it has a powerful ideological and political pull. The *mass media* provide a powerful source of sex stereotyping.

sexism: discrimination against a person or group on account of biological sex. Most sexist practices have historically been aimed against women, and they can either be deliberate or unconscious. Deliberate sexist practices and ideas are often drawn from fundamentalist interpretations of religion, in which women and men have clearly separate and unchallengeable roles, with women in the subordinate position. Though there are examples of overt sexism, sexism most frequently operates in Western democracies through unconscious *sex stereotyping*.

sexual division of labor: where work in its most general sense is divided between what is seen as women's work and what is men's. The most basic sexual division of labor is between paid employment and *domestic labor*, for which women have traditionally been allocated prime responsibility. In more recent times, the sexual division of labor has expressed itself in paid employment, where some jobs have come to be seen as primarily women's work. It is particularly in the lower levels of the caring occupations, such as nursing or cooking, that men and women have become occupationally segregated. (See *glass walls*.)

sexual harassment: the use of language or actions to denigrate and humiliate a person on account of *gender*. Arguments over the extent and importance of sexual harassment have made it a *site of ideological struggle*, as different groups insist on its widespread prevalence or argue that it is much exaggerated. While sexual harassment undoubtedly does take place, sociologists have tried to establish its incidence in a variety of situations, most notably the workplace.

sexual orientation: used as a general term in sociology to describe the direction of an individual's sexual drive. Though it is an individual characteristic, sociologists are interested in the way that groups develop around sexual orientation. While heterosexuals, whose orientation is toward the opposite sex, might be expected to form one group, there are obvious divisions within it, such as between men and women. Similarly, within the homosexual identity there are many divisions, the main one being between gay men and lesbians.

sexuality: see *sexual orientation*

shanty towns: an old and now little-used term for *favelas*, or unorganized housing areas that emerge in the *third world*, and have few amenities such as running water or electricity. The term has fallen into disrepute as these areas become more established and serviced by the city councils of the area.

shift work: the organization of labor such that production is maintained around the clock, with the workers working in units of about eight hours. Workers usually have to take alternating turns at the different shifts, with the night shifts being the least popular. New computer technologies have allowed the intensive production that is associated with shift work, and *high-tech* industries are often therefore associated with an intensification of shift work.

sick role: a social *role* legitimized by the medical profession that allows people to withdraw temporarily from their social duties and obligations. As a functionalist, *Parsons* believed that society would only work properly if all people fulfilled their social obligations to the rest of society. Illness allows a legitimate, usually temporary, withdrawal from at least some of these obligations (e.g. going to work). Parsons suggested that by bringing sickness within the domain of doctors, people would be encouraged to "become well" and take up their social duties again as soon as possible.

sign: a symbol that stands for or represents something else. A sign indicates a relationship between a *signifier* and the signified. A sign may be a mark on a paper or a sound, and is a central concept in *semiotics*. The meanings attached to signs may be direct and fairly obvious or they may be mediated, so that the meaning depends on social convention rather than direct symbolism.

significant others: a term for those who are given importance in a person's life, perhaps acting as *role models*, but also constituting an important audience for a person in a particular role.

signification: the way that cultural *signs*, such as pictures and words, create meaning. For example, television images are not just windows on the world but are imbued with ideological meanings, which can be read like a *text*. Much of the signification of advertising is mythological, referring to an idealized past or setting, as in the use of pastoral scenes to sell factory-farmed produce.

signifiers: images, objects, or words that bring to mind other ideas or meanings (the "signified"). For example, a pastoral scene may be associated with freshness or pureness and therefore may be an important signifier for an advertising campaign for food.

signs proper: a term used by Saussure to indicate meanings derived from agreed conventions in society, such as red indicating "stop." (See *icons; index.*)

single-issue politics: political views and actions based on one overriding concern, such as the environment, animal rights, or gay/lesbian issues, rather than on the full spectrum of political issues.

single-parent families: families consisting of a dependent child or children living with only one parent, usually the mother. The proportion of single-parent families in the US has been growing since the 1970s, and in 1990 the proportion of children living in one-parent *households*, was more than 25%. About 90% of single-parent households are headed by single mothers. While the media *stereotype* of the single-parent family is often of the young, unmarried mother, single-parent families are more likely to be created by the *divorce* or separation of the parents, or the death of a spouse. While some single-parent families may enjoy a reasonable standard of living, as in families where the single parent is a well-paid professional worker, many single-parent families are in, or on the margins of, *poverty*. In many cases, this is a result of the problems of finding and being able to afford suitable *child care.*

site of ideological struggle: a social *location* in which the ideas and beliefs of different social groups compete to establish precedence and domination. Schools and universities are often cited as sites of ideological struggle, in which advocates of different conceptions (of, for example, history) attempt to establish themselves as the legitimate holders of the subject. So traditional conceptions of history, such as those based on the exploits of great men, battle it out with those that emphasize black history, women's history, social history, and so on.

site of struggle: a term to describe any *location*, either geographical or social, that is contested by different social groups. For example, housing is a site of struggle among different *housing classes* over access to various types of housing.

situatedness: a term used by postmodernists to describe where an individual stands in social formations. Our situatedness is defined by our position in economic and social relationships, which groups we identify with or belong to, and so on. The importance of our situatedness is that it will affect the understanding we bring to bear on our experiences and create a partial knowledge of the world around us, distinct from (but no better than) other partial knowledge derived from the situatedness of others.

situational constraints: circumstances in which people find themselves that limit their course of action. For example, motherhood acts as a situational constraint to getting involved in political activity, though this does not usually apply to fatherhood. Situational constraints can be permanent or change as people move through their *life cycle.* (See *institutional barriers.*)

situational constraints theory: an explanation of *poverty* that rejects the idea that it is the *culture* of the poor that is responsible for deprivation, but argues that it is the circumstances in which the poor find themselves that are the cause of their poverty. In particular, it is the fact of low wages or *unemployment* that forces the poor to act the way they do. The poor therefore do not have a distinctive culture, but share that of mainstream society. They simply do not have the resources to finance the lifestyle associated with mainstream culture.

situational criminology: see *administrative criminology*

situational rules: the guidelines to behavior that actually operate in any given circumstance, as opposed to the formal rules that are supposed to be operating. The concept was developed by ethnomethodologists such as Bittner to explain how individuals made sense of their everyday activities. Bittner argued that individuals used or ignored formal rules according to the situation in which they found themselves and according to which rules best suited their intentions. The point that was important for the ethnomethodologists was that formal rules do not determine individuals' behavior in *organizations*. Rather, they are used by individuals *reflexively* (referring to oneself and the position one is in) to justify any decision or course of action. Critics of this approach argue that it places too much emphasis on the *rationality* and spontaneous thought processes of social *actors*, while ignoring aspects of behavior such as tradition or emotion.

situational withdrawal: a reaction to *total institutions* in which the inmate withdraws attention from everything except the immediate events concerning the body, and becomes a "silent" and minimal participant in the everyday activities of the institution.

skewed deviants: according to *Durkheim*, deviants that appear when society allows individual passions to have a free rein and the inappropriately socialized individual engages in deviant activity. Thus, the skewed deviant emerges in a society characterized by *anomie*.

skilled labor: work in which workers need a high level of training and specific capabilities in order to perform their tasks. Traditionally, skilled labor attracts higher wages and better conditions, although some highly skilled occupations may not be rewarded to the extent expected. (See *semiskilled labor, unskilled labor*.)

skills: the abilities that individuals have, which occupations demand to varying degrees so that effective performance can be achieved. There are many different types of skills, which exist in a *hierarchy* of *esteem*, and which can be concerned, for example, with manual dexterity, intellectual thought, and design talent. Skills have been a focus for sociologists of education, while vocationalists have argued for a greater emphasis on the skills needed for industry in a postmodern world.

skills crisis: a reference to the shortage of workers with the particular skills needed by employers. Despite the high number of workers who are unemployed, some employers find difficulty in filling vacancies because the applicants lack the required skills.

slavery: an extreme form of *stratification* in which the enslaved have no rights or freedom, and are subject to total control by their masters. Slaves are often drawn from a conquered people, and enslaved by the conquerors. Slavery appears to have existed before recorded history, and therefore is found in many different forms. An extreme form of slavery, in which the slave is regarded as the property of the master, and something to be bought and sold, is known as "chattel slavery."

sleeper effect: where the effects of media content are delayed, with the messages initially rejected, and then accepted, as inhibiting factors are worn down by repetition of the message. (See *drip effect*.)

snowball sampling: a *sampling* method in which a researcher gains access to a group and then uses members of this group to make contact with others, and then in turn uses the new group to make further contacts, and so on. Although the method obviously does not result in a *random sample*, it is sometimes the only way to gain access to sufficient numbers from a particular kind of group, for example members of a religious *cult*, or people engaged in deviant activities.

social action: action affected by the existence of others, involving the understanding and interpreting of their behavior. Social action therefore involves interaction, either directly or indirectly. An example of the direct form might be talking with another person. An example of indirect social action might be writing those same words in a letter, to be read by someone else later.

social benefits: a term usually referring to benefits, particularly financial ones, received through the *welfare state*. (See *means-tested benefits*; *universal benefits*.)

social capital: the existence of established and well-integrated family and community networks, which act as a support mechanism for people in times of difficulty. The presence of such capital leads to feelings of security. The absence of social capital is a crucial component of *social disorganization*.

social change: the process whereby societies or aspects of society move from one state to another. The study of social change was central for the *classical sociologists*, because society was undergoing massive changes when the early sociologists were writing. Sociologists who emphasize social change at the expense of *social order* tend to focus on *conflict* in society, and the contradictions that exist between social groups and interests. However, there is also a difference between those who stress social change through evolution and those who focus on revolutionary change. (See *consensus*.)

social class: any one of the hierarchical divisions of a capitalist society, in which *wealth, income,* and *occupation* form the defining characteristics of each group. The classic formulation of social class in Western capitalist society is of a three-class society – upper, middle, and working class – in which the largest concentration of people is in the *working class*. As a rough rule-of-thumb, the distinction between manual and nonmanual occupations can be seen as the dividing line between the middle and the working class. For the *upper class*, concentration of wealth, *power*, and *status* are important as defining characteristics. Social class, however, is subject to change, and some sociologists have suggested that society has developed so that the middle sector has grown large enough for some to claim that "we are all *middle class* now." Others argue that the significant development in social class has been the appearance of an *underclass*, with little prospect of full-time employment.

social closure: a term used by Weberians to indicate the attempts by social groups to monopolize privileges and rewards by closing them off from other groups. Any social group can practice social closure, though the tactics employed tend to differ according to whether the group is at the top or bottom of the occupational *hierarchy*.

The importance of the concept is that it helps to explain divisions within classes as well as between them and can take into account gender and ethnic complexities. (See *credentialism*; *exclusion*; *solidarism*.)

social construction: the process whereby a phenomenon is built up through social processes rather than being a natural occurrence. The use of the term social construction has become popular as sociologists have focused increasingly on *identity* as an organizing principle of postmodern life. The term was originally used to describe the ways in which, for example, statistics did not always represent the real rate of what they were supposed to describe, but were the product of social processes involving many decisions by many individuals. In terms of identity, the concept is used to illustrate the view that an individual's character is not totally given, but is built up by the individual in terms of different conceptions of gender, ethnicity, sexuality, and other factors, which are influenced by personal preference and the reactions of others.

social consumption: a term to denote the use of goods and services beyond what is needed for basic subsistence. For example, consumption concerned with meeting religious or kinship obligations is social consumption, the demands of which can sometimes be met at the expense of individual consumption.

social contract: the agreement assumed by utilitarian theorists to exist among individuals when they come together to form a society. According to Hobbes, individuals in a *state of nature* are antisocial, and liable to pursue their own selfish interests at the expense of others. However, this leaves individuals open to physical violence and threats. In order to avoid this, people form a society, in which they agree to respect the lives and property of others in return for being left in safety to pursue happiness, within limits. This does not mean that there is a real contract, but rather an implicit understanding that those who offend the social contract by engaging in crime should be punished in order to protect all the other members of society. (See *utilitarianism*.)

social control: the process whereby society seeks to insure *conformity* to the dominant *values* and *norms* in that society. The processes may be informal, relying on the force of public or peer opinion to insure compliance, or formal, employing specific social agencies to encourage or enforce conformity. The tactics adopted to establish social control may include a mixture of negative *sanctions,* which punish those who transgress the rules of society, and positive policies, which seek to persuade or encourage voluntary compliance with society's standards.

social disorganization: a situation in which there are conflicts in social codes and confusion about the proper way to behave. In such a situation, there is little stability in social relationships and the individual stands out as a separate entity, motivated by unregulated impulses and drives. The resulting loss of organization, according to Cavan, can lead to increased *suicide* rates, as individuals become unable to cope with the instability. To Cavan, social disorganization leads to personal disorganization and increased suicide. (See *ecological fallacy*.)

social division of labor: a concept developed to explain occupational differences in society. It is used as a more sophisticated version of the idea of *specialization* and in contrast to the *detailed division of labor*. In traditional societies there is only a limited social division of labor, with very little occupational specialization. As societies become more complex they develop many more differences in occupations.

social engineering: planned social change brought about by the implementation of particular social policies. Some argue that social engineering is a legitimate and even desirable role for governments, while others are concerned by the potential for the abuse of such power, citing examples such as Nazi Germany as evidence. Education policies in particular are often viewed as social engineering, such as the policy of *busing* children to achieve greater racial integration in schools.

social facts: phenomena that are external to the individual, but act upon him or her in a constraining way. A good example of a social fact is a law, as it exists independently of any individual yet shapes the way he or she acts. *Durkheim* argued that sociologists should "treat social facts as things" – in other words, deal with them as if they were actually real, with an objective existence beyond individual subjectivity. (See *reification*.)

social forces: a term used by *Durkheim* to indicate aspects of society external to the individual that act upon the individual. An example of a social force might be a wave of patriotism that could sweep up the individual, who would then both contribute to and be propelled by it.

social inequality: the skewed distribution of the scarce resources in society, which is reflected in an unequal distribution of prestige and feelings of superiority and inferiority among individuals.

social mobility: movement up and down the *class structure*. The study of social mobility is one of the central concerns of social *stratification* theorists. The amount of social mobility is a measure of how rigid a society is and how locked into traditional structures it is. A high degree of social mobility therefore makes the drawing of class boundaries difficult, because of the fluidity it engenders. It is also difficult to measure the extent of social mobility, because it relies on *occupational scales*, with all the problems that these have. (See *intergenerational mobility*; *intragenerational mobility*.)

social order: the patterned *action* or regularities that people display in their social lives. It is social order that allows a degree of predictability in social life and therefore allows much social life to proceed. A focus on social order by sociologists tends to lead to conservative perspectives about the social world, emphasizing integration and cohesion at the expense of *conflict* and change.

social policy: the actions of governments and their agents in relation to their citizens. While social policy is usually associated with the legislative activities of the *state* in the area of the *welfare state* (housing, health, etc.) the term covers wider activities than these, such as taxation, pension policies, and employment laws. In academic terms, social policy is the subject of economic, sociological, and political study about the impact of planned government activity. The relationship between social policy and sociology is seen differently by various sociologists:

- Some argue that there is a direct input into social policy by sociologists, especially those who are used by the government as consultants or employees.
- Others argue that the importance of sociology for social policy is in creating a climate of opinion that influences the development of policies.
- Yet others argue that sociology should have little or no effect on social

policy, because sociologists should stand aside from government and be critical of its actions.

social problem: as distinct from a sociological problem, a phenomenon that society identifies as being in need of remedial action, because of its negative effects on individuals or on society as a whole. Although social problems such as *poverty*, ill-health, and delinquency are often the focus for sociological study, sociologists do not confine their interest only to the problematic features of social life. They are equally interested in the positive aspects.

social science: a general term for subjects of study that are concerned with the workings of society in some respect, and seek to establish general propositions about them. The term usually covers sociology, psychology, economics, and politics.

social security: in the US, a federal system of old-age, unemployment, health, and disability insurance paid for by mandatory contributions from employers and workers. In general, all industrialized countries have some type of social security system.

social segregation: a feature of urban living, the separation of social groups into distinctive neighborhoods, with a lack of social interaction between them. Wirth argued that as cities grow the degree of social segregation increases, so that any relationships among different social groups in the city are composed of emotionally empty contacts, with only segmental and instrumental involvement.

social status: the honor or prestige given by members of society to groups or individuals. This is based not just on economic standing but on social standing as a whole, and has a real manifestation in the lifestyles of the groups or individuals associated with a particular status. The concept is particularly associated with *Weber*, who used it to obtain a finer analysis of social differentiation than class analysis allowed. Moreover, Weber argued that social status was a firmer basis for the analysis of *social action* than class itself.

social structure: see *structure*

social surveys: the systematic collection of information about a given population. The term is commonly used in connection with surveys using standardized *questionnaires*. Social surveys usually result in *quantitative data* about the population studied, and are widely used, not only in sociological research but also by government departments and in market research. Although most social surveys gain their information from *sampling* the population, the largest social survey in the US is the ten-yearly *census*, which attempts to include all members of society.

social system: patterned regularities and relationships between individual *actors* and collectivities, reproduced over time and space. They are thus relatively permanent features of society that individuals invest with an external existence, talking about them as if they were real.

social world: used as contrast to the *natural world*, a term for the world constructed by human beings and their activities. It includes physical artifacts that people manufacture, and also patterned regularities that we create through our interactions. The social world is therefore composed of buildings, *institutions*, *structures*, dyads, triads, etc.

socialism: a political philosophy that stresses the communal ownership of the *means of production* and communitarian policies. It has many variations, ranging from the complete control of all productive processes to more utopian notions of communal living, in which individuals take responsibility for their own decisions within a *frame of reference* that includes the collective.

socialization: the process whereby the young of a society learn the *values,* ideas, practices, and *roles* of that society. The socialization process is a semiconscious one, in that the major agency for socialization, the family, would not necessarily see itself in this role, while some *secondary socialization* agencies such as *education* are deliberately set up for this purpose. The socialization process is never total, as the young take on some of the lessons but reject, adapt, or expand on others. In this way, societies retain some continuity but also progress.

socially aspiring worker: a member of the *working class* who seeks to join the *middle class,* either economically or socially. The concept is used to distinguish workers who wish to be mobile (whether they are accepted by the middle class as equals or not) from those who are happy to remain working-class and have no ambitions to be socially mobile. (See *assimilated workers.*)

society: the social totality of all the relationships in a given space. The notion of a society exists at several different levels. In the main, it is used in conjunction with the term *nation-state,* since within the boundaries of a nation-state, a distinctive society is likely to form. However, there is also a sense in which there is a "human society," consisting of all human relationships together. In the Durkheimian sense, society has a real existence outside of the individuals who form it. Sociologists may also use the term society in a non-nation-state sense, for example in defining "Jewish society."

sociobiology: an approach to social behavior based on the belief that patterns of human conduct can be explained by biological imperatives such as the drive to spread genetic inheritance as widely as possible. It was developed from Darwinian notions, but goes much beyond these, seeking to explain social arrangements as the inevitable consequence of biological inheritance. It has been criticized by sociologists because:

- it is deterministic in identifying patterns of behavior that cannot be altered by free choice
- it ends up defending the status quo and traditional gender roles
- it does not explain the mechanisms whereby biological drives can only be satisfied in particular ways.

(See *genetics.*)

sociocultural deference: an acceptance of a traditional social and moral order, sometimes known as "traditionalism." (See *ascriptive sociopolitical deference, political deference.*)

sociodrama: a term for group role-playing that helps individuals to deal with problematic relationships and issues; developed by Moreno.

socioeconomic group: a broad collection of individuals who share similar occupational positions in the social hierarchy. It is thus wider than an occupation but smaller than a class and constitutes a subgroup within a *social class.* For example, skilled manual workers form a socioeconomic group distinct from unskilled manual workers.

sociogram: see *sociometry*

sociolinguistics: the study of *language* in its social and cultural context. Sociolinguistics has been particularly concerned to examine the class, ethnic, and gendered forms of language that individuals create and develop, which are transmitted through everyday life and through *cultural reproduction*.

sociological imagination: the ability to link the experiences of individuals to the social processes and structures of the wider world. It is this ability to examine the ways that individuals construct the social world and how the social world impinges on the lives of individuals that is at the heart of the sociological enterprise.

sociological myth: the belief held by some teachers and drawn from misconceived lessons in sociology that children from low-income families will underachieve. It is mythical because many such children are highly successful within the education system. However, this sociological myth plays an important part in the *labeling* and *self-fulfilling prophecy* processes, which may influence certain students so that they accept the label of "failure" and act accordingly.

sociology: the study of individuals in groups and social formations in a systematic way, which grew out of the search for understanding associated with the industrial and scientific revolutions of the 18th and 19th centuries. It is now an established discipline in education and has offered generations of students insights into the social world they inhabit. Often accused by the right of being left-wing, it includes individuals of every political opinion, who are united by a commitment to search for knowledge and understanding, through providing evidence for the theories and insights they offer.

sociology as a science: one of the key theoretical debates in sociology, namely whether it should follow the principles and practices of the *natural sciences*. Those sociologists who argue that it should are called "sociological *positivists*," while those who do not believe that sociology should be a science are generally called "antipositivists." However, the terms positivist and antipositivist hide a variety of positions. Positivists can be functionalist in their approach or Marxist. Antipositivists include those who wish sociology could be a science, but feel that it is impossible because of the nature of the subject matter, and those who believe that sociologists should never try to be scientific, because human beings cannot be studied in a scientific way. The crucial difference between the two positions concerns their attitude toward their subject matter. Ultimately, positivists believe that there is sufficient regularity of behavior among people to generate *laws* about them. Antipositivists argue that human beings have *free will*, and are awkward and contradictory, so that laws about them can never be sustained.

sociology of the underdog: a term used by Becker to describe his sociological approach, based on taking the side of the powerless in society. Becker argued that, since *value freedom* was impossible, it was imperative that all sociologists declare their allegiances. For him, this meant looking at social phenomena from the perspective of those most disadvantaged in society, with his sociology geared toward bettering their position. Gouldner criticizes this as not being a simple sociology of the underdog, but a sociology *for* the underdog by well-paid, well-meaning, middle-class sociologists. (See *hierarchies of credibility*.)

sociometry: a method developed by Moreno for gaining information about how the members of a group feel about each other, in order to identify types of relationship within the wider group. It is widely used in education and the workplace to study group dynamics. The method involves asking members of the group questions like "Who are your best friends?" or "Whom do you least like to be with?" The replies are plotted on a diagram, known as a sociogram, and individuals can be identified as "stars" (those who receive lots of positive choices) and "isolates" (those who receive few, if any, friendship choices). The sociogram also allows friendship groups or clusters to be identified, which can be useful when asking people to work collaboratively in teams.

soft statistics: statistics that are particularly prone to *subjectivity* in both their collection and their presentation. These are usually statistics that describe aspects of society in which the potential for value judgments on the part of those who collect and those who interpret the data is very high, either because of the nature of the phenomenon under consideration, or as a result of political motivation. Examples of soft statistics are those on *crime, suicide, strikes*, and *poverty*. (See *hard statistics; official statistics*.)

solidarism: a tactic of *social closure*, in which a social group acts collectively to gain increased rewards, usually from superordinate groups. It is mainly associated with the working-class *labor unions*. Solidaristic tactics include *collective bargaining*, striking, and demarcation disputes. (See *credentialism; exclusion*.)

solidarity: the feelings of identification and mutual interest manifested by a group. It is usually associated with the working class and has a real existence in the actions that they employ to defend their interests, such as unionism or political activities.

space–time distanciation: the ways in which time and space have been transformed by new technologies, so that objects are separated from their original locations and distance is no longer a problem for communication between individuals. An example of the former is the way that digital technologies allow us to listen to, or view, text and images whenever we want, regardless of where they came from. In the latter case, new communications technologies bring the world into our living rooms almost as soon as events happen, and modern travel allows people to traverse the globe with relative ease. (See *disembedding*.)

span of control theory: the theory that workers work best when the span of control, or the ratio of workers to managers in an organization, is large, and therefore supervision is light. Likert, for example, showed that both morale and productivity were higher when control was carried out with a light touch. It is a contrast to *scientific management* which argued for a narrow span and tight control over the activities of workers. (See *Taylorism*.)

spatial boundaries: a term used by postmodernists to refer to the distinctions in location in which activities are carried out. Modernity is typified by boundedness in which different activities would have particular spaces given over to them. As an example, in schools this might be the science laboratory or the sociology department. It is argued that in postmodern societies these spatial boundaries dissolve so that rigid distinctions of location no longer exist. (See *temporal boundaries.*)

special needs: a term applied to the requirements for those who, usually because of a disability, have needs additional to those of others. It implies a duty on the part of the relevant institution or organization to meet those needs. The term is particularly used in the context of *education,* where it is correctly known as "special educational needs," and is applied to students with either physical disabilities or learning difficulties or a combination of both.

specialization: the narrowing down of work tasks into their smallest constitutional parts. Though specialization is sometimes referred to as the *division of labor,* the two are not quite the same thing. Specialization is a central feature of *Taylorism,* and describes the ways in which any work task can be broken down into smaller tasks. This means that workers will specialize in a work activity that is less and less skillful, so that less training and financial reward for the worker is needed. Specialization therefore contributes fundamentally to the profitability of companies that are mass-producing standardized goods.

spiralists: identified by Watson as those who are upwardly mobile through climbing *hierarchies* in large-scale *organizations.* They tend also to be geographically mobile and rely on expert knowledge in making claim to a higher *status.* (See *burgesses.*)

spirit of capitalism: the ideas, values, and typical modes of behavior associated with Calvinist Protestantism that underlie the practices of *capitalism.* The ideas of thrift, self-discipline, and a capacity for hard work were seen by *Weber* as the source of the patterns of behavior appropriate for the development of the capitalist system of production. However, this idea has been criticized from a variety of positions:

- Some sociologists have argued that Weber does not show that the early capitalists, although Protestant, actually held these ideas in any depth.
- Others have argued that it was not the Calvinist ideas that were important for the Protestants' behavior, but their marginality in a Catholic-dominated world that led them to capitalist practices.
- Still others have argued that the ideas came from the practices of capitalism and did not cause it.

spiritualism: belief, and practices arising from such belief, in the existence of the disembodied "spirits" of people now dead, and in the ability of certain people to communicate with them. While it is difficult to obtain figures, spiritualism appears to have a considerable number of believers in contemporary Western societies. The belief in spiritualism is used by some to cast doubt on Weber's idea of *disenchantment.*

spurious correlation: a situation in which there appears to be a correlation between two or more variables, but in fact no causal relationship exists. For example, it might well be shown that the rise in the number of cohabiting couples has been accompanied by a rise in the ownership of mobile telephones, but it would be most unwise to suggest that one was caused by the other.

square of crime: the network of relationships among the state, informal control mechanisms, the criminal, and the victim, which are the basic factors to be considered by sociologists of crime.

stages of development: see *five stages of economic growth*

standardized interview: see *structured interviews*

state: a wider term than *government* that includes all the organizations that are agencies of the governing institutions in society and their activities among the general populace. Thus, Congress and the President are obvious parts of the state, but so are federal agencies, the military, and the public education system. The growth of state activity in the 20th century has been enormous and sociologists have been interested in the extension of state *power* and attempts to roll back the frontiers of the state. The political balance between the state and the individual has been a focus for sociological investigation, as well as being politically controversial in itself. (See *centralization*.)

state capitalism: a term used by Barrington-Moore to denote the development of private industry in Japan, sponsored and guided for political reasons by state sup-port. The political leadership of 19th-century Japan saw rapid *industrialization* as the only way to avoid the imperialistic tendencies of the Western powers and therefore grafted onto the traditional great houses of Japan a system of industrial develop-ment, which left large numbers of companies concentrated in private hands. However, plans for industrial development were determined centrally in the national interest, rather than occurring piecemeal as individual capitalists saw oppor-tunities to profit. (See *state socialism*.)

state-centered theories: analyses of power that start from the idea that the *state* is the most powerful institution in society, and that it has interests of its own, inde-pendent of groups and classes in society as a whole. It is thus an anti-Marxist view of the state.

state-dependent population: those who rely on public provision for their major services. For example, the elderly receiving supplemental security payments are part of the state-dependent population. Welfare recipients and anyone else who needs state support for their main source of *income* are part of this group. (See *welfare dependency*.)

state of nature: a hypothetical situation referred to by philosophers as the condi-tion in which there is no society. It is assumed that, since basic human nature is selfish, the state of nature is a war of all against all, in which unconstrained desire leads to a life which is "nasty, selfish, brutish and short." Society is therefore brought into being to avoid the state of nature. (See *utilitarianism*.)

state socialism: a term used by Barrington-Moore to describe industrial develop-ment in which enterprises are sponsored and directly owned by the *state*. This leads to a centrally planned economy, in which the national development plan determines where resources should be placed, which sectors should be developed, and which should be neglected. This centralization allowed heavy industrial development to take place in the Soviet Union, but at the expense of consumer products and meet-ing the material needs of the population. (See *state capitalism*.)

status: a position in society associated with particular *roles* and duties. It is not the same as *social status*, which is associated with Weberian sociology.

status consciousness: a belief that individuals can advance by their own actions, and achieve improvement in their lot by virtue of their own efforts. (See *class consciousness*; *labor union consciousness*.)

status frustration: where individuals have their aspirations to a particular position in the social *hierarchy* blocked by circumstances, such as a lack of qualifications, *social closure* by superior groups, or even bad luck.

status group: a collectivity distinguished from others by the amount of *prestige* or honor that is accorded to it. Social positions such as occupation or class position have negative or positive estimations of honor attached to them and these are grouped into a *hierarchy* of superior and subordinate status groups.

status inconsistency: where the estimation of *prestige* given to individuals does not accord with some other social position associated with them. For example, status inconsistency is accorded to those black individuals who occupy high occupational positions in the *professions*.

status passage: a term developed by the *Chicago School* to indicate the transform-ation of an individual into a "professional." The Chicago School argued that professionalism was a state of mind, into which individuals (both professionals and *clients)* had to be inducted. This was achieved with professionals through intensive training and socialization into professional *culture* and ethics. It was this process that took the individual from a "lay" frame of mind to the status of professional.

status predicament: a term used by interactionists to describe the contradictions in consciousness experienced by those in middle-class occupations, who are subject to *proletarianization* forces. For example, the traditional middle-class orientation of clerical workers has been challenged by changes in their objective circumstances, so that they have been pulled toward a working-class consciousness. The dilemma for them is how to reconcile their historical allegiances with their changed circumstances.

status situation: a term used by Lockwood to describe the identification of clerical workers and their relationship with their employers. Traditionally, clerks have been close to employers, both physically, in terms of their *work situation* and ideo-logically, in the sense that they identified their fortunes as resting with the employers. The status situation implied a sense of superiority in the consciousness of clerks over manual workers. The *proletarianization* thesis suggested that this identification was being replaced by a solidarity of consciousness with the *working class*. (See *market situation*.)

statutory services: services that the *state* undertakes to provide for citizens as a right of *citizenship*. Examples of statutory services are education and welfare programs. (See *nonstatutory services*.)

stereotyping: the process whereby groups or individuals are characterized in simplified and often pejorative terms, so that all members of the category are seen in one particular way. For example, popular stereotypes of gay men include some indication of effeminate behavior, so that all gay men become associated with feminine characteristics, regardless of their actual behavior.

stigmatization: the process whereby individuals are labeled with some marginalizing characteristic, such as "deviant," "crazy," etc. Causes of stigma may vary from negative signs or names to some physical attribute, such as "staring eyes." The result of stigmatization is usually the prevention of full acceptance by the rest of society. Where the stigma is accepted by the person being stigmatized it becomes an important part of the *self-fulfilling prophecy*.

stimulation effect: the effect of violence in the media on audiences, based on the idea that watching violence on television or in movies increases the likelihood of violence in the real world, since aggression is encouraged by exposure to realistic depictions of violence. (See *catharsis effect*.)

stratification: the hierarchical division of societies on the basis of a social characteristic. Social differences are stratified in societies when the relative possession or nonpossession of a social characteristic such as *wealth* or *status* becomes the distributing principle for individuals within a system of unequal rewards. Different societies use various organizing principles for slotting individuals into the *hierarchy*. Traditional societies have often used hereditary characteristics as the basis for distribution, while more modern societies often use wealth or income. The importance of stratification is that those at the top of the system have greater access to scarce resources than those at the bottom.

stratified diffusion: a term for the spread of particular cultural beliefs and practices from the upper social groups down through the status *hierarchy* to lower groups. It is thus believed that many practices that are first observed in the middle classes will filter down to the working classes. Bott believed that the *joint conjugal roles* that she observed in middle-class couples would eventually replace the working-class *segregated conjugal roles*, and it is suggested that the "*new man*" will begin to emerge in working-class families. However, critics claim that the evidence shows that this is a grossly oversimplified view of the spread of cultural beliefs and practices, and it is by no means a simple one-way process.

stratified sampling: a form of *sampling* in which the *survey population* is first divided into mutually exclusive groups and then a *sample* is drawn from each, the size of the sample in each being proportionate to the number of members of that group in the survey population. For example, a survey of a school in which there were 2,000 students, equally divided between males and females, might be conducted by drawing a simple random sample of 100 male and 100 female students. However, if the students were drawn from three distinct and very different neighborhoods, in the proportion of 1,000 students from neighborhood A, 800 from neighborhood B, and 200 from neighborhood C, the students could first be divided into three groups, A, B, and C, reflecting their home neighborhoods. A sample could then be drawn from each group, with 100 from A, 80 from B, and 20 from C, with equal numbers of male and female students in each, assuming that each group had a roughly equal balance of males and females. This arrangement is likely to be more *representative* than a simple *random sample*.

street crime: one of the most visible forms of crime that is associated with violence, including activities such as mugging, robbery with violence, and snatching.

strike duration ratio: an indicator of strike activity obtained by dividing the number of working days lost by the number of workers involved in strikes for a particular year. It was used by Ross and Hartman to show that there had been a gradual decline in the striking habit in Britain since World War II.

strike-proneness: the propensity of workers in a particular industry or country to go on strike. Industries associated with high strike-proneness are mining, ship-building, and other heavy manufacturing occupations. Those with low strike-proneness are agriculture, and most types of office work. (See *cohesive mass segregation*.)

strike rates: the measurement of recorded withdrawals of labor that allows comparisons to be made among different companies in the same industry, different industries, and different societies. Raw strike statistics tell sociologists very little about the propensity to strike and do not allow interindustry or intersocietal comparisons. The production of strike-rate statistics allow such comparisons to be made, through taking into consideration for example, the numbers of days lost per 1,000 workers. (See *membership involvement ratio; strike duration ratio*.)

strike statistics: the number of stoppages of work reported to a government in any one year. The problem with strike statistics is that they are a *soft statistic*, with problems about the *reliability* of collection and therefore questions about their validity. For example, different governments use different definitions of what constitutes a reportable strike and it is therefore difficult to make cross-cultural comparisons of strike rates. Moreover, many strikes go unreported as the management neglects to inform the government. It is thought therefore that the total number of strikes is underestimated. Some sociologists argue that the strike statistics are subject to social negotiation and are therefore not very valid.

strikes: a form of *industrial conflict* in which workers withdraw their labor in order to achieve their goals. Strikes may be official, or held with the support of the *labor union*, or unofficial. Sociological interest in strikes is threefold:

- as a measure of industrial discontent in a society
- in the causes of strike action
- in the experience of being on strike.

(See *wildcat strike*.)

structural differentiation: the historical process whereby social structures become increasingly specialized and segregated from each other. It was seen as an important part of the *modernization* process by *Parsons*, who argued for example that as religious institutions withdrew from nonreligious functions such as welfare, they became more effective institutions, focusing only on their core activities. Structural differentiation therefore produced purer, more spiritual religious organizations.

structural-functionalism: the form of *functionalism* associated with *Talcott Parsons*, with an emphasis on the way that *structures* in society interact with each other to perform positive roles for society as a whole. The distinctive feature of structural-functionalism is the notion that everything that exists in society has a positive function to perform. This has been criticized, not least by other functionalists, as providing justification for the existence of such phenomena as the Mafia, child abuse, etc.

structural location: the position of individuals in the social arrangements of a society. Structural location may include a whole range of factors ranging from the size of the workplace of the individual to whether a person lives in a rural or urban environment.

structural position: see *structural location*

structuralism: in sociology, a general term for theories that give priority to the analysis of social structures, rather than the individual. There are many variants of structuralism, but they all operate from the premise that there are underlying rationales or formations in society that are initially hidden from the individual, but can be explored by sociologists and laid bare by them. The individual is thus unimportant except in so far as he or she carries out the *actions* dictated by their structural position. More recently, structuralism has become closely associated with the analysis of *language* through the work of Saussure and Barthes. Language is seen as the fundamental structure in society, with all human products being a form of language. So, while every sentence may be a "speech act," it is drawn from an underlying structure of language, made up of the rules about the relationships of sounds to ideas. (See *icons; index; signs proper.*)

structuration: a theory developed by *Giddens* to dissolve the structure–action dualism that stresses the mutual interdependence of *structure* and *action*. It is based on the idea that structures are created by the patterned activities of individuals, who call upon structural forms in order to perform those actions.

structure: a term widely used in sociology to indicate a social formation that is more than just a collection of individuals or groups. Social structures are relatively permanent features of society that take on new characteristics different from the individuals who make up the social structure. So, a structure will survive the death of any individual member, will have a history of its own, and has a role to play in society beyond that played by any individual life. Examples of structures are the *family*, the *education* system, and language itself. *Language* is a structure because it is made up of words, which when placed together in sentences take on a meaning beyond the individual words that compose the sentence. Language changes over time (it has a history), it extends across *generations* (it survives the death of any individual member), and it is the means by which individuals are able to act together in society (it has a role to play). However, it is important to recognize that a structure is not a thing and does not have thing-like attributes. Structures are found in the continued activities of individuals across time and space.

structure–action dualism: one of the central debates in sociology that concerns whether it is the actions of individuals that are the prime social phenomena, or the social structures that are the more important aspect of social activity. Sociologists are divided on this issue to become structuralists or interactionists. However, the distinction is in many senses a false one, with most sociologists dealing with both aspects in their work, even when they do focus their attention on one level at the expense of the other.

structured interviews: *interviews* typically used in large-scale *social surveys*, in which *respondents* are asked the same questions in the same order and their replies codified. It is argued that this type of interview helps to reduce significantly the degree of *interviewer bias*. However, structured interviews by their nature do not yield the kind of in-depth information that can be gained from an *unstructured interview*.

structured questionnaires: questionnaires that use closed, precoded questions.

style: in sociology, a word to describe the features of *subcultures* in symbolic form. A style is composed of the dress, speech, behavior, and leisure interests of subcultural groups. When placed together they form a distinctive image that identifies an individual immediately as a member of the subculture. The style adopted can also indicate the subculture's attitudes toward mainstream society, and whether this is *oppositional* or *conformist*. (See *resistance*.)

styles of life: a term associated with *Weber* that denotes the patterns of consumption carried out by particular status groups in society. On a mundane level, the style of life is associated with the goods that people consume and the taste that they exhibit. At a deeper level, they are the standards of propriety, judgment, and good taste that each group holds to. The problem with the concept is that it is difficult to determine who decides what constitutes good taste.

subcontracting: the company practice of giving out parts of the production process to other independent companies or individuals, usually because it is cheaper for them to do it than the main company carrying it out itself. Nonessential processes, such as catering or cleaning, are often subcontracted, which has the effect of downsizing the main company's workforce. (See *periphery workers*.)

subcultural signs: symbols that denote membership of a specific group, separate from the rest of society. They are often symbols like dress, music, ways of behaving, or a particular form of slang.

subculture: an identifiable group within a society, whose members share common *values* and have similar behavior patterns. Subcultures can be based on social characteristics, such as ethnicity, or on *styles* generated by the individuals who make up the subculture, as in the case of punk. Subcultures usually share some features with the host culture, but may also be oppositional to it.

subemployment: a term developed by Braverman to indicate those who are not in full employment, but who do not register as officially unemployed. These are:

- those long-term unemployed who have given up looking for work and therefore cease to register as unemployed. This group is particularly large among the black and Hispanic populations
- part-time workers, who are low-paid
- those paid below the minimum wage, often illegal immigrants.

subject–object dualism: often written as S–O, the dilemma inherent in the fact that the world (the external object) is only experienced by the individual (the internal mind of the subject). The problem is whether the categories of the social world would exist without the subject, or the subject instead imposes categories onto the external world in a way that is open to change and negotiation.

subjective poverty: the state of feeling poor by comparison with a particular *reference group*. Thus a family with a car might experience feelings of subjective poverty if they lived in a neighborhood in which the majority of families had two or three cars.

subjective social class: a person's position in the social *hierarchy* as identified by the individual himself or herself. The significance of subjective social class is that for sociologists it is the most important *indicator of class,* because the class people place themselves in is likely to affect their behavior more than *objective social class.*

subjectivity: an individual's perspective or point of view about a thing. Subjectivity is also defined as a lack of *objectivity* – that is, where the individual's own view influences the approach taken to an issue. The attitude toward subjectivity that is taken in sociology is ironically affected by the sociological position of the sociologist employing it. For positivistic sociologists, subjectivity is something to be looked down on, as tainting "objective" social scientific research. It is thus to be avoided. For interactionists, the subject's subjectivity, or individual viewpoint, is exactly what should be examined by the sociologist. It is only the subjectivity of the individual that gives meaning to the social world.

subordinate value system: a set of ideas associated with the *working class* that recognizes that the system is unfair, but also recognizes the limitations of political action to change it. The subordinate value system is therefore not oppositional, but is more concerned with community values and *solidarity.* (See *dominant value system; radical value system.*)

subsistence economy: see *peasant economy*

substantial rationality: a term used by Mannheim to indicate the comprehension of the individual of the whole work process. Where substantial rationality is lacking, *alienation* is likely to result.

substructure: the economic base of society, called the "Unterbau" by *Marx*, that lies beneath and gives rise to all other social phenomena. The idea of substructure as the cause of the social totality has led to the criticism that it is a deterministic concept, allowing no independence to other social and cultural structures such as the education system, architecture, etc. (See *superstructure.*)

subterranean theologies: a term used by Pin to describe the existence of much magical and superstitious belief among the urban *working class,* who are otherwise unconcerned with formal religious beliefs. The survival of such nonrational beliefs among large numbers of people is problematic for those sociologists of *secularization,* who argue that there is a decline in *supernatural* beliefs.

suburbanization: the process whereby cities develop outlying districts, connected to the center through employment and transportation systems. Suburbanization may occur as a result of the specific development of housing on the outskirts of towns, or by the growth of cities in the process of so-called "urban sprawl."

suburbia: a term to describe the surrounding areas of cities and towns, in which the majority of the population live. Suburbia is associated with the lower-middle and middle class and contains the more desirable residential areas of the town or city. It is associated also with a particular style of life, which is home-centered and family-oriented. In American sociology, suburbia can be said to represent one aspect of the *American Dream*.

succession of goals: an explanation for what happens when an *organization* achieves its *goals* – that is, new goals are devised so that the organization can continue to exist.

suicidal act: a term used to denote suicide that takes into account the various circumstances in which an individual might attempt to take his or her own life. The actual moment of *suicide* is surrounded by other events and circumstances, which give meaning to the suicidal act itself – for example, whether it is a serious attempt to take one's own life or whether the chances of detection are high. (See *gambles with death*.)

suicide: in *Durkheim*'s classic definition, this is any case of death where the victim has acted, either directly or indirectly, positively or negatively, to bring about the death. Durkheim was thus offering a wide definition of suicide, including events where the victim carried out the action himself or herself, or where the actions of others might result in the victim's death. Actions that avoided lifesaving action were also included. Durkheim's interest in suicide arose out of the very individual nature of the suicidal action. He wanted to show that, even with gun in hand, the individual was caught up in social processes. Types of suicide can be illustrated by the following diagram:

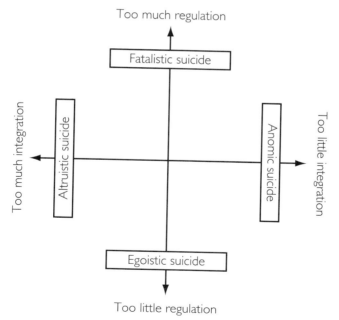

Types of suicide

suicide rate: the number of suicides per million population in a society. The suicide rate, rather than the total number of suicides in any society, is an important measure for sociologists for two reasons:

- It allows the comparison of societies in terms of how suicidal the population is. The result is that sociologists can identify high- and low-suicide countries.
- It allows the comparison of the incidence of suicide in any one country over time to see if it is on the increase or decrease.

The idea of a suicide rate has come under attack by many interactionist sociologists who argue that it is a *social construction,* made up of thousands of individual decisions by coroners who have different *operational definitions* of what is a suicide. It does not therefore count the *real rate of suicide.* However, though the statistics are socially constructed in this way, it is all the more impressive that, year in, year out, they stay remarkably stable in different societies.

suicidogenic impulses: a term used by *Durkheim* to describe the *social forces* in society that impel individuals toward *suicide.* These might be such forces as the degree of *integration* in a society, or the amount of regulation. To Durkheim, these social forces were real, not theoretical, and were linked to the fundamental natures of different societies. They accounted for the different *suicide rates* in different societies.

sunrise industries: a term for the industrial sector associated with computer technology and the development of new forms of production such as bioengineering. Some sociologists argue that the sunrise industries constitute a new *Industrial Revolution* that will transform the way we live in the same way that the first one did. Others argue that the effect of the sunrise industries will be to reinforce the divisions in society, as more and more people are made unemployed by the development of automated processes.

supernatural: that which lies outside the "laws of nature," and can only be explained by reference to magical or divine forces.

superstructure: all the social and cultural activity in society, called the "Überbau" by *Marx,* that arises from the economic activity of the *substructure.* In one sense, the superstructure is the social world, apart from economics, and is the product of labor in the widest sense.

surface reality: a term used by postmodernists to describe the appearance of the world as it is presented through media images. They argue that it is impossible to penetrate this surface reality to find out what is really underneath, because there is nothing underneath these surface images. Things are as they appear in *hyperreality.*

surface world: a term to describe the kaleidoscope of everyday life as it is experienced – chaotic and meaningless. The implication of the concept is that there is no structure to the social world, only life as it is lived. (See *poststructuralism.*)

surplus repression: an idea developed by Marcuse that capitalist society is engaged in keeping down the *proletariat,* above and beyond what is necessary for the continuation of the capitalist system. In particular, the capitalist system suppresses the erotic instinct in society. (See *eros.*)

surplus value: the difference between the worth of the *capital* employed at the beginning of the productive process and the worth of the goods produced at the end. The difference is accounted for by the purchase by capital of the labor power of the worker. Labor power is itself wealth-producing, as it accounts for the profits that accrue to the capitalist. Therefore, the difference between the price of purchasing labor power and the worth of the final commodities is the rate of appropriation of the worker's labor power. *Exploitation* can be intensified by increasing the length of the working day, thus expanding the time that labor power is operative without increasing the cost, or by increasing the productivity of the worker by, for example, changing the organization of work or using new machines.

Surrey occupational scale: a way of classifying the *occupational structure* developed by a team of sociologists from the University of Surrey in Great Britain. An important feature of the scale is that occupations are classified in such a way that those occupied mainly by members of one sex are shown separately. The resulting data show clearly the predominance of men in the upper and lower groups, and that of women in the intermediate group. The occupational classes devised by the Surrey group are as follows:

1 higher professionals
2 employers and managers
3 lower professionals
4 secretarial and clerical
5 foremen; self-employed manual
6 sales and skilled manual
7 semiskilled
8 unskilled.

(See *occupational scale.*)

surrogate religiosity: the situation in which, for an individual, secular beliefs or *ideologies* take the place of religious beliefs in providing meaning and purpose for that individual's life.

surveillance: a term used by postmodernists to describe the type of social control exercised in postmodern societies, in which individuals police themselves through the operation of ways of thinking and behaving that define what is normal in society. The shaping of behavior in postmodern societies is thus established through *discourses*, by which individuals channel their own activity into socially acceptable forms. This is in contrast to the *social control* by force used in preindustrial societies and social control by the rule of law associated with *modernity*.

survey: see *social surveys*

survey population: all of the members of the group in whom a researcher is interested when conducting a *social survey*. The survey population will form the basis of the *sampling frame*, although not all members of the survey population will necessarily be in the sampling frame.

sustainable development: where the process of *industrialization* does not result in damage to the environment or the loss of natural resources, so that progress can be maintained over a long period of time. It is particularly concerned with the rational exploitation of replaceable resources, especially in agriculture and fishing, so that a constant source of revenue can be sustained. However, it has also come to signify the sensible use of irreplaceable resources such as minerals and the search for alternatives to, for example, finite mineral oils.

suttee: a ritual in India, in which the widow of a recently deceased husband throws herself onto his funeral pyre, as a matter of honor. It is often used in the sociology of *suicide* as an example of how social pressures can overcome individual instincts.

symbiosis: a term used by the *Chicago School* to describe city living, in which members of different cultures come to live together within the same habitat, or zone of the city. The idea is based on the assumption that natural areas grow up within the city.

symbol: see *sign*

symbolic annihilation: a term used to refer to the underrepresentation of women in media texts, especially television, so that they become virtually invisible. (See *invisibility of women.*)

symbolic control: a type of power, usually exercised in the higher parts of an *organization,* in which *prestige,* acceptance, and *status* operate as the incentives and therefore as a control. (See *material control; physical control.*)

symbolic interactionism: a theoretical approach in sociology that draws its inspiration from *Weber,* and starts from the assumption that we inhabit a symbolic world in which symbols have shared meanings. Language is one set of symbols that we share. The social world is therefore constructed by the *meanings* that individuals attach to events and phenomena and these are transmitted across the generations through the language. A central concept of symbolic interactionists is the *self,* which allows us to calculate the effects of our actions. The perspective has been criticized because:

- it has not elaborated its methodology sufficiently
- it ignores the emotional side of the self as a basis for social action
- it has no proper concept of the self.

symbolic referent: an idea or *sign* to which individuals refer or give acknowledgment when they are negotiating courses of action. They help individuals to justify the decisions they make. For example, ethnomethodologists use symbolic referents in the sociology of organizations when examining goals. They argue that the goals of the organization are employed as bargaining counters by participants when they are seeking to achieve particular outcomes, in negotiating with other individuals and groups.

system: see *social system*

systematic sampling: a sampling method frequently used when the *survey population* is on a list, such as a school list or a voting register. If the *sampling frame* contains 5,000 names, and the sample size has been agreed as 200, then the sample will be 1 in 25 people on the list. A random number is selected between 1 and 25, say 14. The 14th name on the list is chosen, then 25 (which is known as the *sampling interval*) is added to this number, thus 14 + 25 = 39. Therefore, the 39th name is included in the sample, and then since 39 + 25 = 64, the 64th name is included, and so on until 200 names have been drawn. This is a very quick and easy way of drawing a sample, but care must be taken if the sampling frame is ranked in any way or otherwise "organized." If one were drawing a sample from a very large school using school registers, for instance, and it was the custom of the school to place boys' names first on the class register, and if the sampling interval were so large that only one name would be drawn per class, the sample could end up containing only students of the same sex.

taboo: that which is forbidden by religious law or by custom.

tactical voting: a strategy in which individuals cast their vote not according to their own political preference, but in order to achieve the best result from their political point of view. This often takes the form of voting for the second party in a constituency, when the political preference is actually for the third party, in order to prevent the election of a more despised first candidate.

taken-for-granted: that which is accepted by members of society without thought and on which much *social action* is based. It is a central concept of ethnomethodological thought because ethnomethodologists believe that social life is carried out on the basis of taken-for-granted assumptions. (See *glossing*.)

takeoff: the crucial and middle stage of Rostow's five stages of economic development. The term described the transformation of an agricultural society into an industrial one. The crucial aspect of the transformation is increasing investment of between 5 and 10% of *gross national product* in the developing sectors of the economy. Another feature of takeoff is the rapid technological developments that take place in the leading sectors of the economy and the consequent development of supportive industries to service these leading sectors. (See *five stages of economic growth; preconditions for takeoff*.)

taking the natural attitude: an expression used by Husserl to describe the situation where individuals take their everyday world for granted, seeing it as the natural order of things and not to be questioned or challenged. (See *Lebenswelt*.)

talent: the usually inborn abilities that an individual might have in a particular field. For example, musical talent or academic talent might be seen as gifts of nature. Sociologists argue that the idea of talent serves an ideological function also, in that it serves to internalize failure for those who do not succeed. If certain children do not succeed in a particular area, they can come to see themselves as untalented in that field, and therefore failure becomes the individual's fault, not the fault of the system.

target group: a group of people with particular characteristics that render them the focus of attention of another individual or group. The purpose of this attention might be to persuade the target group to accept advice or recommendations (e.g. persuading homosexuals to practice safe sex as a way of limiting the spread of AIDS) or to buy a product or service, or to obtain information from them (e.g. by means of a *social survey*), in which case the target group would be the population.

taste: associated with the idea of styles of life in sociology, a term for what is stylish in a particular time. Taste is a very elusive concept, because it is socially constructed and therefore varies from time to time and place to place. In postmodern sociology, taste has become a very important concept as attention has switched to consumption rather than production. Therefore the arbiters of taste in a society have become the new capitalists in postmodern societies, as they define what is seen as worthy and worthwhile in terms of culture and art.

tax threshold: the level of income at which a person starts to pay tax.

taxonomies: classifications of social life devised by sociologists from their studies. Taxonomies are one of the basic ways in which sociologists seek to place an order on the often chaotic social world, and are a first step in the development of *theories*.

Taylorism: the name given to a *management* system developed by British sociologist F.W. Taylor, in which the activities of workers are tightly controlled according to principles generated by the application of scientific observation to the workplace. Sometimes known as *scientific management*, Taylorism is associated with time-and-motion studies and increasing *specialization* of tasks. Braverman argued that the most important consequence of Taylorism was the *deskilling* of workers. Sociologists dispute the importance of Taylorism, with some arguing that the principles did not spread very far in British industry, and that where they were implemented, they were strongly resisted by workers.

teachers' expectations: see *Pygmalion effect*

technicism: the sociological term for red tape, or an abundance of rules and regulations in *organizations* that can stifle the ability of the organization to deliver its *goals* to its *clients*. (See *displacement of goals; formalism; ritualism.*)

technological determinism: the idea that similar machines, related to each other in similar ways, always produce similar types of work organization and similar attitudes among the workers who operate them. The concept is built upon classifications of technology into *craft, machine-minding, assembly-line, continuous process,* and *automated* technologies. Each of these is associated, according to technological determinists, with different organizational structures and worker *consciousness*. In the case of attitudinal effects, Blauner argued that *alienation* reaches its height in assembly-line technology and decreases with the introduction of automation. For organizational structure, Woodward argued that the more complex the technology (from craft to automation) the more complex the *management* structure needed. However, technological determinism has come under a great deal of criticism from various sociological positions:

- Some argue that the empirical findings of the technological determinists are mistaken, and that high levels of alienation are to be found in automated industries.
- Some argue that technological determinists ignore the importance of individuals and the way that they can choose to react to different technologies.
- Others argue that similar technologies in different societies lead to different management styles – that is, there is an element of managerial choice in deciding on structures.
- Yet others argue that technological determinism is a myth and that the process is the reverse of what the technological determinists say. That is, it is technology that is determined by social and economic forces, rather than the other way around.

technology: the application of technical and scientific knowledge to the systems of production. In a more specific sense the term can be used to describe the machines that are used, both in production and in everyday life, and the way that they are organized. Sociologists have always been interested in the effects of technology on society, but they have difficulty in defining what exactly it is. The narrow definition focusing only on the machines themselves and on their degree of complexity tends to be the definition taken by *technological determinists*. A more Marxist and/or inter- actionist definition tends to include the social and economic forces that shape the development of the machines. Other sociologists include a more ideological element in defining technology, arguing that technologies provide the justification for capitalists controlling workers, through the need for coordination and *efficiency*.

technoscapes: sites for the flow of machines and new technologies through a *globalized* economy.

teenage economy: a term used by Abrams to describe the development in the post- war period of a market for goods specifically aimed at *adolescents*. It is the result of growing *affluence* in the economy and the emergence of a *youth culture* with a dispos- able income at its fingertips. The teenage economy has been particularly associated with the *media industries*, especially music.

teenage marriage: a marriage in which at least one of the partners is under 20 years of age. These have declined in number since the 1960s, and part of the reason for this is the lessening of the *stigma* attached to unmarried mothers, since many teenage marriages in the past took place to legitimate a pregnancy. Social attitudes toward *cohabitation* have also relaxed.

teleological explanation: the explanation of a phenomenon by reference to the end it serves. So functionalist theory is teleological in that it explains the existence of social customs through the purpose they serve for the maintenance of society as a whole. The problem with this is that it implies that all action is purposeful and deliberate. However, action is more complicated than seeing a problem, thinking up a solution, and acting upon it. People do not always act purposively or from conscious motivation.

televangelism: the use of television to reach a mass *audience* for the preaching of evangelical or fundamental *Christianity*. The term is particularly relevant in the US, where so-called televangelists like the Rev. Jerry Falwell, Jim Bakker, Oral Roberts, Pat Robertson, and Jimmy Swaggert regularly broadcast on prime-time television. It has been estimated that about 25% of Americans are evangelical or fundamental Christians, so the potential audience is very large. However, in the 1980s, when televangelism was at its height, figures showed that only about 8% of the total American viewing public (15 million people) were regular viewers of such programs. This figure fell after both Jim Bakker and Jimmy Swaggert were involved in sex scandals toward the end of the 1980s. Research indicates that televangelism does not convert nonbelievers; rather, it is watched by those who are already followers, who enjoy the particular mix of gospel music, homespun philosophy, and fiery preaching that forms the staple diet of such programs. However, the members of the *new Christian right* are now using religion-based programs to "cross over" into mainstream television, and are producing soap operas and game shows with a religious message that are proving increasingly popular with audiences.

temporal boundaries: a term used by postmodernists in describing the division in time among different activities. Modernity is characterized by strict separation of activities into slots of time. For example, school subjects have distinct units of time (class periods) given over to them. In postmodern societies, these boundaries are dissolving as the distinctions between traditional subjects disappear. (See *spatial boundaries*.)

Tepoztlan: a village in Mexico that was studied by anthropologist Redfield in the 1930s and then studied again in the 1940s by Lewis. The village is important because it provides one of the few cases of *replication* in sociology. In this case, the results found by each sociologist were different from the other. Critics argue that these differences were the result of the different expectations of the two researchers.

tertiary health care: long-term health care aimed at rehabilitation or maintaining the quality of life, e.g. care provided in nursing homes or residential homes for the elderly.

tertiary sector: in the *occupational structure*, service jobs that are usually carried out in offices, such as banking. (See *primary sector, secondary sector*.)

text: used in sociological analysis of the media to denote any program, book, magazine, movie etc., that has to be "read" by the *audience*. Texts in this sense are much wider than suggested by the traditional use of the word and imply that messages may be transmitted by a whole variety of media, not just the written word. (See *decoding, encoding*.)

thaumaturgical sects: *sects* that promise their members a variety of personal benefits that will occur through *supernatural* or miraculous intervention.

theocracy: a society ruled by the priestly caste, who use religious ideas to control the population and establish dominance through the manipulation of religious *symbols* and *rituals*.

theodicy: in religion, explanations for the contradiction between the supposed existence of a just and benevolent god and the existence of evil and suffering in the world. The contradiction is at its most acute when the pain and suffering are inflicted on the innocent, particularly children.

theodicy of disprivilege: a term used by *Weber* to refer to religious explanations that legitimize social inequalities. Weber argued that certain *sects* would have a particular attraction for the poor and socially deprived because they explained social deprivation as God's way of testing faith, and also promised a reversal of fortunes in the next life. Worldly suffering can thus be endowed with a moral justification.

theological stage: the earliest of *Comte's three stages of human development*, distinguished by the explanation of phenomena by reference to the *supernatural* world. Religious authority is therefore the ultimate source of explanation for the social and natural worlds. (See *metaphysical stage, positive stage*.)

theories of the middle range: identified by Merton as explanations derived from empirical data in specific areas of social life. They are attempts to bridge the gap between *high theory* and *empiricism*.

theory: a systematic and general attempt to explain phenomena and, in the case of sociology, the social world around us. Theories are advanced to cover general areas of social life, yet they are often partial in that they are put forward by sociologists from a particular sociological perspective. There are different levels of theory in sociology, from *high theory* to *taxonomies*.

theory x: a term developed by McGregor to denote the philosophy behind those traditional *organizations* that ignored their workers' needs for *self-actualization*. Such organizations tended to treat workers as rational economic beings, motivated by money and nothing else. (See *theory y*.)

theory y: the alternative to McGregor's *theory x*, a term to define the principle behind organizations that recognized their workers as more than just there for the money. Theory y organizations therefore rejected the *detailed division of labor*, in favor of *job enlargement, participative leadership*, and *decentralization* of responsibility.

third world: a popular term for the less developed areas of the globe, in which *poverty* and lack of *development* is predominant. The term is usually applied to the poorer countries of Asia and Africa, which are heavily reliant on agriculture in their economies. The term "third world" has come under heavy criticism for its all-embracing nature. Critics argue that it is wrong to lump all African and Asian countries together in this way. Each country has its own history, *culture*, and problems, and to use an umbrella term like this is likely to result in general solutions to poverty that do not fit the needs of individual countries. However, proponents of the concept argue that the major problem that countries of the third world face is their relationship with the *first world*, and it is therefore appropriate that they develop a common strategy in dealing with the richer nations. (See *second world*.)

this-worldly orientation: a term used by Pfautz to indicate the attitude of individuals who focus on the present in dealing with the world around them. Social action is therefore shaped by a pragmatic ethic, in which satisfaction here and now is an important component. (See *other-worldly orientation*.)

three roads to modernity: three suggested alternative ways in which a society could industrialize, i.e. *capitalism, state socialism*, and *state capitalism*. Barrington-Moore argued that historical evidence suggested that these were the models that societies had adopted when industrializing. Britain and the US were used as an example of capitalist development, Russia as an example of state socialist development, and Japan as an example of state capitalism. They were therefore presented as "roads to modernity" for undeveloped societies. Critics of this approach argue that all the models are inappropriate for modern times, because they describe situations where for one reason or another the industrializing society had little competition from more developed societies. In the case of the Western capitalist societies, they industrialized early, while Japan and Soviet Russia remained relatively isolated from more developed societies and were able to industrialize with little exposure to competition. Critics also suggest that undeveloped societies were also trying to develop their own roads to modernity through such policies as *intermediate technology* development or third worldism. (See *development*.)

three stages of human development: a set of distinctions used by Comte to explain the way that human societies have developed. He argued that it was the change in ideas that led to progress in the material world. In particular, it was the relationship of ideas about the control of the environment that were crucial for the social actions characteristic of each stage. (See *metaphysical stage, positive stage, theological stage*.)

three systems theory: a theory developed by black feminists to argue that class, gender, and ethnicity interact in complex ways to produce differences in the social positions of various women. It is a reaction to the way in which radical, but white, feminists have seemed to assume that the experiences of black women were similar to their own. (See *dual systems theory.*)

tiger economies: a term for those once-poor countries of the *third world* that exhibited high rates of *development* in the 1980s and 1990s. Countries such as South Korea, Taiwan, and Singapore have placed *industrialization* at the forefront of their policies, with the result that they have surged ahead of neighboring countries in attracting foreign capital and investment. Some sociologists have argued that a common feature of these economies is an authoritarian state that has kept labor cheap and inhibited the development of independent *labor unions.* Others have suggested that it is the openness of these countries to capitalist penetration from *first-world* companies that has led to successful development. (See *Pacific rim.*)

time: the measured passage of existence, which for sociologists also has social dimensions. Time can be seen as the *durée*, which is the flow of everyday life, and the *longue durée*, which is the rise and fall of social institutions. Time is also divided by humans into historical epochs such as the Modern Age, which are divisions of convenience, but which also encapsulate the *Zeitgeist.*

time-and-motion studies: the use of scientific observational techniques to study people working, in order to establish the most efficient and therefore profitable organization for a production line or office. Time-and-motion studies are traditionally associated with *scientific management* techniques, where their purpose is to control the minute-by-minute actions of the worker. They have been met with great suspicion by workers who have been subject to them, who view them as eroding the traditional rights of workers to control the pace of their work.

time-budget studies: the investigation by sociologists of the *domestic division of labor* by asking spouses to record the amount of time they spend on particular domestic tasks during a set period of time. The results of such studies produce remarkably similar findings in which women, regardless of whether they work outside the home or not, are shown to bear most of the burden of household tasks.

total institutions: organizations in which individuals spend their entire time, either permanently or temporarily. Organizations such as prisons, asylums, or army camps control the whole life of inmates while they are part of the institution. Though there are different types of total institution, they are similar in their all-encompassing nature and in their residential aspect. Inmates therefore participate in such organizations as whole persons. Total institutions are usually divided into the following groups:

Type of total institution	Example
For the incapable and harmless	Home for the blind
For the incapable and unintentionally harmful	TB hospital
For the capable and intentionally harmful	Prison
For the more efficient pursuit of tasks	Boarding school
For those who wish to retreat from the world	Monasteries

total quality management (TQM): an industrial principle transferred to education that seeks to involve all members of the organization in the production of a valuable product by making each individual responsible for his or her own part in the process. In education, this involves placing the learner at the center of educational procedures and giving the individual ownership of his or her own learning. This is achieved through providing arrangements that allow students to adapt learning programs to their own needs so that a quality education results.

totalitarianism: a situation in which absolute *power* is held by a group in society, which seeks to control as many activities and ideas of the citizens as possible. The totalitarian group may be an aristocracy, the military, a political party, or a minority ethnic group. Totalitarian regimes take control of the media and other ideological agencies in an attempt to control the minds of the population.

totemic religions: see *totemism*

totemism: a system of beliefs and practices based upon the notion of a mystical relationship between the members of a social group, such as a tribe or clan, and an object or class of objects, usually a particular species of animal or plant. The totem is an object of *ritual* and worship for the group. *Durkheim* argued that the totem came to symbolize the whole group, and in worshipping the totem, the group was actually worshipping and revering itself, which he believed led to increased social solidarity.

tracking: an organizational device used in some schools by which students are divided into separate tracks according to their supposed ability. Tracks often prove quite rigid, in that a student will remain in the same track across all areas of the *curriculum*. Tracking is an extremely controversial practice and many believe that it promotes inequalities, with students in lower tracks suffering from a less challenging academic environment. Research studies have shown that tracking can have a negative influence on the students in lower tracks. (See *labeling theory*.)

traction: a term developed by Baldamus to describe the feelings of pleasure that a worker could gain from the rhythm of work. Baldamus identified several types of traction:

Type of traction	Description
line-traction	where the rhythm is established by the product moving down the assembly line
process-traction	where the rhythm is established by the nature of the physical changes going on
object-traction	where the rhythm is established by the picture of the work-object in the worker's mind
machine-traction	where the rhythm is established by a constantly running machine on which a worker is working

traditional action: a form of *action* in *Weber*'s typology where behavior is governed by customs and where beliefs are habitual rather than rational. Weber saw pre-modern societies as characterized by traditional action, with actions influenced by the way things have always been done. Such actions are often very resistant to change. (See *affective action*.)

traditional societies: those social arrangements in which behavior is governed by tradition, or "what has always been done." The important rules governing social behavior have been passed down from generation to generation and are distinguished by a high degree of *ritual*. Such societies do not change very quickly and tend to be characterized by *mechanical solidarity*. Though there is a tendency for traditional societies to be seen as "primitive," they have their own high culture and level of sophistication that can be dismissed as old-fashioned, but actually show efficient adaptation to natural conditions.

traditional teaching: see *chalk-and-talk*; *pedagogy*

traditional voters: those who vote consistently for the same party. These are the strong supporters of a given party, and though often associated with traditional class or social affiliations, they can be found in all parties from all social groups. Often traditions of voting extend across generations, with sons and daughters following their parents in voting habits. Traditional voters are in decline as *volatility* increases.

traditional working class: a term applied to those manual workers in heavy manufacturing or extractive industries, who have historically exhibited high levels of solidarity. They have been the backbone of *labor union* development. (See *privatized working class*.)

trained incapacity: a term coined by Veblen to describe the situation where an individual's skills and abilities can lead to inadequate performance in an *organization*. Veblen used the concept to explain how *actions*, while successful in the past, may become inappropriate in changed circumstances and lead to inefficiency rather than efficiency. An example might be that chickens can be trained to respond to a bell by offering food as a reward. The same bell can also be used to summon them to have their necks wrung.

training: a conception of education as a preparation for a life of work, which has traditionally appeared in the further education sector but which has increasingly penetrated secondary schools in the form of vocational education. The idea of training is to provide the next generation with the appropriate *skills* to function effectively in work.

trait theory: an approach to the sociology of the *professions* in which the characteristics of many professions are examined to produce an *ideal type*. The problem with the approach is that there are so many traits identifiable that it is difficult to know when to stop. Millerson, for example, identified 23 traits of the professions, taken from 21 different writers on professions.

transcendental ego: identified by Husserl as that which all minds have in common – in other words, the essential properties of the mind. Husserl argued that it was the transcendental ego that led us to the truth about things – to knowledge itself. The transcendental ego is therefore the way in which our mind necessarily knows the world because of the way the mind is organized in all humans.

transferable skills: the nonspecific abilities that are carried by the worker from one job to another. Transferable skills are developed to meet the needs of postmodern industry, which requires flexible workers whose skills are not rooted in traditional work practices but can be employed in different work circumstances. Critics of the notion of transferable skills argue that they have the effect of *deskilling* workers, because skills that can be used by anyone have little market value. Nontransferable skills are those from which workers derive their power and monetary rewards.

transformative capacity: the ability of something to effect social change in a large-scale fashion. *Weber* identified the ideas of *Calvinism* as having this transformative capacity, though other sociologists have argued for other social formations and ideas as the main cause of the change from *feudalism* to *capitalism*. (See *spirit of capitalism*.)

transnational companies: those companies that carry out their business on a global scale. This term has largely replaced *multinational companies* because it has been seen as a more accurate description of such companies. Transnational companies (TNCs) operate in a global marketplace, aided by the *information technology* revolution, and are able to switch resources and personnel to those areas of the world where the greatest profit beckons. Sociologists have tended to focus on the activities of the transnational companies in the *third world*, although they have an impact on social life in the *first world* as well.

- Some sociologists argue that the role of the transnational companies in the third world is an exploitative one. Susan George, for example, has suggested that the transnational companies use the third world as a dumping ground for possibly unsafe products, which do not have permission to be sold in the *first world*. It is also suggested that transnational companies pursue profit in the third world regardless of the harmful effects of their products on the people. Through the power of advertising, people in the third world are persuaded to buy products they do not need and cannot really afford, such as cigarettes, when the money would be better spent on local produce.

- Other sociologists see the activities of the transnational companies as beneficial, because they provide third-world economies with *capital* and entrepreneurship, so that they actively contribute to the development of third-world countries. The model put forward here is one of reciprocal benefit, in which the transnational companies gain a decent profit and the third-world countries are helped to industrialize. The *tiger economies* of the *Pacific rim* are said to have developed as a result of this relationship.

- A third aspect of transnational companies in which sociologists have been interested is their power. While most TNCs are controlled by individuals from one particular society, such companies are responsible to their shareholders rather than to any particular national interest. They therefore have the power to affect the lives of millions through their investment decisions, such as where to locate industry or to concentrate production. The result of such decisions is that thousands may be thrown out of work or gain new opportunities, depending on where investment is made. It is also argued that the global effect of such power is to depress the real incomes of workers as the TNCs switch investment around the world in pursuit of the lowest possible costs.

(See *coca-colonization*.)

triangulation: the practice of using more than one, and usually at least three, different research methods when carrying out a piece of research, so that the different kinds of data will complement each other. Triangulation is also likely to increase the *validity* of the research.

trickle-down effect: an assumed process by which the *wealth* of the richer members of society filters down to the poorest. A belief in this process was used by Conservative governments in Great Britain from 1979 to justify cuts in income tax, particularly for very high earners. It was argued that by reducing very high levels of taxation, the wealthy would be encouraged to use their entrepreneurial skills to generate more wealth. This would trickle down to those below in the form of more jobs within a generally more prosperous society. There is little evidence to show that this process has taken place; in fact much evidence points to the contrary, i.e. that richer people have become more wealthy while the poorest groups in society have become relatively poorer.

trivialization: the process whereby oppositional *subcultures* are neutralized through being made a spectacle or reduced to what Barthes calls the "status of clown." This often means the transformation of the subculture into an exotic form. (See *domestication.*)

trust: said to be a key feature of late-modern societies, the reliance on knowledge about the world that is beyond the ordinary individual's grasp. There has been such an explosion of scientific, industrial, social, and technological knowledge that any individual cannot hope to understand it all. We must therefore have trust that the application of this knowledge is not harmful. (See *risk.*)

truth: that which conforms to fact. In another sense the term describes beliefs that are held to be correct. The issue of truth is a critical one in epistemology. There are different bases for what is held to be true, such as intuition, faith, tradition, and most importantly for sociology, science. The attraction of science as a basis for truth compared to faith, for example, is that it is *verifiable.* By knowing something is true for certain, sociologists hope to understand and therefore control the social world. However, postmodernists argue that this dream of the *Enlightenment,* that human beings can know something for certain, is itself a fallacy. They argue that there are no *meta-narratives* that can explain the whole of the social world and that therefore there is no such thing as truth.

turnout: the proportion of the registered electorate who vote in elections, expressed as a percentage. Turnout is important because different turnout among the supporters of political parties can affect the outcome of elections.

two faces of power: a phrase expressing the idea that *power* can be exercised not only by getting your own way against opposition (the first face) but also by preventing an issue ever being raised as controversial in the first place (the second face of power). It is argued that this second face is more powerful because it insures that society is run in favor of the dominant group without opposition, as policies that benefit that group are unchallenged and accepted as the normal running of society.

two-step hypothesis of the flow of information: the idea that media information does not have a direct effect on the whole of a media *audience,* but is mediated through *opinion leaders*, who absorb the information and pass it on to their immediate group. It stands in contrast to the idea that the media influence everyone directly and therefore that political media campaigns directly affect the way that people vote. The two-step hypothesis suggests that opinion leaders are the crucial conduit for political information. (See *hypodermic syringe approach.*)

two-way convergence: a type of *convergence theory* that accepts that all industrial societies will end up being like each other, but suggests that there is a new synthesis to emerge, which takes elements from all existing societies. The result will be a new type of highly industrialized society, with its own distinctive characteristics.

typification: the organization of *knowledge* in terms of the typical features of phenomena rather than their individual characteristics. It is a process that both sociologists and lay people engage in, as they seek to make sense of the social world in which they live. Typifications therefore cover a whole number of cases and seek to encapsulate what is common about them.

Überbau: see *superstructure*

unconscious motivation: the reasons for why we do what we do that are hidden even from ourselves. These lie below the conscious rational motivations we employ, and Giddens argues that sociology has historically neglected this part of *action*. (See *discursive consciousness; practical consciousness.*)

underachievement: the failure of a person or group of people, particularly in an educational context, to perform as well as expected or as well as indicated by their potential. Traditionally, the main groups of underachievers in the education system have been girls, lower-class students, and children from some *ethnic minority groups*. These are not, of course, mutually exclusive groups. Recently, however, the academic achievement of girls at school have outstripped those of boys, with the result that there is growing concern over male underachievement. The relative underachievement of children from the working class and some ethnic minority groups is still apparent, despite the existence of various "enrichment" programs. (See *ethnic underachievement; female underachievement.*)

underclass: a highly controversial term applied to a group or groups of people at the bottom of the class system. The concept is associated with, among others, the American writer Charles Murray, who identified the lifestyle of the underclass as characterized by high levels of *illegitimacy*, violent crime, and dropout from the labor force. He argues that it is the "deterioration of the family" in the lower classes that has led to the creation and growth of the underclass. Murray has also stated that one can see evidence of a growing underclass in Britain. Murray claims that the growth of the underclass has profound implications for the class system and for society as a whole, arguing that the physical segregation of the classes will become more extreme, with the middle classes moving to "*gated communities*," i.e. residential areas surrounded by physical barriers to prevent unauthorized access. There are a number of criticisms of Murray's views, including the following:

- his arguments are based on moral, rather than scientific and logical, reasoning
- he ignores the real constraints on some people, such as a lack of available jobs
- much of the squalor and blight of urban areas is a result of lack of investment
- it is unhelpful to describe such disparate groups of people as young unemployed males, female heads of single-parent families, the chronically sick and disabled, and the impoverished elderly as a "class." Their experiences and their goals are likely to be very different.

underdevelopment: the process whereby *third world* countries are exploited by the *first world*, and end up worse off than they were previously. The term was used by *underdevelopment theorists* and *dependency theorists* to explain how, prior to colonization by the first world, third-world countries often had industrial sectors of their own.

When third-world countries became colonized, the laws governing trade between the two societies were altered to favor first-world goods, with the consequent destruction of the indigenous third-world industries. Dependency theorists therefore argue that the state of undevelopment characteristic of third-world countries is not a "natural" state, but is the result of relationships with the first-world countries. (See *colonialism*; *development*.)

underdevelopment theory: a view that it has been in the interests of capitalist countries to keep their colonies, both former and current, in a state of submission. Arising directly from the *Marxist* tradition, the theory was developed in the 1950s by Paul Baran, who explored the strategies that the colonial powers used to exploit both those countries that were still directly ruled by a European power and those that had gained their independence. These strategies included the direct exploitation of the *third world*'s natural resources and the use of "clients" in the third world. The aim in either case was the "patriation" or return to the *first world* of as much surplus profit as possible. (See *patriation of profits*.)

underemployment: the situation in which people have jobs that do not fully employ them. It often takes the form of low-paid, part-time work and accounts for the emergence of a growing *informal economy*.

undeveloped societies: a term used to describe an assumed "original state" for all societies, in which the potential of those societies is not realized. The term is associated with *modernization theory*, which suggests that the development of societies from an agricultural basis into an industrialized state is central to societal progress. This perspective emerged from the *evolutionary theories* of early sociology, which under the impact of Darwin's theory of evolution saw societies following the same route of progress as had the human species. This theory therefore compared, usually unfavorably, the "primitive" state of undeveloped societies with the sophistication of developed societies. Undeveloped societies were seen as primarily agricultural, with a large peasant sector and a strong influence by traditional religious beliefs. The natural resources of undeveloped societies are unexploited by the inhabitants, who are seen as being content to follow a subsistence lifestyle. (See *development*.)

unemployment: the state of being without work. Sociological interest in unemployment has grown as the proportion of the population out of work in various societies has grown. Attention has been focused first on the *validity* of the unemployment statistics, as governments often change the definition of being unemployed, and second on the experience of being unemployed. Unemployment also has an ethnic dimension, with varying rates on unemployment among different minority groups.

unintended consequences: the outcomes of *actions* that were not meant and usually unanticipated. Since *Weber*'s work, most sociologists have viewed social actions as *rational* – that is, calculated to achieve particular effects. A course of action is therefore chosen to result in specific outcomes. However, all social actions also result in other outcomes that were not intended by the *actors* involved. Some of these outcomes may be the opposite of what the social actors meant to happen.

unionization: the process whereby members of an occupational group join a *labor union* in such numbers that the occupation is said to be unionizing. The concept is often used in reference to the *semiprofessions*, which are located between the powers and high rewards of traditional *professions* and the industrial muscle of the unions, which can often produce affluence for their members. Unionization is one of the tactics that members of the semiprofessions may turn to in order to attempt to protect and improve their financial rewards and working conditions. (See *density of membership*.)

unitary elite theory: an approach to the issue of *power* in society, which suggests that there is a single group, or *elite*, that rules, whose members are to be found in the key institutional positions in society. The unitary elite theory rejects ownership as the distinguishing characteristic of the ruling group, and instead argues that *location* is the important dimension, thus allowing the possibility of meritocratic movement. However, in the main, the unitary elite theorists see the main interests of the ruling elite as defending their own power and passing on their privileges to their children. There are thus limitations to the amount of *meritocracy* in a society, although there are alternative ways of replacing and renewing elites. Unitary elite theory has been criticized because:

- it assumes that just because people know each other, they operate as an elite, which is not necessarily the case
- social change at the top occurs more than unitary elite theorists allow
- it denies the importance of the representative tradition in democratic societies.

(See *circulation of elites*; *pluralism*.)

unitary theory: an approach to *industrial relations* that sees the company as analogous to the family, in which any opposition to management is seen as hostile and unacceptable. The unitary theorists emphasize common purpose and unity in the company and are antagonistic to the idea of workers linking up with each other in any way other than approved by management. *Labor unions* are only tolerated when they are "moderate" and serve the interests of the company.

universal benefits: welfare benefits that are available to everyone as a right of *citizenship*. (See *means-tested benefits*.)

universal church: see *ecclesia*

universal functionalism: a principle of *functionalism* that states that all activities in society positively contribute to society as a whole. It is criticized because nonfunctional patterns of behavior can be shown to exist.

universal laws: statements of cause and effect that apply to all situations in which similar conditions exist. Laws at this level of generality exist as the outcome of the scientific method, which takes verified instances of specific knowledge and generalizes them to apply to all similar circumstances. Universal laws therefore allow the scientist to examine a situation previously unseen and to predict the outcome of the events. By so doing, the scientist can know things for certain and thus control the future. A classic example of a scientific universal law emerges from the consideration of what happens when sulphuric acid is mixed with sodium hydroxide and the result is sodium sulphate and water. By examining other situations in which an acid and a base are mixed together, the scientist might generalize to reach the universal law that any acid added to any base will always produce a salt and water. (See *generalizability*.)

universalism: where the rules of a society are applied equally to all, with no fear or favor. Personal relationships are given no advantage in public affairs, and individuals are dealt with in terms of the rules generated to insure fair dealing. This, along with *particularism*, constitutes one of *Parsons' pattern variables* for traditional and modern societies.

universality of the family: an argument put forward by the functionalist George Murdock, based on the notion that some form of family exists in every society. It is generally agreed that whether this argument is regarded as true or not depends on the definition of "family." While all societies have rules governing sexual relationships, the responsibility for rearing children, and the inheritance of property, there are very wide variations in all of these arrangements. (See *core functions of the family*.)

universities of crime: a popular description of prisons that implies that one of their main, if unintended, functions is to teach inmates how to be better criminals. The term is used in the debate between those who see prisons as vehicles of retribution and those who argue they should be for rehabilitation.

unobtrusive methods: methods of research that are used without the subjects being aware that they are bring studied. Unobtrusive methods usually form part of a *qualitative research* study, and include observation (provided that the observation is unnoticed) and *covert participant observation*. It is claimed that the main benefit of unobtrusive research methods is that they avoid possible changes in the subjects' behavior or conversation which could arise if they knew they were being studied (i.e. the *Hawthorne effect*).

unskilled labor: work for which there is no training or talent required. The term is often applied to the most lowly paid of occupations and is associated with the basic working class. (See *semiskilled labor, skilled labor*.)

unstructured interview: an *interview* that usually has as its aim the probing of emotions and attitudes rather than the gathering of factual information. Unstructured interviews are usually tape-recorded, to allow the interview to resemble as much as possible a normal conversation and also to allow other researchers to listen later on. There is no interview plan; rather, the interviewer has a mental list of topics or headings around which he or she will try to direct the interview, as unobtrusively as possible. Skilled interviewers conducting unstructured interviews "listen with the third ear," i.e. note not only what is being said, but how it is being said, and what is being omitted, and also take note of nonverbal information, such as facial expressions and other *body language*.

unstructured questionnaires: a term usually applied to *questionnaires* that contain all, or a large majority, of *open-ended questions*. The term is not really accurate, as a questionnaire by definition has a structure.

Unterbau: see *substructure*

upper class: a term used to denote the dominant social group in society, but more specifically employed to indicate the aristocratic *elite* that controlled capitalist societies in Europe until World War II, sometimes alone and sometimes in alliance with other classes.

upward social mobility: the phenomenon of individuals or groups moving from a subordinate social position to a higher one. Upward mobility can occur for a number of reasons. In modern societies, education is the main vehicle for upward mobility, though marriage and enterprise can be alternative routes. There are also structural factors that affect the chances of mobility in a society. For example, change in *occupational structure,* when middle-class jobs expand, can create more openings for those in subordinate positions. (See *downward social mobility.*)

urban apartheid: a term referring to the growing trend in large cities to segregate space in a class-specific way, with gated communities and guarded private spaces for the rich and powerful, and heavily policed, or even sealed off, ghettos for the poor.

urban areas: localities characterized by high population *density,* in which large numbers of people coexist who are likely to be engaged in manufacturing or service industries.

urban blight: a blanket term used to describe the situation in certain parts of large cities, which have become ugly, inhospitable, and even dangerous places in which to live, and where residents are poorly served in terms of employment opportunities and amenities like transportation, shopping and community facilities, and play areas for children. The blight is often a result of a combination of bad planning, corruption, poor housing, and low investment, and reflects the fact that many of the residents of these areas are among the most poor and deprived in the population.

urban cowboys: a term used by Simmel to describe the streetwise and successful individuals of the city environment. In the fast-moving world of the city, the urban cowboy is able to manipulate the life of the street to his own advantage.

urban crisis: a term developed by Castells to suggest the crises that *capitalism* periodically undergoes, which are manifested most of all in the city areas of the nation. That is, the city is the main arena of modern *class struggle.* Castells argues that cities go into crisis when basic services are no longer met through *welfare,* and when *unemployment* rises fast. The crisis leads to disorder on the streets. In these circumstances, the *state*'s response is repression, with riot shields and new forms of police weapons and tactics being used. Critics argue that this account is a very simplistic one, in which the state can do no right. However, Castells' view of the state is that, whether it is providing welfare or quelling urban riots, it always serves the interests of capitalism.

urban dispersal: the process by which residents of urban areas leave the towns and cities and move to the suburbs or rural areas. The trend has been noticeable from the 1970s, and reflects the increasing tendency of businesses to relocate in rural sites. For the companies, it is suggested that one reason for this is the pool of cheap labor available in these areas, much of it female. For many workers, it provides the opportunity to fulfill the dream of the "rural idyll."

urban ecology: a sociological approach to a city in which the social characteristics of an area are investigated; it is associated with the *Chicago School.* (See *concentric zone theory; symbiosis.*)

urban managers: a term developed by Pahl to describe those people in positions of influence over the housing market in cities. People like mortgage assessors, planners, architects, and social workers are all involved in the housing market and have their own goals and interests, which they impose on the less powerful individuals in the housing marketplace. Pahl argues that sociologists need to examine the activities of such groups to see how they distort and manipulate the market.

urban social movements: a term developed by the Marxist writer Castells to refer to activism on the part of urban dwellers, who form groups to pursue their collective interest, usually regarding an aspect of life in their *community* about which they feel concern. Areas of interest are typically transportation, education, housing, and concern over crime and vandalism. Urban social movements are essentially local *pressure groups*, and Castells considered them an important source of *social change*.

urban villagers: a term coined by Gans to describe the existence of communities in city environments. It emerged from a study of Boston and New York, where Gans found lively ethnic and working-class communities, very different from the isolated individuals that the *loss of community thesis* suggested.

urban zones theory: a theory developed by Burgess to explain urban processes, based on the idea that cities are spread out in successive zones, each occupied by a particular type of person. The theory, based on Chicago, suggests that all cities develop in this way. However, other sociologists have tried to apply the theory to other cities with limited success. Even in the US, where most cities have been planned carefully, the concept of concentric ring development does not work uniformly. The theory has therefore been criticized for being simplistic, since it assumes that development is natural rather than the result of the exercise of political and economic *power* by social groups in cities.

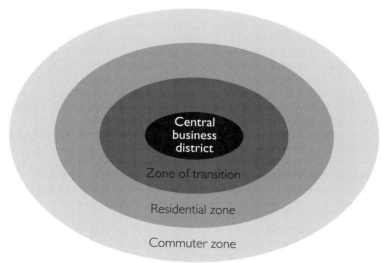

A representation of urban zones theory

urbanism: a term used by Wirth to emphasize that living in urban areas was a distinctive way of life, separated from rural living by a variety of factors. Urbanism is characterized by the collection of heterogeneous individuals in a large, dense, and permanent settlement. These features produce a distinct pattern of life, shown in its *impersonality* and *social segregation*. (See *density*.)

urbanization: the process whereby populations increasingly live in towns and cities rather than in villages and the countryside. Urbanization is arguably one of the greatest changes that has occurred during *industrialization*. The process is enormous, creating a great deal of dislocation and causing many social problems. Urbanization can occur in a planned fashion, but is more often than not unplanned, with towns growing rapidly into cities and cities into *conurbations*. The flight to the city can occur in any situation but is particularly associated with industrialization. Nevertheless, cities attract people from the land because of the opportunities they represent, whether the society is industrializing or not. (See *urban dispersal*.)

urbs in rure: literally "the town in the countryside," a term developed by Gans to describe the invasion of the countryside by many of the alienating features of urban living. The crucial development for the urbs in rure is the opening up of small towns to the city worker, so that in many towns the majority of the population no longer work in the locality but commute to the city. Gans also noted that there was conflict between the incoming commuters and the original inhabitants of the towns, particularly over the way the local housing market is distorted by the commuters, raising prices to levels the original inhabitants are unable to afford.

uses and gratification approach: a theory associated with the sociology of the media that argues that individuals used the media to satisfy certain psychological and social needs in their lives. It is an individualistic approach, which has been criticized for ignoring the social context in which individuals use the media.

utilitarian power: a type of control in which money or material rewards are used to direct the activities of individuals. This type of *power* relies on the calculation of individuals that the money reward is worth giving up freedom of action. (See *coercion*; *normative power*.)

utilitarianism: a political philosophy that stresses the rational self-interest of individuals in coming together in society. Starting from the premise that people are naturally self-interested, the utilitarians argue that it is in the self-interest of all to form a society in which everyone might pursue individual happiness within certain constraints, rather than accepting the "law of the jungle." (See *state of nature*.)

utopian sects: *sects* that withdraw from the world in order to develop a new, ideal way of living, in the hope that the superiority of the new model will become so apparent to others that they also will seek to adopt it. (See *new religious movements*.)

validity: the ability of a test or research method to measure what it sets out to measure. For example, IQ tests are often contested with regard to their validity, as there is no consensus over what IQ tests are actually measuring – is it "intelligence," or the ability to do well in IQ tests? Research into the motives of juvenile delinquents carried out by standardized *questionnaires* would probably be less valid than research using in-depth *interviews,* or covert *participant observation.*

value consensus: a general agreement about what are the things of worth in society. To *Parsons,* the value consensus was the basis of *social order* as it integrated disparate individuals and reduced *conflict* between them. The value consensus is not a conscious one, in that individuals do not have to think about what their *values* are, but it emerges from the past, as the best, most effective way of getting things done. The extent of a value consensus in society has been challenged, with many sociologists denying that it exists at all:

- Some argue that values are imposed upon the rest of the population by those at the top.
- Others suggest that the value consensus is a useful ideological device for keeping the compliance of those at the bottom of society.
- Postmodernists argue that in a society that is fragmented and composed of many different groups, there is little general agreement among the composite parts as to what constitutes the "good life."

value freedom: the idea in sociology that research should be carried out without the researcher's beliefs and ideas intruding into the research and influencing the design and execution of the project. Value freedom is a central characteristic of *positivism* but is influential right across the sociological spectrum. For positivists, value freedom is a desirable aspect of research, and achieved by following objective procedures that emulate the *natural sciences.* For some antipositivists, value freedom is not possible because of the human agency involved, and therefore the best that can be obtained is for the sociologist to declare his or her values to allow others to decide if these have interfered with the work. Still others argue that value freedom is impossible and therefore commitment should be substituted. As long as that commitment is made clear, the research can be checked and verified. (See *sociology of the underdog.*)

values: ideas or beliefs that are thought to be valuable by those who hold them. There is an ethical dimension to the concept of values, in that beliefs about goodness are often attached to them. In functionalist sociology, values have a central place, as they are thought to be crucial in forging social solidarity among disparate individuals. (See *norms; value consensus.*)

variable: a characteristic that can be measured and thus subjected to numerical analysis. Common variables in sociological research include age, social class, educational qualifications, ethnic group, support for a political party, income, and marital status. Variables are, by definition, not constant, but reflect differences within a given population. One of the important advantages claimed for *laboratory experiments* in natural science is the ability of the researcher to control and manipulate the variables, particularly the independent variable (the variable considered able to bring about changes in other variables, known as dependent variables). One of the objections to sociology being regarded as a science is the inability of sociologists, when carrying out research, to control the variables in the situation. (See *hypothetico-deductive method.*)

verifiability: in research, the process whereby an *hypothesis* can be shown to be true through experimentation. It is verifiability that is at the heart of the traditional view of *positivism.* This approach stresses the need for scientists to demonstrate that their hypotheses are true by designing experiments that verify them. (See *hypothetico-deductive method.*)

verstehen: literally "to understand," in sociology a term for putting oneself in the shoes of another in order to appreciate their particular experiences and perspectives. It is perhaps best understood as *empathy*, the feeling that one person can have for another's subjective being and objective circumstances. *Verstehen* was suggested by Dilthey as the way in which the sociologist can access the subjective world of the individual *actor,* and thus to understand the intentions and meanings behind his or her actions. It is thus a central concept in sociology, because, unlike the natural world, the social world exists both as an objective reality and in the subjective consciousness of the people who inhabit that world. (See *erklären.*)

vertical segregation: the distribution of social groups differentially along the levels of hierarchy in employment. It is generally women and ethnic minorities who are found in the lower levels of organizations. (See *glass ceiling; horizontal segregation.*)

victim-blaming: explanations of social phenomena that place responsibility on the people who most suffer from them. Victim-blaming theories are often found in the sociology of *poverty,* where the poor themselves are seen as responsible for their own poverty. For example, explanations that argue that poverty is the result of individual fecklessness are said to be victim-blaming, because they see poverty emerging from the poor's own behavior patterns and not from structural causes.

victim studies: canvasses of the public that request people to report any crimes they have experienced, whether or not they have reported them. This is one of the main ways in which the amount of criminal activity that never appears in crime statistics is exposed, particularly in cases of rape. Such surveys usually show that the real rate of criminal activity is at least double that which appears in the official crime statistics. Victim studies have been criticized because there is no way of verifying the information given by *respondents.* (See *self-report studies.*)

vital statistics: the official records of important demographic trends such as death and birth rates.

volatility: in politics, changes in voting behavior between one election and the next. It is often a symptom of a decline in *political identification.* (See *gross volatility; net volatility.*)

voluntarism: the belief that individuals are completely autonomous and able to exercise free will and choice. It was an attitude held by action theorists to show that what people did actually mattered in terms of the creation of history. It was developed by *Parsons*, who believed that the freedoms that *capitalism* gave could lead to the good society through the actions of autonomous individuals. (See *determinism*.)

voluntary associations: organizations, either political, recreational, or social, for which membership is optional rather than compulsory. They are seen by many sociologists as central to the operation of democratic societies, standing between the individual and the power of the *state*.

voluntary minorities: a term used by Gibson and Ogbu to describe those groups who have recently migrated to a host country and who tend to see education as a way of improving their situation. Regardless of qualifications gained elsewhere, voluntary minorities tend to start in the *occupational structure* somewhere below where they should be and therefore see education as a ladder of *social mobility*. (See *involuntary minorities*.)

voting register: the list of those eligible to vote. Its importance is that firstly it does not cover all of those eligible to vote, as some fail to register, and secondly, that it is already out-of-date before it is used, as some electors die and others move away. The voting register, however, can constitute a prime *sampling frame* for sociologists, as it does encompass a significant number of those over 18.

vulgar Marxism: a term used to describe the most deterministic of the variants of *Marxism*, which put forward the idea that everything in society was directly influenced in the most fundamental way by economic circumstances. It has been attacked for reducing history to a conspiracy theory, in which the *ruling class* manipulates members of the subordinate classes and exploits them in every sphere of social life.

W, X, Y, Z

wealth: the total value of the possessions held by an individual or a society. It is usually distinguished from *income,* because wealth can itself be income-generating, for example where an individual owns a factory. Sociologists have mainly focused on the distribution of wealth in two ways:

- In a global sense, interest has focused on the inequality in wealth held by countries of the *first world* compared to those in the *third world.*
- In a societal sense, the distribution of wealth in a country has been a constant focus of sociological interest, in particular with regard to whether the gap is increasing or decreasing. Wealth in many Western capitalist societies is very unevenly divided among the population.

A major problem with examining the distribution of wealth is that there is no general agreement among sociologists and economists as to what constitutes wealth. Part of the problem is that wealth can actually be hidden from statisticians, in order to avoid taxation. The emergence of a global economy has allowed the transfer of wealth across national boundaries with ease.

Weber, Max: one of the *classical sociologists* whose work is often seen as a counterpoint to that of *Marx* in its attempt to move away from the economic *determinism* of Marx toward a more complete and voluntaristic approach to the investigation of society. Weber was concerned to establish the importance of ideas rather than material forces as a vehicle for *social change.* To this end, he argued that religious ideas were important in shaping the practices that led to the development of capitalist society.

welfare: a general, popular term for government aid programs for the poor, especially Aid to Families with Dependent Children.

welfare dependency: a situation in which personal or household income is solely from welfare payments, e.g. the state retirement pension or unemployment benefit. Such people are likely to be among the poorest in society. The term is particularly associated with the *New Right,* who argue that overgenerous welfare benefits have made many people too reliant on the *welfare state.*

welfare state: a society in which the state, in the form of the government, accepts the responsibility of insuring a minimum standard of living for all people as a right of *citizenship.* Although particularly associated with the payment of welfare benefits to the needy, a welfare state delivers a range of services, including health care, education, housing, and leisure services. LeGrand argues that although the welfare state is presumed to cater primarily for the poorer groups in society, the middle classes actually benefit more, through their greater use of health, education, and transportation services and tax subsidies on mortgages. The precise nature of the role of the welfare state is the focus of intense political debate and struggle, both between and within political parties. There are four main perspectives on the role of the welfare state:

- Liberal: the welfare state is there to provide a safety net for those in need, and to help redress the worst economic injustices and inequalities in society.
- Social Democratic: there are certain inalienable rights of citizenship in a modern democratic society that are the duty of the state to protect. The welfare state should play a redistributive role with regard to *wealth* and *income,* with a view to moving toward greater equality.
- Marxist: the main function of the welfare state is an ideological one. By providing workers with a certain basic level of income and lifestyle it encourages them to accept *capitalism,* and indeed gives them an incentive to help to make it work. It therefore reduces their revolutionary tendencies.
- New Right: the welfare state is overprotective and too generous in its benefits and has led to the formation of a *dependency culture.* People should be made to focus less on their "rights" and more on their "duties" to society. The welfare state should be greatly scaled down, with people made to turn to the private, rather than the public, sector for the majority of their welfare needs.

Weltanshauung: literally meaning world view, a term used by *Weber* to describe the particular way of looking at things associated with a specific social group. Sociological interest has focused on the origins of different world views and their effects on the behavior of those who hold them.

Wertrational: actions guided by logic that are aimed at achieving or promoting a particular value or idea. Defending the homeland by taking up arms is seen by *Weber* as the ultimate *Wertrational* action, as it may involve the death of the individual, but would be a rational death if it saved the thing that was valued. *Wertrational* is one of the two types of *action* that typifies modern societies for Weber. (See *Zweckrational.*)

white-blouse workers: female workers in routine, lower-grade, middle-class occupations, particularly clerical and secretarial work. Workers at this level of nonmanual work have traditionally been known as *white-collar workers,* but as a high proportion of them are female, the term white-blouse workers is increasingly adopted, particularly in American literature on the subject.

white-collar crime: criminal acts committed by middle-class people in the course of their work. The term was introduced by Sutherland in the 1940s as a contrast to working-class crime. He argued that the sharp business practices of many business people were often illegal. Attention was drawn to such activities as price-fixing, embezzlement, fraud, and invisible crimes connected with substandard goods. Sutherland argued that white-collar crime was pervasive but did not appear in the criminal statistics because it was difficult to detect and to convict the perpetrators even if it was detected. (See *corporate crime, work crime.*)

white-collar unions: representative organizations for workers in clerical or professional occupations. They are historically latecomers to the *labor union* movement, of which they now constitute an important element. White-collar unions are important to sociologists because they seem to represent a move away from middle-class *consciousness* by those who join them. Traditionally, labor unionism is associated with the *working class* and therefore any increase in the numbers of white-collar workers joining unions is seen as a significant development. Some sociologists argue that this indicates an increasing identification by many members of the *middle class* with the working class. Other sociologists argue that all it means is that more white-collar workers are seeking to improve their pay and conditions through collective action rather than individual bargaining. They still keep their consciousness of superiority over *manual workers*.

white-collar work: a term to describe occupations situated in offices. These are also known as desk-jobs and are usually designated as middle-class, nonmanual occupations. (See *manual work*.)

white-collar workers: a group of workers usually conceived of as belonging to the lower middle class, representing the clerical workforce and occupying a crucial *structural location* between the *working class* and the traditional *professions* of the old middle class. More recent formulations of *class structure* tend to place white-collar workers in the intermediate class. (See *white-collar work*.)

whitelash: a shortened version of "white backlash," a term to describe the reaction against *affirmative action* programs that give preferential treatment, particularly in the labor market, to members of minority groups. The whitelash has been criticized as racist, but it accounts for the Republican domination of Congress in the early part of the 1990s, as many whites voted against the affirmative action programs of the Clinton administration. (See *positive discrimination*.)

wildcat strike: a work stoppage started by workers without authorization by the national union. Most wildcat action is of short duration. Sociological interest has focused on how conditions can emerge that lead workers to be so angry that they indulge in wildcat action. (See *strikes*.)

Wissensociologie: a term used by Scheler to indicate the sociology of knowledge. (See *knowledge, relativ-naturliche Weltanschauung*.)

withdrawals from work: a term developed to take account of the situation when workers may have stopped work, but are not yet on strike, either officially or unofficially. In many disputes at work, workers may stop to complain about an issue. Though production has stopped it is not yet a strike until management takes the workers "off the clock," from which time wages will not be paid. Thus, many withdrawals from work never end up as *strikes*, because the management is able to resolve the issue immediately, or to promise enough for the workers to go back to work.

work: a difficult concept for sociologists to define, but usually conceived of as paid employment. The difficulties in defining work in a sociological way stem from two issues:

- The relationship between work and *leisure* is not always clear-cut, for example with some people being paid for carrying out activities that for most others would be conceived as leisure (sports, for example).

- The relationship between *housework* and work is also problematic. While it is formally unpaid, housework can be conceived as receiving indirect payment, and it is certainly physically arduous, like many manual jobs. Yet housework is not usually seen as work. Therefore, sociologists break classifications of time down into the following categories:

	Element of compulsion	No compulsion
Element of payment	Work	Work-related time
No payment	Nonwork obligations	Leisure

Work and nonwork

work crime: lawbreaking in the workplace, ranging from the trivial, such as taking paper clips home from work, to the serious, such as embezzlement. The interesting thing from the sociological point of view is the distinction between the kind of work crime that is seen as acceptable by everyone and work crime that is condemned. (See *corporate crime; white-collar crime.*)

work enrichment programs: approaches in industry based on the idea that in order to increase production, workers need to be given much more responsibility in their jobs, so that they become involved and committed to their work. The work enrichment program was developed in opposition to *scientific management,* which sees the increasing *specialization* of tasks and *deskilling* of workers as taking control over work away from them. Proponents of work enrichment therefore argue for the *reaggregation of tasks.* The most famous experiment in work enrichment was at the Volvo car factory in Sweden, which reintroduced work teams to build cars, rather than the extremely specialized *assembly line.* Though eventually abandoned, the Volvo experiment was used to show that the *detailed division of labor* was not the only way that efficient production could be organized.

work motivation theories: explanations developed in early forms of industrial sociology for what makes workers work harder. Though there were various types of work motivation theory, such as *expectancy theory* or *incentive theory,* all were based on underlying assumptions of the basic nature of human beings. So, for example, sociologists who saw human beings as basically economically rational tended to put forward types of incentive theory when explaining work motivation.

work-related time: the period of the working day where the worker is not at work, but is carrying out activities necessary to do work. For example, getting the bus to work would be work-related time. (See *leisure.*)

work satisfaction: basically, a condition in which workers are happy in their work. However, sociologists dispute what actually makes workers happy in this sense. While some sociologists focus on the material rewards of work as the key element in promoting work satisfaction, others argue that other factors such as *intrinsic satisfaction* are equally important. The assumption behind the concept of work satisfaction is that satisfied workers will be productive workers. (See *alienation; work motivation theories.*)

work situation: a term used by Lockwood in his consideration of the *proletarianization* of clerical workers to describe the physical environment in which men and women labor. Lockwood included a whole range of factors in the work situation, such as the size of offices, the degree of automation, the extent of *bureaucratization* etc. (See *market situation; status situation.*)

work-to-rule: where workers take industrial action by obeying exactly the rules of the enterprise. This has the paradoxical effect of slowing down production. The reason for this is that rules are developed over time and many survive in the rule-book long past the time they have served any useful purpose. By implementing every single rule, the workers are able to disrupt production, yet do not lose basic pay. (See *strikes.*)

working class: the position in the social structure that is characterized by manual labor. The numbers in the working class have been declining as manual work is replaced by automated machines. (See *middle class; proletariat.*)

working class subcultures: groups within the *working class* who share similar attitudes, styles, dress, and identity that separate them both from the majority of the working class and from the rest of society. The *subculture* exists within the dominant culture, though it may be resistant to it. Members of working-class youth subcultures often dress in a similar fashion, so that they are easily identifiable.

world-accommodating sects: see *new religious movements*

world-affirming sects: see *new religious movements*

world-rejecting sects: see *new religious movements*

world system theory: a theory that approaches *development* from the viewpoint of a global economy, seeing the economies of the world as interconnected and inter-dependent in many ways. World system theory differs from both *modernization* and *underdevelopment* theory in resisting a simple and fixed division of the world into two or three "worlds." Rather, it argues that there are core and periphery countries in the global economy and that these change constantly under the dynamic global impact of *capitalism.* The historic role of capitalism has been to transform traditional and feudal societies into modern capitalist ones. The result of capitalist development has therefore been to extend the reach of capitalist *relations of production* into every corner of the world, to produce a constantly changing and ambiguous world.

xenophobia: fear of foreigners or those from a distinctly separate ethnic back-ground, which often leads to hatred of members of these groups.

youth culture: a concept of a shared way of life and similar attitudes among all the young people in a society at any one time. The idea of a youth culture emerged in the postwar period, when there seemed to be a rebellious spirit among young people. The extension of youth into the late teens, as the time of compulsory edu-cation was extended, also influenced the development of a youth culture. Another important factor was the relative *affluence* of the postwar period, when young people had disposable income to spend on leisure activities. This led to the development of a *popular culture* among the young, largely based on music. However, the notion that all young people have something in common has been heavily criticized, especially by those who argue that it ignores real differences in class, gender, and ethnicity. It may be that young people are generally more affluent than in previous generations, but some are still more affluent than others. (See *generational units.*)

youth unemployment: a situation where significant numbers of people under 21 years of age who are not in higher education are without a job. The appearance of significant youth unemployment in some societies, particularly among socially disadvantaged groups, has led to the concern that large and sustained levels of youth unemployment could produce a generation without experience of work. This has led to sociological investigation of the idea of an *underclass.*

Zeitgeist: literally "spirit of the time," a term used to describe the feeling of an era, its sense of art, *culture,* right/wrong, optimism/pessimism, etc. The *Zeitgeist* is encapsulated in the *language* of a society, in which the spirit is given concrete expression.

zero-sum relationship: a situation of *power* between two individuals or social formations in which the winner in the struggle takes all that the loser can offer. The balance of the outcome of the power struggle is always zero, with the loser registering all the minuses and the winner all the pluses. The implication of this view of power is that it is always exercised over someone for the benefit of the winner in the struggle. (See *nonzero-sum relationship.*)

zero tolerance: a policing policy in which all criminal violations, no matter how trivial, are acted upon. The idea is that attention to even minor infringements of the law will result in a decline in more serious crimes as well. Partly this is because of the certainty that the police will proceed with action against offenders, but also because of an increase in local pride that follows from clearing up graffiti, dealing with litter dropping, etc. The policy was claimed to have been a great success in New York, but concerns have been raised about the abuse of power by the New York police in implementing the policy.

zone: an area of a city that has some particular characteristic to provide it with a unity and identity. Zones are therefore "natural" areas of cities, composed for example of similar housing stock, or inhabited by people of similar ethnic origin.

zone of transition: one of the areas suggested by Burgess in his *urban zones theory* that is characterized by social disorganization, and therefore high rates of *suicide* and *crime.* The zone of transition is often inhabited by recent immigrants into the city, who are forced to take low-cost housing in the least desirable area. There is also a high turnover of people in the zone of transition, as groups move up to better housing or seek work in other locations or other cities.

Zweckrational: logical behavior that is aimed at achieving a specific end result. For example, building a bridge in order to cross a river is *Zweckrational* action. *Weber* identified *Zweckrational* action as one of the two types of *action* that are dominant in modern societies and stand in contrast to *traditional* and *affective action.* (See *Wertrational.*)